✤

A LIBRARY OF PROTESTANT THOUGHT

✤

A LIBRARY OF PROTESTANT THOUGHT

✤ ✤ ✤

The Social Gospel in America
1870–1920

GLADDEN ✤ ELY ✤ RAUSCHENBUSCH

EDITED BY

ROBERT T. HANDY

New York

OXFORD UNIVERSITY PRESS

1966

PRINTED IN THE UNITED STATES OF AMERICA

A Library of Protestant Thought

A LIBRARY OF PROTESTANT THOUGHT is a collection of writings intended to illumine and interpret the history of the Christian faith in its Protestant expression. It is as variegated in its literary forms and theological positions as is the movement it mirrors. Tracts, letters, sermons, monographs, and other types of literature comprising the heritage of Protestant thought find a place in this series. Works that were originally composed in English, whether in Great Britain or in the New World, and works that were originally written in other languages, many of them not previously translated into English, are included. But it is neither necessary nor desirable that every segment of Protestant theology, piety, and ethics receive equal space. The trite theology, the conventional piety, and the platitudinous ethics always bulk larger in any tradition, also in the Protestantism of the past four centuries, than does the creative output of the religious spirit. The latter is our primary interest in this Library. While we have not felt obligated to grant them equal attention, we have included works that are typical of the more commonplace literature of the Protestant tradition. On the other hand, some works which logically belong in this series have not been included because they are readily available elsewhere.

In keeping with the fundamental purpose of this Library, the voices of Protestantism are allowed to speak for themselves, with only as much introduction, commentary, and exposition as will in fact allow them to do so. Wherever feasible, documents are reproduced in their entirety. A few representative selections have been preferred to more numerous but shorter passages, for the Library tries to depict the structure of thought rather than the genetic development of a man or a movement. Nevertheless, the variety of Protestant forms precludes a uniform treatment throughout. Our aim has been to be representative rather than exhaustive and to employ the best available tools of critical historical scholarship. Despite its ambitious scope, A Library of Protestant Thought is not an encyclopedia of Protestantism. It is a series of volumes from which not only clergymen and theologians, but students of philosophy, history, literature, political science and other disciplines can gain a more balanced view of how the Protestant mind has thought and spoken since the Reformation.

The Board is grateful to the Hazen Foundation for an initial grant enabling it to begin its work; to the Sealantic Fund, Inc., for a grant making possible Board meetings, consultations, and editorial assistance in the preparation of specific volumes; and to the Oxford University Press for undertaking the publication of the Library.

THE   EDITORIAL   BOARD

Acknowledgments

The personal papers of the three men featured in this volume are well kept: the Washington Gladden Papers at the Ohio Historical Society Manuscripts Collection, Columbus; the Richard T. Ely Papers at the State Historical Society of Wisconsin, Madison; the Walter Rauschenbusch Papers at the American Baptist Historical Society, Rochester, New York. For the courtesy and help of the curators of those collections I am very grateful. Much of the work of research has been done in the Library of the Union Theological Seminary, New York; for the untiring assistance of the librarian, Robert F. Beach, and his efficient staff I am much indebted. Professor Winthrop S. Hudson of the Colgate Rochester Divinity School has made many helpful suggestions; my sincere thanks go to him, and to Professors Sydney E. Ahlstrom of the Yale University Divinity School and Robert S. Michaelsen of the University of California at Santa Barbara, for serving as an editorial committee for this volume in A Library of Protestant Thought. Mr. Wilbur D. Ruggles and his associates at the Oxford University Press have been most cooperative throughout. Special thanks go to Mrs. Margaret Apgar and to Miss Amy Clampitt for their patience and care with many details in the preparation of this book.

Publishing houses have been most cooperative in granting permissions for quotations and selections. My thanks go to the following publishers for certain specific items:

The Association Press, for the selection from *The Social Principles of Jesus*, by Walter Rauschenbusch.

The Christian Century Foundation, for quotations from articles by John C. Bennett in the November 8, 1933 issue of *The Christian Century*, and by Martin Luther King, Jr., in the April 13, 1960 issue of the same journal.

Harper and Row, Publishers, for quotations from *The Great Tradition of the American Churches*, by Winthrop S. Hudson; from *Southern White Protestantism in the 20th Century*, by Kenneth K. Bailey; and from the introduction to the Torchbook edition of Rauschenbusch's *Christianity and the Social Crisis*, edited by Robert D. Cross.

The Macmillan Company, for selections from *Christianizing the Social Order* and *A Theology for the Social Gospel*, by Walter Rauschenbusch.

United Church Press, for quotations from *The Interpreter* and *Ultima Veritas and Other Verses*, by Washington Gladden, both originally published by The Pilgrim Press.

University of California Press, for quotations from *The Protestant Search for Political Realism, 1919–1941*, by Donald B. Meyer.

University of Minnesota Press, for a quotation from *The Paradox of Progressive Thought*, by David W. Noble.

Yale University Press, for quotations from *The Rise of the Social Gospel in American Protestantism, 1865–1915*, by Charles Howard Hopkins.

R. T. H.

Table of Contents

Part Three

WALTER RAUSCHENBUSCH (1861–1918)   251

❖

A LIBRARY OF PROTESTANT THOUGHT

❖

Introduction

THE STORY of the rise, spread, influence, and decline of the social gospel in America is one of the most distinctive and fascinating chapters in the history of Protestant social concern. The social gospel reached its peak of influence in the United States in the first two decades of the twentieth century. Protestants were facing the new century with a high expectancy that the nation and Christianity would both richly prosper. One who was in his prime in those years later wrote of them:

> The first fifteen years of the twentieth century may sometime be remembered in America as the Age of Crusades. There were a super-abundance of zeal, a sufficiency of good causes, unusual moral idealism, excessive confidence in mass movements, and leaders with rare gifts of popular appeal. The people were ready to cry "God wills it" and set out for world peace, prohibition, the Progressive party, the "New Freedom" or "the World for Christ in this Generation." The air was full of banners, and the trumpets called from every camp. It was a brave time in which to be alive.
>
> The churches shared the general crusading zeal and inaugurated enterprises of their own.[1]

Not only did they share in the mood of the time, but they also did much to stimulate it.

Although the prospects for Protestantism in the young nation had not seemed very bright at the opening of the nineteenth century, the various movements of revivalism and missions soon were not only causing the churches to grow faster than the general population, but were also having a strong influence upon the culture as a whole. By the latter decades of the nineteenth century, however, certain threats to the great hopes for making America into an ever more Christian nation had appeared. An influential group of Protestant leaders regarded as especially serious the problems arising from the struggle between capital and labor and from the spreading blight of urban slums. They led a Protestant crusade for the kingdom of God and against social evil, which did much to prepare

---

1. Gaius Glenn Atkins, *Religion in Our Times* (N.Y., 1932), 156.

Americans who had been reared in an individualistic ethos for the tensions and conflicts of twentieth-century industrial life. The social gospel was particularly important in that it helped individuals and institutions to make the transition from a rural and small-town America to an industrialized and urban society with its inescapable social problems and regulations.

The social gospel in America was part of a developing world-wide interest in social Christianity. The impact of the industrial revolution had led to the formation of Christian social movements in many countries. The central concern was with the human problems arising from industrial strife, from the unequal distribution of wealth, and from the worsening of urban conditions for the poor. American Protestants had some acquaintance with the growing Christian social interest on the continent of Europe. They were more familiar with its development in Great Britain. The work and writings of such diverse men as Thomas Chalmers, Frederick Denison Maurice, Charles Kingsley, John R. Seeley, and Henry Scott Holland, for example, provided some stimulus for the rise of Christian social movements in the United States.[2]

Though these influences from abroad should not be minimized, the Christian social movement in the United States was fundamentally indigenous. The response to the problems of an urbanized and industrialized society was shaped by the patterns of thought and action that had long been characteristic of American Protestantism. A fascinating feature of the social gospel movement was that it flowered at a moment when many middle-class Americans were exhibiting an unusual degree of moral idealism and exuberant optimism and were ready to respond to pleas for social reform. This climate of opinion, itself in part a compound of the

---

2. See the works of Maurice B. Reckitt, especially *Faith and Society: A Study of the Structure, Outlook and Opportunity of the Christian Social Movement in Great Britain and the United States of America* (London, 1932), and *Maurice to Temple: A Century of the Social Movement in the Church of England* (London, 1947). Chalmers (1780–1847) was a prominent Scottish churchman who had done much through his efforts and writings to improve the plight of the poor. Maurice (1805–72), a seminal Anglican theologian, and Charles Kingsley (1819–75), a clergyman remembered especially for his social novels, were leaders in the Christian socialist movement in England (1848–54). Sir John Seeley (1834–95) published anonymously on both sides of the Atlantic *Ecce Homo: A Survey of the Life and Work of Jesus Christ* (Boston, 1866). Calling attention to the social aspect of the ethics of Jesus, the book popularized the phrase, "enthusiasm for humanity." Henry Scott Holland (1847–1918), a scholarly Anglican, was the founder of the Christian Social Union, of which an American branch was formed.

Protestant crusading spirit and the mood created by remarkable scientific and technological advances, gave to the movement its air of excitement and eager expectancy.[3]

The term "social gospel" did not come into common use until after 1900. Before then, the designation most widely used was "social Christianity." The new term came to be applied chiefly to a particular kind of Protestant social concern. There was, on the one hand, a social Christianity which was cast in a "conservative mold."[4] Its exponents recognized social problems but sought to deal with them without sharply challenging the dominant individualism. Joseph Cook (1838-1901), an immensely popular lecturer, and Minot J. Savage (1841-1918), a widely read minister who included social topics in his writings, were typical spokesmen for this position. That one was an orthodox Protestant and the other a Unitarian shows that differing theological backgrounds could support a basically conservative social Christianity. Important movements such as the Salvation Army and the rescue missions reflected fundamentally the same position.[5]

At the other extreme were those who tended to reject existing social and economic institutions in favor of sweeping reconstruction. Often they called themselves Christian socialists, though their socialism was usually mild, evolutionary, and non-doctrinaire. Perhaps because of the influence of Christian socialism in the Church of England, this movement had a following in the Episcopal Church. James O. S. Huntington, founder of a monastic order, gave much attention to social issues in the 1880's. In 1887 he founded the influential Church Association for the Advancement of the Interests of Labor, which included men with less radical views than his. W. D. P. Bliss (1856–1926), a tireless laborer in social Christian causes, formed the Society of Christian Socialists in Boston two years later. The most widely known Christian socialist in the 1890's was George D. Herron (1862–1925), whose radicalism was to lead him out of the church entirely. In the early twentieth century, a group of Christian socialists formed a fellowship somewhat more militant than preceding ones,

3. The standard account of the social gospel is Charles Howard Hopkins, *The Rise of the Social Gospel in American Protestantism, 1865–1915* (New Haven, 1940). For analogous Roman Catholic trends, see Aaron I. Abell, *American Catholicism and Social Action: A Search for Social Justice, 1865–1950* (Garden City, N.Y., 1960).

4. Henry F. May has discussed the development of this and the other major forms of social Christianity in *Protestant Churches and Industrial America* (N.Y., 1949).

5. Aaron I. Abell supplies much information on these and other groups in *The Urban Impact on American Protestantism, 1865–1900* (Cambridge, Mass., 1943).

frankly supporting political socialism.[6] Numerically these movements were small, and their influence was rather short-lived.

Occupying a position somewhere between the conservative and radical extremes were the advocates of what Henry May has called "Progressive Social Christianity." They were acutely aware of the social questions of the time but took a moderately reformist tone. It is to this broad, general movement that the label "social gospel" is most applicable. Its advocates pressed for social improvement, drawing upon the currents of Progressive thought which were flowing freely in the last decade of the nineteenth century and in the early years of the twentieth.[7] Their attitudes were essentially middle-class, combining a call for social action with an emphasis on the importance of the individual, his rights and responsibilities. For many Protestants who were rooted in the older individualism, the insistence that the gospel had its social aspects and the clamor for reform nevertheless seemed radical indeed. But though it had its opponents, the social gospel flourished in the early twentieth century. It took variant forms, but these all had recognizable characteristics in common. For a few years the social gospel was the most conspicuous phenomenon in American Protestantism. Even after its decline and virtual disappearance, its legacy of social thought and tradition of involvement has continued to be evident in many ways in American life today.

The thinkers associated with the social gospel were generally adherents of the "new" or liberal theology. Representatives of this theology, which became important in many evangelical denominations in the half century between the Civil War and World War I, were careful to distinguish it from the earlier forms of liberalism represented by Unitarianism and Transcendentalism. They sought deliberately to mediate between inherited Christianity and modern thought. They strove to center its renovated theological system around the person and work of Jesus Christ. Theirs was an "evangelical" or "Christocentric" liberalism.[8] For some, to

6. See Vida D. Scudder, *Father Huntington: Founder of the Order of the Holy Holy Cross* (N.Y., 1940); Robert T. Handy, "George D. Herron and the Kingdom Movement," *Church History*, XIX (1950), 97–115, and "Christianity and Socialism in America 1900–1920," *ibid.*, XXI (1952), 39–54.

7. Advocates of the social gospel both drew on Progressivism and contributed to it. In his thoughtful book, *The Paradox of Progressive Thought* (Minneapolis, 1958), David W. Noble focuses on nine central figures in the thought of the Progressive movement, two of whom, Richard T. Ely and Walter Rauschenbusch, are represented in this book.

8. See Kenneth Cauthen, *The Impact of American Religious Liberalism* (N.Y., 1962), 26–30, for a distinction between "evangelical liberalism" and "modernistic

be sure, this form of liberalism was no more than a halfway house to a more radical, humanistic liberalism; but for many others it was a satisfying and defensible position. During the ascendancy of the social gospel, its theology was largely evangelical liberal. A number of its leading spokesmen, beginning with Washington Gladden — who is often described as "the father of the social gospel" — were also well known for their liberal apologetics.

There have been many efforts to state the essence of the new theology. One of the earliest was by Theodore T. Munger (1830-1910), a Congregational pastor in New England and a friend of Washington Gladden. According to Munger, the new movement did not propose to do without a theology, did not part with the historic faith of the church, did not reject the specific doctrines emphasized by the church in the past (such as Trinity, Incarnation, and Atonement), was not iconoclastic, and did not intend to find its field outside of the existing churches. In less negative terms, he explained that the new theology made a somewhat larger and broader use of reason than had been customarily accorded to theology, that it sought to interpret the Scriptures in "a more natural" (i.e. historical) way, and that it aimed at replacing an excessive individuality with a truer view of the solidarity of the race. The new theology offered a contrast to the old theology in calling for a wider study of man; it recognized the necessity of a restatement of eschatology, the doctrine of last things.[9]

Another early effort to define the new theology was undertaken by the editors of *The Andover Review*, and was published under the title *Progressive Orthodoxy*. Its authors, all professors of Andover Theological Seminary, were convinced that ". . . theological progress does not involve or require any break with the faith of the church catholic, any recasting of the primitive ecumenical creeds, any departure from the fundamental principles of the Reformation." [10] They believed that what

liberalism." See also H. Shelton Smith, chap. xvii, "The Christocentric Liberal Tradition," in Smith, Robert T. Handy, and Lefferts A. Loetscher, *American Christianity: An Historical Interpretation with Representative Documents* (2 vols., N.Y., 1960–63), II, 255–308. Sydney E. Ahlstrom, "Theology in America: A Historical Survey," in James Ward Smith and A. Leland Jamison, eds., *The Shaping of American Religion* (Princeton, N.J., 1961), 232–321, discusses liberalism and the social gospel in relation to what preceded and what followed them on the American theological scene.

9. *The Freedom of Faith* (14th ed., Boston, 1886), 7–44.

10. *Progressive Orthodoxy: A Contribution to the Christian Interpretation of Christian Doctrines* (Boston, 1886), 5.

stamped their new divinity was its "reality." They wanted theology to
deal more with beings than with abstractions, more with actual processes
than with a priori assumptions, more with persons than with things or
words, more with the progressive unfolding of Christian truth than with
static categories. These men made such passionately Christocentric statements as that "everything in Christianity centers in Christ" and that "the
ultimate test of progress is Christological." [11] They put special emphasis
on the doctrine of the Atonement, affirming that "a truly Christocentric
system will be won when, and not until, the person of Christ rather than
his work is made central in redemption, and is seen at the same time to be
central also in creation, revelation, and the universal kingdom of God." [12]
Philosophically, they were seeking to modify the prevailing conception
of the divine transcendence with a richer appreciation of the immanence
of God, a fuller awareness of his nearness and ongoing activity.

These efforts to define evangelical liberalism belong to a day when the
new theology still had the freshness of a rising movement. A recent statement of the essence of liberalism, now that it has long been under attack
and in decline, has re-emphasized its mediating character. Henry P. Van
Dusen sees liberalism as "bridge theology," with "one foot firmly planted
in Modern Thought, the other deeply rooted within Christian experience." [13] From each side of the bridge there are four distinct contributions to the liberal tradition. From modern thought come fidelity to
truth, deference to science and the historical movement, tentativeness
concerning metaphysical certainty, and the assumption of continuity (between revelation and reason, Christ and other men, God and man). From
religious evangelicalism stem the authority of Christian experience, the
centrality of Jesus Christ, loyalty to the historic faith, and moral and social compassion and dedication. It should be added that the whole liberal
mood was strongly influenced by a rather general but pervasive philosophic current: romantic, monistic idealism.

Though the thinking of the social gospel fell within this liberal frame
of reference, by no means all evangelical liberals became advocates of the
social gospel. Sydney E. Ahlstrom was dealing primarily with the earlier
liberalism when he called attention to a "lack of social emphasis" as a

11. *Ibid.*, 7, 13.

12. *Ibid.*, 14. On the Andover development, see Daniel Day Williams, *The Andover
Liberals: A Study in American Theology* (N.Y., 1941).

13. *The Vindication of Liberal Theology: A Tract for the Times* (N.Y., 1963),
22.

"prominent characteristic of liberalism." [14] But even when the social gospel seemed to be carrying the main thrust of liberalism, there were many who did not go along. Much of Protestantism, both conservative and liberal, remained attached to old laissez-faire views, and argued that the enlightened individual who served his own interests would be serving the good of the whole. Sidney E. Mead has summed up much study of the later nineteenth century in affirming "the general agreement that at the time Protestantism in America achieved its greatest dominance of the culture, it had also achieved an almost complete ideological and emotional identification with the burgeoning bourgeois society and its free-enterprise system." [15] Those liberals who worked out new patterns of social thought and action struggled against powerful resistance, since social conservatism could be allied with theological liberalism as well as with the "old theology."

Yet the pioneers of the social gospel were determined not to retreat. The labor strife that erupted in the last quarter of the nineteenth century thrust the problem before them in a dramatic way. The terrible railway strike of 1877, the most destructive in the history of American labor, the labor troubles of 1886, the year of the Haymarket riot, and the series of strikes in the early 1890's, shocked these Protestant leaders into a reconsideration of their social views in relation to their faith.[16]

A less intense but still notable pressure upon social thought was the awareness that the expanding cities were breeding poverty, misery, vice, and crime. One of the powerful early voices of the social gospel was that of Josiah Strong (1847–1916), whose widely read book *Our Country* discussed seven perils threatening the American land of promise. He argued that the last and greatest of these perils was the city, which had become a serious menace to civilization, for "the dangerous elements of our civilization are each multiplied and all concentered in the city." [17] Various other exposés told in lurid detail of the poverty, suffering, and ignorance of the slum. Such books as William T. Stead's *If Christ Came to Chicago!* were controversial, but they sold well. Several hundred thousand of the

14. *Loc. cit.*, 294.

15. *The Lively Experiment: The Shaping of Christianity in America* (N.Y., 1963), 142.

16. Henry May has discussed these developments under the heading "Three Earthquakes" (*Protestant Churches and Industrial America*, 91–111).

17. *Our Country: Its Possible Future and Its Present Crisis* (N.Y., 1885), 133. On Strong, see Dorothea R. Muller, "The Social Philosophy of Josiah Strong: Social Christianity and American Progressivism," *Church History*, XXVIII (1959), 183–201.

English journalist's work, originally published in 1894, were issued in England and America.[18]

These problems drove many liberals to search in the biblical, theological, and historical resources of their faith for a social philosophy and program more adequate to their times than those in which they had been reared. Stimulated often by Christian social literature from abroad, assisted by contributions from progressive elements among sociologists and economists, and startled by the criticisms of the social order from the then avant-garde socialist movement, social gospel thinkers advocated positions sharply at variance with the older, individualistic social attitudes associated with laissez-faire. Convinced that they were right, and troubled by what they could see only as stubborn conservatism, they assailed those who resisted change in church and society.

A complex and dynamic movement in history, the social gospel was variously expressed by its several generations of leaders, yet its main emphases can be rather briefly stated. These include a conviction that the social principles of the historical Jesus could serve as reliable guides for both individual and social life in any age. Central to his teachings, so these liberal social Christians believed, was a stress on the immanence of God, the goodness and worth of man, and the coming kingdom of God on earth. Indeed, they affirmed, at the very heart of his gospel was the message of the kingdom, which they interpreted as a possibility within history. Though the church had long ago lost the true key to the kingdom, now that key had been recovered. The spokesmen for the social gospel expected that, through the efforts of men of good will, the kingdom of God would soon become a reality, bringing with it social harmony and the elimination of the worst of social injustices. Some who heralded the coming kingdom were less guarded than others, yet there was a high expectation of a much improved if not perfect social order. Thus the whole movement had something of a utopian cast. Spokesmen for the social gospel believed wholeheartedly in progress. Their faith was not, as a rule, in automatic or inevitable progress, for they normally saw progress as conditional upon man's response to divine leading. But along with liberal theologians generally, they were so confident of human goodness as to be sure that men could be educated to choose the good and to contribute directly to "the building of the kingdom." Sin they regarded primarily as selfishness. Through education, men could be led to

18. On Stead, see below, 112–13.

prefer social good to private advantage. The spokesmen for the social gospel were aware that sin could be transmitted corporately through social institutions, yet they believed that these institutions too could come under the law of love. Through determined moral effort, men could hasten the day of the coming of the empire of law and love, the kingdom of God. The ethics of the social gospel stressed Christ's way of love, which could lead men toward the glorious reign of love. In this coming order, socialized and enlightened men would work for the good of all.

The foundations of the social gospel were laid in the 1870's and 1880's, but the breakthrough to a more significant role in the life of the churches came in the 1890's. The editors of a well-known denominational periodical made a comparative study of topics treated in religious gatherings of all kinds in 1894 with those of twenty-five years before, and found that questions scarcely mentioned a quarter century earlier, notably concerning the relation of the church to labor and to social movements, were dominating religious assemblies by the latter date. The movement was pervasive: "Never, perhaps, were the themes of discussion so nearly alike in church assemblies of all denominations as now." [19] Reviewing the books for that same year, another journal found that it had "been most prolific in the production of books, good, bad, and indifferent, on the subjects most near to the public heart — socialism, social reform, sociology, political economy, and social aspects of Christianity." [20] Then came the flood of sermons, articles, pamphlets, and books advocating the social gospel; and by the early twentieth century the movement was powerful in American Protestantism.

Though the social gospel did call for action and did encourage responsible participation in philanthropic and political causes for the righting of social wrongs, its leaders were not so much activists as they were preachers, proclaimers, and educators. They sought to change men's views and attitudes, to win them to a new religio-social faith. The movement was strong in the pulpit and on the platform, and in the seminaries.[21] At its peak it had considerable support among the laity, especially among those who had been influenced by the Progressive movement. Lay leaders of

19. "Changes in Religious Thinking," *The Congregationalist*, LXXIX (July–December 1894), 580.

20. "Notices of Recent Publications," *Bibliotheca Sacra*, LII (1895), 205.

21. See James Dombrowski, *The Early Days of Christian Socialism in America* (N.Y., 1936), chap. v, "The Seminaries Discover a Social Problem," 60–73; Abell, *The Urban Impact on American Protestantism*, chap. ix, "Changing Trends in the Seminaries," 224–45.

the social gospel often came from the ranks of liberal social scientists, who are represented in this book by Richard T. Ely. The high tide of general Protestant interest in the social gospel probably came with the "Men and Religion Forward Movement" of 1911–12. A highly organized crusade to win men and boys for Christ and the church, the movement carried on intensive eight-day campaigns in sixty cities. Along with the familiar themes of evangelism and missions, there was a new stress on social issues at these meetings. Through them, the social gospel was carried to a wide audience.[22]

In some denominations the social gospel became especially conspicuous, as in the Congregational, the Episcopal, and the northern branches of the Baptist, the Methodist, and the Presbyterian churches. Of course, the movement was resisted by some within these bodies, and its proponents remained a minority — but for some years a highly influential and articulate one. Nor were the Southern branches of the last three denominations unaffected, though they were slower and more cautious in giving a place to the trends. Kenneth K. Bailey has summed up the matter in these words:

> Hence, between the turn of the century and World War I, the three major southern white Protestant groups underwent significant changes in program and outlook. Absorbed at the turn of the century in evangelism and little mindful of social needs beyond blue laws and prohibition, they emerged during the next fifteen years as advocates of social justice, proclaiming the Christian obligation to fashion Christ's kingdom on earth. . . . Southern Protestant social pronouncements mirrored the Progressive movement in tenor and phraseology.[23]

These years can indeed be referred to as "the era of the social gospel" in American Protestantism.

Interdenominational agencies gave even more emphasis to the social gospel than the denominations were able to do. The Federal Council of the Churches of Christ in the United States of America, founded in 1908, was a channel both for the movement for cooperative Christianity and for the social gospel. The two were often closely related. Many prominent advocates of the social gospel were conspicuous among the pioneers of Christian unity. The leaders of the various groups that joined in 1908 to form the Federal Council included a number of men prominent for

22. See Clarence A. Barbour, ed., *Making Religion Efficient* (N.Y., 1912).
23. *Southern White Protestantism in the Twentieth Century* (N.Y., 1964), 42–43.

their stand on the social gospel in their own denominations. For example, from the Congregationalist ranks came Gladden, Strong, and Graham Taylor. Among Northern Baptist participants were Rauschenbusch, Samuel Zane Batten, and Shailer Mathews. The Methodist contingent was a strong one, including Frank Mason North, Harry F. Ward, and Francis J. McConnell. Charles L. Thompson and Charles Stelzle were Presbyterians conspicuous both for preaching the social gospel and for interdenominational work.[24]

At the first meeting of the Federal Council of Churches a report was adopted on the Church and Modern Industry, containing the famous "social creed of the churches." This was a declaration that the church must stand (among other things) for the right of workers to some protection against hardships resulting from the swift crises of industrial change, for the principles of conciliation and arbitration in industrial dissensions, for the abolition of child labor, for the reduction of the hours of labor to the lowest practicable point, for a living wage as a minimum in every industry, for the most equitable division of the products of industry that could be devised, and for the abatement of poverty. In a critical study, John A. Hutchison has found that "the Council has provided a kind of laboratory or demonstration station for the Protestant churches, in which new ideas in many realms, especially social ethics, might be tried out. Possessing a measure of independence, it has been able to pursue experiments in both ethics and theology which would have been impossible to an organization tied more closely to the official denominational bodies." [25]

24. Taylor (1851–1938) was professor of social economics at Chicago Theological Seminary and founder of a settlement house, Chicago Commons. Batten (1859–1925), a close associate of Rauschenbusch, long served as chairman of the Social Service Commission of the Northern Baptist Convention. Mathews (1863–1941), was dean of the Divinity School of the University of Chicago, and served as president both of the Northern Baptist Convention and of the Federal Council of Churches. North (1850–1935) and Ward (1873——) were co-founders of the Methodist Federation for Social Service; the former was largely responsible for the draft of what became known as "the social creed of the churches," and among the latter's many books concerned with the social gospel was one explaining its creed in full. Bishop McConnell (1871–1953) was a vigorous leader in the Federation, in the Federal Council, and in many other socially concerned agencies. Thompson (1839–1924), as president of the Presbyterian Board of Home Missions, appointed and supported Stelzle (1869–1941) to head a new Workingmen's Department, later renamed the Department of Church and Labor. Dr. Thompson was also the chief founder, and for many years president, of the Home Missions Council. (The Episcopal Church was not formally a part of the Federal Council until 1940.)

25. *We Are Not Divided: A Critical and Historical Study of the Federal Council of the Churches of Christ in America* (N.Y., 1941), 311.

Other interdenominational bodies also demonstrated the close relation between the concern for Christian cooperation and the social gospel. [26]

After World War I, the social gospel entered a different and difficult phase. Donald B. Meyer has said, "Much of the labor of the social-gospel idealists, from Washington Gladden's first work in the 1870's to Walter Rauschenbusch's *Theology for the Social Gospel*, published in 1917, had gone into defining, defending, and preaching their vision of the ideal goal. By the end of the First World War, however, the pastors had come to be dominated by questions of strategy, and so they were to remain, moving from hope to anxiety, for the next twenty-three years." [27] The general disillusionment of the postwar decade greatly affected the Protestant churches. Very soon after the close of the war, it was evident from the collapse of the Interchurch World Movement, in which millions of dollars to undergird a forward thrust of the churches were to have been raised, that the crusading mood was over. Winthrop S. Hudson has summarized the ebbing of Protestant idealism in these words:

> Nothing is more striking than the astonishing reversal in the position occupied by the churches and the role played by religion in American life which took place before the new century was well under way. By the nineteen twenties, the contagious enthusiasm which had been poured into the Student Volunteer Movement, the Sunday School Movement, the Men and Religion Forward Movement, the Laymen's Missionary Movement, the Interchurch World Movement, and other organized activities of the churches had largely evaporated.[28]

Not that the social gospel disappeared in those years — far from it, but it elicited a less enthusiastic response, and lost much of what lay support it had had. Indeed, in the early 1930's the influential editor of *The Christian Century*, Charles Clayton Morrison, wrote: "The social gospel up to date has been a preacher's gospel. It has not been the church's gospel. The laity

26. Especially the Home Missions Council; see Robert T. Handy, *We Witness Together: A History of Cooperative Home Missions* (N.Y., 1956), in particular chap. II, "Building the Kingdom of God," 29–63.

27. *The Protestant Search for Political Realism, 1919–1941* (Berkeley, 1960), 3. Other works dealing with the social gospel between the two world wars are Paul A. Carter, *The Decline and Revival of the Social Gospel: Social and Political Liberalism in American Protestant Churches, 1920–1940* (Ithaca, 1954); Robert M. Miller, *American Protestantism and Social Issues, 1919–1939* (Chapel Hill, N.C., 1959); John A. Hutchison, ed., *Christian Faith and Social Action* (N.Y., 1953), especially Hutchison's preliminary essay, "Two Decades of Social Christianity," 1–22.

28. *The Great Tradition of the American Churches* (N.Y., 1953), 196.

have little share in it. They do not know how central and dominant it is in the thinking of their ministers." [29]

But by that time the liberal theology on which the social gospel had rested was losing its appeal for many. Liberals, with their optimistic orientation and heritage of idealism, were finding it hard to deal satisfactorily with the realities of depression and the rise of totalitarianism. One careful observer, himself nurtured as a liberal, declared in 1933: "The most important fact about contemporary American theology is the disintegration of liberalism. Disintegration may seem too strong a word, but I am using it quite literally. It means that as a structure with a high degree of unity theological liberalism is coming to pieces." [30] This shaking of the liberal foundations of the social gospel was continued throughout the 1930's as neo-orthodox theology upset much of Protestant thinking. The thought and strategy of the social gospel received a full dose of neo-orthodox polemics.[31] By the 1940's the social gospel as a distinct, self-conscious movement with a clear sense of direction had largely disappeared. Its major contention, however — that Christian churches must recognize and deal responsibly with social and economic questions — has not been forgotten, but has been continued in many ways in quite different theological settings. The social gospel has left a lasting impression on American church life.

The focus of this book is on the development and mature expression of the social gospel before World War I, and prior to its transition, decline, and reorientation. The speeches and writings of the two major spokesmen among the clergy, and of the most influential lay exponent of the movement, are a mass of material indispensable to a full understanding of the social thought of their times. In his perceptive study of American religion from 1892 to 1932, Gaius Glenn Atkins has pointed out that two men "did more between them to direct the mind of the churches toward the social problem than any of their contemporaries." After listing many

29. *The Social Gospel and the Christian Cultus* (N.Y., 1933), 42.

30. John C. Bennett, "After Liberalism–What?" *The Christian Century*, L (1933), 1403.

31. See, e.g., J. Neal Hughley, *Trends in Protestant Social Idealism* (N.Y., 1948); on the general shifts in theological thought see Arnold S. Nash, ed., *Protestant Thought in the Twentieth Century: Whence and Whither?* (N.Y., 1951); Herbert W. Schneider, *Religion in 20th Century America* (Cambridge, Mass., 1952); Smith, Handy, Loetscher, *American Christianity*, II, Part vi, 419–611; George Hammar, *Christian Realism in Contemporary American Theology: A Study of Reinhold Niebuhr, W. M. Horton, and H. P. Van Dusen* (Uppsala, 1940).

others, he returns to the thesis that "Washington Gladden and Walter Rauschenbusch . . . deserve a place apart." [32] He does not mention Ely, only a relatively small part of whose brilliant career was devoted to Christian social concerns. Yet in assessing the academic contribution to the social gospel, Henry May's judgment is sound: "Far more important than any other member of the group was Richard T. Ely, who was, in fact, one of the most important single influences on Christian social thought." [33] A study of representative selections from the voluminous writings of these three men can be a very profitable approach to the theology, the ethics, and the program of an important movement in the history of Protestant thought.

32. *Religion in Our Times*, 46–47.
33. *Protestant Churches and Industrial America*, 40

PART ONE

❖

Washington Gladden

1836-1918

WASHINGTON GLADDEN

AN INTRODUCTION

Washington Gladden was born in Pottsgrove, Pennsylvania, on February 11, 1836. His father, a New England schoolteacher, had moved westward a few years earlier. After a period of turmoil because of his father's death when the lad was only six, he was settled on an uncle's farm near Owego, New York. Since his labor was needed on the farm, his education for years was limited to the winter term at the district school. Happily, his uncle was an avid reader, who gathered his family on winter evenings to listen while good books were read aloud. As he grew older, Gladden was asked to take his turn as reader, and he later observed that "in that practice I learned most of what I have known of the art of oral expression." [1] As a result of the habits thus nurtured, Gladden was a voracious reader for the rest of his life.

Both his father and his uncle were men of sincere piety. While on the farm, Gladden regularly attended the two Sunday services of the Presbyterian church at Owego, and went through the Bible four or five times with the family at worship. From being required to memorize long portions of the Scriptures and the whole of the Westminster Shorter Catechism, Gladden early learned the main articles of Christian belief as stressed in the Reformed tradition. "It would be difficult to convey to most of those who will read these pages," he wrote in his autobiography, "any adequate sense of the positiveness with which those doctrines were held in the circle in which my life was spent. We did not admit to ourselves the possibility of any error in their statement, and we guarded ourselves carefully against any influences which would tend to weaken our hold upon them." [2] Yet the lad, try for it though he might, did not undergo the emotional experience of God's favor which he had been taught was necessary for salvation.

1. Gladden, *Recollections* (N.Y., 1909), 25. 2. *Ibid.*, 37.

At sixteen, Gladden was apprenticed to a newspaper publisher in Owego. He began writing for publication there rather incidentally, when his employer accepted a column dealing with local affairs and encouraged him to write more. At first, like so many young men freshly on their own, he stayed away from church, but he was won back by a famous evangelist, Jedediah Burchard, who had long been associated with Charles Finney.[3] Burchard had been known earlier for the rigor of his views; but perhaps he had mellowed by 1853, for Gladden found his mild Calvinism and his ideas concerning Christian experience reasonable and appealing. So the young printer joined the Congregational church where he had been won, a body whose original members had separated from the Presbyterian Church over the issue of slavery. In this atmosphere Gladden later resolved to enter the ministry: "I wanted to be — if I could make myself fit — the minister of a church like that. I could not think of any life better worth living." [4] An unexpected opportunity permitted him to prepare for college at Owego Academy. After a year and a half of hard study, he was ready to enter the sophomore class at Williams College in September 1856.

He did well at Williams, where his activities outside the classroom included debating, journalism, and music. Two men especially influenced him intellectually. The president, Mark Hopkins (1802–87), conducted memorable Saturday morning discussions for seniors based on the Shorter Catechism, thereby providing instruction in systematic theology. John Bascom (1827–1911) was then professor of rhetoric, a field he found "partially distasteful," and which he enlivened by introducing work in English literature and aesthetics. He was a man of wide interests and somewhat unorthodox religious views. He later served as president of the University of Wisconsin (1874–87), and eventually returned to Williams as professor of political science. He wrote on many subjects, including political science, philosophy, ethics, and theology. Bascom and Gladden remained lifelong friends.[5]

After his graduation in 1859, Gladden taught public school briefly in Owego. Here he formed a warm friendship with Moses Coit Tyler (1835–1900), who later became famous as an historian of American life

3. On the career of Burchard (1790–1864), see Whitney R. Cross, *The Burned-over District: The Social and Intellectual History of Enthusiastic Religion in Western New York, 1800–1850* (Ithaca, 1950), 188–89.

4. *Recollections*, 64.

5. See Frederick Rudolph, *Mark Hopkins and the Log: Williams College, 1836–1872* (New Haven, 1956); John Bascom, *Things Learned by Living* (N.Y., 1913).

and literature, and who at that time was pastor of the Congregational Church to which Gladden belonged. Under Tyler's guidance, the young man read in theology, delivered his first sermon, and was licensed to preach. After a temporary charge in a Pennsylvania town, he was called to the pastorate of a small church in Brooklyn, New York. On November 15, 1860, he was ordained to the Congregational ministry. Several weeks later he was married to a former schoolmate in Owego Academy, Miss Jennie O. Cohoon. His congregation was soon hard hit by the dislocations following the outbreak of the Civil War. The strain of this, coupled with the anxieties of the war itself, brought the young pastor to a nervous collapse, and he resigned his charge.

He was fortunate enough to be called soon to a less troubled church in the "quiet suburb" of Morrisania, then a small village north of New York City. Here he had time for rest and study. He attended lectures at Union Theological Seminary. In those years of growth, he read works of two men who decisively shaped his understanding of Christian faith and theology: Robertson and Bushnell.

Many men have fallen under the posthumous spell of Frederick W. Robertson (1816–53), the gifted preacher of Brighton on England's south coast. His early faith had been largely dissolved by the acids of nineteenth-century modernity. He then thought and felt his way through to a Christocentric liberal position which allowed him to bring the gospel to bear on the difficult moral and intellectual problems of his day. After he died at an early age, an admiring biography and the published collections of his sermons made him known to a wide public.[6] For Gladden, Robertson's honest, thoughtful interpretations of the faith were vitally in touch with reality, rather than divorced from it as was so much of traditional religion.

If Robertson opened Gladden's eyes, it was Horace Bushnell (1802–76) who taught him to use them. His first encounter with Bushnell, through a volume of sermons, led Gladden to read *God in Christ*, a book that absorbed him for months. The "Preliminary Dissertation on Language" became for him "a 'Novum Organon,' giving me a new sense of the nature of the instrument which I was trying to use, and making entirely clear

6. Stopford A. Brooke, ed., *Life and Letters of Frederick W. Robertson, M.A.* (2 vols, Boston, 1865); Robertson, *Lectures and Addresses on Literary and Social Topics* (Boston, 1866), and *Sermons Preached at Brighton* (N.Y., 1870). See Hensley Henson, *Robertson of Brighton* (N.Y., 1916), and James R. Blackwood, *The Soul of Frederick W. Robertson, the Brighton Preacher* (N.Y., 1947).

the futility of the ordinary dogmatic method." In the three discourses that made up the main part of the book, Gladden found an "emancipation proclamation which delivered me at once and forever from the bondage of an immoral theology" [7] — which, Gladden believed, attributed injustice to God, whereas Bushnell's interpretation of the faith stressed divine love and justice. Bushnell advocated a "subjective-objective" view of the Atonement, maintaining that Christ's work was to renovate man's character and restore him to fellowship with God.[8] A pioneer of liberal theology, Bushnell was a controversial figure, whose loyal follower and friend Gladden became. One of his first magazine articles was a defense of Bushnell's theology. In 1866 Gladden was called to the pastorate of the Congregational Church in North Adams, Massachusetts. The next year, when the time came for his formal installation, he invited Bushnell to preach the sermon.

In North Adams the young pastor became acquainted with the struggle between labor and capital, which was to concern him for the rest of his life, when a disagreement about wages in a shoe factory led to a lockout, followed by the importation of Chinese workers from the West Coast. Gladden left North Adams in 1871 to serve (until 1875) as religious editor of *The Independent*. Published in New York, at first under Congregational auspices, this well-known weekly had cast off its denominational allegiance, and its articles and editorials covered a wide range of religious, social, and cultural topics. The large-scale municipal corruption carried on by the Tweed ring was soon absorbing much of the new editor's attention. Through his editorials on the subject, he became an active participant in the struggle against that infamous organization.[9]

Other controversies also claimed his attention in the exciting years of Gladden's editorship. The theological waters had already been stirred by reaction against some of the traditional dogmas of Calvinist theology. When *The Independent* called the doctrine of infant damnation immoral, replies were soon pouring in. In one of the early "heresy trials" that marked the emergence of the new theology, *The Independent* backed David Swing, who disappointed Gladden by withdrawing from the battle.[10] Gladden's eventual departure from *The Independent* came about

7. *Recollections*, 119. Bushnell, *God in Christ: Three Discourses delivered at New Haven, Cambridge and Andover* (Hartford, 1849).

8. There are many books by and about Bushnell; for an excellent introduction with selections from his writings, see H. Shelton Smith, ed., *Horace Bushnell* (N.Y., 1965).

9. E.g., see below, 33–37.

10. Swing (1830–94), a Presbyterian pastor in Chicago, was critical of the doctrine

over another controversial matter: he deplored the practice of disguising paid advertisements as editorials, and when his protests were not heeded, he resigned.

He was then called to the pulpit of the North Congregational Church in Springfield, Massachusetts, where tension between labor and capital was acute. A long industrial depression had followed the financial panic of 1873; many men in Springfield, then a city of about 30,000, were unemployed. Invited to address a group of unemployed workers, Gladden promised also to address the employers, on the following Sunday night. Thus began a pioneering series of lectures on the labor question, later published as *Working People and Their Employers* — the first of what came in time to be a mountain of books about the social gospel. In it he called for the application of Christian law to industrial society.[11]

Gladden was also becoming a conspicuous spokesman for liberal theology. During his Springfield years the question of the inerrancy of Scripture began seriously to trouble the churches. In England, a company of scholars were busy revising the English translation of the Bible; but the very idea of the revision of a sacred text was disturbing to many. Scholarly criticism of the Bible was beginning to inform the writers of biblical commentaries. Discovery of manuscripts still more ancient than those used in the preparation of the King James Version led some to question theological views which rested on the old translation. In 1877 at Indian Orchard, near Springfield, the Reverend James F. Merriam was refused ordination by a Congregational council because he was unwilling to assert that all who died impenitent suffered everlasting conscious torment, but he preferred to believe that the incorrigible might suffer extinction. The Merriam case became a theological *cause célèbre*. Gladden, from his pulpit, expressed the minority view in no uncertain terms:

> The man who believes in Christ, who has the spirit of Christ in him, who shows in his life the fruits of that spirit, who, denying himself and taking up his cross, is following Christ in toilsome but loving labor for the salvation of men — he is my brother, and nothing shall

---

of inspiration held by conservative elements in his communion. After he had been acquitted by presbytery of the charge of heresy, and his accusers had announced that they would appeal the case to a higher judicatory, Swing withdrew from the Presbyterian Church. He continued to preach from the platform of Central Music Hall, where he attracted considerable attention. See Lefferts A. Loetscher, *The Broadening Church: A Study of Theological Issues in the Presbyterian Church since 1869* (Philadelphia, 1954), 13–15.

11. For more about the book and a selection from it, see below, 38–48.

hinder me from offering him the right hand of fellowship. I do not care what name they call him by, whether he is Churchman or Quaker, Universalist or Roman Catholic, he who is united to my Master shall not be divided from me.[12]

To those who suggested that men who disagreed with the "theological consensus" ought to withdraw from the Congregational ministry, Gladden replied stoutly that the consensus was a changing thing, and that the terms of fellowship ought not to follow a too rigid theological line.

Late in 1882 Washington Gladden, now in his prime, accepted a call to the First Congregational Church in Columbus. Then a growing city of over 50,000, the capital city of Ohio was to be his home for the rest of his life.

Throughout his long ministry in Columbus (he became pastor emeritus in 1914), Gladden was one of the most influential ministers in America. He preached regularly, twice a Sunday, made many addresses on occasions of all kinds, and gave several important series of lectures. He was twice Beecher lecturer at Yale. He had written half a dozen books before he came to Columbus; more than thirty were yet to come from his pen. Most of these were compilations of his addresses from pulpit and platform. As he put it, "Of the thirty-one volumes [as of 1909] of which the encyclopedias accuse me, all but six have gone through my pulpit, and are printed as they were preached, with almost no revision." [13] It was his custom to preach on Sunday morning on some aspect of personal religion; he would speak in the evening on any of a wide range of topics, religious, theological, social, biographical. His sermons and addresses were often first published as articles or pamphlets, and later compiled into books. Gladden was a wide reader but not a careful, critical, or original scholar. Much of his preaching and lecturing served to popularize ideas from the books current in his day, especially in the fields of religion and social thought. He wrote his messages out in full, and read them to his auditors.[14]

12. *Recollections*, 263–64.
13. *Ibid.*, 411. Gladden thought a collection of sermons on personal religion, *Where Does the Sky Begin* (Boston, 1904), was his best book. A number of the others had a wider circulation and were much more influential.
14. The bulk of Gladden's sermon and lecture manuscripts are preserved in the Ohio State Historical Society manuscripts collections at Columbus, together with thousands of letters received by him, reviews of his books, clippings, and so on — sixty-three boxes in all. There is also important material in the archives of the First Congregational Church at Columbus. An excellent biography is "Washington

Much of his public speaking — and thus of his published work — was devoted to clarifying and defending the "new theology." Upon finding that the theory of evolution had shaken the beliefs of Christians and made faith difficult for young people in college, Gladden gave a series of lectures to the students of Ohio State University; these later appeared in periodicals and then as a book, both in the United States and in England, under the title *Burning Questions*. Here his work as a Christocentric, liberal mediator between inherited faith and modern thought can be clearly seen. At the outset he said that he proposed to discuss "some of the fundamental doctrines of Christianity, as they appear under the light of modern science." He found that the basic religious beliefs remained:

> This modern science which has been supposed by some persons to have banished God from the universe, has not, then, banished order from the universe; it has given us revelations of the order and system which pervades the whole far more impressive than our fathers ever saw. It has not banished purpose from the universe. For though it has set aside that somewhat childish notion of design in nature which Paley unfolded, it has opened to us vistas far down the ages, and has shown us how an increasing purpose runs through them all, shaping the issues of organic life with Divine patience and unwearied power. Nature as Paley saw it exhibited intelligence, order, purpose. Therefore he believed in an intelligent Creator. Nature as Darwin saw it, exhibits a grander order, a more far-reaching and comprehensive purpose. Why, then, should we cease to believe in an intelligent Creator?[15]

Again and again Gladden explained how a person could accept the teachings of modern science and the theory of evolution and emerge with faith intact — purified, and stronger than before.[16]

Gladden had long emphasized the value of the historical approach to the Bible, and believed that many young people were indifferent to the Scriptures because views of the origins of the sacred book inconsistent with its own inner witness were being forced on them. Hence he gave a

---

Gladden: Prophet of the Social Gospel, 1836–1918," by Jacob H. Dorn, III (typed Ph.D. dissertation, University of Oregon, 1965).

15. *Burning Questions of the Life that Now Is, and of that Which Is to Come* (N.Y. [1889]), 5, 28–29. William Paley (1743–1805) was a British apologist whose writings were standard in Protestant education for over a century. In his *Evidences of Christianity* (1794) and *Natural Theology* (1802) he utilized extensively the argument from design.

16. As in *How Much is Left of the Old Doctrines? A Book for the People* (Boston, 1899), and *Present Day Theology* (3rd ed., Columbus, 1913). On the latter book, see below, 154–69.

lecture series on "Who Wrote the Bible," putting "into compact and popular form, for the benefit of intelligent readers, the principal facts upon which scholars are now generally agreed concerning the literary history of the Bible." [17] A later series on the subject was focused on particular books.[18]

In his theological popularization, Gladden drew freely on the work of the liberal religious thinkers of his time, such as T. T. Munger, Newman Smyth, William Newton Clarke, A. M. Fairbairn, William Adams Brown, R. J. Campbell, and Henry Churchill King. The same basic religious ideas are expressed again and again in his sermons and lectures, now briefly, now at length. Never denying God's transcendence, he laid stress on the divine immanence: "Surely if God is in his world, he must be revealing himself to us in all its laws and forces, and therefore all ordered knowledge of the world must be bringing him nearer to our thought, and every science must be tributary to that great unifying revelation wherein faith and knowledge are no longer twain, but one." [19] Under the influence of the romantic idealism of much of modern liberal religious thought, he minimized discontinuities between man and God, between nature and the supernatural, between reason and revelation. God as loving Father — this he never tired of articulating as the central theme of his religion: "Fatherhood is the fundamental idea of the new theology; and the sovereignty has to be interpreted through the Fatherhood." [20] Intimately related to this was his doctrine of the brotherhood of man — men are children of God, they are of the same nature as the Father, and as they progress toward the ideal, toward the perfect Man, brotherhood is gradually realized. He summed up his Christological thought in these words: "The manifestation of the life of God in Jesus Christ we call the Incarnation; and it was a manifestation so much more perfect than any other that the world has seen, that we do well to put the definite article before the word. Yet it is a mistake to overlook the fact that God dwells in every good man, and manifests himself through him." [21] Hence he could conclude that modern theology tends to find "the revelation of essential truth in the social consciousness." [22] In his view, then, the Atonement becomes

17. *Who Wrote the Bible? A Book for the People* (Boston, 1891), 1. For the book's concluding chapter, see below, 84–101.

18. *Seven Puzzling Bible Books. A Supplement to "Who Wrote the Bible?"* (Boston, 1897).

19. *How Much is Left of the Old Doctrines?*, 27.

20. *Present Day Theology*, 30.

21. *The Church and Modern Life* (Boston, 1908), 24–25.

22. *Present Day Theology*, 67.

"the reconciliation through suffering of holiness with love. And it is by bringing us into the same mind with himself; by filling us with his own abhorrence of sin; by bringing us to look upon the selfishness and animalism of our own lives with his eyes, and to recoil from them as he recoiled from them, that he saves us." [23] As for grace, it "is not what Augustine figured it — a vast, all-compelling energy, which overbears and submerges and sweeps away the human personality in its resistless onset; it is rather the helper of our infirmities, the prompter of our better thoughts, the quickening influence that reinforces all that is best in us and makes us strong to achieve and overcome. We are saved by grace, and grace is help." [24]

Salvation was always both personal and social, Gladden believed. He assumed as a truth that "the relations of men to one another in society are not contractual, but vital and organic; that we are members one of another; that no man reaches perfection or happiness apart from his fellow men; that no man liveth to himself, and none dieth to himself." [25] Salvation, he declared, drew near with the kingdom of God, which was present, at work, and steadily increasing among men. "The thought of this world is gradually being freed from superstition and prejudice; the social sentiments are being purified; the customs are slowly changing for the better; the laws are gradually shaped by finer conceptions of justice." [26] Finally, and in the not very distant future, the kingdom would come to its glorious fulfillment, when the law of love was fully recognized as the law of all life.

In this work of religious reinterpretation, Gladden was convinced that he was not diluting or repudiating Christian faith. He was sure he was saving it, making it intelligible to modern man, and relating it to the best of contemporary scientific and scholarly work. He was personally deeply devoted to Jesus Christ, but his Christocentrism (Jesus as the summit of human perfection by the grace of the Father) was of a theological nature quite different from the evangelical theology of the nineteenth century — or from the neo-orthodox theology of the mid-twentieth.

As Gladden's career as liberal apologist came to its climax in the Columbus pastorate, so did his role as social prophet — and for him they were always inextricably intermingled. In his congregation were both employers and employees. In the times of industrial strife he "witnessed with sorrow and alarm the widening of the breach between these classes." So,

---

23. *How Much is Left of the Old Doctrines?*, 194.   24. *Ibid*, 216-17.
25. *Ruling Ideas of the Present Age* (Boston, 1895), 285.   26. *Ibid.*, 290.

"as a Christian teacher, as the moral counselor and guide of the men under my care," he had to understand and "get at the rights" of the labor question.[27] In a number of evening addresses focusing on the labor problem, subsequently published in periodicals and ultimately as *Applied Christianity*, Gladden expressed his conviction that the teachings of Jesus contained the fundamental principles for the right ordering of society, and that when they were applied to the industrial situation, its deeper problems would be solved. "Christianity is a law, as well as a gospel," he insisted. "And the Christian law, faithfully preached, as the foundation of the gospel, will put an end to all this trouble."[28] The Christian law of love he preached as faithfully as he knew how, applying it to the problems of industrial life in many sermons and addresses. A number of books were the by-product of his concern with social problems: his first Lyman Beecher lectures, *Tools and the Man: Property and Industry Under the Christian Law* (Boston, 1893); *Social Facts and Forces: The Factory, the Labor Union, the Corporation, the Railway, the City, the Church* (N.Y., 1897); *Social Salvation* (Boston, 1902), the second set of Beecher lectures; *Christianity and Socialism* (N.Y., 1905); *The Church and Modern Life;* and *The Labor Question* (Boston, 1911). He was convinced that cooperation must replace competition in the realm of industry. He was no socialist; as he told the students at Drew Theological Seminary, "I think that for the normal development of human character, and the stable and fruitful organization of human society, it is necessary to have private property firmly safeguarded and private enterprise strongly encouraged by the state." Yet he believed that many industries could be managed cooperatively; in them "all the people should unite to furnish the capital and direct the work." He believed that the railways, the telegraphs, the mines, and the public service industries of the cities should come under governmental control and ownership. "Any business which is actually or virtually a monopoly must ultimately be owned and managed by the government." In so far as these developments were socialistic, thus far was he prepared to go, but always leaving "a great many important industries to be managed by private persons under the system of individual initiative."[29] The socially concerned Christian should not hesitate to involve

27. *Recollections*, 294, 295.
28. *Applied Christianity: Moral Aspects of Social Questions* (Boston, 1886), 169. For an important chapter of this book, see below, 49–71.
29. *Christianity and Socialism*, 123, 126–27. On his understanding of cooperation in industry, see below, 45–48.

himself in politics, Gladden asserted, thereby seeking to bring the political realm also under the law of love. To those who said that the Christian had no right to meddle in politics, that Christ's kingdom had nothing to do with the kingdoms of this world, Gladden replied bluntly, "This is nothing but flat rebellion against the express command of God, who bids every ruler to rule with diligence." [30]

Gladden also preached that international relations should be brought under the law of cooperation. He distrusted militarism and hated war; during World War I he called for the creation of a League of Peace with an international police force to make its policies effective. He believed that the whole world should become one in which the distinctions of caste, the repugnances of race, and the barriers of nationality were broken down. "If anything is central in Christianity," he said as war raged in Europe, "it is this obliteration of the lines of divisions between races and nationalities and the inclusion of the world in one brotherhood." [31]

Gladden did not speak only in generalities about racial brotherhood, but showed serious concern for the situation of Negroes in America. In the 1960's, with their struggle for full civil rights for all citizens, there has been sharp criticism of the social gospel's preoccupation with the industrial scene to the neglect of racial justice.[32] The proponents of the social gospel did tend to center their attention on the labor-capital problem and to touch upon other causes, including race and woman suffrage, only in passing. They tended to accept the views of race held by progressives generally. Josiah Strong was closer to being obsessed with the idea of Anglo-Saxon superiority than most other advocates of the social gospel, though there was some reflection of his sentiments in what they had to say. As the early social gospel leaders saw it, a major step had been taken for the Negro with the abolition of slavery; now it was the turn of wage-slaves to be freed. Gladden was troubled by the plight of the Negroes, and he did not ignore the racial situation entirely, even though he did not focus on it. In an address commemorating the Emancipation Proclamation, he declared, "The Negroes are in a condition far less free and prosperous and happy than we could desire . . . I can see how the black man has been from the beginning the victim of wrongs un-

30. *Ruling Ideas of the Present Age*, 175.
31. *The Forks of the Road* (N.Y., 1916), 123–24.
32. See, e.g., Thomas F. Gossett, *Race: The History of an Idea in America* (Dallas, 1963), chap. VIII, "The Social Gospel and Race," 176–97.

speakable, at the hands of the whites." [33] He sincerely believed that the two races could live together in peace and with mutual respect.[34]

Gladden was primarily a preacher — a spokesman for a liberal and social interpretation of evangelical Christianity. But as the head of a large downtown church he was also what the late H. Richard Niebuhr has called a "pastoral director." Two of his books especially reflect his knowledge of church administration: *Parish Problems: Hints and Helps for the People of the Churches* (N.Y., 1887) and *The Christian Pastor and the Working Church* (N.Y., 1898). He not only preached and wrote about municipal affairs and reform, but served for two years (1900–1902) as a member of the Columbus city council, on which he was especially active in working for the reduction of street-railway fares, and for improvement in gas and lighting facilities. A fair-minded man, Gladden forcefully protested the anti-Catholic feelings stirred up in the early 1890's by the American Protective Association. The protest cost him the opportunity of becoming president of Ohio State University, for the legislature had many members in sympathy with the A.P.A. Gladden later observed that "free speech, it is clear, is sometimes a costly luxury to those who indulge in it, but it is worth all it costs." [35] In 1905, the University of Notre Dame remembered the occasion in awarding him an LL.D.

As a writer, Gladden occasionally ventured a work of the imagination. The chief of these were *The Christian League of Connecticut* and *The Cosmopolis City Club*.[36] He loved poetry, and quoted it frequently in the pulpit. His own verse, which often reflected the sentimentality of the time, included the Williams College song and other pieces concerned with his alma mater, as well as on the Civil War. Two poems have long been favorites. One, "The Disciple," set to music under the title "O Master, let me walk with Thee," is among the best-loved of modern Protestant hymns. The other, "Ultima Veritas," expressing his unshakable faith in God's goodness, concludes with the words:

> And fierce though the fiends may fight,
> And long though the angels hide,
> I know that Truth and Right
> Have the universe on their side;

33. Gladden Papers, Box 58.

34. See his article, "The Negro Crisis: Is the Separation of the Two Races to Become Necessary?" *The American Magazine*, LXIII (November 1906–April 1907), 296–301.

35. *Recollections*, 415.   36. See below, 72–83.

> And that somewhere, beyond the stars,
> Is a Love that is better than fate;
> When the night unlocks her bars
> I shall see Him, and I will wait.[37]

Gladden was a rather reserved and dignified man, who did not often speak of wife and children; throughout his long ministry, his private life was largely kept so. The files of his correspondence preserve some letters written during his several trips abroad, in which may be sensed a father's deep love for his two sons and two daughters.

In 1904 Gladden was elected moderator of the National Council of the Congregational Churches. The most exciting event of his three-year term in that office was his protest against the acceptance by the foreign missions board of his denomination of a gift of $100,000 of what he called "tainted money" from the president of the Standard Oil Company.[38]

Washington Gladden had been reared in the Protestant America of the nineteenth century, and his faith that the United States would one day become a fully Christian land was unbounded. Though the country was rapidly shifting from the essentially Protestant pluralism of the nineteenth century to the more radical, "Protestant-Catholic-Jewish-Orthodox" pluralism of the twentieth, few of his time anticipated what this was to mean. His dream remained undimmed that a united, holy, socialized America would one day fulfill the Protestant hopes for the coming of the kingdom of God.[39] He saw the church not as an end in itself, but as an instrument, a means toward the building of the kingdom. "The kingdom of heaven is not an ecclesiastical establishment; it includes the whole of life — business, politics, art, education, philanthropy, society in the narrow sense, the family; when all these shall be pervaded and controlled by the law of love, then the kingdom of heaven will have fully come. And the business of the church in the world is to bring all these departments of life under Christ's law of love." [40] So he spoke in all sincerity for the continuation and extension of the "Christendom" of nineteenth-century American Protestants. To the day of his death in Columbus on July 2, 1918 — troubled though he was by the war — his faith never weakened. These words from the closing pages of his last collection of sermons

37. *Ultima Veritas and Other Verses* (Boston, 1912), 3–4, 67–68.

38. On this incident and the writings connected with it, see below, 119–34.

39. See especially his sermon, "The Nation and the Kingdom," reproduced below, 135–53.

40. *The Church and Modern Life*, 85. See also his earlier address, "The Church and the Kingdom," reproduced below, 102–18.

gather up many of the central interests, passions, and hopes of his life into
a prophecy of the coming kingdom of God:

> If the churches of your city, gathered in a federation, could but
> get the vision of this divine possibility, and with one heart and one
> soul could throw their energies and their resources into the realiza-
> tion of it, no one can tell what the issue might be. With such a work
> on its hands and such a fire in its heart, the church would get atten-
> tion to its message; the carping voices would be silenced; the chasm
> which divides the working classes from the church would shrink
> to a fissure; men would cease to think of God as careless or unkind;
> the Brotherhood, when we realize it, will prove the Fatherhood.
>
> A light like this could not be hid. If the churches of one city began
> to seek first the kingdom of God, the story would spread; glorious
> things would be spoken of that city; other cities would be caught
> by the flame; for this is a good that cannot be monopolized; you could
> no more stop it once it was started than you could stop a prairie fire;
> and the area of good will would soon be nation-wide.
>
> And it is coming. It must come. There is no other way for the
> children of men to live together. This dreadful war is the expiring
> spasm of the individualism which culminates in militarism and
> nationalism, and threatens the extinction of the race. God has some-
> thing better for the world than this. This is the time to believe it.
> If we ever doubt it, may God forgive our faithlessness! Lift up your
> hearts, O beloved! It is nigh, even at the doors! [41]

So "the father of the social gospel" summed up much of the message of
his life. Not a profound or original thinker, he nevertheless became one
of the most effective interpreters of liberal and social Christianity in a
critical period in American Protestant life. No account of the religious
history of that important time of transition is complete without serious
attention to him.

41. *The Interpreter* (Boston, 1918), 267–68.

✥ ✥ ✥ ✥ ✥ ✥ ✥ ✥

WHAT WE ARE GOING TO DO ABOUT IT [1]

Editor's introduction. During his first year as religious editor of *The Independent*, Washington Gladden met at first hand with an unforgettable example of the problem of corruption in municipal government. Headed by William Marcy Tweed, state senator and head of Tammany Hall, a conspiracy that included New York's mayor, treasurer, and controller had been defrauding the city of millions of dollars. *The New York Times* and *Harper's Weekly* crusaded against the Tweed ring; George Jones of the *Times* refused a five-million-dollar bribe to suppress information he had in his possession. Tweed, thinking he could ride out the storm, responded to attacks with the cynical question, "What are you going to do about it?" This was the occasion for Gladden's editorial. References to the crises of the Civil War, which made an indelible impression on the young man, were frequent in Gladden's work. The Cooper Institute meeting of Monday, September 4, 1871, mentioned in the editorial, proved to be an important step in the defeat of the ring. Several of its members escaped abroad; Tweed himself died in prison in 1878.

✥ ✥ ✥ ✥

The king of the ring, brought to bay by the press, turns and hurls back upon his pursurers the defiant question, What are you going to do about it? The challenge is accepted; and the best wits of the best men of New York are busy finding out what to do about it. A definite and feasible plan of attack will shortly be matured, but, while we are waiting for the lines of battle to be drawn, it is well to reflect for a moment upon the nature and the significance of the fight.

Nothing is risked in saying that the issue now made up between the honest men of New York and the officials by whom we have long been plundered is the most important question now before the public. Indeed, it is quite impossible to exaggerate its importance. All other questions dwindle into insignificance when compared with it. All matters of finance

1. *The Independent*, XXIII (August 31, 1871), 4.

and economy, of debts and revenues that can present themselves to the mind of the statesman; all discussions of doctrine or polity that can ask the attention of the religionist, are for the moment of trivial consequence when placed alongside the problem of municipal reform now awaiting the solution of the people of New York City.

The first duty of the people is the preservation of the nation. When the Southern rebels struck at the nation's life, every Christian patriot confessed that there was no obligation to church or family so sacred as that which he owed to his country. Between patriotism and religion there was no conflict; his patriotism was part of his religion, his religion inspired and consecrated his patriotism. To many a man in the Union army enlistment was a sacrament, and battle was a holy obligation. The parallel lines of obligation to God and man converged for the time into the one supreme duty of upholding the nation with whatever gift, by whatever sacrifice.

The life of the nation is again assailed. The assault is more insidious, but no less deadly, than that of Mr. Jefferson Davis and his friends. They are blind who cannot see that the political corruption which infests the land is a foe more dangerous and more difficult to fight than secession or rebellion. This evil is already widespread, and every day it is spreading more widely. Every legislature has its lobby, every city its ring, almost every considerable town its knot of scheming officials who fatten on the public spoils. Sober men have long been watching with dismay the progress of this iniquity. "What shall the end be?" they have asked themselves. "Will the intelligence and virtue of the land never rise in revolt against this reign of robbers?" The answer for which they have impatiently waited has come at last. New York City, cursed for years with the domination of a gang of thieves, who count their plunder by millions, and whose partnership with the baser elements of our society has been of the most shameless sort — New York City, whose councils and whose courts have come to be the byword of civilization — has risen in rebellion against the rule of the ring, and promises its plunderers the retribution of which they have long been defrauded. The heartiness and the unanimity with which the people of the city have risen to this work is the happiest omen the land has seen for many a day. At last, we trust, free government is to be vindicated, and the reproach which the condition of our municipality had cast upon Republicanism is to be wiped out.

In Sumter days the world beheld the uprising of a great people. It was then doubtful, for a time, on which side New York City would be found.

The Southern rebels confidently counted on the alliance of this city. There were newspapers here which proposed that the city should secede from the state, and join its fortunes with the Southern Confederacy. The mayor [2] was accused, whether justly or not, of plotting with the rebels for some such end. But the country was not left long in suspense concerning the position of our people. It was quickly discovered that the New York *Herald* and the Common Council did not represent New York. Into the faces of the eager throng a new light suddenly flashed — the light of patriotic resolve. The shuffling feet struck into marches; and a dense crowd gathered about the office of the organ of secession, and waited in grim and ominous silence till the American flag was thrust from the window. Hailing the old banner with a cheer, they went their ways; but from that hour it was plain to the dullest passenger that New York City would not join the Confederacy. A few days after the great meeting was held in Union Square, and the resolve of the people found a fit expression. That was the first victory — it might almost be claimed as the decisive victory — of the war. There was little room for doubt after New York had spoken what the issue of the fight would be.

The war against bad government begins here in New York. This city was thought to be the stronghold of secession in the North; it has long been known to be the stronghold of political corruption. The rebels relied on New York for aid and comfort; the rogues and plunderers of the land have been strengthened in their iniquity by the success of our ring. And now there is a promise of a grand uprising against these thieves and their misrule, and in behalf of good government — an uprising which, we trust, in its earnestness and its determination will rival that of the days of Sumter. There is not so much in this contest as there was in that to kindle the imagination; but there is even more to arouse the conscience, and the public conscience is very thoroughly aroused. Moreover, this issue appeals to the pockets of the taxpayers far more cogently than that one did; and, if we may not trust the moral sense of the people, we may confidently rely upon their regard for their own interest.

On next Monday evening we are to have an expression of the public mind about these matters. The call for the meeting will present an array of signatures representing the property, the brains, and the character of New York, such as never was appended to any similar call. Without distinction of party, the solid men of New York have put themselves in

2. [ED.] A. Oakey Hall.

column, and are moving directly on the enemy's works. Our German fellow citizens have shown an especial readiness to identify themselves with the movement, and, in spite of the maneuvers of the ring to preserve their allegiance, there is a fair prospect that they will enlist in a body against the common foe.

Honest men of New York! We expect to see you all at the Cooper Institute next Monday evening. We expect to find that place of meeting crowded, and acres of the surrounding space filled with your faces. We expect to hear from you a voice that shall assure the lords of misrule here, and everywhere throughout the land, of a swiftly coming retribution.

Meantime, let us make the most of our opportunity. Let every man speak to his brother, and every man to his neighbor, pledging one another to diligence and fidelity in this good cause. The ministers have their text for next Sunday; let none of them fail to use it. And, while the meeting is in progress next Monday evening, why may not meetings be extemporized in other cities and towns throughout the country, to join in the condemnation of these master workers of corruption, and to swell the general voice that calls for the purification of our politics?

So, then, gentlemen of the ring, we can tell you only in part what we are going to do about it. For further particulars you will not, however, be obliged to wait very long. But we are ready now to let you know a few things which we greatly hope to see accomplished, and to the doing of which we shall devote our best energies.

We are going to turn you and all your creatures out of your offices. That we can do, and shall do, please God, before the new year is a week old.

We are going to get back as much as we can of the booty you have stolen. We know the job will not be an easy one; but you may depend on us not to give it up without a fair trial.

We are going to use our best endeavors to send you to your own place, the penitentiary. You have been guilty of the most staring and stupendous frauds; and we do not intend to admit, until we are compelled to do so, that men in office can commit such frauds without incurring the vengeance of the law.

At any rate, we are going to make this city and the whole country too hot for you. There is some conscience left in this land yet, and you will find it out before you die. Upon you shall rest, heavy and immovable, the load of a nation's curse! You have trafficked in injustice. You have perverted our laws. You have corrupted our young men. You have done what in you lay to destroy our government. There are some sins that a nation may never forgive, and yours is among them. It is our solemn charge to hold you up while you live to the scorn and contempt of mankind. God may have mercy upon you; but as for us, we promise you that your ill-gotten booty shall be but a poor compensation for the inheritance of shame which shall be yours forever.

LABOR AND CAPITAL [1]

Editor's introduction. "Now that slavery is out of the way," wrote Gladden in the preface of his first major statement of social Christianity, "the questions that concern the welfare of our free laborers are coming forward; and no intelligent man needs to be admonished of their urgency. They are not only questions of economy, they are in a large sense moral questions; nay, they touch the very marrow of that religion of good will of which Christ was the founder." [2] Always central to the social gospel were the relations of labor and capital. That is the major theme of *Working People and Their Employers*, "a book which became one of the first mileposts set by American social Christianity." [3] Gladden later wrote of this pioneering work that "the attitude of the discussion toward labor unions is not quite so sympathetic as it ought to have been," but it pleased him that he had maintained at that early date the right of the men to organize for their own protection.[4] The addresses that made up this book were originally given to audiences that included mechanics and factory operatives.

❖ ❖ ❖ ❖

History shows us three different systems by which capital and labor have been brought together — the system of slavery, the wages system, and the system of cooperation.

In the first of these there is no conflict between capital and labor, because the capitalist owns the laborer. On the one side is force, on the other side submission. Labor and capital are indeed identified, because the laborer is part of the property of the capitalist which is engaged in production. There is no dispute about wages; the word is never heard.

This system of slavery is recognized and regulated in the legislation of the Bible, just as polygamy and blood vengeance are recognized and regu-

1. *Working People and Their Employers* (Boston, 1876), chap. II, 30–51.
2. *Ibid.,* 3. 3. C. Howard Hopkins, *The Rise of the Social Gospel,* 27.
4. *Recollections,* 256.

lated. The laws of Moses do not sanction either of these evils: they only set bounds to them, and secure their administration on certain principles of justice and humanity which will in due time put an end to them. And when these principles begin to root themselves in the convictions of the people, prophets arise announcing the higher law of perfect righteousness, of which the Levitical legislation was only the precursor; and bidding the people, in the name of the Lord, to undo the heavy burdens, and to let the oppressed go free.

Under such a moral regimen, slavery could not thrive. And when Christ appeared, declaring that the law and the prophets were all summed up in the rule which bids us do to others as we would have others do to us, the doom of the system was sealed. There is no express legislation against it in the New Testament; but there is no great need of express legislation against wearing fur overcoats in July. What Christianity did was to create a moral atmosphere in which slavery could not exist.

Men have always been quoting the Bible on the side of slavery; but, while pettifogging theologians have been searching its pages for texts with which to prop their system, the spirit of the book has been steadily undermining the system.

There are those who still choose to represent Christianity as the ally of despotism. A newspaper published in this Commonwealth made, not long ago, the sweeping assertion that "freedom and Christianity are fundamentally and irreconcilably antagonistic; and that whoever strikes a blow for the one strikes a blow against the other." In contradiction to this statement, we may quote the whole of history. Go back to the dark ages, to the period when the church was most corrupt and faithless, and you will find that even then it always was the champion of the oppressed. Mr. Fitzjames Stephen, one of the most brilliant of living English writers — himself a barrister and a student of ancient law, though a skeptic as regards revealed religion — bears this testimony to what Christianity has done for liberty: "The glory of the medieval church is the resistance which it offered to tyranny of every kind. The typical bishop of those times is always upholding a righteous cause against kings and emperors, or exhorting masters to let their slaves go free, or giving sanctuary to harassed fugitives. . . . What is true of the bishops is true in a still more eminent degree of the religious orders."

Read Guizot's *History of Civilization in Europe* for abundant confirmation of these statements. The power of the keys which the church put into the hands of the priests was used in behalf of the enslaved, in unlocking their shackles and in lightening their burdens. The destruction of the feudal system in Europe, and the abolition of serfdom, was, in considerable part, the work of the Christian church.

I have dwelt upon this fact of history, because I wish to make it plain to workingmen that the religion of Christ is not hostile to their interests; that it has indeed done more for the mitigation of their hardships, and the enlargement of their privileges, than any other power on earth. The suspicion with which the laboring classes, especially in Europe, have been taught by some of their leaders to regard Christianity, may be excusable in view of the corrupt and perverted nature of the Christianity by which they are surrounded; but it would surely be impossible, if they had any clear notion of what the religion of Christ is, and of what it has done for them.

If, then, this first system in which history brings together the capitalist and the laborer, the system of bondage, be largely a thing of the past; if the workman has now, in many lands, been emancipated — this result is due, in great part, to the prevalence of the Christian religion.

The second of these systems is that in which, throughout the civilized world, we now find capital and labor, in which they freely exchange services. The workman gives his work in exchange for the employer's money. There is a contract between them, by which the rate of remuneration is fixed. The fundamental principle of this wages system is competition, that is, conflict. If all men were benevolent, if the Golden Rule were the rule of all exchanges, of course this need not be; but unfortunately, the business of the world is for the most part organized on a basis of self-interest; and thus, by the wages system, the interest of the employer and the interest of the laborer come directly into collision. The laborer wants to get all he can for his labor, the employer wants to give for it no more than he must; and between the two there is an unceasing struggle for advantage and mastery. How sharp and fierce this struggle is, let the history of England and America for the last twenty-five years bear record.

Thus the second stage in the progress of labor is a stage of conflict. Slavery first, then war. All the kingdoms of the world's industry are now in a state of war. Sometimes the strife is suppressed, and there is apparent peace; sometimes the warfare is only one of words or of unfriendly combinations: but very often, as lately in the Pennsylvania coalfields, the parties come to blows. Violence is constantly resorted to when the contest waxes hot. Either between the employers and the laborers there is a direct issue of force, or else part of the laborers take the side of the employers, and are attacked as traitors to the army of labor. But even when the arbitrament of brickbats and bludgeons is not appealed to, there is none the less a state of war. Capital will assert and maintain its claims, so will labor; and neither will yield to the other more than it is compelled to do. Labor and capital work together in production. They must work together. Capital is worth nothing without labor; labor cannot subsist without capital. The contest arises in dividing the profits of this joint production. Over these profits there is a perpetual quarrel. It is generally believed among workingmen that the capitalist gets the lion's share of them; it is commonly asserted nowadays by capitalists that business cannot be done without a loss on account of the high rate of wages. I do not pretend to know which side is right: I only see the quarrel going on, and wish that it might in some way be stopped. Can it be stopped? That is the question.

I have read what the political economists have to say about this matter, and I confess that it does not help me very much. There is much learned talk about the wages fund; and no little dispute among the professors as to what this wages fund is, and whether the laborers are paid out of it or out of the product. Indeed, it would seem that the warfare of which the wages system is the occasion is not confined to the factories, but extends to the universities as well. They tell us that a certain part of the profits of production is set aside by the capitalists to pay future laborers, and that the price of wages depends upon the relation of this wages fund to the number of laborers, and can depend on nothing else; that when the wages fund is large, and the laborers are few, the wages will be high because each man's share will be larger; that, on the other hand, when the wages fund is small and the laborers are many, the wages must be low because each man's share will be small. Accordingly, they tell us, the whole question is one of supply and demand: the rate of wages is determined by fixed economical laws; the will of the employer cannot alter it; no combinations of workmen can affect it; it is just as vain to undertake to control it by legislation or by organization as it would be to control the winds or the tides in that way.

Well, that may be true, and probably is true if men are not moral beings; if the doctrines of materialism or of high Calvinism are true, and if the actions of men are determined by forces outside of themselves. But we shall venture to assume for a little while longer that the wills of men are free; that their choices have something to do with their destinies; and that by the presentation to them of truth, by an appeal to their reason and

their moral sense, their conduct may be influenced. The questions of social science or of political economy are in part moral questions; and my
business is to find out what are the moral considerations that enter into
this problem, by which the strife between labor and capital may be
tempered, and the good of both parties may be promoted.

In the first place, then, it would appear that what the economists call
the wages fund — that portion of the capital which is devoted to the remuneration of labor — does depend somewhat on the will of the capitalist. It depends partly on his habits of living whether it shall be increased
or diminished. If he is lavish in his personal expenditures, he will not of
course have so large a wages fund as if he is economical. Here is an employer who during the year spends ten thousand dollars in the merest luxuries of life — in feasting and in dressing — in that which is consumed
and cast aside with the using: must not his power to remunerate his
workmen be reduced by that amount? Might he not, if he had chosen,
have used this money in increasing the wages of his laborers?

"But that is all nonsense," answers the capitalist. "Business is business.
Supply and demand, my dear parson! Supply and demand! Every man
must pay the market price for labor, and any man is a fool who pays
more." No, my friend: you do yourself wrong. You are not wholly the
victim of these economical laws; you resist them and rule them sometimes,
in the interest of humanity. There is a poor man in your employ who has
been partly disabled. In the market, he could get almost nothing for his
labor. But you take pity on him and his household, and continue his wages
at the rate you paid him when he was in health. That is not "supply and demand" at all. Another law comes in here, a better law — the law of love.
You do bring it in, now and then, to alleviate the hardships that would
result from the inflexible enforcement of those economical laws of which
you speak. The question is, whether you might not bring it in a little
oftener; whether, indeed, you might not incorporate it into all your dealings with your workingmen; and instead of saying, "Business is business,"
say, "Business is stewardship: business is the high calling of God, into
which I am bound to put conscience and benevolence, as well as sagacity
and enterprise." This is just what Christian principle ought to effect on
the side of capital, in the relation between capital and labor; just what it
does effect in some degree: but if, on the present basis of production,
there is to be any enduring peace between these now warring parties,
there must be on the part of capitalists a good deal more of this interven-

tion of Christian principle, to hold in check the cruel tendencies of the economic forces.

Not only on the side of the capitalist must this spirit of sweet reasonableness find expression: the workman must govern himself by the same law. If employers are sometimes heartless and extortionate, laborers are sometimes greedy and headstrong. I have known of more than one case in which workmen have demanded an increase of wages when the business was yielding no profits; when the balance every month was on the wrong side of the employer's books; when with the strictest economy in his personal expenditures, and the most careful attention to his affairs, he was growing poorer instead of richer every day. I have known other cases, in which workmen have resisted a reduction of wages, when that was the only condition on which the business could be carried on without disaster. As a mere matter of policy, this is suicidal. For workmen to exact a rate of pay that shall destroy the business by which they get their living, is simply to kill the goose that lays the golden egg every day, because she does not lay two every day. It is not, however, with the policy of the transaction that I am chiefly concerned, but with the rightfulness of it. Grave wrongs are often in this way inflicted upon employers: their business is paralyzed, their credit is impaired, their property is swept away; and, in the destruction of the enterprises which they are carrying on, their power to help and serve their fellow men is crippled. For nothing is plainer than that a man who organizes and carries on any honest business, in which he gives employment and fair remuneration to laborers, ought to be considered a public benefactor. All depends, of course, upon the manner in which he manages his business. If it is managed in the spirit of Shylock, it may be an injury to the community; but if it is based upon principles of justice and fair play, it is a benefit to the community, and the destruction of it is a calamity and a wrong, not only to him, but also to the public. Any combination of laborers that undertakes to cripple or to kill an enterprise of this kind is engaged in a bad business.

"Is this meant, then, for a condemnation of strikes?" asks somebody. Not necessarily. I have no doubt that such combinations of laborers are often unwise and unprofitable; that, as a general thing, they result in more loss than gain to the laboring classes; but it does not appear to me that they are always morally wrong. This is a free country: if you do not choose to work for a man unless he will pay you a certain rate of wages, no one can compel you to do so; and if ten or twenty or two hundred of your fellow workmen are of the same mind, and prefer to be idle for a season rather than to take less than the price demanded for their services, they have a right to do it. But it seems to me that you ought to consider whether by your combination you may not be inflicting serious damage upon the whole community, and that you ought to have some regard to the public good in what you do. If the Christian law governs your conduct, you will think of this. But if you can satisfy yourself that the public welfare will take no serious detriment from your action, I do not know that it can be shown to be morally wrong. You and your fellows may find it for your advantage to take this course; and it is a lawful means of securing your own advantage. On the other hand, it may be for your disadvantage; you may be worse off in the end: but that is your concern and the concern of those dependent on you. So long as you pay your honest debts, and support your families, no one else has a right to complain if you do take a course which results in loss and damage to yourself.

Certain measures are, however, frequently resorted to at such times that are morally wrong. You have a right to refuse to work for less than a certain rate, and you have a right to *influence* others to join with you in this refusal; but you have no right to use force or intimidation to keep any man from working for less. Nobody has any right to force you to work: you have no right to compel anybody to idle who is satisfied with less wages than you demand. He may be a poor workman; but that is his employer's concern, not yours. If you can persuade him to join you, very good; but you have no right to lay a straw in his way if he refuses to join you. We believe in free labor in this country, do we not? And that belief implies that no laborer ought to be enslaved or coerced by his employer or by his fellow laborers.

If, now, workmen will endeavor to deal with their employers and with one another without threatening or violence, in a spirit of good will and fair play; recognizing the important service that is rendered them by the men who organize the various industries by which they get a living, and trying to render a fair equivalent in work for the wages they receive; they will do *their* part toward terminating this unhappy strife which has so long prevailed between labor and capital. It is a most melancholy quarrel: society is disturbed and unsettled by it, and the human brotherhood is rent into discordant and hostile factions. If the capitalist would measure his profits, and the workingman his wages, by the Golden Rule, there would be instant peace. And that is the only way to secure peace on the basis of the wages system. Political economy cannot secure it: its maxims breed more strife than they allay. Political economy only deals with natural forces; and the natural forces, even those which manifest themselves in society, often seem to be heartless and cruel. The law of nature would appear to be the survival of the strongest; and it is the workings of this law with which political economy has to do. Legislation cannot stop this strife. What, indeed, is law but an edict of force? Behind every law is the policeman's billy or the soldier's bayonet. It has no meaning, no efficacy, unless there is force behind it. And you cannot make peace with a sword between these contending interests. A gentler influence, a subtler but a mightier force, must take possession of the minds and hearts of the combatants on either side before the warfare will cease. If the spirit that dwelt in Christ be in you — if you will learn to "look not every man on his own things, but also on the things of others"; to love your neighbors as yourselves; to put yourselves in their places now and then, and judge their conduct and yours too from their point of view — you will speedily come to terms in all your quarrels. And is it not about time for all of you, capitalists and laborers, in view of the wasting warfare that you have so long been waging, to lay to heart the injunction of Paul, "If ye bite and devour one another, take heed that ye be not consumed one of another"?

I must own that I have not much hope, however, that the war to which the wages system gives occasion will ever cease until the system is abolished or greatly modified. Christian principle can do much to mitigate the strife, so far as it gains control of the lives of men; but it will be a good while before the masses of men, whether capitalists or laborers, are so fully governed by the Christian law that they will cease to struggle for the advantage and mastery. The wages system is better than slavery, because conflict is better than apathy; but there is something better than the wages system, and I hope that we some time shall reach it.

The subjugation of labor by capital is the first stage in the progress of industry; the second stage is the warfare between labor and capital; the third is the identification of labor and capital by some application of the principle of cooperation. This is what we are coming to by and by. The long struggle between these two conflicting interests promises to end by uniting them, and making the laborer his own capitalist.

I need not stop to describe this system to you: you are all familiar with the principles on which it rests. By combining their savings, the workmen employ themselves, and divide the profits of the business among themselves.

Not only will peace be promoted by such an organization of labor, but thrift and morality also. None but those who have a mind to save their earnings can become members of such an association. Business requires capital, and the capital must be provided from the savings of the workmen themselves. In furnishing a strong motive to economy, cooperation will do good. The miseries of the working people in this country are often due to extravagance and improvidence, rather than to insufficient incomes. Besides, it is always necessary in these associations to enforce rigid rules of moral conduct. Drunkards or idlers are immediately turned out. Sober and steady workers are not at all disposed to divide their profits with the lazy and dissolute.

We may hope, too, that cooperation will secure greater economy of material, and better work. The workmen working for themselves, and having a direct interest in the profits of their work, are likely to be careful about waste. This carefulness will be of advantage not only to them, but to everybody else. The world is enriched not only by the discovery of new wealth, but by the frugal use of that which is already in men's hands. All waste makes the world poorer.

For the same reason, because each man is working for himself, it is directly for his interest to make all his work as nearly perfect as he can; and that is a result at which the whole world ought to rejoice.

Such are some of the results which may be expected from the success of industrial cooperation. The expectation is not based upon theory, but upon accomplished facts. Already in France and in England the experiment has been tried with remarkable success. A year ago, Mr. Thomas Brassey, M.P., in an address before the Cooperative Congress, stated that there were in England and Wales 746 cooperative societies, with more than 300,000 members, the share capital amounting to nearly $14,000,000; and that during the previous year they had transacted a business amounting to nearly $57,000,000. The larger part of this business, however, was in the mercantile rather than in the manufacturing line. In England the system has worked better in distribution than in production; but there has been considerable success in both directions.

But some of you may ask why a system so excellent has not been universally adopted. There are two or three reasons. So far as this country is concerned, the wages of labor have hitherto been so large that workingmen have been pretty well satisfied with their condition, and have not been driven to devise new ways of gaining a livelihood.

In the second place, workingmen everywhere lack confidence in the honesty and fidelity of one another. They hesitate to risk their savings in such enterprises, for fear some faithless treasurer will default and run away with them. Very many of the cooperative stores in this country have come to grief in this way.

In the third place, in the members of such an organization, a certain trait is essential which I may find it difficult to describe in one word, and which is not so fully developed as it might be among our working people, or among our people who do not work, for that matter. It is the trait that makes a man work well in harness. It is the spirit of concession, the spirit of subordination, the spirit that thinks less of personal power or gain or glory than of the common good. It is the spirit that we ought to find as the bond of union in all our churches, and *do* find sometimes, thank God! It is the virtue Paul inculcates when he bids the Romans, "Be kindly affectioned one toward another with brotherly love, in honor preferring one another." Where this spirit abounds, there is always unity and fruitfulness; where this spirit is not, there is confusion and all kinds of evil. And it is the absence of this spirit that hinders the success of many of our cooperative societies.

There is or was an Iron-Workers' Cooperative Association in Troy, New York, whose success at the beginning was quite remarkable. Last summer I wrote to a gentleman living there, to inquire how it was flourishing; and he replied that it seemed to be losing ground. Dissensions among the members were killing it. There had been frequent changes of managers, and it appeared that every man wanted to be boss.

More than one association of the kind has met its fate in this way. You cannot have cooperation till you can find men who can cooperate. How can you?

Add to these considerations, the fact that comparatively few among our workingmen have the intelligence and sagacity requisite to organize and manage a large business, and you have a pretty clear explanation of the reasons why cooperation has not been more generally introduced. Before the production of the country can be carried on in this way, there must be a great improvement in the mental and moral qualities of working people. But this improvement is steadily going on; our free schools and our open churches are offering to the children of our mechanics and operatives a culture in morality and intelligence that we may hope will qualify them after a while, to take their destinies into their own hands. The hour is not yet come, but it is sure to come; and the bell that strikes it will

Ring out the feud of rich and poor.

The transition from the wages system to the system of cooperation is likely to be made through the introduction of what are called industrial partnerships: by which the work people in a manufacturing establishment are given an interest in the business; and, in addition to their wages, a stipulated portion of the profits is divided among them at the close of every year, in proportion to the amount of their earnings. It would seem that the times are fully ripe for the adoption of this principle. I have no doubt that many of our manufacturers would find it greatly to their advantage to introduce it; that it would result in securing steadier workmen and better work, and that it would put an end to strikes and all other forms of strife.

But, if I am right, workingmen, as to the obstacles that hinder your entrance upon the better system, they are mainly such as arise out of your own defective conduct toward each other; they are such, too, as the Christian religion is calculated to remove. Indeed, is it not just because the Christian principle does not govern your lives, that you cannot cooperate? If the law of love ruled your treatment of each other, you would have no difficulty whatever in working together; in taking into your own hands all the grand industrial enterprises of the age, and carrying them forward with a vigor and a success that the world has never seen under the principle of competition.

For let no one fail to see that cooperation is nothing more than the arrangement of the essential factors of industry according to the Christian rule, "We being many are one body in Christ, and every one members one of another." It is capital and labor adjusting themselves to the form of Christianity; and, like every other outward symbol, is a false deceitful show, a dead form, unless filled with the living spirit of Christianity itself.

Workingmen, I ask you to ponder these things. There are those who seek to make you think that the church of Christ is an enemy, or at best but a heartless stepmother, greedy to get your service, but careless of your welfare. I know that there are elements in the church — corrupted fragments of the church — against which such a charge as this might be truly brought; but it is not true of the Christian doctrine or the Christian system. The power that has stricken the shackles from the laborer, that has lightened his burdens, that has lifted him up to a happier and a nobler life, and that has put into his hands the key of a great future, is the power that came into the world when Christ was born.

IS IT PEACE OR WAR? [1]

Editor's introduction. The year 1886 was a stormy one on the industrial front. Early in the year the Knights of Labor lost a bitter strike against the Gould railway interests. This was only the most conspicuous of hundreds of strikes. In the spring of that year of conflict, Gladden was invited to speak to a mass meeting of laborers and employers in Cleveland. A fierce strike had been raging there, and the atmosphere was tense. Gladden faced an audience in which workingmen predominated, and he succeeded in convincing them of his fairness and understanding. "If war is the order of the day," he declared in words often quoted since, "we must grant to labor belligerent rights." [2] He was asked to repeat the address several times in Boston — first to a gathering primarily of employers, then to one chiefly of employees. The address was published in *The Century Magazine* for May 1886. It appeared at a timely moment indeed, for in the hysterical public reaction to the disastrous Haymarket riots of May 4, the difference between strikes and anarchy had become obscured for many. "Is it Peace or War?" then became a chapter in one of Gladden's best-known books, *Applied Christianity.* The title put a new phrase into circulation. The reader for the publisher (Houghton Mifflin Company) at first hesitated over the title, but was convinced by Gladden's assertion that "the thing the world needed most was a direct application of the Christian law to the business of life." [3]

The question of peace or war between capital and labor includes several questions: whether there is at the present time peace or war between these two great powers, and if it is war, what they are fighting for; whether war is better than peace, and if not, how the war is to be brought to an end and peace is to be made — whether by capital subjugat-

1. *Applied Christianity: Moral Aspects of Social Questions* (Boston, 1894), 102–45.
2. *Ibid.,* 125.   3. *Recollections,* 298.

49

ing labor, or by labor subjugating capital, or by finding some way of uniting their interests.

The question whether peace or war now exists in the industrial realm need not detain us long. The answer is too easy. Optimists have been diligently assuring us, for a score of years, that there was no such thing as a labor question, except in the minds of a few crazy agitators; that everything was lovely in the industrial world, and constantly growing lovelier; that those beautiful harmonies of the French economist were sure to make everybody rich and contented and happy very soon. Few are now heard talking in this strain. Everybody admits that the relations between the working classes and their employers are extremely uncomfortable; the strikes, the lockouts, the boycotting, the rioting here and there, make up a large share of the telegraphic news in our daily papers. The state of industrial society is a state of war, and the engagement is general all along the line.

This state of things is the natural result of a system of pure competition. Competition means conflict. The proposition is disputed, but if any philosopher wishes to test its truth by a scientific experiment, let him gather a crowd of twenty urchins together upon the sidewalk and address them as follows: "Here is a handful of coppers, which I propose to divide among you, and I wish to tell you how I am going to make the distribution. To begin with, you have all got to stand back on the other side of the curbstone; then I shall heap the coppers on that flat stone; then, when I give the word, let each one of you come forward and take what he can get. The only principle, my dear young friends, that we can recognize in the distribution of this fund is the principle of competition. Neither justice nor charity can have anything to do with it. Under competition, the political economists tell us, everybody gets a reasonably fair share. All ready! One, two, three — grab!" If our philosopher will stand by now and watch his experiment, he will see reasons for believing that competition is not uniformly a beneficent force. In the first place, it will turn out that the biggest boys will begin at once, while he is talking, to crowd themselves up nearest to the curbstone, and nearest to the pile of coppers, pushing back the smaller boys. Likely enough they will have a fight for this vantage-ground while he is making his speech explaining the beauties of competition. When he gives his signal they will rush in at once, trampling on one another, the strongest, of course, seizing the largest share, and many of the little boys getting only a stray copper or two that may be dropped from the hands of their more greedy and powerful companions as they make off with their booty. This is the way that competition works. The whole story of the competitive régime is outlined in this thumbnail sketch of the curbstone financiers. Competition means war. And the law of war is the triumph of the strongest.

What is it that the scientific people tell us always happens in the struggle for existence? Is it not that the strongest individuals and the strongest races kill off the weakest? Competition is the struggle for existence, which is the law of the inferior races, adopted as the law of industrial society. It works in society exactly as it works among the inferior races. I will not stop to argue whether or not it is a good thing to kill off the weaker classes; my only point now is that under a system of which competition is the law this is the tendency. Naturally, the weaker classes object to being killed off, and fight against it with what strength they have; hence the conflict which always must accompany a system of pure competition.

It may be admitted, however, that a system of fair competition would work better than the existing system. If all the competitors were equally intelligent and equally strong, and if our laws were able to prevent classes among them from securing by unjust means unfair advantages, then we should see a different state of things from that with which we now have to deal. For, bad as unrestricted competition would be, we have something now that is worse. Fair competition between the strong and the weak, between men of trained faculty and men of low intelligence, is pretty sure to result in combinations on both sides, by which the bitterness of the conflict is greatly intensified. This is what we are confronting today. Competition, as the regulative principle of our industry, has utterly broken down, and combination has taken its place. It began with the establishment of those great financial and industrial corporations in which capital was encouraged by the state to combine, and, thus organized, was exempted from certain liabilities and given advantages which the individual proprietor does not possess. And these corporations, and the great business firms and banking institutions in which the savings of many are consolidated under the management of one, have learned the art of combining among themselves, so that, in all branches of industry and commerce, competition is greatly crippled where it is not killed, and prices as well as wages are largely fixed by conferences, and syndicates, and pools of all sorts. Is it competition that determines freight rates and railway fares? Not at all. The best part of the railroad business of the country is done under agreements between the great companies. The

price of oil, the price of coal, the prices of many of the common
necessaries of life are determined much of the time by combinations
among the producers or the dealers. "Our various industries," says the
Reverend Josiah Strong, "are combining to force down production
— that means that workingmen are thrown out of employment; and to
force up prices — that means increased cost of living. There are lumber,
coal, coke, oil, brick, nail, screw, steel, rope, fence-wire, glass, wallpaper,
schoolbook, insurance, hardware, starch, cotton, and scores of other combinations, all made in the interests of capitalists. Small dealers must enter
the 'pool,' or be crushed. Once in, they must submit to the dictation of
the 'large' men. Thus power is being gathered more and more into the
hands of conscienceless monopolies." [4] On the other side, there are powerful combinations among the workingmen which seek to control the rate
of wages and the hours of labor, and sometimes to prevent improvements
in industry — combinations rapidly increasing in numbers and in power.
Under this reign of combination there is no longer any such thing as free or
fair competition. The individual coal operator in the Hocking Valley [5] cannot compete with the other operators for the labor of the miners; he is tied
up by an agreement to pay no more than a certain price. The individual
miner cannot compete with his fellows for the wages offered by the operators; he is bound by his union to take no less than a certain price. And
these combinations on all sides are made for fighting purposes. The big
dealers combine that they may crush out competition, and kill off the
small dealers. The employers combine to fight the workmen, and the
workmen combine to fight the employers. Doubtless it is an illusion to
suppose that competition, under the best conditions, while human nature
remains what it is, would ever give us peace; however that may be, it is
certain that the combinations which have so largely supplanted competition are calculated to give us nothing else but war. And war it is, bitter,
and destructive, and desolating. "Masters and men," says a great Belgian
economist, "are in a state of constant warfare, having their battles, their
victories, and their defeats. It is a dark and bitter civil war, wherein he
wins who can hold out longest without learning anything; a struggle far

4. [ED.] Josiah Strong (1847–1916), one of the most prominent of the early social
gospel leaders, wrote *Our Country: Its Possible Future and Its Present Crisis* (N.Y.,
1885), from p. 105 of which Gladden drew this quotation.

5. [ED.] There had been serious labor troubles in Ohio's Hocking Valley in 1884–
85. The coal operators failed in their effort to keep out the union, the demands of
which were finally submitted to arbitration, with results generally favorable to the
miners.

more cruel and more keen than that decided by bullets from a barricade; one where all the furniture is pawned or sold; where the savings of better times are gradually devoured, and where at last famine and misery besiege the home and oblige the wife and little ones to cry for mercy."

The war arises in the division of the product of industry. The capitalist employer on the one side, and the laborer on the other, are fighting over the wealth produced by their joint exertions. The capitalist says that the laborer wants more than his fair share, and the laborer says the same thing about the capitalist; the capitalists, on the one side, combine to keep the laborers from getting any more, and the laborers, on the other side, combine to get as much more as they can. Then the question of the hours of labor comes in; the laborers contending that the world's work can be done in fewer hours, and the employers as a general rule resisting that demand. Still other matters in dispute are the right of the workingmen to combine, and their right to dictate to the employer whom he shall employ. The workingmen think that if they are to succeed in this conflict they must be able to combine and to bring the whole force of labor into the combination; and the employers think that if they are to succeed they must prevent the combinations of laborers by some means or other. Perhaps both are right. I cannot see how the workingmen can win the battle without uniting; and I am equally unable to see how the masters can win unless they can break up the unions. Such attempts as that of the manufacturer in Springfield, Ohio, to crush the labor organizations, are perfectly logical if war is the proper relation between labor and capital. Such attempts as those made by the employees of the Third Avenue railroad to compel the company to discharge some of its old hands because they would not join the union are natural and legitimate, if war between employer and employee is the necessary and normal condition of things. These are war measures on both sides. Are they right? They are right, if war is right. Is it right to march through the country, destroying barns and grain-ricks, appropriating the farmer's pigs and chickens, driving off his cattle and horses, and pillaging the stores and the smokehouses in the cities and villages? It is right, if war is right; it is a common and sometimes a necessary war measure. Is it right to kill men who have been guilty of no crime by thousands and tens of thousands? It is right, if war is right; this is the immediate object in view when people go to war. Is it right for the labor unions to endeavor to coerce men to join their ranks under pain of starvation? It is right, if war is right; it is a natural war measure. Is it right for an employer to discharge men because they belong to a union? It is right, if war is right; it is attacking the stronghold of the enemy. Many things which, in a state of peace, are inexcusable and even criminal, are justified, as everybody says, by the laws of war. Falsehood, deception, violence, homicide are the very substance of war. In a state of peace it would seem an abominable piece of tyranny to insist that no man should be permitted to earn his daily bread in the trade which he had practiced all his life, unless he would join the trades union. In a state of peace it would be a gross outrage upon personal liberty for an employer to discharge his workmen for belonging to a society which they had formed to promote their own interests. These are war measures. This fact cannot be too strongly emphasized. Let us get clearly before our minds exactly what we are doing and why we are doing it.

Of course, both parties to the conflict claim that this warfare is purely metaphorical; that they neither propose nor condone illegal measures. But it is hard, in such a deadly controversy, to keep within the law. It is inevitable that coercion should take violent forms. Society must deal sharply with such disturbances, but it is not easy to prevent them. They are indefensible, they are criminal, yet they are terribly logical. But even those coercive measures on both sides which keep within the law can be justified only as war is justified. If war is a good thing, they are good things. If war is evil, they cannot be good. What, then, shall we say about this fundamental question?

Is a state of war the natural and proper state of mankind? Are the happiness, the prosperity, and the morality of the people at large promoted by the maintenance of warfare? We shall agree, doubtless, that war is not the best employment for human beings; that it is not, on the whole, a good thing for people to be divided into classes and arrayed in armies for the purpose of encroaching upon one another's liberties or possessions. Surely the world is not enriched by warfare; it is impoverished, rather. While men are fighting they are not producing wealth; they are consuming what has already been produced, and they are very likely destroying, wantonly, about as much as they consume. This war between labor and capital, as we have seen, is about the division of the product of industry; and it is certain that the more they fight the less they will have to divide. The more constant and persistent the fighting is, the smaller every man's share of the world's wealth must be.

But this is not the worst of it. Such a warfare as this destroys the moral wealth of the nation even faster than its material wealth. It tends to make men bitter, suspicious, cruel; it turns neighbors against each other; it keeps the embers of resentment and hate all the while smoldering. This is the saddest part of the whole business. Those who have some knowledge of the temper of the combatants know that suspicion and distrust and ill will have been steadily growing more intense on both sides. Surely it cannot be well for men to cherish such feelings toward one another, and one cannot help wondering whereunto this will grow. In a recent letter from over the sea, written by one who is giving his life for the welfare of the working people, are these solemn words: "There is a strong feeling among employers and employed that the cruel conflict between capital and labor, aggravated by competition, is destroying some of the best elements in human character." This is the kind of destruction most to be dreaded. When the old feelings of friendliness are gone, when a sullen envy and a rankling hatred have taken their places, the very foundations of the social order will be gone, and chaos and anarchy will be at hand. None of us will be very rich or very happy when that time comes.

War is not, then, a good thing. Yet there are evils worse than war. In the olden times the men who did the world's work were mainly slaves. There was no warfare then between capital and labor, because labor was owned by capital. That was not a good state of things for the laborer, and it was no better for the capitalist, though Carlyle lauded it and longed for its return. It is better that the laborer should be a free man, even though some measure of conflict and suffering be the price of his emancipation. And if the laborer could see that the tendency of the industrial system under which he was living was to reduce him to a state little better than slavery, so that he would be dependent upon his employer, so that his chances to rise in the social scale would grow steadily less — if the laborer could see that this was the steady drift of the existing system, then, I think, he would be justified in fighting against that fate; in being willing to die rather than submit to it.

War is always a terrible evil; but it is sometimes the lesser of two evils. The degradation of a large class in society would be a greater evil than a war undertaken by that class to prevent such degradation. Now, it is certain that the wage-workers of this country feel that they are in danger of social degradation; in danger of falling behind the rest of the community in the march of industrial progress; in danger of becoming, to a great extent, dependent upon their employers, or upon the community at large, for subsistence and livelihood. We must do them the justice of recognizing this as the real reason of the widespread discontent that exists among them. The certainty that they are losing ground socially, and the fear that they may come to want and dependence, are the sources of the present tendency to combine for offensive and defensive warfare.

I am not referring to any such outbreak as that which, at this writing, is taking place in Chicago. That is not war; it is rapine, assassination, savagery. It is not the work of the Knights of Labor, nor of any other labor organization; it is led by men who, in the brutal harangues by which they stirred up the mob, denounced the Knights of Labor; men who have no part nor lot in the legitimate labor organizations; who, by creed and profession, are simply destroyers.[6] It is a cruel injustice to identify these miscreants with the army of labor. The labor forces sometimes make sad mistakes and commit serious offenses, but nothing like this fiendishness can be charged upon them. It is not with such weapons that they are waging war. No wrongs ever existed in any state of society which could justify the methods of these men. I am not, then, discussing their complaints. I am considering how the matter lies in the minds of the great body of sober, industrious workingmen.

Some time ago Mr. Powderly described the working classes in this country as the "army of the discontented."[7] He meant that there were enough of the discontented to make a large army; but it is also true that it is their discontent that is leading them to organize themselves into an army, that they may the better do battle against the evils which cause their discontent. If they are right in thinking that they are losing ground, if they are reasonable in their fears about the future, then they are justified in organizing thus for protection and defense.

Are they right? I will not try to answer so large a question; I will only indicate the answer that the thoughtful workingman is inclined to give. To begin with, the fact that this country is rapidly getting rich is a fact that the workingman, though not a political economist, knows very well. The evidences of this growing wealth are before his eyes. I will not rehearse the familiar figures paraded during the last two years by so many persons, for so many purposes; by Mr. Blaine, to prove that national salvation could not be found in any other than the Republican party; by Mr. George, to show that poverty and progress advance with equal step.

6. [ED.] The reference is to the Haymarket riot of May 4, 1886, during which a bomb was thrown at the police, precipitating violence that left more than ten people dead and over a hundred injured. Anarchists were blamed for the outbreak. Gladden here reflects the conventional Protestant opinion, which was rather generally held.

7. [ED.] Terence V. Powderly (1849–1924) was the head of the Knights of Labor, which attempted to combine all labor in a national body. Formed in 1869, it declined after the failure of its last strike against the Gould railroad system in 1886.

Unless the figures of the census are greatly at fault, the wealth of the nation is increasing much more rapidly than its population. With this great increase of wealth, with the enormous development of lands and mines, and with an improvement in machinery which is said to double the productive power of our manufacturing industries every seven years, it would seem that the average annual income of the individual must be greatly increased. Of some classes of the population this seems to be true. To speak of the class with whose circumstances I am most familiar, I should say that clergymen must be receiving incomes at least fifty per cent larger than they were receiving twenty-five years ago. It is certain that they are living much more expensively now than they were living then; that they can afford many luxuries of furniture and decoration and travel that they could not then afford. This is not probably true of all the country ministers, but of the clergy as a class I believe it is true. The clergy are not exceptionally prosperous; the same is true of the other professions. The average lawyer or the average physician gets a far better living today than he got twenty-five years ago. I think that the salaries of teachers, and salesmen, and bookkeepers, and clerks in the great offices have also been considerably advanced. Besides these, between the capitalists on the one hand and the wage-laborers on the other, there is a large class of persons who render professional and personal services of various sorts, many of whom are well remunerated. Such are musicians and teachers of music, artists and teachers of art, actors, and purveyors of public diversions. This class has greatly increased within the period under consideration, and is much better paid for its services now than formerly. A large share of the national income falls into the hands of such persons.

Without considering the condition of the employing classes, it is evident, therefore, that signs of increasing prosperity are visible in other parts of society. But how is it with people who work for wages? Some of the English statisticians have been trying to prove that the income of the wage-laborers in that country has increased as rapidly as that of any other class; but the validity of this cheerful conclusion is by no means established. The latest and apparently the most thorough investigation, by Professor Leone Levi, shows that the actual money wage of the English laborer has increased during the past twenty-seven years about thirty per cent, while the cost of meat and other necessaries of life has also risen almost but not quite as much; so that the English laborer is a little better off today than he was twenty-seven years ago.[8] Is this the case with the

8. [ED.] Levi, professor of the principles and practices of commerce at King's Col-

American wage-laborer? The statistics do not permit us to dogmatize. Professor Richmond M. Smith has shown us some of the fallacies of the labor figures.[9] The doctrine of averages has not been well understood by some of our statisticians, and their conclusions are not trustworthy. Two or three considerations must be borne in mind in determining this question.

The first is the fact that in most industries work is much less continuous and stoppages are far more frequent and more prolonged now than formerly. If the day wages are larger, the annual wages may still be smaller. The precariousness of employment is now a serious matter to most workingmen.

The second fact to be considered is the effect of machinery in reducing the demand for skilled labor. To take a single example: the ironwork of carriages was nearly all made by hand twenty-five years ago; and the blacksmiths employed in the carriage-shops were skilled workmen, who could forge any part of the ironwork of a carriage, and who commanded good wages. Most of these irons are now stamped out by machinery, and the handwork is so subdivided that very few skilled men will be found in a large factory; the hand who tends a machine, and who can learn his work in a week or two, cannot, of course, obtain the remuneration paid to the superior mechanic of the days before the war.

The third fact is the increased cost of many of the necessaries of life. Clothing and flour and some groceries are somewhat cheaper; rent, which is the largest item in the poor man's expenditure, has increased, and meats, vegetables, butter, milk, and fuel are much dearer. On the whole, then, it may be questioned whether the average annual wages of the average workingman will purchase for him any more of the necessaries of life today than it would in the year before the war.

Mr. Carroll D. Wright, the most experienced and the most judicious of our labor statisticians, estimates that from 1860 to 1881 wages increased about thirty-one per cent, and prices about forty-one per cent.[10] If this estimate is to be trusted, the workingman was a little worse off in 1881

---

lege, London, was author of *Wages and Earnings of the Working Classes* (London, 1885).

9. [ED.] Richmond Mayo-Smith, professor of political economy at Columbia College, was later to write *Emigration and Immigration: a Study in Social Science* (N.Y., 1890).

10. [ED.] Carroll D. Wright (1840–1909), was then U.S. Commissioner of Labor, later president of Clark College.

than in 1860; and the year 1881 was an exceptionally prosperous year for the working people.

Nevertheless, as I have said, it is not well to dogmatize. We need more light on this question. Overconfident statements on either side are not to be encouraged. All I can say is, that such light as I can get inclines me to the belief that the real annual wages of labor are little, if any, higher to-day than they were in 1860. If this is all that can be said, then the wage-workers are falling behind the rest of the community; for, between 1860 and 1880 the wealth of the whole country increased from sixteen billions of dollars to forty-three billions, or one hundred and seventy per cent, and the average income must have been very considerably increased.

In 1860 the value of the manufactured goods produced in this country was eighteen hundred millions of dollars; in 1880 it was fifty-three hundred millions, almost three times as much. This is the pile to be divided. The number of the persons among whom it is to be divided has grown about sixty per cent — but not half as fast as the pile has grown. And now, when the working classes come up to get their share of the pile, they complain and rebel. "What is the matter with you?" asks some rather thoughtless onlooker. "Are you not getting as much as you ever got?" "Perhaps we are," is the answer, "but that pile was produced very largely by our labor; it is about three times as large as it was twenty-five years ago, and it looks to us as though we ought to get a good deal more than we got then. Other people, who do not labor with their hands, are getting more out of it now than they got then; the traders as a class, the professional people, the people on salaries, most of them, are able to live in a great deal better style now than they could afford a quarter of a century ago; while as for the capitalists and employers, they certainly show us many evidences of greatly increased wealth. Some of us can remember the social conditions of twenty-five years ago, and the signs of opulence and splendor then visible were few and insignificant, compared with what we see nowadays. We can compare in our memory the most luxurious sections and environs of New York and Boston and Philadelphia and Cleveland and Chicago then with what we see today, and the increase in the magnificence is amazing. There were a number of fine turnouts at Saratoga and Newport in 1860; but the luxury of that day was plebeian simplicity compared with the extravagance of today. Long Branch was a cluster of simple wooden cottages then; travel up and down the Jersey coast today, and see the oriental pomp and magnificence that spread themselves all over that favored region. Much the same can be said of the

Atlantic coast north of Boston. Such sights are common. We should know by the evidence of our eyes, if the census had nothing to say about it, that the wealth of this country is increasing very fast; we can see where the bulk of it is going; and we know, by a bitter experience, that we are getting a very small share of it.

"We read the newspapers too, and know something of that class of plutocrats which has sprung up in this country within twenty-five years. Some of us can remember the time when there were only one or two men in the country worth a million dollars; now there are hundreds of them. We pick up a newspaper and read such an item as this, which appeared in many of the journals in the month of January 1880: 'The profits of the Wall Street kings the past year were enormous. It is estimated that Vanderbilt made thirty millions; Jay Gould, fifteen millions; Russell Sage, ten millions; Sidney Dillon, ten millions; James R. Keene, eight millions; and several others from one to two millions each, making a grant total for ten or twelve estates of about eighty millions of dollars.' We know, of course, that there is some exaggeration about this; but if half of it is true, the story is ominous. What is more, we know that these rich men are gaining control of our courts and our legislatures, and of the Congress of the United States, and they get the legislation that protects their interests and builds up their fortunes, and that taxes us to enrich them. It looks as though we had a system of things under which the rich were sure to grow richer, and the poor, at the best, to remain as they are, shut down to a bare subsistence. We do not like the prospect. We think it is not fair. We are not going to submit to it, if we can help ourselves; and we see no other way but to band ourselves together for mutual protection and defense, and fight against this adverse fate."

Such is the reply of the more intelligent and sober of the wage-workers to the critic who cavils at their discontent. I submit that they make out, at any rate, a prima facie case. I submit that what they say has so much reason and justice that no right-minded man can dismiss it with a growl and a sneer. Their fears of social degradation are not groundless. As things are going now, it looks as though they would steadily be forced by the combinations above them to remain at the very bottom of the ladder, while the rest are climbing over their heads to independence and opulence. And since this is the day and age of combinations, since capital in a thousand ways is forming combinations for its own advantage, who will deny to labor the right to combine for the assertion of its just claims?

Combination means war, I admit. Combinations, whether of capital or of labor, are generally made in these days for fighting purposes. And war is a great evil — no doubt of that. But it is not the greatest of evils. The permanent social degradation of the people who do the world's work would be a greater evil. And if, by combination, the wage-workers can resist the tendencies that are crowding them down, and can assert and maintain their right to a proportional share of the growing wealth, then let them combine, and let all the people say, Amen!

The state of the industrial world is a state of war. And if war is the word, then the efficient combination and organization must not all be on the side of capital; labor must be allowed to make the combinations necessary for the protection of its own interests. While the conflict is in progress, labor has the same right that capital has to prosecute the warfare in the most effective way. If war is the order of the day, we must grant to labor belligerent rights. The sooner this fact is recognized, the better for all concerned. The refusal to admit it has made the conflict, thus far, much more fierce and sanguinary than it would otherwise have been.

So far as the students of political economy are concerned, it is now, I believe, universally agreed that the right of the workmen to combine cannot be questioned. Professor Sumner, who represents the old school of laissez-faire economists, and President Walker, who represents the new historical school, are equally emphatic in their assertion of the right of the workmen to stand together in trades unions for the defense of their own interests.[11] And the more reasonable of the employers are also beginning to see the point. Mr. James Means, a leading shoe manufacturer of Massachusetts, in an address to his employees last autumn, uttered these sensible words:

> If the public assumes an attitude of antagonism toward trades unions as a whole, the sense of injustice felt by the working people will bring them at last to seek redress by extreme measures. I believe that orderly trades unions are to be encouraged. . . . Labor is the poor man's commodity; it is the only thing he has to sell; he must get the highest price for it that he can by legitimate means. The price which labor will bring is the market price. What is the market price of any commodity? It is the point where the "bull movements" and the "bear movements" exactly counterbalance each other. The fact that labor brings a certain price in the market does not mean that such is a fair market price. It may be a price based upon in-

---

11. [ED.] William Graham Sumner (1840–1910) was professor of political and social science at Yale; Francis Amasa Walker (1847–97) was president of Massachusetts Institute of Technology.

justice. If there is any one who does not believe this, let him consider
what would be the effect upon the market price of wheat, or
any such commodity, if such price were governed entirely by
the "bears" and if the "bulls" were to cease their action. What is a
trades union? It is a "bull movement" in the labor market. Can any
one wish to see the price of that commodity which we call labor
governed by the "bears" alone? The "bears" organized, and no
one complains. Is it fair that the price of labor should be fixed by
powerful organizations opposed by weak individuals? Is it not
rather to be desired that a more reasonable price should be fixed by
organization met by organization?

Other utterances of the same tenor might be quoted.

The indications are, then, that in this warfare the belligerent rights of
the wage-workers will soon be recognized. Strong combinations of employers still insist that they will never recognize them, but they are fighting against fate; the community at large concedes the right to the
workingmen, and those who stand out will find it hard to stem the
current.

So the battle is joined. Capital and labor confront each other, both organized and resolute, both determined to win. What will be the issue? A
year or two ago we should have said without hesitation, Capital will win;
it is stronger and better organized, and it has the sinews of war. Up to
that time the victory had almost always been on the side of capital. The
great majority of the strikes had been unsuccessful. But within the last
year matters have taken a turn. The organization of the laborers is much
more perfect and more formidable now than ever before. It is by no
means clear that it may not prove a match for its antagonist. At any rate,
things have now assumed such a shape that we may fairly expect to see
some destructive fighting. The combinations on both sides are so strong
that they ought to be able to do each other, and the whole country, a great
deal of damage. It must be possible for them to paralyze the industries of
the nation; to waste a good part of its savings; to dig the chasm that separates the employer from the employed a great deal deeper and wider
than it now is; and to sow seeds of jealousy and spite that will bear a woeful harvest through many generations. *Is it not a good time to stop and
ask the question whether this warfare is really worth while?*

When people go to war, they generally have before them one of two
possible issues of the conflict. Each combatant may be determined on a
complete triumph over the other — a triumph that shall result in extermi-
nating or subjugating or enslaving the other; or each combatant may de-

sire to make an exhibition of his strength which shall enforce the respect of the other and secure honorable terms of peace. It is well for these combatants to determine, before they go any farther, whether they desire to subjugate one another.

Do the employing class think it would be a good thing to subjugate the wage-laborers — to reduce them to a condition in which they would be practically slaves or dependents? Do the employing class want to keep the wages of the laboring class down as nearly as they can to the level of subsistence? Doubtless there are selfish and greedy men among them who would care very little what became of the working people, so long as they were able to make themselves rich. But I am sure that the employers of labor as a rule cherish no such heartlessness; they know that it would be fatal to our national life if the class of wage-laborers became a permanently degraded class; they know that peace and prosperity cannot abide in the land unless all classes have an equal chance and a fair prospect. What is more, when they look at the matter from the lowest materialistic standpoint, they know that the wage-laborers constitute a very large share of the consumers of goods; that if they are able to purchase nothing but the bare necessaries of life, trade will be dull; that when they have plenty of money in their pockets trade will be brisk; that it is not, therefore, for the interest of the manufacturing and mercantile classes that the laboring classes should be reduced to the verge of starvation. Capital is not such a fool as to wish to push this war to the subjugation of its antagonist.

Neither does labor, I trust, desire to subjugate capital. That, to be sure, is the socialistic program: the theory of socialism is that the capital shall all belong to the state, and shall be owned and controlled by the workers; that there shall be no private enterprise; that all the business of production and transportation and exchange shall be managed by state officials. But we are not ready yet for such a revolution. Beyond all question, the industrial system which is based on private enterprise is the best system practicable at the present time, and will be for a long time to come. It needs to be modified, but it cannot be overthrown without disaster to the working classes. Business will be managed for a good while yet by captains of industry; and it is for the interest of the people who do the world's work that it should be. Larger gains, on the whole, will come to them through this management properly modified than through any which they could substitute for it. The attempt to destroy or even cripple capitalistic enterprise is suicidal. So then it is absurd and even monstrous for either of these combatants to dream of subjugating the other. It is for the interest of each that the other should be free and prosperous and contented and hopeful.

The other rational object that men have in fighting is the assertion of their rights and the demonstration of their prowess. They want to make it evident that it is not safe to encroach upon their liberties; they want to lay the foundations of an honorable peace. Have not these two combatants been fighting long enough to accomplish this object? Surely labor has reason enough to respect and even dread the power of capital; and is not capital by this time sufficiently impressed with the power of labor? Is it not a good time for the contending parties to ground their arms, and shake hands, and sit down, and have a frank and friendly conference? Is not this business of war a senseless, brutal, barbarous business, at best? Does either side expect to do itself any good by fighting the other? It is about as rational as it would be for the right hand and the left hand to smite each other with persistent and deadly enmity, or for the eyes and the ears to array themselves against each other in a remorseless feud. It is a sorry comment on our civilization that here, at the end of the nineteenth Christian century, sane and full-grown men, whose welfare depends wholly on the recognition of their mutual interests and on the cooperation of their efforts, should be ready to spend a good share of their time in trying to cripple or destroy one another. It is not only wicked, it is stupid; it is not simply monstrous, it is ridiculous.

Are not the employers ready, by this time, to hear reason? Have they not had fighting enough for the present? Are they not willing to make peace? If so, the first thing for them to do is to face the fact that the wage-workers, by whose labor they are gaining their wealth, are entitled to a little better share of the joint product than they are getting now; that they have a perfect right to expect it, to ask for it, and to combine for the purpose of getting it. When that fact is frankly admitted, arbitration of labor disputes will follow as a matter of course.

The demand for fewer hours of labor must also be fairly considered. It does not seem, on the face of it, altogether unreasonable. With the continual improvements in machinery it is not at all incredible that the world's wants can be supplied by eight hours' work in a day. Would it not be vastly better for the health, the morals, and the thrift of the community to have our shops and factories going eight hours a day all the year round than to have them go ten hours a day for nine or ten months, and be idle all day for two or three months in the year, which is the present order in large sections of the country? The question whether the daily working time can be reduced one-fifth with no diminution in the daily wage is, of course, a question that must be settled on economical rather than sentimental principles. But some interesting experiments tend to show that, even when machinery is a large factor in production, the product of eight hours' work will be much more than four-fifths of the product of ten hours' work. The reduction of the time will not proportionately reduce the product, and should not, therefore, proportionately reduce the wage.

It is often said that increased wages and shorter hours will only promote recklessness and dissipation among the men; that the addition to their income would go to the saloons; that the enlargement of their leisure would result in debauchery. Such statements are too sweeping. Some of the more ignorant and degraded of the men would be affected in this way, no doubt, but it would not be true of all of them; it would not, I trust, be true of the majority of them. The new hope, the enlarged opportunity, would make the better elements among them self-respecting and frugal; their leisure would not all go to the uses of the flesh. The most careful English student of this question, Professor Leone Levi, bears this testimony:

> As a rule, and in the long run, scarcity, low wages, and scantiness of food go hand in hand with high mortality, drunkenness, and crime; while abundance, high wages, and full consumption go hand in hand with low mortality, temperance, and good behavior. A sudden increase of wages, as in the colliery districts in 1872–73, may find the recipients utterly unprepared for their good fortunes. And so we have heard of miners indulging in champagne wine, and of puddlers purchasing for themselves sealskin waistcoats. But reason speedily asserts her higher sway. The housewife eagerly arrests a portion of the higher wages to furnish the bare rooms, to fill the empty cupboard, and to clothe the children. Little by little, as the novel condition with its bountiful stores is realized, self-respect increases, sobriety of conduct is induced, and the family as a whole rises to habits of virtue and prosperity.[12]

This is the result which we have good reason to expect, not by any means universally, but on the whole, and in the long run, from the improvement in the laborer's condition. Some laborers cannot bear prosperity; some employers cannot. Most employers, I dare say, have an abiding conviction that it would not hurt them in the least to be a little better off,

12. *Wages and Earnings of the Working Classes*, 35.

and they may safely reason in the same way with regard to their men. On the whole, and in the long run, happiness is better for men than misery, plenty better than want, hope better than despair. Every effort that is made for the amelioration of humanity rests on that assumption.

Some employers chafe under the new demands of labor. Doubtless these demands are sometimes arrogant and unreasonable; is this to be wondered at? War is an essentially unreasonable business; it is not by reason that its issues are determined, but by force. "It is a pity," men say, "if an employer cannot manage his business to suit himself." It may be a pity, but it is true. If by this phrase is meant managing his business solely in his own interest, that is exactly what he cannot do. The assumption that he can is one of the bottom causes of all this trouble. It is true that employers have long been taught that if they were perfectly selfish in the management of their business, the results would be beneficent; that this kingdom of industry is the one department of human activity with which conscience and good will have no normal relation; that self-interest is and must be the sole ruler of this realm. Most of them have believed this doctrine; some of them have acted accordingly; but many of them have behaved a great deal better than the theory required them to behave, and have mixed not a little humanity with their business, thinking, no doubt, all the while that they were doing a silly thing. It was not a silly thing. The wisdom of their hearts was sounder than the theories of their heads. The doctrine which bases all the relations of employer and employed upon self-interest is a doctrine of the pit; it has been bringing hell to earth in large installments for a good many years. There is no department of human conduct in which pure egoism is a safe guide. No employer can manage his business exclusively in his own interest. It is not exclusively his business. The men who do the work are in reality his business partners, and he is bound to think of them, and care for them, and manage the business in their interest as well as his own. This is what employers must do if they want peace. You can have hell in your factory, or you can have heaven there, just which you please. If it is hell that you want, build your business on the law of hell, which is simply, "Every man for himself and the devil take the hindmost!" Out of that will come wars and fightings, perennial and unrelenting. If it is heaven that you want, then build your business on the law of the kingdom of heaven, which is, "Thou shalt love thy neighbor as thyself." That will put you in the path of peace.

If peace is better than war, the employer's first problem must be to find a way of getting his enterprise on a peace basis. He can only do that by identifying his men with himself in the hopes, the prospects, the rewards of their joint undertaking. It begins to be evident to many employers that industrial partnership in some form is the next step in the evolution of our industrial system. This method has been thoroughly tried in scores of establishments, large and small, upon the continent of Europe, with splendid and almost unvarying success. Multitudes of people, who never have tried it, and have never seen it tried, and who know nothing about it, are free to say that it would not work; but what is the judgment of such doctrinaires worth in the face of the almost unbroken experience of the hundreds who have tried it? It is hard to keep one's patience when those who profess to be "practical men" set up their ipse dixit against the solid achievements of thirty years of peaceful and prosperous industry conducted upon this basis.

I have called attention in another chapter to the inspiring recital by Mr. Sedley Taylor of the progress of this principle in Europe.[13] Quite a number of important firms and companies in this country have been practicing it with entire success for several years; and the rapidity with which the movement has been advancing since the beginning of the present year is something notable. We shall soon have a chance to see for ourselves whether profit-sharing will work in this country.

The common objections to this method are easily answered. "Some years there are no profits to divide," it is said. True; and in such years the workmen would get their regular wages, but no bonus at the end of the year.

"But this would make them dissatisfied and rebellious," it is urged. "They would think they had been cheated." This is assuming that they are hopelessly unreasonable and unjust. It is probable that if the employer really wishes to make his men the sharers of his prosperity, he will be able to make them believe it, and that they will forego their dividend without complaint.

"But there are sometimes losses," it is said, "and it is not fair that the men should share in the profits unless they share in the losses also." Let that be granted. But the system provides for laying aside a reserve fund in the prosperous years, out of which losses could be made up in the unprosperous years. Thus the workmen do share in the losses.

"But the profits are none too large now," it is urged; "to lessen them by an additional dividend to labor would cripple many industries." The

13. [ED.] Sedley Taylor, of Trinity College, Cambridge, was author of *Profit-Sharing between Capital and Labour* (London, 1884).

census makes it plain that the laborer might have a larger share of the profits without doing anybody any injustice; but this point may be waived. It is enough to say that all the economists declare that whatever renders labor more efficient is a clear gain both to labor and capital; it makes a larger product to divide between them. And it is the general testimony of those who have tried profit-sharing, that it makes the laborer more industrious and more economical of materials and tools; that the expense of superintendence is largely reduced; that the employer has as much left after he has paid the laborer his share of the profit as he had before. A slight acquaintance with human nature would make it easy to believe that this might be.

It does not seem at all incredible that business might be more prosperous on a peace basis than on a war basis; and it is at least possible that the employer could put it on a peace basis by making his men his business partners, and letting them share with himself in the rewards of their joint industry. I will venture to predict that peace will never come to stay until this principle, under some form, has been introduced into the industrial order.

What answer now shall we hear from the men of toil to this burning question? Shall it be peace or war? Before they give their voices for the continuance of war, some things should be well considered.

In the first place, they ought to see that the employing class is not their worst enemy. It is not the employing class, as such, that is absorbing the wealth of this country, so much as it is the gamblers and the political corruptionists. A pretty large share of the plutocrats have gained their wealth by gambling operations in the stock and produce exchanges, and by bribing city councils and legislatures and courts and congresses. With franchises and legislative favors and judicial decisions thus obtained, they have robbed the public for their own benefit. The net profits of industry are not excessive, but the plunder of these parasites is enormous. After they have filled their pockets out of the product of industry, there is a good deal less to be divided between employers and laborers. The working classes are just as much responsible for their existence as their employers are. If workingmen had been as careful in choosing men to represent them in the city councils and the legislatures as they ought to have been, this class of parasites could never have flourished as they have done. The first fight for them to make is against these parasites of industry.

In the second place, the workingmen should make up their minds before they push this fight any further, whether they wish to overthrow the present system of industry, or whether they prefer to modify it, so that it shall be more favorable to their interest. They may be able to destroy it; but it will be well for them to count the cost before entering on that campaign. Samson overthrew the temple of the Philistines; but it is instructive to remember what became of Samson.

In the third place, if workingmen do not want to exterminate private enterprise, and if they expect to have business relations with the employing class, they cannot too soon unlearn the bitter and violent habits of speech and thought into which they have been falling of late in their discussion of the labor question. The sweeping denunciations of the capitalists as thieves and swindlers and robbers, in which some of them are wont to indulge, are both unwise and unjust. Successful business relations cannot be maintained among men who cherish such feelings toward one another. There are heartless and selfish men among employers; so there are among laborers. Wrongs are done on both sides; people who are at war are not apt to be scrupulous about respecting one another's rights. Many employers are heartily desirous of doing their men full justice; and the men by no means always show a proper appreciation of this good will. Permit me to say that I know something about this war; I have been in the thick of it for thirty years, trying to make peace, and helping to care for the sick and the wounded; and I know that the wrong is not all on one side, and that the harsh judgments and the fierce talk of both sides are inexcusable.

In the fourth place, if workingmen want business put on a peace basis, let them say so, and show that they mean it. If they desire to have labor disputes settled by arbitration, let them frankly and good-naturedly ask for arbitration, and show that they have a reasonable temper and a purpose to stand by a fair award. If they want profit-sharing, let them put that into their platforms, and make it clear to their employers that they can be trusted to give the scheme a fair trial. Some of them are hoping for cooperation; for an organization of industry in which the men who do the work shall own the capital, and receive both profits and wages. To every such enterprise, Godspeed! It takes a high degree of intelligence and self-control to cooperate in production; workingmen are gaining these qualifications steadily; they will be ready for it before long. But production, on any basis, requires capital — capital to purchase the plant, and capital to live on while the product is maturing; and capital can be got by those who are not born rich in only two ways — by saving, and by stealing. Workingmen cannot afford to steal; they will never prosper if they do. It is true that many of our plutocrats got their money by stealing from the people at large, but their prosperity is a blight upon them and upon the nation. If they have been unjust, our workingmen cannot afford to rebuild the industry of the country on the same foundation of injustice. It is only by economy that the capital can be accumulated by which they can cooperate; and it is to be hoped that profit-sharing will put them in the path that leads to this goal.

The present appears to be a critical time in the history of labor. Within the past few months our workingmen have suddenly come to the consciousness of great power. Their more compact organization, their more effective weapons of war, have given them advantages that they never had before. The question of the hour is whether they can use this power temperately and wisely. There are ominous signs of a disposition to employ it passionately and vindictively. Men who speak in the interests of selfish capital are heard to express the confident hope that the workingmen will soon overstep the bounds of prudence and justice, and ruin their own prospects. That is the real danger. Doubtless, it is hard for those who are smarting under a sense of injustice to be always temperate and judicious; but the welfare of these men depends on keeping their heads cool. Vengeance does not belong to them; and they are strong enough now to be magnanimous.

It is easy for the organizations of labor to cripple by unreasonable demands the industries of whole sections. They have done this thing already more than once. In the stoppages and readjustments thus occurring, great suffering is caused and no advantage is gained. An unjust demand, even if it be temporarily enforced, always reacts on those who make it. The working classes have now tremendous power; they may easily employ it for self-destruction. It is quite possible for them to use their power tyrannically; and tyranny will not thrive in this day, the tyranny of a mob no more than the tyranny of an autocrat. This weapon of the boycott with which the labor unions have lately armed themselves is pretty sure to prove a boomerang. If they use it recklessly, there may easily arise a consumers' union, to fight them with their own fire — to patronize those whom they proscribe. Already the popular indignation at the unscrupulous use of this weapon is so strong that the publication of a boycott has proved, in several cases, an excellent advertisement of the boycotted dealer.

With all the improved enginery of war the labor unions are sure to find that war is dangerous business. It is all the more dangerous because of these improved weapons. It can never be anything else but perilous and destructive business. Let not these combatants on either side suppose that they can hurt and maim their antagonists and get no harm themselves!

Over all this wretched strife one can imagine those "better angels of our nature," whose ministry Abraham Lincoln once pathetically but vainly invoked, bending with divine compassion and crying to the embattled hosts with solemn rebuke and benignant appeal: Is it well, brother men, is it well to fight? Is it not better to be friends? Are you not all children of one Father? Nay, are you not, as the great apostle said, members one of another? Your war is not only wholesale fratricide, it is social suicide. It is little to say that you cannot afford to fight: you cannot live apart; you must live for one another. That is the way you were made to live; and you will never have anything but trouble and sorrow till you learn that way and walk in it. The stars in their courses will fight against you until you make peace with one another. Have we not had more than enough of war and its dismal noises and its spectral train of woes; more than enough of silent looms and fireless forges; of children's faces pale with hunger, and women's sunken eyes; of hearts made fierce and hard by long-cherished enmities; of class arrayed against class and neighbor against neighbor? Oh, put it all away from you — the hate, the suspicion, the scorn; stand here together, brethren as you are, helpers of one another as you must be, and promise one another that you will do what you can, every one of you, to bring the day when between Labor and Capital there shall be no longer war, but peace for evermore.

THE CHRISTIAN LEAGUE OF CONNECTICUT [1]

Editor's introduction. One of Gladden's close friends was Roswell Smith (1829–92), president of the Century Company. Smith asked Gladden to write for *The Century Magazine* a story of how people in some New England town got together and united their forces in practical Christian work. Gladden responded with what proved to be one of his most successful fictional works. Much interest was stirred by his imaginative tale. He said later:

> The series of four articles attracted more attention than any other magazine work of mine had done; not only church people, but all sorts of people, appeared to be interested in them. The practical question of Christian cooperation which they raised was one that appealed to many. To a large extent they were taken for veritable history; I received many curious letters both from this country and from England, where they were republished, asking for further information concerning the experiment.[2]

Published without an explanatory preface, again the story was often read as though it were factual. There were enough Christian unions of various kinds to make it plausible; for example, one man wrote to Gladden that there had been a group in Danbury, Connecticut, much like his fictitious league.[3]

A flood of imaginative writing in the United States on behalf of social Christianity followed Gladden's example. Such diverse figures as Edward Everett Hale, Katherine Pearson Woods, Albion W. Tourgee, Florence Converse, the American Winston Churchill, Vida Scudder, Susan Glaspell, and Charles M. Sheldon contributed to a genre that can be broadly described as "the social gospel novel."[4] Ten years after his first success of this sort, Gladden wrote another story for *The Century Magazine*, this

---

1. *The Christian League of Connecticut* (N.Y., 1883), chaps. XI and XII, 110–29.
2. *Recollections*, 274–75.
3. D. M. Hodge to Gladden, October 23, 1882, Washington Gladden Papers, Box 2.
4. Hopkins, *The Rise of the Social Gospel*, 141–48; cf. Walter B. Rideout, *The Radical Novel in the United States, 1900–1954: Some Interrelations of Literature and Society* (Cambridge, Mass., 1956).

time focusing on urban problems. Republished in book form at a time of growing interest in municipal reform, it gave impetus to the founding of certain organizations devoted to city improvement.[5]

The story of *The Christian League of Connecticut* is told chiefly in the form of reports on the meetings of the imaginary organization. According to the story, the idea of an association representing the various churches of the town of New Albion originated in the minds of the Reverend Theodore Strong, a Congregational minister, and his prominent parishioner, Mr. Walter Franklin. They called together a representative gathering which drew up a constitution for "The Christian League Club of New Albion." It was to be concerned with such things as evangelization and missions, social problems and youth activities. There was to be no creed, nor was theological discussion allowed in the club. As the story unfolds, the league is found to be successful in bringing Christian work to neglected areas in the town. A union church is planted in the neglected suburb of Cyprusville. A church struggling with a heavy debt is helped by the combined forces of the association. Joint effort in law enforcement and in the relief of the poor is undertaken. Then the nearby town of Monroeville hears about the league, and talks are held with several of its leaders. The selection that follows begins with a meeting of the club in New Albion, at which the Monroeville situation is discussed. Of the characters who appear, Dr. Sampson is the Baptist pastor, Dr. Phelps serves the historic First Church (Congregational), Mr. Hartwell is the Methodist minister, Mr. Peters speaks as a layman, and Dr. Strickland is the rector of the Episcopal Church.

❖   ❖   ❖   ❖

XI

The report of the conversation in Dr. Sampson's study furnished a theme for the next meeting of the club.

"Since our talk that morning," said Dr. Sampson, "I have taken great pains to get at a few of the facts about the small towns in this county. Monroeville is the type of a class. There is Stapleton, with a population of eleven hundred and with four churches; Scantico, with six hundred people and three churches; Rowell, with nine hundred people and four churches; and so on. Eight towns in this county, with an aggregate popu-

5. *The Cosmopolis City Club* (N.Y., 1893).

lation of nine thousand one hundred and thirty-four, support thirty-seven religious societies. Of these, at least fifteen are receiving more or less aid from the various home missionary organizations."

"Even when the societies are self-supporting," said Dr. Phelps, "the support is generally meager, the membership is small, and the terms of the pastorates are lamentably short."

"It is plain," said Mr. Hartwell, "that the churches in these small towns ought to unite. What hinders them?"

"First," answered the doctor, "is the strength of the sectarian prejudice — always more intense in the small places than in the large ones. Then there is a sentiment much less reprehensible — the attachment to the local organization, around which many grateful memories cling. The people do not like to give up a church which may have a noble history, and which is sure to be the shrine of sweet associations."

"Certainly," said Mr. Hartwell; "those hindrances are obvious. They may be called sentimental; even so, they are not easily overcome. Are there any other practical obstacles?"

"In most of these towns," said Mr. Peters, "the only way of uniting would be to abandon the old organizations and form a new one — a union church, like ours at Cyprusville."

"But do you know," Mr. Franklin broke in, "that it is legally impossible to do anything of the sort?"

"What do you mean?" demanded three or four voices.

"Just what I say. The union of two churches of different denominations is a proceeding so rare that no provision for it is made, so far as I can learn, in our statutes, nor in those of any other State. Secular corporations can be legally consolidated, but church corporations cannot be. Christian union seems to be regarded by our legislators as against public policy. Churches have sometimes been brought together, but the act was unwarranted by law. Any troublesome member of either church could have procured an order from the courts tearing them apart again."

"Then," said Mr. Strong, "it is high time that we had an act before the legislature, enabling churches to obey the Christian law. I hope that unanimous consent will be given to the appointment, by this club, of Mr. Franklin as our agent, to secure the passage of such a law at this session."

Consent was readily given. Concerning the work of Mr. Franklin in the lobby of the Connecticut legislature the historian of the club is not fully informed; but the facts to be recorded below indicate that he must have been successful.

"There is another practical difficulty," said Mr. Franklin, picking up the thread of the discussion where Mr. Peters had dropped it, "more serious than the legal disability. When you have got your union churches formed, they belong nowhere. Now, people like to feel that they do belong somewhere. If they are weak and small themselves, they enjoy the knowledge that they are members of some respectable body in whose interests they have a part. These union churches have nowhere to go, unless we invite them into our Congregational conferences, as we generally do. But then the other sectarians say that a union church is nothing but a Congregational church. There is truth enough in what they say to make it necessary to devise some means by which these union churches may find a less ambiguous fellowship; and I propose a convention of all the churches in the county, to meet twice a year, for consultation about Christian work in the county."

"Who should call such a convention?" asked Mr. Hartwell.

"This club," answered Mr. Franklin. "A committee, consisting of the minister and one layman from each of our churches, should issue the call, summoning every church in the county to send its pastor and a lay delegate to such a convention, at which a permanent organization should be effected."

"What churches should we invite?"

"I would put the Apostles' Creed into the call, and send it to every church in the county — Protestant or Roman Catholic — with a sentence explaining that any church which accepts this creed and conforms to it in its teaching would be welcome in the convention."

"Do you suppose that the Romanists would come?" queried Dr. Strickland.

"I fear they would not; but I would invite them."

"Would you dare to open the doors to heretics?" asked Mr. Peters.

"Any church that makes its teachings conform to the Apostles' Creed is orthodox enough for me. I mean that I am willing to make that Creed the basis of union in Christian work. Are not you?"

"I'm not at this moment prepared to say that I would not."

"I trust," said the banker, dryly, "that you never will be any better prepared than you are at this moment."

The club discussed the proposed convention vigorously for an hour, and then, no one dissenting, the committee was appointed and the call was speedily issued. The object of the convention, as stated in the call, was "to promote union and efficiency in Christian work, and to secure a more systematic evangelization of the destitute neighborhoods throughout the county." The organization effected was simple. It was named "The Christian League of Bradford County." The only permanent officer was the secretary. An outlook committee of five was to be appointed at each meeting, whose duty it should be to make inquiry respecting the feeble churches, and to secure, so far as possible, cooperation or consolidation. Meetings were to be held twice a year, on the first Tuesdays of April and October. Papers and addresses showing the waste and mischief caused by sectarian divisions, and the need of unity, were to be provided by the outlook committee for each meeting. The principal object of the League, as defined in the preamble, was "to generate and disseminate right opinions respecting the duty of Christians to cooperate, to see that the waste places are cultivated, and to extend the fellowship of all believers to those churches that have no denominational fellowship."

There was some hesitation, at first, about this project; but the representatives of the New Albion churches all threw themselves into it with such heartiness that the doubts and scruples of the rest were vanquished, and the constitution was adopted with some enthusiasm.

Not many days after this, a letter from Monroeville invited a deputation from the churches of New Albion to come up and hold a public meeting in the interests of Christian union. The three ministers who had part in the accidental conference in Dr. Sampson's study responded to this call, taking with them Dr. Strickland, of the Episcopalians, and Elder Bates, of the Adventists. They found the town hall crowded with a curious and not very sympathetic assembly. It was evident that there were not a few of these auditors who were quite of the mind of the historic deacon: they were ready to be convinced, if they were in error, and would like to see the man that could do it. But the New Albion delegation had no misgivings. They knew that the idea they advocated was right and reasonable, and they talked like men who expected to carry their point. The speech of the evening, all things considered, was that of Mr. Hartwell. Several years of his earlier ministry had been spent in these small towns, and he spoke from a full experience of the evils of sectarian division.

"I was never in Monroeville before," he said; "but I have lived in towns just like it, and I can tell something about the state of things in this town which will be no news to you, but which it may do no harm to hear. Your five little societies, living here at a poor, dying rate, do not have a very good time. You cannot live without help from outside; that is confessed. With all the help you can get, none of these churches is able to offer its pastor a decent living. The salaries are so small that the grade of men you are able to secure is extremely low. Now and then a man of good gifts and great fidelity, like the venerable pastor of the Baptist Church, settles in a town like this and stays many years; but the great majority are young men who will not stay more than a year or two, or men who have failed everywhere else, and who sometimes fasten themselves on you and give you plenty of trouble in getting rid of them. The Methodists have a way of managing such cases; but the Methodist churches in these small towns rarely keep a man through the three years that the discipline allows, unless he is a man they do not want. Is not that true?

"The consequence is that your Christian work is poorly done. Many waste places in the corners of these towns are sadly neglected, and are becoming rapidly heathenized. The religious wants of these communities are not so well provided for as they were in the days when there was but one church. You say that you are sending down to the cities a constant stream of your young men, and that is true; but the young men that you are sending us nowadays are not of so good a quality as those you sent fifty years ago. The young men of your town do not get so much benefit from your churches as they got fifty or sixty years ago. How can they? What have you here to attract the attention and command the respect of intelligent young men? Your feeble, half-alive churches, that struggle for existence and are afflicted with chronic debility, do not strongly appeal to the enthusiasm of young men.

"The social life of your town is marred by these hateful divisions. The people of each church are a little clique; there are not enough of them to make it lively when they get together; petty sectarian jealousies keep you apart. If the Methodists have a fair or a supper, very few go but their own folks; if the Congregationalists try to have a course of lectures, they must depend mainly on their own congregation for an audience. Of course, there is some denominational reciprocity, but it is limited. The barrenness of your social life is largely due to these sectarian divisions. They constitute one of the principal reasons why life here is undesirable — why people, especially young men, get away as soon as ever they can.

"So, then, even as things are now, with all the help you are getting, I am sure that you yourselves can see that you are not succeeding in doing for your town, with your present machinery, what needs to be done.

"The devotion and the earnestness of many men and women here is worthy of all praise; but the results of their work, as they will admit, are meager and unsatisfactory. If, then, things could go on upon the present basis, there would not be much encouragement in the prospect; but I am bound to tell you that I doubt whether things can go on much longer upon the present basis. I do not believe that the Christian people of the country will be willing much longer to contribute money for the perpetuation of these sectarian divisions. Many are beginning to see pretty clearly the foolishness and sin of them, and to demand that they shall cease. This is a fact to which you must give due heed. You are wise enough to make a virtue of necessity.

"Think, if you can, how much better it would be to have one religious society here instead of five. You could have one good church edifice; you could take the largest and best of your three and renovate and beautify it for your place of worship, and fit up one of the others for a lecture hall and for other social purposes. You could have one first-rate minister, and pay him a good salary, and not need to beg a cent of it from anybody. You could have your pick of all the singers in town for your choir. You would have one fine congregation — large enough to make preaching and listening, too, much more inspiring. Your minister would be likely to remain with you several years — long enough to get acquainted with the absentees of the out districts, to gain their friendship, and to mature plans of successful work among them. Your social life would be improved. By combining all your forces, you could have singing schools, concerts, courses of lectures, reading circles, various literary and musical diversions of an excellent character. Monroeville would be a pleasanter place to live in; people would not be in such a hurry to get away; property would cease to depreciate.

"What is the condition of all this gain? Simply that you should drop your small, sectarian prejudices, and begin to be what the disciples were called at Antioch — Christians, nothing more nor less. Simply that you should learn to love Christ and his cause better than you love your own pet peculiarities of doctrine or worship. Is that impossible? Does anybody mean to say that the members of these churches in Monroeville are so narrow and obstinate that they cannot make so small a sacrifice for so great a good; that they will insist on maintaining in a town of eight hundred inhabitants five separate, starving, sectarian organizations instead of one vigorous Christian church? Does any man tell me that the people of Monroeville, after coming together and looking this question in the face, are going away to say, 'It is of no use; we are too selfish and bigoted; we cannot live together peaceably; we must stick to our separate churches, though they perish, and religion and virtue and social life perish with them'? No, my friends. I have a better opinion of you. You have remained in this unhappy condition because you saw no good way out of it; now the way is open, and you will walk in it."

Mr. Hartwell's speech carried the day. A committee, consisting of the pastor and two members from each of the societies, was named on the spot and instructed to mature a plan of consolidation, to be presented to each of the churches. Within two months, all the old societies had been disbanded, and a new one formed under the style of Unity Church. The meetinghouse of the Congregationalists, which was largest and most central, was retained as the house of worship; that of the Baptists was refitted as a social hall, and that of the Methodists was purchased by the town for a schoolhouse — the money thus obtained being devoted to the renovation of the other houses. The Apostles' Creed served the new church for its confession of faith, and its organization was in most respects similar to that of the church in Cyprusville. Mr. Slade easily found another field of labor in Kansas, the end of the conference year terminated Mr. Towne's stay in Monroeville, and Elder Crane, who continued to reside in the town, gratified the universal wish by taking charge of the new organization until a pastor could be found.[6] The behavior of the good old clergyman in all this experience was eminently judicious and Christian. His rhetoric was turgid and his opinions were not modern, but his heart was sound and the people loved him.

Thus it was that five feeble bands of sectaries in one small town were united into one efficient and self-supporting Christian church.

XII

A little more than two years after the union mass meeting in the town hall at Monroeville, on a delightful October evening, old Major stopped at the parsonage door, and the parson took his seat in the open buggy.[7]

"Let's see; how long have you been gone?"

"Eighteen months, next Monday."

6. [ED.] Mr. Slade was the Congregational pastor in Monroeville, Towne the Methodist, and Crane the Baptist.

7. [ED.] The assumption here is that the reader will remember the opening pages of the story; "old Major" is Mr. Franklin's horse, and the returning parson is Mr. Strong.

"And you've seen pretty much all that's worth seeing of Europe, Asia, and Africa?"

"Not quite, but enough to think of for some time."

"And you're thoroughly rested and well?"

"Never was so well in my life."

"Good! We were very anxious about you at first, but the later news comforted us. The people have taken solid enjoyment all the while in the knowledge that you were resting and recovering your health. They will give you a hearty welcome at the prayer meeting tomorrow night."

"Bless their faithful hearts!" said the pastor, his eyes filling. "How gladly will I spend and be spent for them in the coming days! But tell me the news. I've had family news often, and church news now and then, but beyond these almost nothing. How goes the club?"

"Gloriously! It is pushing right on to conquest. At every meeting we have news of some good fruit that has grown from its sowing."

"How fares the work among the poor?"

"We've got that into excellent shape. Mendicancy and pauperism are pretty effectually suppressed. There are no more beggars at our back doors; the tramps give us a wide berth. We hammered at the overseers of the poor till we got them to stop their careless largesses of alms to the idle and the vicious; they employ our visitors, now, to investigate their cases, and the amount of outdoor relief has been reduced sixty per cent."

"But I hope you haven't ended with suppressing pauperism?"

"Oh, no. Our visitors are beginning to take hold of the work of caring for the sick, and of helping the poor and the discouraged and the shiftless, in a most intelligent way. The work that has been accomplished, not only in ministering to the helpless, but in lifting up degraded families and inspiring the miserable with hopefulness and courage and self-respect, is the most genuine Christian work that has ever been done in New Albion."

"How about Dr. Strickland's kindergarten?"

"There are three of them now, all doing excellently."

"The Young Men's Club — is that thriving?"

"It has a membership of six hundred."

"And the County League — how is that flourishing?"

"Now you begin to get down to business with your catechism. The County League, sir, has its foot upon its native hills, but its fame has gone into all the earth. Didn't you hear of it in Moab?"

"Not a syllable," answered the parson, laughing.

"Well, sir, the Moabites may as well set their meetinghouses in order, for it will be after 'em shortly. See. You helped to reconstruct Monroeville. Scantico followed suit; but that was before you went away. Then the outlook committee got its eye on Rowell and began to put on a gentle pressure. The result there was different from that in the other two towns. The Methodist Church was pretty strong — much stronger than either of the other three, and the Committee recommended elimination by subtraction instead of substitution. The Methodist Church kept its organization, but broadened its methods somewhat, and the other people gave up their own churches and went in with the Methodists. Of course, the Methodists did everything they could to make it agreeable for the others; put them into offices, got a quiet, broad-minded man for their next minister, and exercised a real Christian hospitality in their reception of the members of the other churches. I hear that they have all learned to sing the Jubilee song:

"A Methodist, Methodist will I live,
And a Methodist will I die,"

with the spirit and the understanding also. That's Rowell. In Woodford, the Baptist Church was found to be the fittest to survive. The Baptist minister exchanges once a month regularly with the Rowell minister, and then the Baptists in Rowell who can't commune with the rest have a special communion service, and the Pedobaptists in Woodford who want their babies baptized have that service performed for them at their houses. In Tuckerton and Millville, union churches have been formed; and of the towns in their county where small populations were once split up among several feeble churches, all but two are now happy in possession of one good church. Besides, our outlook committee has been spying out the neglected districts, and stirring up the people of the towns to occupy them; we have reports from them in the meetings of the County League, and I am sure that a great many more people in Bradford County are now under religious influences than there ever were before."

"Good!" shouted Mr. Strong.

"But you haven't got the whole of it yet," said Franklin. "To the next meeting of the County League, after you went away, a delegation of Dunham County folks, from Samsonville and Knox and other places, came in, and they got into the spirit of the movement, and went back and formed a Christian League in Dunham County. The matter began to be talked about all over the State. The newspapers took hold of it, and pushed it hard; the business men perceived the reasonableness and justice of it, and made their influence felt in favor of it, and soon every county in the State had swung into line. Midland County was the last to organize, and their league was formed last April, five months ago. And week before last the secretaries and outlook committees of all the county leagues held a meeting in Bradford, and formed 'The Christian League of Connecticut.' Its object, as stated in the constitution, is 'to promote efficiency and economy in Christian work, by the suppression and extinction of superfluous organizations, by the occupation of destitute fields, and by the concentration of the efforts of Christian people." We are to have one mass meeting every year, in November, to hear reports from the county secretaries, to read and discuss papers, and to devise measures for the prosecution of our work."

"*Laus Deo!*" exclaimed the parson. "Who would have believed it! Why, this is more of a miracle than your telephone, that has sprung into being since I went away. *Gloria in excelsis!* The unity of believers in this commonwealth is no longer merely a sentiment; it is a solid fact. Have they heard of this yet up in Massachusetts?"

"Oh, yes, they are talking about it there, and out West, too. The West, you know, is a great deal worse sect-ridden than we are, and sensible people out there are beginning to see that they must organize to protect themselves against the nuisance. A keen fellow from Dakota, a leading man in one of the churches out there, was in our bank the other day, talking it over. 'Your outlook committees may do very well for this region,' he said; 'what we've got to have is a vigilance committee. I go in for hanging every man that proposes the second church in a town of less than five hundred people. On one of our railroads, the other day, away out on the prairie, fifty miles from anywhere, the surveyor got off the train to stake out a new town. He drove four stakes and went away to eat his dinner by a spring, and, bless my soul! when he come back, there was a church extension agent a-sitting on every one o' those stakes — a Baptist on one and a Presbyterian on another and a Methodist on another and a Congregationalist on another. They'd all come to locate churches in the new town. That's about the way they do it,' said my friend, 'and they've got to stop it.'"

"That will pass, for Dakota," laughed Mr. Strong. "There are facts, no doubt, under your friend's hyperbole. But we will trust that something less sanguinary than a vigilance committee may serve to restrain the rampant sectarianism of the West."

"Ay, ay," cried the banker. "A little patience and sweet reasonableness, and a great deal of pluck and perseverance will do the business. Let people once see how much better and more Christian is cooperation than competition and conflict, in doing Christian work, and the battle is won."

"I always knew that the millennium was coming," said Mr. Strong, slowly, resting his eye for a moment on the mingled pearl and gold in the cloudless sky, out of which the sun had just sunk, and then dropping it to take in the soft, purple haze of the hills and the shining depths of the placid river; "I always knew that it was coming, but I never knew before just how it was coming. Now I see."

❖ ❖ ❖ ❖ ❖ ❖ ❖ ❖

HOW MUCH IS THE BIBLE WORTH? [1]

Editor's introduction. Gladden's pioneering with the social gospel was intimately bound up with his work as an interpreter of liberal theology. His social interpretation of Christianity was directly informed by his historical and critical understanding of the Bible. He believed that the effort to cling to the doctrine of the infallibility of Scripture was doing great harm, especially among intelligent young men who simply could not accept the old view. The Columbus pastor resolved to speak the truth as he saw it to his people. The series of Sunday evening lectures attracted larger audiences than usual. In published form, *Who Wrote the Bible?* was widely used as a text in Bible classes and Y.M.C.A. groups. It enjoyed the largest circulation of his many books. It was widely reviewed in the press, drawing many positive but also a number of sharply negative reviews. The favorable reviews often commented on Gladden's skill as a mediator between inherited orthodoxy and advanced biblical studies.[2] The work was not very original; Gladden drew much from such American scholars as Charles A. Briggs and Newman Smyth, and from such British authorities as Arthur P. Stanley and W. Robertson Smith. The concluding, climactic chapter of the book is presented here. A few years later, Gladden wrote a somewhat more specialized sequel.[3]

Of the Bible as a book among books, of the human elements which enter into its composition, some account has been given in the preceding chapters. But in these studies the whole story of the Bible has not been told. There is need, therefore, that we should enlarge our view somewhat,

1. *Who Wrote the Bible? A Book for the People* (Boston, 1891), chap. xiii, "How Much is the Bible Worth?", 351–81.
2. Many reviews of this and others of his books have been preserved in the Washington Gladden Papers, Box 62.
3. *Seven Puzzling Bible Books: A Supplement to "Who Wrote the Bible?"* (Boston, 1897).

84

and take more directly into account certain elements with which we have not hitherto been chiefly concerned.

Our study has, indeed, made a few things plain. Among them is the certainty that the Bible is not an infallible book, in the sense in which it is popularly supposed to be infallible. When we study the history of the several books, the history of the canon, the history of the distribution and reproduction of the manuscript copies, and the history of the versions — when we discover that the "various readings" of the differing manuscripts amount to one hundred and fifty thousand, the impossibility of maintaining the verbal inerrancy of the Bible becomes evident. We see how human ignorance and error have been suffered to mingle with this stream of living water throughout all its course; if our assurance of salvation were made to depend upon our knowledge that every word of the Bible was of divine origin, our hopes of eternal life would be altogether insecure.

The book is not infallible historically. It is a veracious record; we may depend upon the truthfulness of the outline which it gives us of the history of the Jewish people; but the discrepancies and contradictions which appear here and there upon its pages show that its writers were not miraculously protected from mistakes in dates and numbers and the order of events.

It is not infallible scientifically. It is idle to try to force the narrative of Genesis into an exact correspondence with geological science. It is a hymn of creation, wonderfully beautiful and pure; the central truths of monotheistic religion and of modern science are involved in it; but it is not intended to give us the scientific history of creation, and the attempt to make it bear this construction is highly injudicious.

It is not infallible morally. By this I mean that portions of this revelation involve an imperfect morality. Many things are here commanded which it would be wrong for us to do. This is not saying that these commands were not divinely wise for the people to whom they were given; nor is it denying that the morality of the New Testament, which is the fulfillment and consummation of the moral progress which the book records, is a perfect morality; it is simply asserting that the stages of this progress from a lower to a higher morality are here clearly marked; that the standards of the earlier time are therefore inadequate and misleading in these later times; and that any man who accepts the Bible as a code of moral rules, all of which are equally binding, will be led into the gravest errors. It is no more true that the ceremonial legislation of the Old Testament is obsolete than that large portions of the moral legislation are obsolete. The notions of the writers of these books concerning their duties to God were dim and imperfect; so were their notions concerning their duties to man. All the truth that they could receive was given to them; but there were many truths which they could not receive, which to us are as plain as the daylight.

Not to recognize the partialness and imperfection of this record in all these respects is to be guilty of a grave disloyalty to the kingdom of the truth. With all these facts staring him in the face, the attempt of any intelligent man to maintain the theoretical and ideal infallibility of all parts of these writings is a criminal blunder. Nor is there any use in loudly asserting the inerrancy of these books, with vehement denunciations of all who call it in question, and then in a breath admitting that there may be some errors and discrepancies and interpolations. Perfection is perfection. To stoutly affirm that a thing is perfect, and then admit that it may be in some respects imperfect, is an insensate procedure. Infallibility is infallibility. The Scriptures are, or they are not, infallible. The admission that there may be a few errors gives every man the right, nay it lays upon him the duty, of finding what those errors are. Our friends who so sturdily assert the traditional theory can hardly be aware of the extent to which they stultify themselves when their sweeping and reiterated assertion that the Bible can *never* contain a mistake is followed, as it always must be, by their timid and deprecatory, "hardly ever." The old rabbinical theory, as adopted and extended by some of the post-Reformation theologians, that the Bible was verbally dictated by God and is absolutely accurate in every word, letter and vowel point, and that it is therefore blasphemy to raise a question concerning any part of it, is a consistent theory. Between this and a free but reverent inquiry into the Bible itself, to discover what human elements it contains and how it is affected by them, there is no middle ground. That it is useless and mischievous to make for the Bible claims that it nowhere makes for itself — to hold and teach a theory concerning it which at once breaks down when an intelligent man begins to study it with open mind — is beginning to be very plain. The quibbling, the concealment, the disingenuousness which this method of using the Bible involves are not conducive to Christian integrity. This kind of "lying for God" has driven hundreds of thousands already into irreconcilable alienation from the Christian church. It is time to stop it.

How did this theory of the infallibility of the Bible arise? Those who have followed these discussions to this point know that it has not always been held by the Christian church. The history of the canon, told with any measure of truthfulness, will make this plain. The history of the variations between the Septuagint and the Hebrew shows, beyond the shadow of a doubt, that this theory of the unchangeable and absolute divinity of the words of the Scripture had no practical hold upon transcribers and copyists in the early Jewish church. The New Testament writers could not have consistently held such a theory respecting the Old Testament books, else they would not have quoted them, as they did, with small care for verbal accuracy. They believed them to be substantially true, and therefore they give the substance of them in their quotations; but there is no such slavish attention to the letter as there must have been if they had regarded them as verbally dictated by God himself. The Christian fathers were inclined, no doubt, to accept the rabbinical theories of inspiration respecting the Old Testament; but they sometimes avoid the difficulties growing out of manifest errors in the text by a theory of an inner sense which is faultless, frankly admitting that the natural meaning cannot always be defended. As to the early Reformers, we have seen how freely they handled the sacred writings, submitting them to a scrutiny which they would not have ventured upon if they had believed concerning them what we have been taught. It was not until the period succeeding the Reformation that this dogma of Biblical infallibility was clearly formulated and imposed upon the Protestant churches. As taught by Quenstedt and Voetius and Calovius, the dogma asserts that "not only the substance of truth and the views proposed in their minutest detail, but even the identical words, all and in particular, were supplied and dictated by the Holy Ghost. Not a word is contained in the Holy Scriptures which is not in the strictest sense inspired, the very interpunctuation not excepted. . . . Errors of any sort whatever, even verbal or grammatical, as well as all inelegancies of style, are to be denied as unworthy of the Divine Spirit who is throughout the primary author of the Bible." [4] This view was long maintained with all strictness, and many a man has been made a heretic for denying it. Within the last century the form of the doctrine has been somewhat modified by theologians, yet the substance of it is still regarded as essential orthodoxy. Dr. Charles Hodge, in his "Theology," Vol. I, p. 152, says, "Protestants hold that the Scriptures of the Old and New Testaments are the word of God, written

---

4. *The Doctrine of Sacred Scripture*, II, 209. [ED.] A two-volume work by Professor George T. Ladd of Yale (N.Y., 1883). Quenstedt and Calovius were seventeenth-century Lutheran theologians; Voetius was Reformed.

under the inspiration of God the Holy Ghost, and are therefore infallible, and consequently free from all error, whether of doctrine, of fact, or of precept." And again (p. 163), "All the books of Scripture are equally inspired. All alike are infallible in what they teach." [5] Such is the doctrine now held by the great majority of Christians. Intelligent pastors do not hold it, but the body of the laity have no other conception.

Whence is it derived? Where do the teachers quoted above get their authority for their affirmations?

Not, as we have seen, from any statements of the Bible itself. There is not one word in the Bible which affirms or implies that this character of inerrancy attaches to the entire collection of writings, or to any one of them.

The doctrine arose, as I have said, in the seventeenth century, and it was in part, no doubt, a reflection of the teaching of the later rabbins, whose fantastic notions about the origin of their sacred books I have before alluded to. It was also developed, as a polemical necessity, in the exigencies of that conflict with the Roman Catholic theologians which followed the Reformation. The eminent German scholar and saint, Professor Tholuck, gives the following account of its origin:

> In proportion as controversy, sharpened by Jesuitism, made the Protestant party sensible of an externally fortified ground of combat, in that same proportion did Protestantism seek, by the exaltation of the outward authoritative character of the Sacred Writings, to recover that infallible authority which it had lost through its rejection of infallible councils and the infallible authority of the Pope. In this manner arose, *not earlier than the seventeenth century*, those sentiments which regarded the Holy Scripture as the infallible production of the Divine Spirit — in its entire contents and its very form — so that not only the sense but also the words, the letters, the Hebrew vowel points, and the very punctuation were regarded as proceeding from the Spirit of God.[6]

The fact that the doctrine had this origin is itself suspicious. A theory which is framed in the heat of a great controversy, by one party in the church, is apt to be somewhat extreme.

5. [ED.] Charles Hodge (1797–1878), professor at Princeton Theological Seminary and defender of conservative Calvinism, set forth his views in full in his magnum opus, *Systematic Theology* (3 vols., N.Y., 1871–72). See I, 152, 163.

6. *Theological Essays*, collected by George R. Noyes. [ED.] August Tholuck (1799–1877), professor at Berlin and Halle, was an evangelical scholar especially influential through his exegetical works. Hodge had studied with him in Germany, as had many American students of varying theological orientations.

The strength of the doctrine lies, however, in the fact that it is a theological inference from the doctrine of God. "God is the author of the Bible," men have said; "God is omniscient; he can make no mistakes; therefore the book must be infallible. To deny that it is infallible is to deny that it is God's book; if it is not his book it is worthless." Or, putting it in another form, they have said, "The Bible is an inspired book. God is the source of inspiration. He cannot inspire men to write error. Therefore every word of the inspired book must be true." That is what the logicians call an a priori argument. The view of what inspiration is, and of what the Bible is, are deduced from our theory of God. It amounts to just this: If God is what we think him to be, he must do what seems wise to us. This is hardly a safe argument. Doubtless we would have said beforehand that if God, who is all-wise and all-powerful, should create a world, he would make one free from suffering and from every form of evil. We find, however, that he has not made such a world. And it may be wiser for us, instead of making up our minds beforehand what God must do, to try and find out what he has done. It might seem to us, doubtless, that if he has given us a revelation, it must be a faultless revelation. But has he? That is the question. We can only know by studying the revelation itself. We have no right to determine beforehand what it must be. We might have said with equal confidence, that if God wished to have his truth taught in the world, he would certainly send infallible teachers. He has not done so. The treasure of his truth is in earthen vessels today. Has it not always been so?

The trouble in this whole matter arises from the fact that men have made up their theories of the Bible out of their ideas about God, and have then gone to work to fit the facts of the Bible to their preconceived theories. This has required a great deal of stretching and twisting and lopping off here and there; the truth has been badly distorted, sometimes mutilated. The changed view of the Bible, which greatly alarms some good people, arises from the fact that certain honest men have determined to go directly to the Bible itself and find out by studying it what manner of book it is. They have discovered that it is not precisely such a book as it has been believed to be, and the answer that they make to those who hold the old theory about it is simply this: "We cannot believe what you have told us about the Bible, because the Bible contradicts you. It is because we believe the Bible itself that we reject your theory. We believe that the Bible is an inspired book, nay, that it is by eminence The Inspired Book; but when you ask us 'What is an inspired book?' instead of making up a definition of inspiration out of our own heads, we only say, 'It is such a book as the Bible is,' and then we proceed to frame our definition of inspiration by the study of the Bible. Therefore, when you say that inspiration must imply infallibility, we answer, No; it does not; for here is The Inspired Book and it is not infallible."

In what sense the book is inspired we may be able, after a little, to see more clearly. For the present I only desire to point out the sources of the traditional doctrine of the Bible, and the sources of the new doctrine. The one is the result of the speculations of men about what the Bible must be; the other is the result of a careful and reverent study of the Bible itself.

What, then, do we find the Bible to be?

1. It is the book of righteousness. No other book in the world fixes our thoughts so steadily upon the great interest of character. Whatever else the Bible may show us or may fail to show us, it does keep always before us the fact that the one great concern of every man is to be right in heart and in life. Righteousness tendeth to life; righteousness is salvation; Jehovah is he who loveth righteousness and hateth iniquity, and in his favor is life; these are the truths which form the very substance of this revelation. It is quite true that in the application of this principle to the affairs of every day, the early records show us much confusion and uncertainty; the definitions of righteousness which sufficed for the people of that time would not suffice for us at all; but the fact remains that the only interest of this book in the individuals and the races which it brings before us is in their loyalty or disloyalty to that ideal of conduct which it always lifts up before us. Righteousness is life; righteousness is salvation; this is the one message of the Bible to men. There are rites and ceremonies, but these are not the principal thing; "To obey is better than sacrifice, and to hearken than the fat of rams." "He hath showed thee, O man, what is good; and what does the Lord require of thee, but to do justly, and to love mercy, and to walk humbly with thy God?" This great truth of the Bible has been but imperfectly apprehended, even among modern Christians; there is always a tendency to make the belief in sound dogma, or the performance of decorous rites, or the experience of emotional raptures the principal thing; but the testimony of the Bible to the supremacy of character and conduct is clear and convincing, and the world is coming to understand it.

Now for any man who cares for the right, to whom character is more precious than anything else in the world, this book is worth more than any other book can be. Even the Old Testament narratives, indistinctly as they reveal the real nature of true conduct to us in this day, show us plainly the fact that nothing else in the world is to be compared with it; and the struggles and temptations of the heroes of that old book are full of instruction for us; their failures and follies and sins admonish and warn us; their steadfastness and fidelity inspire and hearten us.

II. The Bible is the record of the development of the kingdom of righteousness in the world. Man knows intuitively that he ought to do right; his notion of what is right is continually being purified and enlarged. The Bible is the record of this moral progress in the one nation of the earth to which morality has been the great concern. We have seen, clearly enough, the imperfection of the ethical standards to which the early Hebrew legislation was made to conform; we have also seen that this legislation was always a little in advance of the popular morality, leading it on to purer conceptions and better practices. The legislation concerning divorce, the legislation regulating blood vengeance, recognizes the evils with which it deals and accommodates itself to them, but always with the purpose and the result of giving to men a larger thought and a better standard. Laws which conformed to our moral ideal would have been powerless to control such a semi-barbarous people as the Hebrews were when they came out of Egypt. The higher morality must be imparted little by little; one principle after another must be drilled into their apprehension; they could not well be learning more than one or two simple lessons at a time, and while they were learning these, other coarse and cruel and savage practices of theirs must be "winked at," as Paul says. Against any rule more strict at this early time the Hebrews would have revolted; the divine wisdom of this legislation is seen in this method which takes men as they are, and does for them the thing that is feasible, patiently leading them on and up to higher ground. If you would seize a running horse by the rein and stop him, you had better run with him for a little. This homely parable illustrates much of the Old Testament legislation which we find so defective, when judged by our standards.

It is in this larger sense that we see the signs of divinity in this old book. It is a book of inspiration because it is the record of an inspired or divinely guided development; because the life it shows as unfolding is divine; because the goal to which we see the people steadily conducted in its vivid chapters is the goal which God has marked for human progress; because it gives us the origin and growth of the kingdom of God in the world.

"Whence came," asks one, "and of what manner of spirit is this *anti-historic* power in Israel and the Bible? Some inner principle of development struggles against the outward historical environment, and will not rest until it prevails. What was it which selected Israel, and in one narrow land, while all the surrounding country was sinking, lifted man up in spite of himself? which along the course of one national history carried on a progressive development of religious life and truth, while other peoples, though taught by many wise men and seers, and not without their truths, still can show no one connected and progressive revelation like this?" [7]

What is the power that has wrought all this but the divine Power? If you ask for a proof of the existence of God, I point you to the life of the Jewish people as the Bible records it. *That history is the revelation of God.* In the record of this nation's life, in its privileges and its vicissitudes, its captivities and its restorations, its blessings and its chastenings, its institutions and its laws, its teachers and its legislators, its seers and its law-givers, in all the forces that combine to make up the great movement of the national life, I see God present all the while, shaping the ends of this nation, no matter how perversely it may rough-hew them, till at last it stands on an elevation far above the other nations, breathing a better atmosphere, thinking worthier and more spiritual thoughts of God, obeying a far purer moral law, holding fast a nobler ideal of righteousness — polytheism gradually and finally rooted out of the national consciousness; the family established and honored as in no other nation; woman lifted up to a dignity and purity known nowhere else in the world; the Sabbath of rest sanctified; the principles of the decalogue fastened in the convictions of the people, the sure foundations laid of the kingdom of God in the world.

We are quite too apt unduly to disparage Judaism. Doubtless the formalism that our Lord found in it needed rebuke; its worship and its morality were yet far away from the ideal when Jesus came to earth; nevertheless, compared with all the people round about them even then — compared with classic Greeks and noble Romans — the ethical and spiritual development of the Jews had reached a higher stage. It is not extravagant to claim for this race the moral leadership of the world. Hear Ernest Renan, no champion of orthodoxy, as you know: "I am eager, gentlemen" — I quote from a lecture of his on The Share of the Semitic

7. *Old Faiths in New Light*, 81. [ED.] Newman Smyth (1843–1925), liberal pastor of the First Congregational Church in New Haven, was the author (N.Y., 1879).

People in the History of Civilization — "to come at the prime service which the Semitic race has rendered to the world; its peculiar work, its providential mission, if I may so express myself. We owe to the Semitic race neither political life, art, poetry, philosophy, nor science. *We owe to them religion.* The whole world — we except India, China, Japan, and tribes altogether savage — *has adopted the Semitic religions.*" Speaking then of the gradual decay of the various pagan faiths of the Aryan races, Renan continues:

> It is precisely at this epoch that the civilized world finds itself face to face with the Jewish faith. Based upon the clear and simple dogma of the divine unity, discarding naturalism and pantheism by the marvelously terse phrase, "In the beginning God created the heavens and the earth," possessing a law, a book, the depository of grand moral precepts and of an elevated religious poetry, Judaism had an incontestable superiority, and it might have been foreseen then that some day the world would become Jewish, that is to say, would forsake the old mythology for monotheism.[8]

Here is the testimony of a man who can be suspected of no undue leanings toward the religion of the Bible, to the fact that the world is indebted for its great thoughts of religion to the Semitic races, and chiefly to the Hebrew race; that the religion of Judaism, brought into comparison with the other religions, is incontestably superior. Now any man who believes in religion and in God must believe that the people to whom such a task was committeed must have been trained by God to perform it. The history of this nation will then be the history of this training. That is exactly what the Old Testament is. No disputes over the nature of inspiration must be suffered to obscure this great fact. The Old Testament Scriptures do contain in biography and history, in statute and story and song and sermon, the records of the life of the nation to which God at sundry times and in diverse manners was revealing himself; which he was preparing to be the bearer of the torch of his own truth into all the world. And I now ask whether anybody needs to be told that these records are precious, precious above all price? Are there any authentic portions of them that any man can afford to despise? Is not every step in

---

8. *Religious History and Criticism*, 159, 160. [ED.] Renan (1823–92), French orientalist, philosopher, and critical historian, was a prolific writer whose works included a controversial *Life of Jesus* (1863). The quotation is from his famous introductory lecture at the College of France, as found in *Studies of Religious History and Criticism* (N.Y., 1864), 159–60, the English translation by O. B. Frothingham of his *Études d'Histoire Réligieuse*. The italics are Gladden's.

the progress of this people out of savagery into a spiritual faith, matter of
the profoundest interest to every human soul? Even the dullness and ignorance and crudity of this people — even the crookedness and blindness
of their leaders and teachers, are full of instruction for us; they show us
with what materials and what instruments the divine wisdom and patience
wrought out this great result. What other book is there that can compare
in value with this book, which tells us the way of God with the people
whom he chose, as Renan declares, to teach the world religion? And
when one has firmly grasped this great fact, that the Bible contains the
history of the religious development of the Jewish people under providential care and tuition, how little is he troubled by the small difficulties
which grow out of theories of inspiration! "We can listen," says Dr.
Newman Smyth, "with incurious complacency while small disputants discuss vehemently the story of the ark or Jonah's strange adventure. . . .
After all the work of the critics, the Bible still remains, the great, sublime,
enduring work of the Eternal who loves righteousness and hates iniquity." [9]

But what have I been vindicating? The Bible? Nay, I have carefully
restricted my argument to the Old Testament. It is in behalf of the Old
Testament writings alone that I have sought to establish this exalted
claim. What I have shown you is only the pedestal on which the beauty
and strength of the Bible rests, the enduring portals which open into the
glory that excelleth. The Old Testament shows us the progressive revelation of God to the Jewish people; the New Testament gives us the consummation of that work, the perfect flower of that growth of centuries.
After shadows and hints and refracted lights of prophecy, breaks at last
upon the world the Light that lighteth every man! When the fullness of
time had come, God sent forth his Son. It was for this that the agelong
discipline of this people had been preparing them. True, "He came to his
own, and they received him not," but where else in the world would the
seed of his kingdom have found any lodgment at all? The multitude rejected him, but there was a remnant who did receive him, and to whom
he gave power to become the sons of God. So the word of God, that had
been painfully and dimly communicated to the ancient people in laws and
ordinances and prophecies, in providential mercies and chastenings, in
lives of saints and prophets and martyrs, was now made flesh, and dwelt
among men full of grace and truth, and they beheld his glory.

It is here that we find the real meaning of the Bible. "The end," as

9. *Old Faiths in New Light,* 60, 61.

Canon Mozley has so strongly shown, "is the test of a progressive revelation." [10] Jesus Christ, who is himself the Word, toward whom these laws and prophecies point, and in whom they culminate, is indeed the perfect revelation of God. From his judgment there is no appeal; at his feet the wisest of us must sit and learn the way of life. With his words all these old Scriptures must be compared; so far as they agree with his teachings we may take them as eternal truth; those portions of them which fall below this standard, we may pass by as a partial revelation upon us no longer binding. He himself has given us, in the Sermon on the Mount, the method by which we are to test the older Scriptures. When we refuse to apply his method and go on to declare every portion of those old records authoritative, we are not honoring him. The mischief and bane of the traditional theory is that it equalizes things which are utterly unlike. When it says that "all the books of the Scripture are equally inspired; all alike are infallible in what they teach," it puts the Gospels on the same level with Deuteronomy and Ecclesiastes and Esther. The effect of this is not to lift the latter up, but to drag the former down. They are not on the same level; it is treason to our Master Christ to say that they are alike; the one is as much higher than the other as the heavens are higher than the earth.

It is here, then, in the simple veracious records that bring before us the life of Christ, that we have the very Word of God. Whatever else the four gospels may or may not be, they certainly do contain the story of the life that has been for many centuries the light and hope of the world. It is the same unique Person who stands before us in every one of these narratives—

> So meek, forgiving, godlike, high,
> So glorious in humility.

What fault has criticism to find with this life? What word or deed is here ascribed to him that is not worthy of him, that is not like him? Is it any wonder to us when we read this record through, that the guileless Nathanael cried out as he communed with him, "Rabbi, thou art the Son of God, thou art the King of Israel."

If, then, the New Testament gives us the artless record of the life and

10. [ED.] J. B. Mozley (1813–78) was Regius Professor of Divinity at Oxford, and a canon of Christ Church. A high churchman, he nevertheless did not follow a partisan line, but found much truth in Calvinism. The title of his *Ruling Ideas in Early Ages and their Relation to Old Testament Faith* (London, 1877) perhaps suggested that of one of Gladden's own books, *Ruling Ideas of the Present Age* (Boston, 1895).

words of this divine Person, the Son of God and the Saviour of the
world; if it brings him before us and manifests to us, so far as words can
do it, his power and his glory; if it shows us how, by bearing witness to
the truth in his life and in his death, he established in the world the kingdom which for long ages had been preparing; if it makes known to us the
messages he brought of pardon and salvation; if it gives us the record of
the planting and training of his church in the early ages, is there any need
that I should go about to praise and magnify its worth to the children of
men? If light is worth anything to those who sit in darkness, or hope to
those who are oppressed with tormenting doubt; if wisdom is to be desired by those who are in perplexity, and comfort by those who are in
trouble, and peace by those whose hearts are full of strife, and forgiveness
by those who bear the burden of sin: if strength is a good gift to the
weak, and rest to the weary, and heaven to the dying, and the eternal life
of God to the fainting soul of man, then the book that tells us of Jesus
Christ and his salvation is not to be compared with any other book on
earth for preciousness; it is the one book that every one of us ought to
know by heart.

The value of the Bible, the greatness of the Bible, are in this life that it
discloses to us. "It is upon Jesus," says a modern rationalist, "that the
whole Bible turns. In this lies the value, not only of the New Testament, a great part of which refers to him directly, but of the Old
Testament as well." Rationalist though he is, no man could have stated
the truth more clearly. "It is upon Jesus that the whole Bible turns." The
Old Testament shows us the way preparing by which the swift feet of
the messengers approach that tell us of his coming; the New Testament
lifts the veil and bids us, Behold the man! The Bible is of value to us, just
in proportion as it helps us to see him, to know him, to trust him. You
may have a cast-iron theory of inspiration with every joint riveted; you
may believe in the infallible accuracy of every vowel point and every
punctuation mark; but if the Bible does not bring you into a vital union
with Jesus Christ, so that you have his mind and follow in his footsteps, it
profiteth you nothing. And if, by your study of it, you are brought into
this saving fellowship, your theories of inspiration will take care of themselves.

I fear that we do not always comprehend the fact that it is this divine
life shining out of its pages that makes the Bible glorious. We strain our
eyes so much in verifying commas, and in trying to prove that the dot of
a certain *i* is not a flyspeck, that we fail to get much impression of the

meaning of the beauty of the Saviour's life. See those two critics, with their eyes close to the wonderful "Ecce Homo" of Correggio, disputing whether there is or is not a visible stitch in the garment of Christ that ought to be seamless. How red their faces; how hot their words! Stand back a little, brothers! look away, for a moment, from the garment's seam; let the infinite pain and the infinite pity and the infinite yearning of that face dawn on you for a moment, and you will cease your quarreling. So, not seldom, do the idolaters of the letter wholly miss the meaning of the sacred book, and remain in mournful ignorance of him who himself is the Word.

There are those to whom the view of the Bible presented in these chapters seems not only inadequate but destructive. "If the Bible is not infallible," they say, "it is no more than any other book; we have no further use for it." In one of the leading church reviews I find these words, the joint utterance of two eminent American theologians: "A proved error in Scripture contradicts not only our doctrine but the Scripture's claims, and therefore its inspiration in making those claims." [11] A proved error in Scripture stamps the book as fraudulent and worthless! Worthless it is then! Proved errors there are, scores of them. It is fatuity, it is imbecility, to deny it. And every man who can find an error in these old writings has the warrant of these teachers for throwing the book away. Tens of thousands of ingenuous and fair-minded men have taken the word of such teachers, and have thrown the book away. May God forgive the folly of these blind guides!

But what stupid reasoning is this! "If the Bible is not infallible, it is worthless." Your watch is not infallible; is it therefore worthless? Your physician is not infallible; are his services therefore worthless? Your father is not infallible; are his counsels worthless? Will you say that the moment you discover in him an error concerning any subject in heaven or on earth, that moment you will refuse to listen to his counsel? The church of God is not infallible, and never was, whatever infatuated ecclesiastics may have claimed for it; are its solemn services and its inspiring labors and its uplifting fellowships worthless?

"A ship on a lee shore," says one, "in the midst of a driving storm, throws up signal rockets or fires a gun for a pilot. A white sail emerges

11. *Presbyterian Review*, II, 245. [ED.] The article, "Inspiration," was by two Princeton theologians, A. A. Hodge and B. B. Warfield (*loc. cit.*, II, [April 1881], 225–60). Gladden did not always transcribe precisely; the original read, "A proved error in Scripture contradicts not only our doctrine, but the Scripture claims, therefore, its inspiration in making those claims."

from the mist; it is the pilot boat. A man climbs on board, and the captain gives to him the command of the ship. All his orders are obeyed implicitly. The ship, laden with a precious cargo and hundreds of human lives, is confided to a rough-looking man whom no one ever saw before, who is to guide them through a narrow channel, where to vary a few fathoms to the right or left will be utter destruction. The pilot is invested with absolute authority as regards bringing the vessel into port." [12] Is this because the man is infallible, because he has never been detected in holding an erroneous opinion? Doubtless any of these intelligent passengers could find out, by half an hour's conversation with him, that his mind was full of crass ignorance and misconception. And nobody supposes that he is infallible, even as a pilot. He may make a mistake. What then? Will these passengers gather around the captain, and demand that he be ordered down from the bridge and thrown overboard if he disobeys? Will they say, "A pilot who is not on all subjects infallible is one whom we will not trust?" No; they believe him to be, not omniscient, but competent and trustworthy, and a great burden is lifted from their hearts when they see him take command of the ship. On all other subjects besides religion, people are able to exercise their common sense; why can they not use a modicum of the same common sense when they come to deal with religious truth?

It is not true, as a matter of fact, that the Bible no longer has any value for those who have ceased to hold the traditional view of it. Not seldom, indeed, those who have been compelled by overwhelming evidence to relinquish the traditional view have been driven by the natural reaction against it to undervalue the Bible, and even to treat it with contempt and bitterness; but even some of these have come back to it again and have found in it, when they studied it with open mind, more truth than they ever before had known. Let me cite an extreme case. I could take you to a society of freethinkers, consisting of people who have long been outspoken in their rejection of all the doctrines of historical Christianity, many of whom formerly flouted the Bible as a book of fables, but who are now studying it diligently week by week, in the most sympathetic spirit. They do not now accept its supernaturalism; but they believe that as a manual of conduct, as a guide to life, it excels all other books. The

12. *Orthodoxy; Its Truths and Errors*, by James Freeman Clarke, 114. [ED.] James Freeman Clarke (1810–88) was a Unitarian minister; the book cited was published in Boston in 1866. Clarke was a Transcendentalist, and a pioneer in the study of non-Christian faiths.

young people of their Sunday school are told that the Bible is not like other books; that the men who wrote it knew more about the human soul and its struggles and its aspirations after good than any other men who ever lived; and they are besought to attend, most carefully, to the lessons of life which this ancient book teaches. I should like to take some of our ultra-orthodox friends, who are pettishly crying out that the Bible, if not infallible, is good for nothing, and set them down for a Sunday or two in the midst of this freethinking Sunday school; they might learn some things about its value that they never knew before.

This incident ought to be of service, also, to those who, having discovered that the Bible contains human elements, have rushed to the conclusion that it is no more than any other book, and who, although they do not cast it from them, hold it off at arm's length, as it were, and maintain toward it an attitude of critical superiority. Even these freethinkers treat it more fairly. They are learning to approach it with open mind; they sit down before it with reverent expectancy. The Bible has a right to this sympathetic treatment. It is not just like other books. Do not take my word for this; listen rather to the testimony of one who was known, while he was alive, as the arch-heretic of New England:

> This collection of books has taken such a hold on the world as no other. The literature of Greece, which goes up like incense from that land of temples and heroic deeds, has not half the influence of this book, from a nation alike despised in ancient and in modern times. It is read of a Sabbath in all the ten thousand pulpits of our land. In all the temples of religion is its voice lifted up week by week. The sun never sets on its gleaming page. It goes equally to the cottage of the plain man and the palace of the king. It is woven into the literature of the scholar, and colors the talk of the street. The bark of the merchant cannot sail the sea without it; no ships of war go to the conflict, but the Bible is there. It enters men's closets; mingles in all their grief and cheerfulness of life. The affianced maiden prays God in Scripture for strength in her new duties; men are married by Scripture. The Bible attends them in their sickness, when the fever of the world is on them. The aching head finds a softer pillow when the Bible lies underneath. The mariner escaping from shipwreck clutches this first of his treasures and keeps it sacred to God. It goes with the peddler in his crowded pack; cheers him at eventide when he sits down dusty and fatigued; brightens the freshness of his morning face. It blesses us when we are born, gives names to half Christendom; rejoices with us; has sympathy for our mourning; tempers our grief to finer issues. It is the better part of our sermons. It lifts man above himself; our best of uttered prayers

are in its storied speech, wherewith our fathers and the patriarchs prayed. The timid man, about awaking from this dream of life, looks through the glass of Scripture and his eye grows bright; he does not fear to stand alone, to tread the way unknown and distant, to take the death angel by the hand and bid farewell to wife and babes and home. Men rest on this their dearest hopes; it tells them of God and of his blessed Son, of earthly duties and of heavenly rest.[13]

This is not mere rhetoric; it is simplest truth of human experience. How is it possible for any man to treat this book just as he would any other book? He ought to come to its perusal with the expectation of finding in it wisdom and light and life. He must not stultify his reason and stifle his moral sense when he reads it; he must keep his mind awake and his conscience active; but there is treasure here if he will search for it; search he must, yet the only right attitude before it is one of reverence and trust. Any man of ripe wisdom and high character, who has been known to you all your life, whose judgment you have verified, whose goodness you have witnessed and experienced, commands your respectful attention the moment he begins to speak. You do not believe him to be fallible, but you listen to what he says with trustfulness; you expect to find it true. To say that you listen to him as you do to every other man is not the fact; the posture of your mind in his presence is different from that in which you stand before most other men. It ought to be. He has gained, by his probity, the power to speak to you with authority. The Bible has gained the same power. You do not use it fairly when you use it as you do every other book.

There is the nation's flag proudly flying from the summit of the Capitol. It may be a banner that was borne upon the battlefield, decorated now with well-mended rents, and with stains of carnage. "Behold it!" cries the idolater. "It is absolutely faultless in perfection and beauty! There is not a blemish in its folds, there is not an imperfection in its web; every thread in warp and woof is flawless; every seam is absolutely straight; every star is geometrically accurate; every proportion is exact; the man who denies it is a traitor!"

"Absurd!" replies the iconoclast. "See the holes and the stains; there is not one straight seam; there is not a star that is in perfect form; ravel it,

---

13. Theodore Parker, *Discourses on Religion.* [ED.] Parker (1810–60), the stormy petrel of New England Unitarianism, was pastor of a church founded primarily to provide him with a platform. *A Discourse of Matters Pertaining to Religion* was first published in 1842. The quotation appears in the third edition (Boston, 1847), 301–303.

and you will find no thread in warp or woof that is flawless; nay, you may even discover shreds of shoddy mixed with the fine fiber. Your flag is nothing more than any other old piece of bunting, and if you think it is, you are a fool."

Nay, good friends, you are both wrong. The blemishes are there; it would be fanaticism to deny them; and he who says that no man can be loyal to the nation who will not profess that this banner is immaculate is setting up a fantastic standard of patriotism. But, on the other hand, this flag is something more than any other old piece of bunting, and he who thinks it something more is not a fool. It is the symbol of liberty; it is the emblem of sovereignty; it is the pledge of protection; it is the sign and guarantee of justice and order and peace. What memories cluster round it, of dauntless heroism, and holy sacrifice, and noble consecration! What hopes are gleaming from its stars and fluttering in its shining folds — hopes of a day when wars shall be no more and all mankind shall be one brotherhood! The man to whom the flag of his country is no more than any other piece of weather-beaten bunting is a man without a country.

Is not my parable already interpreted? Are not the idolaters who make it treason to disbelieve a single word of the Bible, and the iconoclasts who treat it as nothing better than any other book, equally far from the truth? Is it not the part of wisdom to use the book rationally, but reverently; to refrain from worshiping the letter, but to rejoice in the gifts of the Spirit which it proffers? The same divine influence which illumines and sanctifies its pages is waiting to enlighten our minds that we may comprehend its words, and to prepare our hearts that we may receive its messages. Some things hard to understand are here, but the Spirit of truth can make plain to us all that we need to know. No man wisely opens the book who does not first lift up his heart for help to find in it the way of life, and to him who studies it in this spirit it will show the salvation of God.

THE CHURCH AND THE KINGDOM [1]

Editor's introduction. The following selection opens with a question that was widely discussed in the 1890's. Gladden originally gave it before the State Association of the Congregational Churches of Ohio on May 9, 1894. Together with "The Law of the Kingdom," a graduation address given at Oberlin Theological Seminary during the same month, it was published as a small book. The tendency of the social gospel to present an instrumentalist doctrine of the church — a view of the church as primarily an instrument to prepare the way for the coming kingdom of God on earth — is illustrated in this essay. Gladden's concept of the kingdom, referred to in so many of his writings, is here developed rather fully.

❖ ❖ ❖ ❖

What is the relation of the church to the kingdom of God? The terms are often used interchangeably; and it is sometimes assumed that the church is simply the kingdom in its organized form. I do not think that this is the true conception. The kingdom of God is the larger term; the kingdom includes the church, but the church does not include the kingdom.

Our Lord's use of the words is significant. "Kingdom" is used by him more than one hundred times, and "church" but twice. "The names," says Dr. Fairbairn, "are either synonymous, or they are not. If they are synonymous, it must be possible to translate the church into the terms of the kingdom and kingdom into the terms of the church. If they are not, then the kingdom, as Christ's most used, most emphasized, and most descriptive name for his society, must contain his determinative idea; i.e., the church must be construed through the kingdom, and not the kingdom through the church." [2]

1. *The Church and the Kingdom* (N.Y., 1894), 5–40.
2. *The Place of Christ in Theology*, 515. [ED.] Andrew Martin Fairbairn (1838–1912) incorporated what he had given as the Morse lecture at Union Theological Seminary and the Lyman Beecher lectures at Yale in *The Place of Christ in Modern Theology* (N.Y., 1893). A prominent mediating liberal theologian, he was the first

Jesus nowhere defines the kingdom; his treatment of it is always concrete and pictorial; he shows it to us in instances and illustrations; but it is not difficult for us to reach through his sayings some clear notion of what it is. Sometimes he gives us just a trait or feature of it; sometimes he shows us how an individual life is related to it; sometimes he unfolds for us the law of its development in the field of the world and through the course of history. In the largest sense of the word we may say that the kingdom of God is the whole social organism so far as it is affected by divine influences.

Human society is an organism; it is a whole whose parts are intrinsically and vitally related to it; humanity is one body with many members. Every organism is the product of one coordinating life force; and the vital principle of this social organism is the life which is in Christ, and which is the light of men. For in him were all things created, and in him all things hold together; in him, Paul says, the whole creation comes to a head. Wherever society exists, wherever men dwell together peacefully and helpfully, there the life that was incarnate in Jesus Christ finds some faint manifestation. In him the world was created, by him it has been redeemed. I do not say that it will be, I say that it has been.

This world is Christ's world. Ever since his feet pressed its stony paths, ever since his voice stirred its conscious air, and his blessed hands broke its loaves and caressed its lilies, and with his precious blood its soil became incarnadine, the world has belonged to him.

> The world we live in wholly is redeemed;
> Not man alone, but all that man holds dear;
> His orchards and his maize—forget-me-nots
> And heart's-ease in his garden—and the wild
> Aerial blossoms of the untamed wood
> That make its savagery so homelike—all
> Have felt Christ's sweet love watering their roots.
> There are no gentile oaks, no pagan pines;
> The grass beneath our feet is Christian grass:
> The wayside weed is sacred unto him.

The world is not saved; but you must say precisely the same thing about it that was said of the men who came into the church at Pentecost — it is "being saved." The work of reclaiming and renewing it is always going on. The race is redeemed, and it is "being saved." Through cen-

---

principal of Mansfield College, Oxford, a Congregationalist theological college. The book cited here quickly went through twelve editions.

turies of strife and confusion, through darkness and dearth, through suffering and sorrow, humanity moves slowly forward in the track of God's great purpose.

The kingdom of heaven is here, just as the spring is here when the crocuses open and the violets and the spring beauties are first in evidence. There is more to follow, but spring is here. We pray that it may come — more and more of it — but always with thanks and praise for what has come already. When it shall have fully come, what will it be? what shall we see?

Every department of human life — the families, the schools, amusements, art, business, politics, industry, national policies, international relations — will be governed by the Christian law and controlled by Christian influences. When we are bidden to seek first the kingdom of God, we are bidden to set our hearts on this great consummation; to keep this always before us as the object of our endeavors; to be satisfied with nothing less than this. The complete Christianization of all life is what we pray for and work for, when we work and pray for the coming of the kingdom of heaven.

Now I do not think that the word "church" can very well be stretched to cover all this. I do not believe that politics and business and art and literature are properly departments of church life. The church is the organization in which religion is made our *special* care; in which we confine our attention to spiritual truths and laws, seeking to comprehend them that we may apply them; in which we study the revelations that God has made to us of his nature and purposes, that we may bring ourselves into communion and fellowship with him through prayer and song and worship, that we may gain inspiration and courage for the work and warfare of life.

It is necessary that religion should be specialized in institutions which are devoted to its interests. The problem is to make all life religious; but in order that it may become so, associations are needed whose function it shall be to cultivate religious ideas and religious feelings.

Electricity, we are told, pervades the whole earth and the whole atmosphere. It is everywhere about us; perhaps the time may come when we can make this *diffused* electricity do our chores and run our errands; but, for the present, we must have the powerhouse with the dynamos, where it is collected and concentrated, and distributed to the places where it is wanted. And, in like manner, although the spirit of Christianity ought to pervade and to some extent does pervade the whole of the society in which we live; though the kingdom of heaven, like the hidden leaven, is here, living and working upon the earth; yet there is need that this influence be gathered up and concentrated in institutions formed for this special purpose, that its nature may be more distinctly seen and its power more wisely directed.

As we study the laws of life, we find the higher orders of being distinguished by what the physiologists call an increasing specialization of function.

"In the progress from the lower to the higher organism," says Mr. Huxley, "there is a gradual differentiation of organs and of functions. Each function is separated into many parts, which are severally intrusted to distinct organs. To use the striking phrase of Milne Edwards, 'in passing from low to high organisms, there is a division of physiological labor.' " [3]

Thus in the lower orders of sentient creatures the nervous system is diffused through the living mass, or distributed over its surface; but as the creatures rise in the scale, the nerves are gathered into knots or ganglions, and their function is gradually separated until in the vertebrates, and especially in man, you find the brain, a great central organ, safely housed in a strong cavity made for its protection, whence it moves and directs the whole body. This separation and specialization of the nervous function does not make the human body less sensitive or less responsive to nervous action than the bodies of the snails and the worms; the contrary is the fact. By concentration the nervous force is increased and intensified.

In the same manner, as society advances, the different social functions are specialized; I think that this is likely to be more and more the case. And although religion ought to pervade and govern the whole of society, just as the nervous system pervades and governs the whole human body, yet religion, for this very reason, needs to be specialized in institutions of its own, as the brain is specialized and localized in the human body. It is thus that it gains power to move and direct human society.

This illustration may suggest to us the relation between the church and the kingdom of heaven. The kingdom of heaven is the entire social organism in its ideal perfection; the church is one of the organs — the most central and important of them all — having much the same relation to Christian society that the brain has to the body. The body is not all brain; but the brain is the seat of thought and feeling and motion. A body

---

3. [ED.] Thomas Henry Huxley (1825–95), was the well-known English biologist, Darwinist, and agnostic.

without a brain could not be a very effective instrument of the mind; society, without those specialized religious functions which are gathered up in the church, would not very readily receive and incarnate and distribute the gifts of the spirit of God.

And yet the brain is of use only as it furnishes to all the other organs and parts of the body, feeling and motion. It must make the eye sensitive to light, the tongue to flavors, the ear to sound, the hands and feet to the volitions of the will which set them in motion. The brain is in one sense the master, in another sense the servant of the whole body. It helps to coordinate all the physical powers, and it supplies them all with the conditions by means of which their work is done. Suppose that the brain undertook to set up housekeeping on its own hook; to look out for itself, and have little relation to the other parts of the body; to assume that the brain was the man, and that so long as the brain was well developed, it mattered little about the other parts of the human economy. Is it not evident that any separation of the brain from the rest of the body would kill the brain as well as the rest of the body? The life and health of the brain are only found in ministering to the whole body.

Exactly in the same way is the church related to all the other parts of human society. Its life is in their life; it cannot live apart from them; it lives by what it gives to them; it has neither meaning nor justification except in what it does to vitalize and spiritualize business and politics and amusement and art and literature and education, and every other interest of society. The moment it draws apart, and tries to set up a snug little ecclesiasticism, with interests of its own, and a cultus of its own, and standards and sentiments of its own, and enjoyments of its own — the moment it begins to teach men to be religious just for the sake of being religious — that moment it becomes dead and accursed; it is worse than useless; it is a bane and a blight to all the society in which it stands.

These illustrations may enable us to see what are the true relations of the church to the kingdom of God. And they will point out two errors, of an exactly opposite nature, both of which are too prevalent.

The first error is that of those to whom Christianity is churchianity; those who separate the church from the rest of the world, and give their whole time and strength to exalting it, and building it up, caring little or nothing for the other departments of life; not wishing or at any rate not trying to establish any vital relations between it and those interests which men call secular. To these persons the church is not a means to an end, but it is an end in itself. The church is not the channel through which the life of God flows into the world; it is the reservoir into which the tribute of the world is to flow for the honor of God. Humanity exists for the church, not the church for humanity. The great object is to make men into good churchmen, not to train churchmen to be good men.

The other error is that of those who think that because it is the office of religion to mingle with and sanctify every department of human life, therefore there is no need that we should have any separate institutions of religion. This is precisely as if one should say: "Because we want the nervous influence diffused through every part of the human body, making it quick and sensitive and responsive, therefore we do not want any brain." I do not think that this is good philosophy. I believe that there is exactly the same need of separate organs for the development and manifestation of the spiritual life in the social organism, that there is for the concentration and diffusion of nervous influence in the physical organism. And I do not think that those are wise who disparage the function of the church, or imagine that we are likely to outgrow it as we go on toward social perfection. We are just as likely to do without it as we are likely, in our ascent toward intellectual perfection, to dispense with brains and return to the condition of the oyster, with the nervous system diffused through the whole molluscous mass.

Let me mention, a little more particularly, some of the functions which the church, as the central organ of the great social organism, is called to fulfill.

The whole Christian body, Paul says, "is fitly framed and knit together, through that which every joint supplieth, according to the working in due measure of each several part" — all the different members performing their several offices — "till we all attain unto the unity of the faith and of the knowledge of the Son of God unto a full-grown man, unto the measure of the stature of the fullness of Christ." That is to say, the ideal of Christian perfection cannot be represented by any single individual. It takes a good many men, dwelling together — worshiping and working together — to exhibit the perfect divine manhood; to show what Christianity is.

Take even the element of worship. It is impossible that this should be realized in all its fullness except in the great congregation. One of the elements of worship is song; but no single voice can express what is expressed by the swelling chorus. There is an inspiration and an uplift in the grand choral song that no man can know anything about who worships by himself in the closet or in the secret place of the forest. There are elements of worship which one finds in the secret place and not in the congregation; but the converse is also true. No man alone can sing "The Heavens Are Telling" or the "Hallelujah Chorus"; no man alone can sing "Old Hundred" or the "Gloria Patri" and find in it the awakening of his higher and nobler feelings which he experiences when he joins with a thousand others in lifting up the mighty harmony.

And the same thing is true of prayer. I do not mean to say that there is no inspiring prayer in which all the voices do not join; I do not even mean that there is no genuine prayer but that which is offered in a public place. Quite the contrary is true. There are some kinds of prayer for which there is no place but the secret place. But on the other hand, we must not interpret those words of our Lord in the Sermon on the Mount as forbidding public prayer. That is a gross misunderstanding of them. Our Lord himself prayed in public more than once. What he forbids is ostentation in praying — praying in public *for the sake of being seen of men.* But there is a kind of prayer, and it is the highest kind, which is never heard and can never be heard in any other than a public place. When the man who prays is able to forget all about the impression which his prayer is making, and simply to gather into his own heart, by sympathy, the needs and the troubles and the burdens and the longings of the multitude who in hushed silence are bowing with him before the mercy seat; when he is able to identify himself with them, to discern, by spiritual insight, the struggles, the sorrows, the hopes, the fears of these human hearts; and when, under the stress of this burden of sympathetic desire, he lifts up to God the voice of prayer, there is something in that voice deeper, diviner, fuller of inspiration, than any man ever knows who worships alone in his closet. I have heard men pray in public as no man ever prayed or could pray in secret. The presence of the worshiping assembly, the overpowering sense of their needs, the wish to bring them, with himself, into the very presence of God, the yearning to make known to them the Father, the subtle response that comes to him in the tides of feeling that flood his own soul and lift up his thoughts — all this is an experience which can come to no man in the closet — which requires the association of men in worship.

I know very well that there is a great deal of what passes for prayer in public places, which is only the saying of prayers, just as there is a great deal of preaching which is no divinely given message, but the mere recitation of what the preacher has been taught to say; but the true prayer which leads the congregation into the very presence of God, is the most sublime and uplifting utterance of which the human soul is capable. It is an act in which love for God and love for man are blended in one pure passion that fulfills the very law of the soul.

Now here is an element of the Christian life for the development of which the worshiping assembly is the necessary condition. The quickening, uplifting, inspiring influences which come into men's lives through the song and the prayer of the great congregation, would never be experienced if men were not gathered together in assemblies for worship. Christian worship, in its highest and noblest forms, requires the association of men for that special purpose.

I think that the same thing is equally true of teaching. The loftiest and most inspiring truth is received into the mind more readily, and makes a deeper impression upon the heart, when it comes from a glowing heart through burning lips, and is enforced not only by the emotion of the speaker, but by the sympathetic interest of a great congregation. The earnest preacher, the responsive assembly form an atmosphere in which all highest truth is more powerfully impressed. It ought to be so. All this highest truth concerns our relations to one another and our common relation to God. When we are all together before God, we naturally feel that truth more deeply than at other times. Our sense of human brotherhood is signified and emphasized by meeting together in such an assembly, and the truths which bear upon this relation necessarily impress us more than they would do in solitary places.

But not only is it true of Christian worship and study that they require the union of men in harmonious groups; it is even more true of the practical side of Christianity. To be a Christian is not only to think the thoughts and cherish the emotions that are Christian, but also and more emphatically to behave like a Christian. The love which is the fulfilling of the law is not merely an idea or a sentiment, it is a kind of conduct. To be a Christian is to govern myself in all my practical relations with my fellow men by the Christian law of love.

Now, doubtless I am bound to observe this law in all my relations with my fellow men, whether they are in the church or not; but those who do not recognize this law may not respond with Christian conduct; the proper reciprocal action of the Christian law may fail to be manifested. And it is evident that in an association composed of those who recognize the Christian law as the law of their life, there would be a better opportunity of illustrating the practical working of that law than in the promiscuous relations of men. A company of men and women, united on the basis of the Christian law, taking that as the rule of their conduct, and living up to it, could give the world such an object lesson of what Christianity is as the world could get in no other way. Imagine what would happen if every Christian church perfectly exemplified the Christian law in all its corporate life. What an impression would be made upon the community! How unnecessary it would be, in the presence of such churches, to discuss the evidences of Christianity!

It must be admitted that our churches, even the best of them, come very far short of realizing this standard in their daily life; nevertheless, I maintain that this is what they are for, and that they do, in some imperfect way, recognize and obey the Christian law. As a rule, in the churches, the law of competition, the law of strife, is in abeyance, and the law of mutual helpfulness is substituted for it. "Every man for himself" is not the maxim that we recognized as binding; we have other and very different rules of conduct from those which prevail in the outside world:

"In love of the brethren be tenderly affectioned one to another, in honor preferring one another."

"Love worketh no ill to his neighbor; therefore love is the fulfilling of the law."

"Let each one of us please his neighbor for that which is good unto edifying."

"Be of the same mind, having the same love, being of one accord, of one mind; doing nothing through faction or through vainglory, but in lowliness of mind, each counting others better than himself; not looking each of you to his own things, but each of you to the things of others."

These are the rules of conduct which we recognize as binding in all our relations with one another in the Christian brotherhood. To say that we live up to them would be a manifest exaggeration; none the less we know that they are the rules by which we ought to live. We do not realize our ideal; but we have it always before us, and it is a very different ideal from that which governs the political world and the commercial world. It is very true that the commercial and political maxims do sometimes intrude into our church life and take control of our church business; it is sometimes true that church revenues are raised by appealing to the competitive principle, and offering privilege and distinction to those who have the most money. It is sometimes true, in the great ecclesiasticisms, that office and station are intrigued for and won by wire-pulling and log-rolling; but these are of the spirit of antichrist; they are the denial of the very foundation on which the church rests; they are more hostile to the life of the

church than any sort of infidelity. When the church life is brought under
the sway of such principles as these, the church becomes the most dangerous enemy of the kingdom of God in the world.

It is to be lamented that there are too many churches which have fallen
into this practical apostasy. But there are churches, I am sure, which are
trying to govern their corporate life by Christian principles; which do
not admit the competitive principle into the regulation of their finances;
which do not offer place and distinction to the longest purses; in which
there is never any strife for honors or offices, nor any political combination and wire-pulling; but in which the members do honestly seek to help
one another, to prefer one another in honor, to bear one another's
burdens, and so to fulfill the law of Christ. Such churches serve a purpose
as illustrations or object lessons of Christianity which no other organizations can serve. They furnish a model after which the whole social order
must be reconstructed. They show the world what society will be like
when Christ comes to his own. If there were not too few churches of this
kind, there would be no social question.

When we get hold of this conception of the kingdom of God as com-
prehending in its idea the entire social organism, and of the church as the
central organ of the social organism, we see at once how erroneous is the
statement sometimes made that the church is the greatest obstacle to the
progress of the kingdom of heaven. I do not believe that there ever was a
day when this was even approximately true. I believe that even in the
Middle Ages the church was doing more than all other agencies put
together to promote the kingdom of heaven. I believe that the church is
doing today the largest part of what is done to supply society with the
vitalizing divine energies by which the kingdom of heaven is extended
upon the earth.

What may be truthfully said is this: that there are local churches — a
considerable number of them — whose administration is such that they
hinder more than they help the progress of the kingdom. And it may also
be said that there is a pretty strong tendency, in many churches, to forget
the instrumental character of the church; to forget that it is a part and
not the whole, a means and not the end; and to be content with building
up the church, or the denomination, instead of studying to make the
church serviceable in building up the kingdom. Just so far as this is true,
the church does become an obstacle to the progress of the kingdom.

There are local churches which are, essentially, religious clubs. The
principles on which they are organized, the methods of their administra-

tion are all assimilated to those of the social club. They admit only those whose opinions and tendencies are similar to their own; they take no pains to attract to their membership those who would not be congenial; they preserve before the community a certain attitude of exclusiveness. So far as ideas and practices like these characterize the life of any church, it is, beyond a doubt, a pretty serious obstruction to the growth of the kingdom.

And it must be admitted that the tendency to hold the church apart from the world, to regard it as having its end in itself, is quite too strong in many quarters. All attempts to maintain a vital relation between the church and the community are regarded by many persons with great disfavor and suspicion. The minister who tries to bring the law of Christ to bear upon trade and industry and politics is very apt to be told that he is getting out of his sphere; that his business is to preach the gospel and leave all these secular affairs alone. The minister who tries in all soberness and devoutness of spirit to apply Christianity to life, is very sure to be described by many pious folk as a "sensationalist." "The secularization of the pulpit" — this is the crime charged upon all those who attempt in any way to make the teaching of the church broadly influential in human affairs. Now, just so far as this sentiment prevails in our churches, they are, no doubt, obstacles in the way of the kingdom of God. A more perverse or mischievous notion cannot well be entertained, than that which stigmatizes as profane the very service which the church is called to render. If the Spirit of God has any message for the church in this day, it is the call to go forth through the gates into the crowded thoroughfares and prepare the way of the people; to cast up the highway and gather out the stones; to lift up an ensign for the people. And they who reprove such service as this will do well to beware lest they expose themselves to a stern condemnation.

As a matter of fact, many of those social functions which pious people now describe as secular were once performed by the Christian church. Mr. Stead has put this very strongly in his chapter on "The Church, Catholic and Civic." The care of the poor, as he shows, was once the exclusive function of the church. The hospitals, also, were church institutions; to some extent they are so today, but many of them have passed under the care of the state. The orphans and all the unfortunate and defective classes were sheltered by the church; now the state provides for them. "Education," says Mr. Stead, is another great department which in early times used to be regarded as much the right and duty of the church as the conducting of public worship is today. . . . The public library formally had no existence except in monasteries. . . . In fact (he continues), the more closely it is examined, the more clearly will the fact stand out that if any of the great saints, who, a thousand years ago, Christianized and civilized Europe, were to come to Chicago, they would, after surveying the whole scene, decide that three fourths, at least, of the work which they did was in the hands either of the city council, the mayor, or the county commissioners, and that not more than one fourth remained in the hands of the clergy and their so-called church. The state, or rather the city, has become the executor of the church for three fourths of the work which the church was instituted to accomplish. This is right enough, for it is the duty of the church ever to press forward, and when it has Christianized the community sufficiently to entrust any of its own duties to the elected representatives of the people, there is always more work to be done farther afield. *But the responsibility for the due discharge of all these functions of which it has relieved itself, remains with it intact yet.*

But unfortunately, no sooner does the church rid itself of the onerous responsibility with which it was formerly saddled, than it seems to abandon all interest and care in what used to be its special work; and what was heretofore regarded as distinctly Christian work, is often handed over to men who have not the slightest trace of Christian principle. In this respect the church behaves not unlike the unfortunate mother of an illegitimate child, who, finding it irksome any longer to maintain her offspring, hands it over to a baby farmer, and thanks God she is well quit of her brat.[4]

Not only so, but when any attempt is made to call the attention of the people of the churches to their continuing responsibility for the care of those interests which were once wholly theirs, but which they have now entrusted to the civic authorities, you hear from a certain class of people loud protests against the treatment of such topics in the churches. "We don't want politics," they cry; "we don't want sociology; give us spiritual sermons; preach the gospel."

Such protests as these are very hard to endure patiently. It is no wonder that when they are loud and frequent, earnest men should be moved

4. *If Christ Came to Chicago*, 280, 281. [ED.] William T. Stead (1849–1912), a crusading English journalist and humanitarian, published his well-known book, *If Christ Came to Chicago! A Plea for the Union of All Who Love in the Service of All Who Suffer* (Chicago, 1894), following his encounter with the city during the exposition of 1893.

to say that the church is a great obstacle to the progress of God's kingdom. But I do not believe that this technical religionism represents the
church of today. An institution must be judged by its tendencies more
than by its achievements. The main question is, "Which way is it going?"
And it seems very clear to me that the church of this time is steadily and
swiftly advancing toward a full recognition of its high calling as the servant of God in witnessing for and helping to realize his kingdom on the
earth. Those belated saints who assert the old traditional conception of
the church as an "Ark of Safety,"and want to be left alone in it with their
pious thoughts and heavenly reveries, are not the representatives of the
church of this day. The truth is beginning to get pretty firm possession of
the mind of the church that we are to seek first the kingdom of God; that
it is to this that our superior loyalty is due; that the church is the servant
of the kingdom; that the usefulness of the church is tested by the amount
and value of its contribution to the kingdom; that no church has any
right to exist unless it is pouring a steady stream of vitalizing and transforming influences into the social and political life of the community. It
has taken Christendom a long time to get hold of the idea that the kingdom of God is represented by a regenerated and sanctified society, rather
than by a mere ecclesiasticism. The breadth and significance of the phrase
which was so often on the Master's lips has been tardily apprehended.

From the acceptance of this idea several important results may be
hoped for.

1. It ought to clear the path that leads to a practical unity of Christians.
The strongest barriers between the disciples of Christ today are ecclesiastical rather than doctrinal. The questions which divide Christians relate
more to the polity than to the faith of the church. If the truth can be
grasped that the church in its best estate is only subordinate and
instrumental — that it is not the kingdom, but the servant of the
kingdom — then the schisms which now exist will appear to be as absurd
and hateful as they are. What gives intensity and stubbornness to these
sectarian strifes is the conviction, in the heart of every sectary, that his
particular ecclesiasticism represents the church of Christ, and that the
church is the one supremely sacred and important thing. If you can make
him see that the church is not the supreme thing; that his church and all
churches are only means to an end; that their value is to be ascertained
not by any traditional or scriptural tests but by what they are now seen
to be doing in building the kingdom of God in the world, it is clear that
the nerve of sectarianism would be cut. And I do not believe that any

other radical remedy for schism will ever be found but that which will naturally spring from a clear apprehension of the kingdom of God as superior to, and inclusive of, all ecclesiasticisms, and as the supreme object of Christian loyalty.

2. Another rational fruit of this new conception of Christian obligation will be an enlargement of the type of Christian manhood. The man whose supreme loyalty is due to the kingdom of God, will be a larger and purer specimen than any mere churchman that ever lived. The ideas among which such a man moves will be ampler, his sympathies broader, his aims more aspiring. To believe that the whole world is redeemed and is being saved; to realize that the reclamation of the whole of life for Christ is possible; to comprehend that the Master whom we serve is subduing unto himself all these interests and powers of the world; that business and politics and education and art and social life are all to be brought under his sway, must awaken energies and inspire heroisms and develop characters such as we have not seen.

3. We shall see also, I think, among the results of this way of thinking, a revival of religion of a far more thoroughgoing type than any which has appeared in our day. There is a gospel of the kingdom, and there is also a law of the kingdom; and both of them must be preached with demonstration of the spirit and with power, before that kingdom can fully come.

The law of the kingdom requires us to love the Lord with all our hearts, and our neighbors as ourselves. It expects us, in every relation of life, to look not on our own things but also on the things of others. It insists that the spirit of this commandment must rule in every transaction between man and man, on week days as well as Sundays, in the market as well as in the home. It absolutely reverses the current maxims and practices of exchange, and expects us, in all our bargains and dealings, instead of getting as much as we can, to give as much as we can. *As much as we can*, I say, in justice to ourselves, and to those who are dependent on us. *As much as we can* without weakening or pauperizing those with whom we deal. A proper self-regard is not abolished; but the whole attitude of the mind is changed; and life, instead of being a discipline of greed, becomes an opportunity of ministry. The fact that so many professing Christians doubt the possibility of maintaining life upon this basis, shows how profound is the skepticism of the human heart. When the Son of man cometh, shall he find faith on the earth? Verily he would find in the earth today a great multitude of those who bear his name, but who do not believe that the world could be governed by his law. This is the one blighting, paralyzing, damning infidelity. It is against this, first of all, that they who believe in the kingdom must lift up the standards of the King. His law must be preached as the law of all life — must be preached till it produces conviction of sin. A great many of the people in the pews need to be convicted; the real meaning of the Christian law has never been brought home to them. A thorough preaching of the law of Christ in its application to the shop and the mart and the mine and the kitchen and the office and the senate and the forum, would be very disquieting, no doubt. Many would be pricked to the heart by such a presentation; not a few would stop their ears and say: "Away with this fellow who profanes the pulpit with secularities!" But some would listen; we might hope to hear them crying, "Men and brethren, what shall we do?"

And then we should hear the blessed gospel of the kingdom. O my brethren, have we heard it? How many of us have it ready on our lips, waiting to leap into winged words? What a message it is, if one could only give it voice! O you that toil and strive, you that labor and are heavy laden, do you know what rest and peace there is for all who will take Christ's yoke upon them and learn of him? Do you know what a change would pass upon all this scene of tumult if good will could take the place of greed, and we could all try, even for a little while, to love our neighbors as ourselves? You masters and workmen, who now stand arrayed against each other in hostile bands, each waiting to take advantage of the other's necessities, and to crowd each other to the wall — have you ever heard the good news that you might be friends and helpers one of another? — that employers might find their highest pleasure in turning their gains into helpful ministries to the welfare of their men? that employees might be as loyal to their employer as soldiers to a trusted leader or pupils to a beloved and honored teacher? that factory and workshop might thus become the very house of God and the gate of heaven? Have you ever heard that with such peace as this, plenty must surely come to the millions of happy workers? And what is needed that it may come? Nothing, nothing on earth nor in heaven but the hearty acceptance of the law of Christ by masters and men — by men as well as masters.

You multitudes that crowd the avenues of trade, elbowing one another, trampling one another, pressing against one another so eagerly and brutally that the ways are clogged and there is no passage, and you stifle and smother one another in your mad rush after profit — have you not heard that this world of exchange might be a happy world, if each, instead of watching to snatch what his neighbor holds, were only willing to share with his neighbor; were only thoughtful, in every exchange, of his neighbor's interest as of his own? This world of trade is not meant to be pandemonium; this is not Christ's way — not the way of the kingdom.

> Rich, through my brethren's poverty?
> Such wealth were hideous; I am blest
> Only in what they share with me,
> In what I share with all the rest.

That is the way of the kingdom. And that kingdom is coming!

And you who look on abashed and humiliated while the temple of our liberties is profaned by throngs of place-hunters; you whose hearts are heavy because partisan madness and selfish ambition have come to be the ruling motives in public life, and the great opportunities of public service are thought of mainly as the stepping stones of personal aggrandizement — do you know, have you heard, that all this turbulent realm belongs to Christ; that he has redeemed it; that the coming of his kingdom means the purification of politics, the substitution of patriotism for partisanship, the exaltation of the common welfare above all schemes of private ambition? Do you not know that the day is coming when the citizens, because they are Christians, will have none but their wisest and best to serve them in the state; and that the wisest and best, because they are Christians, will leave the desk or the bench or the pulpit when their fellow citizens summon them to serve the state, as promptly as Cincinnatus left his plow in the field for the service of old Rome? Do you not know that the time is coming when the service of the state will be regarded as not less holy than service at the altar; when the same kind of consecration will be thought needful in a magistrate that we now expect in a missionary; nay, that the people, with the ballot in their hands, will be saying, "Lord, what wilt thou have me to do?" as devoutly as when they take into their hands the bread and the cup of the holy sacrament? If Christ's kingdom in the world means anything, it means this; and the gospel of the kingdom is simply the good news that this time is coming — coming with every revolving day, with every overturning of the hosts of organized selfishness.

Now it is the firm hold of these great realities of the kingdom, present to faith though far from sight, and the dauntless preaching of them, with conviction and fervor, that is going to bring revivals of religion of a different sort from those which have been common here — revivals like those by which John the Baptist prepared the way of the kingdom, and

Savonarola, four hundred years ago, revolutionized Florence. The fruits of these revivals will be found not merely or mainly in lengthening church rolls and more people at the prayer meeting, but in the good will that takes the place of strife in mill and factory; in the heroic and consecrated service of humanity that supplants our lazy and aimless almsgiving; and in the new ideals of public life that will banish the boss and the corruptionist from politics, and make the city hall the citadel of righteousness.

Revivals of religion like these are what the weary world is waiting for. Not until religion is manifested as the power that is able thus to subdue the kingdom of this world, will it command the respectful attention of men. And when you have made it mean all this — nay, when you have even made it manifest that this is what you mean by it, and are bound to make it stand for, the question about reaching the masses will drop out of your programs; the masses will come as clouds and as doves to your windows.

Christian men, this is no mere vision; it is what Christianity means; what it has meant ever since John the Baptist, in the wilderness of Judea, proclaimed that the kingdom of heaven was at hand. The kingdom is here, even now, in many beautiful beginnings; in homes which its love has sanctified; in neighborhoods where its peace is revealed in blessed deeds of kindness; in many a sign in the realm of industry of growing good will and "toil cooperant to an end"; and in groups of men and women here and there who are rising to wrest from hands profane the scepter of the civic power.

It is thus that the kingdom cometh, without observation, indeed, but not without transforming might; it is thus that the New Jerusalem, with homes of comfort, and palaces of beauty, and temples of praise, is silently coming down from heaven. O beloved, believe in it; look for it; build its foundations; lift up its standards; tell out its messages, till the day shall come for which the whole creation waits, and he whose right it is shall reign over all the earth.

❖ ❖ ❖ ❖ ❖ ❖ ❖ ❖

SHALL ILL-GOTTEN GAINS BE SOUGHT
FOR CHRISTIAN PURPOSES? [1]

Editor's introduction. One of the most heated controversies in which
Gladden was involved took place while he was serving as moderator of
the National Council of the Congregational Churches. In "Tainted
Money," an article published in 1895, he had declared that "the gold and
the silver that have been obtained by wrong are corroded with a rust
which eats the flesh like fire." [2] Ten years later, in the spring of 1905, the
American Board of Commissioners for Foreign Missions — the overseas
missionary arm of the Congregational Churches — announced that it had
received a gift of $100,000 from John D. Rockefeller of the Standard Oil
Company. The sources of the Rockefeller wealth, which had earlier been
criticized by such writers as Henry D. Lloyd in his *Wealth Against Commonwealth* (1894), were then under fresh scrutiny as a consequence of
Ida Tarbell's heavily documented two-volume *History of the Standard
Oil Company* (1904). Along with a number of other Congregational leaders, Gladden protested the acceptance of the gift. "The Church which
accepts the Standard Oil Company as its yokefellow can hardly hope to
keep the respect of right-minded young men and women," he exclaimed.[3] But there were others who sprang to the board's defense, insisting that it was not the role of churches or their agencies to judge those
who offered gifts. In a widely quoted editorial, *The Outlook* exploded:
"If one has acquired his money unjustly, he is to be condemned for the
injustice. If he is spending his money beneficently, he is to be com-
mended for his beneficence." [4]

The controversy dragged on for many months. The Prudential Com-

1. *The New Idolatry and Other Discussions* (N.Y., 1905), 57–87.
2. Originally published in *The Outlook*, November 30, 1895, the piece appears in
The New Idolatry, 17–29.
3. "Standard Oil and Foreign Missions," *ibid.*, 48.
4. "Judge Not," *The Outlook*, 79 (1905), 871–73. For an idea of the extent of the
controversy in the religious press, cf. also 767–69, 867–69, 922–24, 926–28, 967–69,
976–79, and 984–88.

mittee of the American Board prepared a "Statement of Principles" to be presented to the full session of the board at its September 1905 meeting in Seattle. The text was as follows:

(1) Organized as a corporation to carry on foreign missionary work and to receive gifts for that purpose, the American Board has not been given the authority to discriminate between those who offer such gifts, and thereby to judge the character or reputation of the donors. It is not a beneficiary from the gift, but only an agent or a trustee for others.

(2) While the board cannot properly accept money from one to whom any of its officers knows it does not belong, it cannot, on the other hand, properly decline to receive money from its legal owner, provided it is given for the purposes for which the board was established and in accordance with its rules. In the absence of legal proof to the contrary, it is necessary to assume that money belongs to the person making the gift. Investigation by the executive officers to determine the sources from which gifts come is neither justifiable nor practicable.

(3) By acting under the above principles, which require the receiving of gifts without compelling its officers to trace the manner in which the donor may have acquired them, the board pronounces no judgment on the character of donors. Nor by the acceptance of gifts are its officers or members stopped from criticizing business methods, or from persistently raising their voices in behalf of the application of the principles of righteousness in all departments and walks of life.

(4) The officers of this board, as of all other similar Boards organized to promote religion, philanthropy, and education, are morally bound to use every legitimate means to secure and convert money from other uses into the direct service of advancing the kingdom of God in the world. It is for the good of all that the way should be made easier, and not more difficult, for all to give of their present possessions and increasing wealth for the noblest purposes.

Gladden countered with a resolution which was brought before the board at the same time, "that the officers of this board should neither invite nor solicit donations to its funds from persons whose gains have been made by methods morally reprehensible or socially injurious." [5]

On September 15, 1905, in defense of his resolution, Gladden made before the board the address reprinted here. After some discussion, the board dodged the issue by tabling both the "Statement of Principles" and Gladden's resolution. The money from Rockefeller had been solicited and

5. The statement and the resolution were both printed with Gladden's address in *The New Idolatry*, 55–56.

portions of it had been spent before the public announcement of the gift, and it was not returned. Gladden later believed that his protest had helped to clear the air, recalling with especial gratitude the hundreds of letters he received:

> The response of the people to this protest was one that touched me deeply. Letters from all parts of the Union literally poured in upon me for months. Once could never have guessed that such an issue would stir the people so profoundly. Among these hundreds of strangers who wrote to express their approval were men and women of all ranks and classes, but the testimony that was most grateful came from those outside the church, who had been repelled by its seeming subservience to Mammon, and who were glad to welcome any signs of the breaking that yoke.[6]

I desire to express my dissent from the "principles" set forth by the Prudential Committee for the government of the board in the gathering of its revenues.

"Why introduce into this assembly disturbing and divisive questions?" I am asked. The answer is first, that those who think as I do are not responsible for the introduction of these questions; the officers of the board themselves have introduced them. The question must mean, then, "Why not agree to this statement of principles without debate, and avoid all unpleasant discussion?" It seems to be assumed that any dissent from this statement can only arise from a litigious and quarrelsome temper, or an undue willfulness or vanity, or some other phase of depravity.

I wonder, dearly beloved brethren, if we are asking too much when we ask to be judged a little less harshly than this. The men who are protesting here today against the policy of the Prudential Committee are not seeking notoriety: they have no particular occasion to do anything of the sort. They are not dissenting because they like to be contrary; they are not unmindful of the injury which such a discussion may inflict upon the work of the board. Perhaps they feel this injury as keenly as others.

Such men as William J. Tucker, and William H. Ryder, and John Bascom, and Reuen Thomas, and Philip Moxom, and William V. W. Davis, and Daniel Evans, and Hugh M. Scott, and E. D. Curtis, and E. G. Updike, and Charles M. Sheldon, and Charles R. Brown, and Sydney

---

6. *Recollections*, 409. Gladden's files of correspondence for 1905 are crowded with letters, some of them critical of his stand.

Strong, and Artemus Haynes, and Lewis O. Brastow, and Newell Dwight Hillis, and Frank S. Fitch — I name but a few out of many — have earned the right to be regarded by you not as pestilent egotists and disturbers of the peace of the churches, but as loyal Congregationalists. They have a right to be fully credited when they say that they dissent from the statement of principles here presented because it is their profound conviction that the policy declared and implied in that statement and illustrated in recent acts of the committee must, if persisted in, work deep and deadly injury to this board, to the Congregational churches, and to all the interests of the kingdom of heaven.

They do not think, and they have never said anything which implies, that the members of this committee or the officers of this board intend any such injury. They know that the interests and purposes of these men are just as honest as their own. It is the tendencies and consequences of their policy that we are discussing; not their intentions. Men with the best intentions may do a great deal of harm; and it is not an unfriendly act to point out to them consequences which they do not see and from which they would surely shrink.

I come now to the "Principles" formulated for the guidance of the board, with what they involve and imply.

Principle One is defective in its statement of the purpose for which the board was organized. It is much more than "a corporation to carry on missionary work and to receive gifts for that purpose." In the words of President Tucker,[7] "The board is not primarily a depository for the reception of unsolicited gifts, nor even an agent or trustee for their disbursement. Primarily the board, as it exists today, is a powerful organization for the solicitation and direction of funds toward missionary ends. Its work in these regards is as positive and aggressive as its work in the field. Principles One and Two virtually ignore the whole matter of solicitation in which present issues for the most part lie." It is this function which we must keep clearly before us in the entire discussion. It is what has been done in the exercise of this function, and nothing else, that has provoked all this controversy. Yet the entire argument of the Prudential Committee, as it has been presented to the public, has ignored this fundamental issue. I think that a great deal of moral confusion has been caused by this

7. [ED.] William Jewett Tucker (1839–1926), Congregational minister and former professor at Andover Theological Seminary, was then president of Dartmouth College (1893–1909). He was an important figure in the development of liberal theology and the social gospel.

evasion; and I hope that we shall be able here to get the main question clearly before us.

I would not, however, evade the question to which the committee has sought to confine our thoughts. If the board were simply, in its home work, a depository for the reception of gifts, the ethical principles which should govern its action are not clearly stated by the committee.

It may be granted that gifts which come from unknown sources, uninvited gifts, like those which are dropped upon the contribution plate, may be taken without questioning. To learn the source of all such gifts would be impossible, and we are not advocating absurdities. Offerings that are made without ostentation, before which no trumpets are blown, which expect no recognition, may be freely received, and no possible harm can be done.

But when the giver comes with his gift and asks us to accept it publicly and formally at his hands, the question is very different. "A gift" — I am quoting from a manuscript in my possession — "a gift requiring an act of acceptance differs in several ways from one that obeys the biblical injunction of not letting the left hand know what the right hand does, in that its effect upon the community at large is to be considered. If the community suffers in its ideals of honesty from such an acceptance, there is a very serious issue raised. Gifts requiring an act of acceptance, and those which do not, belong to different categories; and there is no use in confusing the issue by talking of them as if they differed only as to size. The offering which comes unostentatiously, through the regular channels, can have no unworthy motive attached to it: the public gift may be prompted by many considerations, some good, some bad and others merely indifferent."

This distinction, by the way, entirely disposes of the contention that we are seeking to prevent unworthy men from doing good with their money. Any rich man who is willing to make his gifts impersonal and secret will find no difficulty whatever in bestowing them.

It is only gifts which require some public recognition of the giver, and which connect themselves with the giver, about which any question can be raised. Every such gift represents the giver. His character is more or less reflected in it. Property, as Hegel has so truly said, is an extension of the personality, and the personality can never be eliminated when gifts are publicly made.

It is often said that one man's dollar is as good as another man's dollar, but that is far from true. One dollar lying in a pile of dollars may be as good as any other dollar in that pile; but one *man's* dollar is not as good as another man's dollar, because the man is the coefficient of the dollar. What did Jesus say about the poor widow's mite? He said that it was more than all the gifts dropped into the treasury by the rich men. It was worth more to the kingdom of God. Would you have replied to him that one mite is just as good as another mite, and that since some of those rich men had cast in a thousand mites, their offerings must be worth a thousand times as much as hers? Would you have argued in that way with him? If you believe that there is any truth in what he says, then one man's dollar is not as good as another man's. It is not only the man behind the gun who makes the difference: it is the man behind the dollar quite as truly. And the church which loses sight of this distinction, or suffers it to be blurred, is on the way to apostasy.

I believe that I am responsible for the phrase "tainted money," and I wish to defend it as the expression of a most important truth. It has been greatly ridiculed; some of those who agree with me have deprecated the use of it, but I think it conveys a meaning which we must not miss.

If money cannot be tainted, then it cannot be sanctified. I hope we are not yet ready to say that there can be no such thing as consecrated money. I trust that that phrase may yet have a real and an inspiring meaning.

Other material things may become morally tainted. No woman listening to me would wish to accept as a gift, and wear with the knowledge of her friends, a fur collar or a diamond brooch of Mrs. Cassie Chadwick's.[8] Why not? It may be just as fine a fur or just as genuine a brooch as any she could buy.

But you say that a personal possession like that is different from a gift of money. Yes; the personal connection is more clearly brought to light, but it exists, even in the case of money.

Here is a Congregational church on the prairies of Kansas, which has become deeply and enthusiastically enlisted in the work of foreign missions. It has established classes and circles for mission study; it has organized methods of collecting funds among its men, its women, and its children; it keeps in closest touch with all the work on the mission field;

8. [ED.] "Cassie Chadwick, a Cleveland woman, induced some important bankers to lend her immense sums on the basis of a relationship she claimed to have to distinguished public men, and the mysterious contents of a safe-deposit box that turned out to be mythical." Mark Sullivan, *Our Times: The United States, 1900–1925;* II, *America Finding Herself* (N.Y., 1932), 631.

the spirit of prayer for missions permeates all its assemblies. Finally it adopts a mission school, somewhere in Turkey, and by the most heroic and self-denying efforts it sends a gift of five hundred dollars for the support of that school.

The teachers and missionaries all know whence the money came; what inspired it and what goes with it. I care not whether the identical dollars and dimes and nickels contributed by the church are sent, or whether the money goes in a draft through a Turkish bank; the source of the gift is known.

Now let us suppose that, one year later, some gambler or keeper of a house of prostitution, moved by motives which we will not explore, sends with some publicity, to the same mission band, the same amount of money; and the missionaries know the source of it.

Is there no difference, to the missionaries, in these two gifts? Shall we say that since one man's dollar is as good as another man's, the five hundred dollars from the gambler's till will do just as much good on the mission field as the five hundred dollars of the praying, loving, consecrated church? I think we all know better.

The one gift comes bringing love and hope and courage with it; every dollar the missionaries use reminds them of the true and tender hearts that are working with them and praying for them; their faith is deepened and their purpose strengthened whenever they think of it.

The other gift brings with it the most painful and depressing thoughts; they may be glad that they have the money to use, but they cannot help remembering how dreadful are the sources from which it has come; how many lies and perfidies and cruelties have gone into the gathering of it; how many souls have been ensnared and defiled in heaping it up.

One man's dollar is as good as another man's dollar? No such thing as consecrated money? No such thing as tainted money? Nobody says so who is not destitute of moral imagination.

Money is a symbol [I am quoting again, at length, from the manuscript of which I spoke], an outward and visible sign, and if the thing which it symbolizes is worthy, then the gift of it is worthy; if the thing it symbolizes is a thing of darkness and crooked ways, the offer of it is an insult and the reception of it is an immorality. If $100,000 is offered a church, the first question to be decided is this: Of what is this money the pledge and token? If it is the sign of hard work, if it tells a story of great energy and much patience, of pluck and endurance, if it means that the possessor of it has refused to be daunted, and has fought a good fight, and that his muscles have endured the strain and his heart has not fainted, then it is a very worthy offering, and the man places in our hands a holy and a sacred thing, the very sacrament of his manhood. The offering of it is a credit to him, and the acceptance of it by the church is to be commended.

If, on the other hand, the money is the outward and visible token of a dishonest career, if the thing it symbolizes is anything that decent men would not touch, if it betokens a life disgraced by remorseless violence and plunder, if it has been wrung from the helpless, and snatched from the unsuspecting, if it is the shameless representation of a combination that crushes out smaller and less powerful combinations, a pirate upon the sea of industrial life, then the offer of that money is a covert sneer, and the acceptance of it stains the hands held out for it. Is there not something ethically wrong and spiritually degrading about accepting for our holy work money that has been made in the devil's way? Is there not a certain blasphemy in thinking that God's work will suffer unless we use such instruments for its advancement as are provided by the enemies of his kingdom?

Suppose such a gift could suddenly assume visible shape of that of which it is the representative, and by some kind of chemico-vital process become the thing it is the symbol of, and right there before the eyes of the recipient he could see, in panorama, the lies, and the heartlessness, the competitive knife dripping with the blood of innocent victims, the despair of the man who has been crushed to the wall, and robbed of his living, the midnight scheming of the rogue, the thefts committed under the shadow by laws passed to prevent them—suppose he could see all these foul shapes before him, a sight more hideous than any in the inferno, think you he would dare accept that for God's work? Would he not with unutterable loathing cry out, "Take away that foul thing! God's work is dependent on no such ministering agents!"

Is not that specter visible, even now, in every part of this continent? I think that it is. It may be that there are some who are too blind to see it and some who even count it a ministering angel; but there are millions who behold it in its true light, and whose minds are filled with amazement, yea and scorn, when they behold the figure of the Bride of Christ drawing near to that horror, and supplicating its aid. Would to God that spectacle could be blotted from the sight of men; but it is there, and no veil of sophistry that we can weave will ever avail to hide it!

I hope I have made plain the truth that money may be and often is a symbol; that it may represent, most vividly, virtuous or vicious character and conduct; and that when it stands for things that are evil and base and cruel, the church must not welcome even voluntary gifts of it. The church cannot do so without compromising herself. The fact that the donor has a legal title to it does not alter the case. To hide behind a bare legality in such a transaction is shameful.

I have dwelt upon this phase of the question, not because it is the real question before us, but because it is the phase of the question which has been continually thrust before us from the begining of this discussion, and because the ethical principles involved greatly need clearing up. The principles which I have laid down have been recognized in all the ages of the church. It has always been understood that the children of God must not be partakers of the rewards of iniquity. From the old day when the children of Israel were forbidden to bring the hire of a harlot into the congregation of the Lord, and when the Psalmist represented Jehovah as crying out, "I hate robbery for burnt offering," down through the days of the early fathers and even in the medieval church, there has been a constant testimony against all partnership or complicity with evil-doers in carrying on the Lord's work. The quality and the curse of tainted money have been well enough known to the saints of all the ages. Even when medieval bandits were acquiring merit by gifts to monasteries, the voice of the church was clear in condemnation. It is to be lamented that these first years of the twentieth century have witnessed the attempt to erase this distinction; to repudiate the symbolical character of money, and to obscure the ethical judgment respecting the use of it which moral teachers have always recognized. It is an unfortunate enterprise and it will not prosper, for God is in his world, even though portions of the church are unaware of it, and the ethical judgments of men are sure to be lifted up and purified.

The reception of voluntary gifts is not, however, the question before us. No gifts from compromising sources have been proffered to this board or are likely to be. The practical issue before us concerns the active solicitation rather than the passive acceptance of gifts. Even granting that "the American Board has not been given the authority to discriminate between those who offer gifts," it is certain that the board has ample authority to discriminate among those from whom it will solicit gifts. It does discriminate among these persons. It has not gone, and it will not go, to great gamblers or liquor-sellers soliciting aid. The suggestion that it might intend to do so has been already indignantly repelled as a slander. The legal title of such persons to the property now in their hands may be perfect, but the officers of the American Board will not seek out such persons and invite their cooperation in its work. It will discriminate against them. The right and the duty of making discrimination among those who are invited to contribute to its treasury will not, I dare say, be disputed on this floor. The line is drawn, and will be drawn. The only question is where it shall be drawn.

The committee say that "investigation by the executive officers to determine the sources from which gifts come is neither justifiable nor practical." However this may be, it is certainly competent and wise for them to make some inquiry respecting the character and reputation of the persons to whom *they apply* for assistance. This is the simple, practical question to which the whole of Principle One and Principle Two must be reduced, and the answer is so obvious that I will not waste a word in arguing it.

Using the discretion which they must use in soliciting donations, there are one or two simple rules by which they should be guided.

In the first place, as we have already seen, they must not seek the cooperation in their work of persons whose gains have been and are being made by scandalous immoralities. About this there is no dispute.

In the second place, they must not invite gifts from persons who are conspicuous enemies of society.

It is a bitter truth that such a class exists among us, and that the nation is now confronting, with anxiety and fear, the problem of restraining its depredations. The class is composed of persons who have rapidly acquired enormous wealth. The number of these persons is not large, but the power which they have acquired is prodigious. No such aggregations of wealth have ever been known.

The existence of such fortunes is prima facie evidence of social injustice. I think that a man may, by means fairly legitimate, accumulate a considerable fortune, but no man can possibly render to society a kind and amount of service which shall entitle him, within a generation, to heap up for himself a fortune of a thousand million or five hundred millions of dollars. The existence of such fortunes is an enormous peril to a democratic state; they could never have been accumulated, in a democracy, without a great deal of social and political rottenness; and the men who have taken advantage of such conditions, or have, perhaps, helped to create them, in the building of their fortunes, are entitled to be regarded as the most dangerous enemies of society.

These colossal gains have, in all cases, been made by practices which are glaringly unjust and iniquitous. By obtaining control of the public highways and levying tribute on the traffic of competitors, and taxing the necessaries of life for the millions; by corruptly controlling legislatures and city councils and thus obtaining franchises and contracts, by which they are able to extort from the people exorbitant compensation for public service rendered; by enormous inflations of capital, and the dishonest manipulation of the stock and grain markets and by the exploitation of trust funds for private gain, these great accumulations have been made. Most of these practices are flagrantly illegal, those which are not covered by explicit legislation are none the less unjust and oppressive.

The true character of these giant combinations, these grasping monopolies, is now pretty well understood by the people at large. It is evident that they must be sharply restrained or our liberties will soon disappear. It is evident that they have narrowed the bounds of individual initiative — that is industrial freedom — and have shut the gates of opportunity upon millions; that they have greatly intensified the strife of classes; above all that they have done more than all other causes put together to corrupt and debauch our governments, municipal, state, and national. The vital relation between big business and political corruption has been brought to light most vividly within the past six months. And the deadly damage that has been done to the nation in dulling the sense of business honor and intensifying the passion of avarice no statistics can ever show.

Against these merciless and portentous powers the conscience of the nation is now pretty well aroused; our President has spoken, again and again, with clearness and emphasis; our ex-President, Mr. Cleveland, has borne strong testimony; the government of the nation and the governments of some of the States are exerting their powers to restrain and punish these transgressors; quite a number of them are now under indictment for crime and many others are dreading it; it begins to be pretty plain that this is not a windmill that we are attacking but a strong and dangerous foe to the national life.

What, now, should be the attitude of the church toward men who stand in this relation to the commonwealth? I think that the church cannot afford to cultivate their friendship or seek their cooperation in its work. They may be courteous and cultivated gentlemen, estimable husbands and fathers and constant attendants upon church and prayer meeting, but if their business methods involve a peril to public morality and threaten the public welfare, the church must not invite their cooperation in its work.

It must not do so because such solicitation involves an endorsement of them which it has no right to give. If the acceptance of a voluntary gift implies no recognition of the giver, the solicitation of a gift puts the matter upon a different footing. The man himself has a right to infer, and the public has a right to draw the same inference, that the church values his friendship and does not disapprove his conduct. No other interpretation can be put upon such an action. The committee affirms in Principle Three that "by the acceptance of gifts the officers and members (of the board) are not stopped from criticizing the business methods" of donors. Will they say that they would feel entirely free to criticize the business methods of a donor whose gifts they have diligently solicited for the space of two years? I will do them the credit of not imputing to them any such conduct. I know that they do not intend to forfeit the respect of gentlemen. It is the simple historical fact that the business methods of such givers are not criticized by those who have solicited their bounty. When an instance of such criticism is produced we may admit the validity of this contention.

The church is not wise to solicit the gifts of multimillionaires because in this quest its own power is apt to be paralyzed and its natural resources dried up. Nothing is more fatal than the habit of dependence on such sources. Even when there is no moral question raised, the exploiting of big donations lessens the interest of the multitude of small givers on whom the work must mainly rest. The gifts of the Congregational churches to missions are less now than they were ten years ago, though their numbers have considerably increased and their wealth has probably doubled. I think that one main cause of this is an increasing tendency to turn to the big givers.

The Baptist churches, according to Dr. Josiah Strong, are giving forty per cent less now than ten years ago, even counting the much heralded donations of their largest giver. Wise men in that church attribute that shrinkage to these big gifts.

Simply as a matter of economy, therefore, the policy which the committee is introducing is likely to prove suicidal. But if this policy is followed, a moral injury is to be apprehended whose effects will be much more disastrous. The result of cultivating friendship with men of low moral tone cannot be healthful to the work of the board. Such an exhibit as has been put forth in connection with this case, of sordid reasons for the propagation of Christian missions, illustrates the tendency to which I am calling attention. There is no help in such alliances; there is weakness in them. One can hear the solemn words of the old prophet: "Woe unto them that go down to Egypt for help; and stay on horses, and trust in chariots, because they are many; and in horsemen, because they are very strong: but they look not unto the Holy One of Israel, neither seek the Lord." "Therefore shall the strength of Pharaoh be your shame, and the trust in the shadow of Egypt your confusion."

A kindred reason why this board should not make friends with predatory wealth is found in the grief and shame and weakness it brings to the churches whose agent the board is, with whose life it is identified, and upon whose strength it must rely. The board is not an independent organization. It is the representative of the Congregational churches. For whatever it does we must bear the responsibility. Of the glorious work it has done, and it has done some of the best work this world has ever seen, we have had the credit. Of the mistakes it has made, and it has made some woeful ones, we have had the blame.

Now, I am aware that there are Congregational churches and Congregational ministers to whom such alliances as we are considering are not offensive. They think them suitable and helpful. I do not judge them. But there are other churches and other ministers, a good many of them, to whom associations of this nature are very unwelcome. I know them, and I have a right to speak for them, for they have told me in many impressive ways what they think and how they feel. Their judgment is summed up in these words of a veteran missionary now in the field: "It seems to me like countenancing evil-doers in their evil doings to solicit and use funds from them for the work of the churches of Jesus Christ." There are a great many thousands of Congregationalists who share this feeling, and I ask the members of this board most earnestly to consider whether the gains they are likely to get from these doubtful sources will compensate them for the injury which they are inflicting upon their loyal friends in the Congregational churches. An injury it is, and a shame it is. You may not understand it, but we must be permitted to testify for ourselves. We know when we suffer, and we know when we are ashamed. The honor and the strength of the Congregational churches is dear to us, and when anything is done in their name that offends our sense of honor the shame is ours.

But it is not only our feelings that are hurt; our power is weakened. We know what our tasks are, and what are the difficulties before us. We are trying to bridge the chasm that divides the great masses of the working people of this country from the church. It is the one urgent business of the Christian church today. We know that the churches, in the view of these people, are in altogether too close relations with the predatory wealth. If we cannot correct this impression, we cannot win these people.

"For years," says a professor in one of our leading New England colleges, "I have been seeing more of the wage-earning people of New England. Their alienation from the church is a fact with us. . . . They are watching to see what decision is to be made of this question of tainted money. If the resolution which you have framed as an offset to the statement issued by the Prudential Committee is rejected, in substance or form, at Seattle, we must expect, in this part of the country, to see the workingmen turn their backs upon our churches."

Not upon our churches alone. Such action will affect not merely the Congregational churches. It will be laid up against all the churches. It will be regarded as indicating the attitude which the Christian church of this country has taken upon this question. And it will send a chill through the frame of every workingman who reads it, and widen and deepen the chasm between the church and the entire class of wage-workers. The task of every man who is trying to close up that chasm, and to convince the working people that the church of today is the church of him who came to preach the gospel to the poor, will be made more arduous, and hope will die in his heart.

Don't tell me I am making too much of a small matter. I know what I am talking about. I have been on the firing line in this warfare for a good many years, and I know how the battle is going. The appalling thing about it all is that so many of those who ought to be our leaders know so little and seem to care so little. But I implore you, as one whose experience is entitled to some credit, that you will not, by your action here today, put any more obstacles in the way of those who seek to make the Congregational church the church of the common people.

I think I have given adequate reasons why the missionary society of the Congregational churches should not cultivate the friendship and cooperation of men who represent the aggregations of predatory wealth which now threaten the life of this republic. It may be asked who these men are. It is not necessary to name them. There are not many of them. It will not be difficult for the officers of the society to learn their names by a little inquiry among their neighbors. With such a caution as the resolution which I am advocating contains, I am willing to leave the matter to the discretion of the committee.

But I shall be asked whether all rich men are not under the same condemnation. I answer no. There are multitudes of them who are governed by no such purposes. There are thousands and tens of thousands of men in large and active business whose methods are in the main honorable and fair.

It may be true, I think it is true, that there have been evil tendencies among them. Some of them have been sometimes tempted to imitate the schemes of the rebate robbers, and the frenzied financiers; and the church may be partly to blame for this, for the churches and the colleges have been giving their certificates of character to the worst of these offenders, and it could hardly be wondered at if ambitious men sometimes assumed that their methods were laudable and exemplary. We owe to our active business men sounder ethical instruction — not such as is expressed in the moral indifferentism respecting the sources of gifts in the statement of principles before us.

It is sometimes implied that if we are shut out from appeal to these doubtful sources, our resources will be crippled. That is a counsel of cowardice and infidelity. We have our Congregational constituency, and how much more do we need? Are not the people of our churches able to support their own missionary organizations? These are vines of their own right hand's planting, they have watched and watered from the beginning; their heart's love is bound up in them; can we not trust them to see that they are nourished and carried on from strength to strength and from glory to glory? The Congregational people are increasing in numbers, and their financial ability has been growing by leaps and bounds. They are well able to do today, not merely as much as they did ten years ago, but twice as much.

I have already said that they are failing in this, sadly failing. I am not quite clear as to the reason of this. I am sure that it is not the fault of the officers of this society. They have done strong work, untiring work, patient and wise and efficient work, in trying to bring the claims of the cause which they represent home to the hearts of the people of the churches. If the churches had responded as they ought to have responded to their appeals, the treasury would have been full continually, and there would have been no occasion to go outside of our own constituency for the means to carry on our work. Because of this failure the officers of this society have often had to carry a heavy burden of anxiety, and they have been forced to turn in many directions for the supply of their necessities. If there is fault here, the beginning of blame is with us, and not with them.

When I say "with us," whom do I include? I include the great majority of the Congregational pastors, and the leading laymen of the churches. I include myself. I am as much to blame as anybody. I have done a little, but not much; and I take to myself shame and confusion of face because of it. We ought to make all this philanthropic and missionary work a great deal more central and prominent than it has ever been in the life of our churches. We ought to develop the missionary resources of our churches, and of our local conferences, as they have never been developed. We ought to do it, and we can do it. We can go before the people of our churches and say to them: "This work of bringing Christ to the world is our work, and we must do it. The good fight is our fight and we can win it. We are not going down to Egypt after chariots and horses; we will fight it out ourselves. We do not need to discuss tainted money; it is enough to say that we need none of it, for we know where there is plenty of good honest money for all this work. It is the Lord's money, and he shall have what he calls for."

When we face the problem in this way, we shall soon find ourselves far beyond the need of discussing the question that has occupied our thoughts today.

Brethren, I have said my word, and I call you to witness that it has been spoken not in anger or bitterness, but soberly and kindly. I have indulged in no personalities, I have aspersed no man's motives. I have been constrained to speak very plainly, for the juncture is a serious one; there are principles at issue which cannot be trifled with, there are interests at stake which ought not to be sacrificed.

Some of you have been kind enough to assure me that I am in a very insignificant minority. That may be; I do not know about that; I leave that to be decided by you. It will not be the first time that I have been in a very small minority, even in this board; but I have seen such small minorities, in a very few years, grow to overwhelming majorities. "The safe appeal of truth to time" is one on which I have learned to rest with hope, and I therefore commit with confidence what I have said, to you, and to the people of the Congregational churches, and to the kindly judgment of all honorable men.

THE NATION AND THE KINGDOM [1]

Editor's introduction. In many respects, the social gospel was an effort to realize the nineteenth-century dream of a Protestant nation in the new America of expanding industry and burgeoning cities. It was the old concept of Christendom, refurbished to fit the realities of a voluntaristic, pluralistic, liberty-loving Protestantism. The advocates of the social gospel hungered and thirsted for a Christian America in an evangelized world. Reared in the intensely missionary atmosphere of nineteenth-century evangelical Protestantism, they put special emphasis on the role of their nation in the saving of the world. Their faith in progress gave them hope that their dreams would soon be largely fulfilled. These ideas have rarely been stated more eloquently than in Gladden's sermon on October 13, 1909, at Minneapolis, before the American Board of Commissioners for Foreign Missions. Now a patriarchal figure in his seventies, Gladden expressed the conviction that the spiritual movement and the national movement were converging toward a glorious climax throughout the world.

Lift up thine eyes round about, and see; they all gather themselves together, they come unto thee; thy sons shall come from far and thy daughters shall be carried in the arms. Then thou shalt see and be radiant, and thy heart shall thrill and be enlarged; because the abundance of the sea shall be turned unto thee, the wealth of the nations shall come unto thee. (Is.LX, 4,5)

This is part of a fervent apostrophe to the nation as the servant of Jehovah, that ideal in which was concentrated the hopes of the great unknown prophet of the exile. What kindles his expectation is his vision of a regenerated society, a society from which injustice and oppression and misery and want and all iniquity and wrong shall be put away; in which peace and good will shall abide and order and security shall reign. The

1. *The Nation and the Kingdom: Annual Sermon Before the American Board of Commissioners for Foreign Missions* (Boston, 1909).

prophet represents Jehovah as pledging his protection and care to this holy nation, this peculiar people; they are indeed to represent him; it is through them that he is to be made known in the earth, and therefore all his resources are at their disposal to enrich them and defend them, and crown them with his benediction. "Violence shall no more be heard in thy land, desolation nor destruction within thy borders, but thou shalt call thy walls Salvation and thy gates praise."

What the prophet beholds in his vision is the kingdom of God, the reign of righteousness and truth and love in the earth. Was it not the same kingdom that John the Baptist announced, and that Jesus described in the Sermon on the Mount, and that the Revelator pictured in his glowing representation of the new Jerusalem coming down out of heaven from God, to fill the earth? In this prophecy, spoken five or six hundred years before Christ, the prophet depicts that glorious society; in his vision he sees it established, and in the words that I have read to you, he is describing the mighty attraction that it is exerting upon the population of the world. They are flocking into it, nations and tribes and peoples. "Who are these that fly as a cloud, and as the doves to their windows? . . . Strangers shall build up thy walls, and their kings shall minister unto thee. . . . Thy gates shall be open continually, they shall not be shut day nor night, that men may bring unto thee the wealth of the nations and their kings led captive." As the prophet conceives it, this transfigured society, when the world once gets a fair look at it, will have irresistible attraction for the children of men. They will come into it in crowds, they will throng its gates, they will bring the strength and the glory and the honor of the nation into it.

Let us get it clearly before our minds what it is that exerts such a powerful influence over the minds of men. Let us listen to what this prophet has to say about it. "For behold," saith Jehovah, "I create a new heaven and a new earth, and the former things shall not be remembered, nor come into mind. But be ye glad and rejoice forever in that which I create. For, behold, I create Jerusalem a rejoicing, and her people a joy . . . And they shall build houses, and inhabit them, and they shall plant vineyards, and eat the fruit of them. They shall not build, and another inhabit; they shall not plant, and another eat; for as the days of a tree shall be the days of my people, and my chosen shall long enjoy the work of their hands. . . . The wolf and the lamb shall feed together, and the lion shall eat straw like the ox; and dust shall be the serpent's meat. They shall not hurt nor destroy in all my holy mountain, saith the Lord. . . . They shall build the old wastes, they shall raise up the former desolations . . . For your shame ye shall have double. . . . therefore in their land they shall possess double; everlasting joy shall be unto them. For I the Lord hate robbery with iniquity, and I will give them their recompense in truth, and I will make an everlasting covenant with them."

The establishment and maintenance of sound and fair social conditions, so that there should be no oppression nor injustice, but a square deal for everybody; so that the strong should not be permitted to prey upon the weak; so that the law of helpfulness should prevail, instead of the law of ravin; this was the primary cause of the phenomena which we are considering. Such sound and fair social conditions would bring to the community in which they were established and maintained, unexampled and marvelous prosperity; and this prosperity and peace and happiness would promptly advertise themselves, and set up an irresistible attraction. Such a society as this would be a magnet that would draw to itself, all the children of men. They would all want to be in it.

It is not necessary to conceive that the peoples from all parts of the world would abandon their homes and flock to the particular territory in which these social conditions were established; that is simply the outward costume of the spiritual fact. Even if the prophet himself conceived of it in this limited way, there is no reason why we should not discern the larger truth, that such conditions established in one community tend to repeat themselves in other communities, and these spread themselves over the world. The movement described is not geographical; it is social, it is moral; the kingdom of heaven is not advanced by gathering all the peoples into one place, but by inspiring them all with a common purpose. If New Zealand, on the opposite side of the globe, sets up a better method of social organization, the nations come to her light, and the kings to the brightness of her rising, by adopting the same methods; by putting in operation on their own soil the principles which have brought to her order and welfare. And such imitation as this is sure to take place. If any people in the world can establish and maintain conditions similar to those which the prophet here describes, the day is not distant when all the other peoples will follow its example. The result will not be immediate; the world may wait for a good while to see how the scheme works before accepting it, but eventually it will win. Righteousness and truth, justice and fair play, kindness and friendship are what the world needs, and when the world sees them organized into society and bringing forth their natural fruits in society, the world will lay hold on them, and cleave unto them. That is the way the kingdom of God is coming, by the mighty contagion of social justice.

It is touching to see the eagerness with which "poor sad humanity" has always turned toward any clear promise of the establishment on earth of this kingdom. When John the Baptist came proclaiming it, the people crowded to listen to him; they thought the real thing which the prophet had foretold was surely coming, and they were in haste to join themselves to it. And when Jesus took up the same theme in his Sermon on the Mount, the multitude thronged to hear him. What would have happened if the social aim of Jesus could have been realized then and there, if the society which is outlined in that great discourse could have been established in that little country of Palestine, we may faintly imagine. But there was simply no room in that quarter, nor anywhere else on the earth at that time, for the establishment of such a social order.

> It is correctly asserted (says Dr. Rauschenbusch) that the apostles undertook no special propaganda. Paul held no anti-slavery meetings, and Peter made no public protest against the organized grafting in the Roman system of tax farming. Of course they did not. Even the most ardent Christian socialist of our day would have stepped softly if he had been in their place. The right of public agitation was very limited in the Roman empire. Any attempt to arouse the people against the oppression of the government or the special privileges of the possessing classes, would have been choked off with relentless promptness. If, for instance, any one had been known to sow discontent among the vast and ever threatening slave population, which was not Negro but white, he would have had short shrift. Society was tensely alert against any possible slave-rising. If a slave killed his master, the law provided that every slave of the household should be killed, even if there was no trace of complicity. Upper-class philosophers might permit themselves very noble and beautiful sentiments, only because there was no connection between them and the masses, and their sentiments ended in perfumed smoke. Under such circumstances, any prudent man will husband his chance of life and usefulness, and drop the seeds of truth warily. If the conviction of William Lloyd Garrison had burned in Paul, we should probably not know that Paul had ever existed. There is no parallel between such a situation and our own in a country where we are ourselves the citizen-kings, and where the right of moral agitation is almost unlimited.[2]

This is the reason why the social aims of Jesus were not realized in his day. Doubtless he knew that they would not be. The seed had to grow

2. [ED.] *Christianity and the Social Crisis* (N.Y., 1907), 152–53.

secretly for many a generation before the blade of the Christian social organism could appear above the earth. The full corn in the ear was millenniums away. It would only be by centuries of indirect influence that liberty would be gradually enlarged, and room made in the earth for the establishment of a Christian social order.

So we have never yet had upon the earth a society representing, on any large scale, the principles of the teaching of Jesus. We have had many societies whose main reliance was on military force; many societies resting upon slavery or serfdom; many societies founded on feudal distinctions of ruling and serving classes; many societies whose regulative principle was competition, or a struggle for advantage and mastery; but we have never yet seen a society which rested upon the law of brotherhood and the principle of service.

Yet it is toward this that we have been steadily traveling ever since the day when the old prophet held up before the eyes of men his social ideal. One obstacle after another has been taken out of the way of its coming. The Roman empire crumbled, under the disintegrating influences which it set in motion; feudalism has disappeared; slavery has been abolished; political democracy with freedom of speech and of the press is the rule of the foremost people of the world; and large elements in our social life have been, to a very great degree, christianized. Philanthropy, the principle of compassion and kindness, has been largely organized into the social life of this nation; the defective and dependent classes are the wards of the state. A considerable part of the life of civilized society is controlled by Christian principle. We have come to a day in which it does not seem quixotic to believe that the principles of Christianity are soon to prevail; that all social relations are to be christianized. Listen to these words spoken a year and a half ago, not at a missionary meeting, not by a minister, but by a journalist who is not a church man, spoken at a political banquet in a western city:

> The whole world is coming into a new era. It is an era as distinct from the nineteenth century as the reformation is distinct from the middle ages. This new era is manifest in Russia as well as in Kansas; in England as well as in Nebraska. It is manifest in religion as well as in politics, in business as well as in art. It is *the era of humanization, the era of brotherhood.* . . . Whether commerce will admit it or not, the chief concern of business today is not so entirely the accumulation of wealth as it was in the latter part of the nineteenth century, but instead, one of the chief concerns of business is the distribution of wealth. . . . The spirit of mutual kindness has been

moving slowly for centuries through the world. The seed was sown two thousand years ago and *the plant is now preparing to burst into bloom*, and the next thousand years may see some real fruit of the spirit of brotherhood.

It is a great testimony, and it is a true testimony. This keen watcher from the mountaintops of the movements of humanity brings in a report which is surely entitled to credit. What is it that he sees and declares? It is the fulfillment of the prophet's vision, the realization of the Master's teaching in the Sermon on the Mount. It is all coming true. It is no longer a dream, it is proving to be a reality. The city of God, the New Jerusalem, which the Revelator saw coming down from heaven, is beginning to materialize before our eyes. It is still very fragmentary, very inchoate; it is like a new building rising on ground that has been occupied, and is but partially cleared; much debris and unsightliness is still visible; but we can begin to discern something of the plan and to rejoice in the beauty yet to be revealed.

While the witness whom I just quoted discerned signs of this dawning in other lands than ours, while, indeed, there are in some other Christian countries omens no less auspicious than those which are visible around us, yet we may thankfully confess that the promise which meets our eyes in our own country is for us the clearest and the most convincing. That the prophecy is beginning to come true of America is not to many of us incredible. These words of the text, as we read them, sometimes sound like a transcript from a current history of the United States.

> Lift up thine eyes round about, and see; they all gather themselves together, they come to thee; thy sons shall come from far, and thy daughters shall be carried in the arms. Then shalt thou see and be radiant, and thy heart shall thrill and be enlarged because the abundance of the sea shall be turned unto thee; the wealth of the nations shall come unto thee.

Have we not thus brought clearly before our minds the fact that the nation is to be an important agency in bringing in the kingdom? Has not the time come when we must learn to look for the employment of the nations by the divine Power, in the evangelization of the world? Is there not work to do in the salvation of the world which can only be done on the scale of the nation, and by the enlistment of national resources; and is it not needful that we, who have this missionary work on our hands, should be well aware of this fact and should make large room for it in all our estimates and endeavors?

This is certainly the prophetic conception. It was through the nation that the kingdom of God was to be set up in the world. The contact of the holy nation, the socialized nation, with other nations was to result in the transformation of the other nations into the same type of national life, with righteousness reigning and plenty and peace prevailing. All these glowing promises made by the old prophets, of the triumphs yet to be won for the kingdom of God in the world, are made to the nation and not to the church. We have given to them so long a purely spiritual significance that it is difficult for us to realize that it was to a political rather than an ecclesiastical organization that all these promises are addressed. You may say that the nation was conceived as a theocracy, and that is true, but that is God's plan for every nation; he desires no other relation to any nation than that which he maintained toward Israel. It was the people Israel, and not the priesthood, which was to be equipped for moral and spiritual leadership; it was of Israel that Jehovah testified. "Behold, I have given him for a witness to the peoples, a leader and commander to the peoples." Any one who will read through these prophecies of the later Isaiah, with his eye upon these references to the part which the nation is to play in the conversion of the world, will get some new idea of the magnitude of the missionary movement.

In truth, the evangel which the divine love is seeking to proclaim to all the peoples, is a truth so large that it can only be adequately uttered by a nation's voice. There is, indeed, a message for the individual, and this the individual can utter, not indeed in its completeness, but in such manner that it may meet the needs of him who hears it. To the individual, in his darkness and his loneliness, bending under a nameless burden, groping in paths that lead he knows not whither, without hope and without God in the world, our gospel has a message of light and comfort and salvation, and blessed is he who hears it, and blessed is he to whom is given the joy of speaking it. This is the message to which the emphasis of our missionary preaching and teaching has hitherto been given, and great and beautiful have been the gains that have been gathered from this sowing, in transformed characters and regenerated homes. God forbid that this emphasis should ever be weakened, or that the brightness of this hope of salvation for the individual should ever be dimmed. How much need there is of filling the world with new life and power, we shall see very soon.

Nevertheless, the gospel has been very imperfectly heard by any one to whom it has brought no other tidings than that of personal salvation. For in truth the individual is saved only when he is put into right relations to the community in which he lives, and the establishment of these right relations among men is the very work that Christ came to do. The individual gospel and the social gospel are therefore vitally related, inseparably bound together, and salvation can no more come to the man apart from the community, than life can come to the branch when it is separated from the vine. And the social gospel can be adequately presented only in the terms of the common life. No man can know what it is except as he sees it exemplified in the life of the community. The family can show it to us in part, but only in part; the church can illustrate only certain of the gentler and humbler phases of the common life; to know what Christianity is, we must see it at work on the scale of the nation. If we want the nations of the earth to understand Christianity, we have got to have a Christianized nation to show them. Small samples will not serve. The real question is, after all, what Christianity is able to do for the civilization of a people. The keen-witted Orientals to whom we are making our appeal, the Japanese, the Chinamen, the Hindus, the Turks, understand this perfectly, and we must be ready for a rigid application of this test. It is perfectly fair. We are judging them in the same way. The religions of the world are forced by the contacts and collisions of world polities into a struggle for existence; the evolutionary processes are sifting them; and we shall see the survival of the fittest — that religion which best meets the deepest needs of human nature. Doubtless each will make some contribution to that synthesis of faith which the ages are working out, but none of us doubts which one of them will stamp its character most strongly upon the final result. But the elements are yet in the crucible, and Christianity is listening to the challenge of the millions to whom it offers the way and the truth and the life. And that challenge, as I have said, is addressed to the larger incarnation of its spirit in the life of the nation. The keen critics, to whom we are proffering our solution of the problem of life, are practically replying to us: "We must be shown. By its fruits we are judging your religion. That is the word of your own Founder. And we must find its fruits in the national life. The individual types that you send us in the missionaries may be satisfactory, but what we need to know is that these are not exceptions, that the society out of which they come is fairly represented by them. Yours is a Christian nation, so we are told. We want to know what a Christian nation is like. We want to see what Christianity is doing for all classes of your people, for all departments of your national life."

This is the challenge by which our missionaries are halted on the frontiers of all the old civilizations. It is a challenge that must be met. If we cannot answer these questions satisfactorily, our missionary enterprise will have no large results.

It is needless to say that we sometimes find such questions embarrassing. For, in truth, as I have already said, our society is yet very imperfectly christianized. That suppositious Chinese official whose "letters" made some stir a few years ago, was within the truth when he said: "You profess Christianity but your civilization has never been Christian, whereas ours is Confucian through and through." [3] It is true that our industrial society has been economic rather than Christian, and that our political society has been too closely assimilated in its ruling ideas, to our industrial society. The Christian conception of human relations has never been consistently applied to these great departments of our national life, and it is the sad truth that the Christian church has only recently begun to see that it is its business to make this application. That critic whose words I was just quoting says again, "Whether your religion be better than ours, I do not at present dispute, but it is certain that it has less influence on your society." This must be confessed to be a grave defect in the type of Christianity with which we are familiar. It has been quite too much employed, not in saving the world, but in saving people out of the world. Of course we have always had some interest in promoting righteousness and justice here on earth, but this has been a subordinate interest; if we could get people ready to die, the question how they lived together here did not so much concern us. Thus it has come about that the influence of our religion on our industrial society and on political society has been a superficial — oblique and not direct, incidental rather than central — and not a controlling influence, and the national life therefore gives very imperfect expression to the Christian ideal. Nevertheless, in spite of our failure to apply our Christianity as thoroughly as we ought to have applied it to these great departments of our national life, its indirect and partial influence has been felt in every part of the life of the nation; and just as it is, we need not shrink from the challenge of the rival faiths. We admit that America is not as consistently Christian, as China is Confucian; if it were, it would be a far better country than it is. We

3. [ED.] First issued anonymously in *The Saturday Review*, the letters, actually by Goldsworthy Lowes Dickinson, were published in London (1901) as *Letters from John Chinaman*, and in New York (1905) as *Letters from a Chinese Official: Being an Eastern View of Western Civilization*.

admit that grave and deadly evils yet mingle with our civilization; that poverty and vice and crime still infest the social order; that our industry in many of its phases is brutalized by greed; that we have harbored the growth of a plutocracy, whose presence on our soil is a shame and a curse to us, and have bred, at the other end of the scale, a proletariat whose helpless misery is the dismay of our philanthropy; we confess our public service is grievously disfigured and debased by inefficiency and corruption, and that multitudes of men seek public office as the opportunity of unscrupulous greed and ambition. With that tariff wrangle still sounding in our ears, in which there were so few public servants who were not ready to sacrifice the good of all to the gain of a few, it is quite impossible for any American to claim that the law of Christ rules our legislation. And yet, while we confess all these things with sorrow and shame, we must not shut our eyes to the saving virtues which do yet appear in the life of our own people. The nation is not yet sanctified, but we may say of it what they said of the people who were added to the church in the Pentecostal revival, that it is being saved.

Most of that which is bad in our present condition was worse two hundred years ago, or one hundred years ago; in spite of all that has been brought to light by pessimists and muckrakers, the health of the nation is sounder, its moral forces are stronger today than they ever were before. Much of that which startles and confounds us is due to the deepened and clarified ethical feeling of the people. The interests were just as selfish and insistent when the Dingley bill and the McKinley bill[4] were framed, as they were last summer, but nobody paid much attention to them; today the people are mad all through at the exhibition of egotism. This does not indicate a falling but a rapidly rising standard of political morality. Most of the other disturbing violations of social and political distemper fall under the same judgment. While, therefore, we acknowledge with humiliation that our nation still falls far below our ideal of a Christian nation, and while we are resolved by the grace of God to bring it a great deal nearer to that standard before this century is very old, yet even now, just as it is, we are not ashamed to put its civilization side by side with any civilization that is not Christian and let the world judge between them. With other Christian lands we make no comparison, that is beside the point; but

---

4. [ED.] The McKinley tariff of 1890 raised duties on many imports; it favored manufacturers and led to a rise in retail prices. The Dingley tariff of 1897 incorporated the particular interests of many members of Congress, and was the highest protective tariff that had yet been passed in America.

where in the world today is there a non-Christian country whose people enjoy so large a measure of well-being as ours possess? Where is the path to life as free as on this Christian soil? Where is property as secure, where is enterprise as unconfined, where is life as precious? Where, in any non-Christian land, is there any such provision as that to which we are accustomed, for the alleviation of human suffering and the care and comfort of the disabled and the unfortunate? Where else are the gates of knowledge thrown wide open to the children of the poor? Tell us of any country outside Christendom where woman enjoys the honor and the freedom that here are her inheritance.

It is not necessary to pause for answer to these questions. The answer is coming in the tides of immigration always pouring into our harbors. Wherever communications are opened between our own country and non-Christian countries, the multitudes that throng to seek the protection and the opportunity which our flag symbolizes are convincing witnesses to the value of our civilization. Defective as our national performance is when measured by the high standards of Christian morality, it yet embodies principles and forces and produces results which appeal, with irresistible power to the heart of universal humanity.

In that great chapter of his on "The Advent of Humanity" in his book on *The New Epoch for Faith,* Dr. Gordon puts high among the agencies which are leading in that advent, the United States of America. It is not, I am sure, the fond conceit of a patriot, it is the reasoned judgment of a philosophical historian. Grievous as her shortcomings have been, I think it is true that "throughout the civilized world, government at the end of the nineteenth century is a very different thing from what it was at the beginning; and in bringing about this vast change, the influence of the United States has been predominant." And I hope that it is not in any petty national pride, but with profound and humble thankfulness for our great inheritance, that we are able to join with Dr. Gordon in saying: "In the ideas upon which it was founded, in the nature and scope of its political institutions, in the striking intellectual hospitality of its people, in the object and issues of its great war, and in the human foundation which it asserts for religion, the United States has been, in this century, the foremost servant of the idea of humanity." [5]

I believe that the people of all the nations are beginning to discern

5. [ED.] George A. Gordon, *The New Epoch for Faith* (Boston, 1901), 95, 99–100. For over forty years minister of Old South Church in Boston, Gordon (1853–1929), was one of the most able thinkers among the evangelical liberal clergy.

something of the loftiness of our national ideals, and to turn with wistful hope to America for leadership. And what has caught the world's attention is the illustration in the life of the nation of the Christian virtues. Dr. Gordon's estimate was made up at the end of the nineteenth century; but the first decade of the twentieth has lifted it into clearer light.

Ask China who it was that sturdily and successfully resisted the attempts of the powers to partition her territory among themselves, and established the policy of the open door; and who it was that sent back a good part of the indemnity money, and who it is that has just been seeking within the last few months to rouse the conscience of the nations of the world against the accursed opium traffic. China knows that in all these matters the United States has been her friend, and she knows that what this nation has done in these great matters has been done because she is, in some imperfect sense, a Christian nation.

Ask Japan what evidence she has had within the last year that this nation means to deal with other nations on Christian principles, and whether Christian principles, thus incarnated in the life of a nation, do not commend themselves to her as sound principles of national life.

Ask the European nations who it was that urged the reassembling of the Hague tribunal, and led the way toward the arbitration of national disputes and the establishment of peace and good will among men.

Ask the whole world who it was that laid a strong but gentle hand upon Russia and Japan when they were devouring each other, and brought them into an honorable peace. It was our President, you say, and he was acting on his own responsibility. Yes, but he never more perfectly represented the spirit of the nation than in that unofficial act, and all the world knows it. And all the world knows that the spirit of the nation as revealed in that act was the Christian spirit, and all the world stood still, reverently beholding a great nation going forth to claim the blessing of the peacemakers.

May we not say that the world has seen in the years just past such a manifestation of the glory of Christianity as it never before has witnessed, in these acts by which, on a national scale, the spirit of Christianity has been exemplified? There have been great preachers of the gospel, great missionaries of the cross, but few, I believe, who have presented the principles of our religion to the non-Christian world more convincingly than William McKinley and John Hay and John W. Foster and Theodore Roosevelt and Elihu Root and William H. Taft. Through the testimony of these witnesses the peoples of the non-Christian lands have gained a conception of the real genius of Christianity which they never had before. This exhibition must have its effect upon all our evangelical enterprises. I cannot doubt that because of these benign interventions of our national government the people of many of the Eastern lands must be more ready than they have ever been to listen to the message of the gospel of Christ.

Perhaps it may occur to some minds that since the nation in these large ways is so effectively witnessing to the principles of Christianity, there is less need of such work as that which this society is organized to promote. I do not so conceive the situation. The government has rendered a mighty service to agriculture in some parts of our western domain, in promoting irrigation, but that does not warrant any relaxation of diligence in the cultivation of the soil. The extensive husbandry which the Lord of the harvest is promoting by the testimony of the nations does by no means supplant that intensive husbandry which these missionary societies are called to practice.

In truth, it must be said that the witness of the nations would have made far less impression on the minds of the Eastern people if they had not had concrete examples of Christian manhood and womanhood living among them and illustrating the religion of Christ in the common affairs of life. They do need, as I have maintained, the demonstration, on the scale of the nation, of the value of Christianity; but their minds have been opened to the sense of that need by what they have seen of the men and women who have come to make their homes among them, and to reveal to them, in the terms of a sacred personal friendship, the reality of the gospel of Christ.

For these men and women, who bear the name of Jesus among these people, have effective ways of making known the significance of that name.

The gospel begins with the statement that Jesus went about in all Galilee, teaching in the synagogues, and preaching the gospel of the kingdom and healing all manner of disease and all manner of sickness among the people. The gospel begins in every mission field with this benign ministry to human suffering. There are few cities in the Orient where the multitude has not learned that the men and women who bear the name of Christ have wonderful power to heal the sick and give strength to the lame and sight to the blind. Everywhere the medical work of our missions is reaching down to the humblest and the neediest and easing their pains and soothing their wounds, and wiping away their tears.

Their experience of a skill which to them is marvelous excites their admiration; but they cannot help seeing that their skill is born of compassion, and that wins their hearts. And when they sit down in the hospitals and the dispensaries to hear the surgeon read to them the gospel story, they find out who it was that awakened in human hearts this impulse to care for the sick and the suffering.

The advent among them of the American family is also a revelation. I am aware that among some of these ancient peoples the family relation is greatly cherished, and there are features of that family life which we might well seek to imitate; but after all that can be said of Confucianism, the Christian home is not to be classed with any other institution on the earth as a training school of human character. How deadly are the evil tendencies which assail the foundations of the family in America, I do not need to try to tell; and the wreckage of households here produces conditions quite as deplorable as any that the Orient can exhibit. When we compare the lowest levels of our own social condition with the lowest coolie of India or Turkey or China, there is not much to choose. It may be that we can show the world a deeper degradation than that into which any Eastern nation has sunk, for the higher and fairer are the social ideals, the fouler is the deformity when they are trampled under foot. The worst is always the perversion of the best. The purest thing in the world is the heart of a good woman, and the vilest is the heart of a bad one. The infidel who scoffs at the God of Horace Bushnell or Phillips Brooks is a more revolting character than was the one who shut his heart against the God of John Calvin.

But civilizations are not rightly estimated on their lowest level; it is by their growth and not by their abortions that we must judge them. And when the best types of the Christian family are set over against the best types of the family in any non-Christian nation, there is no call for argument or demonstration. Certain it is that nothing can be done for China or for India or for Turkey, comparable with that which is done when the Christian family is transplanted to their soil, and they are permitted to look upon it with their own eyes, to witness its blossoming and its fruitage; to see for themselves what Christianity makes of womanhood and childhood; to feel the force of the mighty contrast between the Christian home and the best form of family life elsewhere existing. We sometimes hear arguments, on the score of economy, for celibate missionaries; and we all share the loneliness and pain of missionary parents in being parted so many years from their children; but, after all, nothing can take the place in our missionary work of that object lesson which the Christian family presents to the non-Christian people. We could not make them understand what our religion means if we could not show them this. It is by just such fruits as these that we wish to have them know it. Doubtless, the Hindus and Confucians are apt to regard their domestic institution as superior to those of other peoples, and there is much superficial comment by Europeans and Americans in which certain features of those systems are eulogized to the disparagement of our own; but all that is needed is that the differing types of family life be placed side by side. The home in which the wife is apt to be a menial; in which it is a very rare thing for her to be able "to read for profit or recreation," from which she can never depart without seeking permission; in which a social meal is a thing unknown, since men and women never eat together; in which the appearance of a girl baby is generally regarded as a calamity, and from which multitudes of them are cast forth to die and many more are sold into degrading slavery; such homes as these need only to stand side by side with the homes in which the missionaries live, in order that those who dwell in them may understand the meaning of the Christian religion. And it is somewhat surprising to hear Americans and Europeans of ordinary intelligence maintaining, in the face of that contrast, that Christianity has nothing to give which these non-Christian peoples need. The Christian school has also been a powerful agency in the preparation of the non-Christian peoples for that larger revelation which is now coming to them in the testimony of the nation. The thousands of primary and secondary schools in which boys and girls are receiving the rudiments of science and literature and history, and thus being prepared to understand something of the meaning of the world and life, and the colleges for men and women in which ideals are lifted up and leaders are trained for a new civilization, are mightily preparing the way of the Lord. It is to this leaven that the healthy ferment now pervading Orient society is largely due. The new spirit in India, which reveals ominous aspects but vast possibilities, is in good part the inspiration of the missionary schools. The awakening in China finds itself in closest relation to the educational work so long prosecuted there, and the progressive forces of the Empire are eagerly seeking today to avail themselves of the aid and leadership of our missionary teachers. Could there be a more impressive testimony to the wisdom and value of our work? The part that missionary schools, and notably the schools of the American Board, have been playing in the regeneration of Turkey is well known. It is the simple truth to say that as in

Bulgaria twenty years ago, so in Turkey today, the leadership of the reform movement is in the hands of young men who have either been educated in our schools or strongly influenced by them.

We may say that the missionary work is in truth a method of revelation. It is, to these non-Christian peoples, God's continuing revelation. God has always been revealing himself to men; he has manifested much of his goodness and truth to these non-Christian peoples. It is part of our great happiness that we, in these latter days, are able to discern this so clearly and to rejoice in it. Our missionaries, above all others, are teaching us to recognize the elements of value in all the other religions. We go forth not to destroy but to fulfill their form of faith. We expect to find in them much that is in harmony with our own belief, and some elements by which our own faith may be strengthened. Nevertheless, we know that we have something to give, something very vital and precious, and we believe that the larger truth with which we have been entrusted is ours that we may share it. This, I say, is God's method of revelation. His word to us is "Freely have ye received, freely give." But the substance of this revelation, now as always, is conveyed by personal contact. "In him was life, and the life was the light of men." There is no way of teaching men what Christianity is except by living it among them. What the missionary says is of secondary importance; what the missionary is and does — the missionary and his wife and children, in the relations of everyday life, in buying and selling, in work and in play, in the home and in the school and in the hospital and in the street, in the presence of sickness and misfortune and danger and death — all this is of primary importance. The missionary may be able to interpret to them, to some good purpose, the law and the prophets and the psalms and the gospels, but the missionary and his family are the living epistles out of which they have the greater part of what they know about Christ and his religion.

It should not be needful to urge that the one great thing that we have to give to these Orient peoples is the knowledge of our God. "There are many glories in the religion of Jesus Christ," says Dr. William Newton Clarke, "and it can do many services for men; but its crowning glory, or rather the sum of its glories, is its God. Christianity has such a conception of God as no other religion has attained, and, what is more, it proclaims and brings to pass such an experience of God as humanity has never elsewhere known. It is in this that we find that superiority which entitles Christianity to offer itself to all mankind." [6]

6. [ED.] *A Study of Christian Missions* (2nd ed., N.Y., 1901), 10. Clarke (1840–

I once heard a brilliant Japanese scholar, who had been lecturing on the Oriental faiths, plumply asked in the presence of his audience, by one who undoubtedly expected a different answer, whether, after all, Christianity was in any respect superior to the other faiths. He hesitated a little, but his answer came at length, clear and frank: "Yes, I think that the Christian faith in the Fatherhood of God is something better than any other religion has to offer." If that is true, there is nothing more to say. The case is concluded. If that is true, our one great business is to reveal this truth to those who do not know it. And it can only be revealed from life to life. Men can never know what friendship with God means except as they see that friendship incarnating itself in the terms and relations of human life; they must see it upholding and inspiring us, giving us comfort and courage, and peace and power. Such lives as these, hid with Christ in God, are the continuing revelation, and it is quite impossible for us, by any other method, to present to the people of other faiths, the real meaning of the Christian religion. This intimate and vital knowledge of what is seminal and essential in Christianity must be communicated to those who need it as we have been communicating it through the consecrated lives of the men and women who become their neighbors and companions, and show them by a testimony which no logic can confute and no prejudice withstand, what it means to have for a friend the God and Father of our Lord Jesus Christ.

It is the patent subsoiling that has been going on for a hundred years, on all the fields of Christian missions, which has opened the minds of the peoples to that great testimony which the nation is now prepared to utter, and which as I have tried to show is destined to appeal, with increasing power, to the great populations of the East.

Thus I have sought to bring before your minds the fact that the work which is so dear to us is going forward along other lines than those we are pursuing, and by the aid of mightier forces than we can muster. When we pray "Thy kingdom come," we are not always awake to the breadth of the grace by which our prayers are answered, "For God fulfills himself in many ways."

I am sure that we can all see how vitally related these two movements are; the spiritual movement, for which we stand; the national movement, which is part of God's providence. He is doing great things through the

1912), professor of theology at Colgate University, is remembered especially for his pioneer work in evangelical liberal systematics, *An Outline of Christian Theology* (N.Y., 1894), which ran through many editions.

powers that be whom he has ordained, but he cannot do them without us. It would be strange if such a vision as this should lead us to disparage our work and relax our diligence; rather, is it a rousing call to us to fling ourselves into it with a courage and a confidence tht we have never known. God has commissioned this nation, within the last few years, in some unwonted and impressive ways, to show the non-Christian nations what Christianity means; and in that call is a mighty summons to the Christians of this country to illuminate and enforce the message of the nation to clothe it with crowning light and constraining love.

It is not a futile or a hopeless enterprise. See what mighty forces God is summoning to carry it forward. For these great nations, the nations that are bearing the standards of modern civilization, are under compulsion to behave like Christians. Their policy must needs be, increasingly, a Christian policy. There is no other way out, for any of them, in God's providence. Look at England! Reeling, alas! and somewhat incoherent, under the obsession of naval supremacy, but that is the bad side of England; we all have our bad sides. Look at what she has had to do for Egypt. Look at that South African nation which she has just welded together out of those peoples with which only yesterday she was in a deadly struggle. Was there ever anything finer than the magnanimity with which England has clothed the conquered Boers at once with full citizenship, trusting them utterly and putting the responsibility of self-government upon them? Could any nation have done this whose mind was not saturated with the Sermon on the Mount? It was Jesus Christ who taught her how to do it. For India, too, she has got to do a great deal of the same sort of thing, and she will do it, yes, she will do it under John Morley's head. John Morley may not be posing before the theological professors as a typical Christian, but for John Morley, as the Secretary of State for India, no path is open but that which is worked out by the ethics of the Christ.[7] Whatever he believes, he has got to behave like a Christian. And this is the way the world is going. Doubt it not, beloved, doubt it not.

7. John Morley (Viscount Morley of Blackburn, 1838–1932) was famous both for his statesmanship and for his contributions to literature. He first became conspicuous as editor of the *Fortnightly Review,* an English journal of liberal opinion which carried many of his own writings. In the 1880's he became active in politics; he was elected to Parliament, and served several times as chief secretary for Ireland, and later as secretary of state for India. During his long career he wrote notable biographies of Burke, Voltaire, Rousseau, Cobden, Walpole, Cromwell, and Gladstone, among others.

The earth is circling onward out of shadow into light,
The stars keep watch above our head however dark the night.
For every martyr-stripe there glows a bar of morning bright,
And love is marching on!

Lead on, O cross of martyr-faith, with thee is victory!
Shine forth, O stars and reddening dawn, the full day yet shall be,
On earth his kingdom cometh, and with joy our eyes shall see
Our God is marching on.

There are just two things for us to do. We must pour the love of our hearts and the strength of our lives into this work of preparing the way for him among the peoples. And we must make this nation fit to be a witness for him, so that when the banner of our country and the banner of the cross are seen floating together, it shall be evident to all men that the day has come when mercy and truth are met together, and righteousness and peace have kissed each other.

THE INCARNATION [1]

Editor's introduction. Central to the understanding of Gladden's version of the social gospel is his Christocentric liberal theology. An important part of his ministry was the explication of the theological basis of his preaching and teaching. He had devoted several series of lectures to this apologetic effort; these were published as *Burning Questions* and *How Much is Left of the Old Doctrines?* He returned to the subject once again late in his life, in a series of lectures at the regular midweek services of his church. They proved so popular that the chapel for which they were scheduled could not accommodate the audience, which thereafter comfortably filled the church auditorium. Something of the basic simplicity of Gladden's theological ideas is evident from his comment that his having gone over this theological ground before made it "somewhat difficult to find fresh material; but circumstances seemed to warrant a restatement of the central truths of our religion, and it was gratifying to see that they had not lost their hold on the human heart." [2] Central to his understanding of Christian faith was his Christology, set forth in the passage that follows. In it Gladden's heavy dependence on the Ritschlian theology, especially as interpreted by William Adams Brown, is evident.[3]

❖ ❖ ❖ ❖

We are to consider tonight the central question of our religion, the question respecting the character of its Founder. We call ourselves Christians, and this implies that we are the disciples and followers of Jesus Christ. The question who he was, and what we ought to think about him, is one to which every disciple of his ought to be able to give an intelligent answer.

Jesus is reported by Matthew as asking the scribes on one occasion, "What think ye of Christ?" That is the way the question stands in the old

1. *Present Day Theology* (3rd ed., Columbus, 1913), chap. vi, "The Incarnation," 123–45.
2. *Ibid.*, v.   3. On the Ritschlian theology, see below, 159, 389.

version. It would seem to the superficial reader to be a challenge to them to give him their estimate of himself. But that was not the precise force of the question. "Christ" is the Greek form of the Hebrew Messiah, and the question put to these Jewish theologians was, "What is your opinion about the Messiah, for whom you are looking? Whose son is he to be?" They did not give the title Christ to the man Jesus, and he was not assuming that they would; he was simply trying to draw out their ideas about the origin of their Messiah. But we do give the title "Christ," which means King, to the man Jesus; most of us use the title, when we speak of him, oftener than we use the name; and if he should put the question to us, as it stands in the old version, it would mean, to most of us, "What do you think of me?" That is the question which I desire this evening reverently to answer.

How many different answers have been given to this question in all the ages of the church! It is often assumed that the teaching of the Christian church through all the centuries on these great themes has been uniform. One of the groundless pretensions often set forth by apologists is that orthodoxy is that which has been believed "always, everywhere, and by all." [4] But there is no statement in the oldest of the creeds of which anything like this is true. The history of doctrine is a record of constant changes in the forms of belief. Harnack has filled seven octavo volumes with the phases of theological development. People sing fervently,

> It's the old-time religion,
> And it's good enough for me;

meaning by that, generally, the old-time doctrine; but if any one should ask them if they meant all the old-time doctrines, and they should answer that they did, they would find themselves encumbered with reams and bales of theological rubbish, of which it would be difficult to make any definite use.

The doctrine of the person of Christ is one of the chief battlegrounds of theology. Through all the generations the theologians have been explaining him; and there are thousands, probably tens of thousands of volumes, in all the languages of Christendom, in which these explanations are set forth. The fiercest controversies of the ages have been fought over these definitions of Christ. "In the course of this controversy," says Harnack, "men put an end to brotherly fellowship for the sake of a nuance;

4. [ED.] The formula was stated in 434 by Vincent of Lérins in a work against Augustine.

and thousands were cast out, condemned, loaded with chains, and done to death. It is a gruesome story. On the question of 'Christology' men beat their religious doctrines into terrible weapons and spread fear and intimidation everywhere. This attitude still continues; Christology is treated as though the gospel had no other problem to offer, and the accompanying fanaticism is still rampant in our own day." [5] These are not figures of speech; they are quite exact and literal reports of what has been going on through all the Christian centuries. Men have been exiled, imprisoned, gibbeted for not holding right theories of the person of Jesus Christ. Armies have been raised to ravage the fields and burn the cities of those whose belief concerning him was supposed to be incorrect. Servetus was burned to death at Geneva because his opinions concerning the person of Christ were regarded as heretical. How strange it seems that he who came to bring peace to earth and good will to men should be the subject of such fierce contentions! How little do the men know of Jesus Christ who think that their loyalty to him requires them to hurl hot words of hate and scorn at all whose opinions about him differ from their own!

When we look back at the theories which men have held concerning him, and observe how far apart and how contradictory they are, it becomes evident that there must have been a great deal of confusion in their thoughts. It has always been believed that he was in some way a link between humanity and divinity; but just how the human and divine natures were united in him it has not been easy to explain. There was a sect in the early church which maintained that Jesus was in no sense a man; that his body was not a real body but a visionary appearance — a kind of apparition by which men's eyes were deceived. These people thought that the flesh was the seat of all evil; that matter was essentially vile, and that therefore no divine being could have any contact with it. The act of deception by which the divine person passed himself off as human these pious theologians seemed to find no difficulty in reconciling with their notions of deity.

At the opposite pole from these were the sects that denied to the man Jesus any divine character whatever. While holding that God and man are contrasted natures, they have maintained that the man of Nazareth

---

5. *What Is Christianity?*, 125. [ED.] Adolph von Harnack (1851–1930), liberal German theologian and historian of the Ritschlian stamp, produced literally hundreds of articles, monographs, and books, of which his multi-volume *History of Dogma* is especially well known and has gone through many editions. *Das Wesen des Christentums* (1900), one of the classic statements of liberal Protestant theology, has been translated into many languages, in English as *What Is Christianity?*

was wholly human and could therefore be in no wise a partaker of the divine nature. They were ready to agree that this man had been raised by God to divine honors, so that he should be worshiped; but this was purely a political act of the divine government, so to speak; and the nature of the being thus exalted was not changed thereby.

About the middle of the fifth century, the Council of Chalcedon formulated the theory which has since been held by many Christians to be the orthodox theory — which affirms "the union in the person of Christ of two complete and distinct natures, one divine and one human, each retaining after the union 'without confusion or change' the same properties which it possessed before." Thus a divine nature and a human nature are bound together in one person, not blended and interfused but kept distinct and separate. It is a difficult thing to conceive, and has always been a subject of controversy. Among Protestants, this debate has been raging for centuries. The Lutherans hold that in the union of the two natures the human is practically submerged, and that the consciousness of Christ is therefore essentially a divine consciousness — that he always knows himself to be omnipotent and omniscient; while the Calvinists insist on keeping the distinction sharp between the two natures, and the psychological difficulties are solved, as Dr. Brown tells us, "by the hypothesis of an alternating consciousness, now divine and now human." [6] Which of these theories is it necessary to believe in order to be orthodox? You cannot believe them both.

Such are some of the metaphysical puzzles with which this subject has been invested. They all start in the realm of abstractions, with the notion that some kind of a philosophical scheme must be framed into which this historical person can be fitted. That is the old way of explaining the universe — think out your theories first and make your facts conform to them. Of course, these theories are all man-made; every dogma is as truly a human product as is a wagon or a clock. And of late years this theory of a dual personality has fallen more and more into the background. It raises so many more difficulties than it solves, that intelligent theologians have ceased to insist upon it.

The changes which have taken place in the conception of the person of Jesus Christ are due largely to this fact, that God and man are, by modern

6. [ED.] William Adams Brown (1865–1943) was Roosevelt Professor of Systematic Theology at Union Theological Seminary in New York City. The quotation is from his *Christian Theology in Outline* (NY., 1906), 336. Brown and William Newton Clarke were the two major liberal systematicians; Brown's work was similar to Clarke's but gave more emphasis to the doctrine of the church.

thinkers, no longer regarded as contrasted natures. The difficulty with the old theories, as Dr. Brown tells us, arose from that great gulf which they placed between humanity and divinity. "Regarding God and man," he says, "as mutually exclusive terms, [the old theology] is forced to conceive of the incarnation as a stupendous miracle, involving the union in a single person of two sets of mutually contradictory attitudes." [7] But when men begin to think of God as immanent in creation — as revealing himself in the order and beauty of the universe, as the indwelling life of the world, as coming to the fullness of his manifestation in humanity — that old dualism sinks out of sight. It is simply impossible for those who have come to believe in the presence of God in his world to express their faith any longer in the terms of the old creeds.

Consequently the modern theologians begin their investigation of this transcendent theme not among the clouds, but on the earth. Instead of starting with speculation they start with history. Instead of figuring out a scheme by which the Absolute can enter into human relations, they begin with the known, and find their way through it to the unknown; they begin with the human Christ, and through his humanity approach his divinity. "The true humanity of Jesus," says Dr. Brown, "has always been a fundamental article of Christian faith." [8] Theoretically it has; practically it has been greatly obscured. For a great many centuries it has been virtually denied. The emphasis has all been put upon his deity, and his true humanity has been ignored. Dante's picture of Christ in *Purgatorio* gives us the notion of him which was really prevalent in the popular medieval theology — a figure with the body of a lion and the head and wings of an eagle. Such a grotesque monstrosity Dante found when he was looking for Christ. The Son of man had ceased to be a friend and brother; he had become a theological symbol. It was because of this dehumanization of him, in a substitutionary theology, that the church turned to the worship of Mary. Something human the soul demanded in its religious loyalties. God was inhuman, as all the theologies proved; Christ had become nonhuman, through their metaphysical and forensic manipulations; Mary the mother was still human, and they clung to her as to one of like passions with themselves, whose sympathy they could trust.

It was because of this sterilization of Christianity by the legalisms and fictions of theology that men began to go back to Christ himself. The humanity of Jesus, they said, is the proper starting point for our study.

7. [ED.] *Ibid.*, 334. In the original, the last word of this quotation is "attributes."
8. [ED.] *Ibid.*, 343.

Let us begin with facts that are level to our intelligence and find our way through these into the deeper mysteries of his being.

I suppose that the name which represents most fully the modern way of thinking about Jesus Christ is that of Albrecht Ritschl, the great German theologian who died in Göttingen in 1889. Ritschl was in many ways a disciple of Schleiermacher, but he thought independently and he has left a deep impression on his generation. Let me give you briefly, in the words of Dr. William Adams Brown, the gist of Ritschl's Christology:

> According to Ritschl the divinity of Christ is not so much a theoretical as a practical conception. . . . It expresses the fact that in Jesus of Nazareth his disciples find the ideal of humanity realized, and are conscious, through him, of being brought into contact with a power which is able to raise them above the law of necessity into the freedom and joy of the kingdom of God. Hence, to the church, Christ has the value of God. For God as he is known in religion, *means just this practical power to help and to deliver*. What God is in himself we cannot say, and it is futile to inquire. Hence any attempt to construct the person of Christ by the aid of abstract conceptions like the Absolute, or the Logos, which have no basis in experience, is to invite failure. The true task of the theologian is to study the human Jesus that he may learn, from an analysis of his life and work, what are the features of his character and ministry which gave him his unique power to uplift and to transform human life. When we have done this we shall have learned how it comes to pass that in him we find that practical power to help which we call God.[9]

Such are the methods by which the present-day theology undertakes to find out what it ought to think about Jesus Christ. It does not go to the councils or the creeds or the philosophers. It finds confusion and darkness in all these speculations. It goes directly to Jesus Christ himself, to the record of him which we find in the gospels. It tries to find out what he said, and what it means; what he did and what it signifies; what he suffered, and what it reveals. It hears him calling, Come unto me; take my yoke upon you and learn of me; I am the Way and the Truth and the Life; and it simply takes him at his word, and goes to him to listen, to learn, to follow. It finds that his gospel is a practical gospel; that it offers help to overcome sin, help to live the good life. That, according to his teaching, is what it is for. The present-day theology proposes to put this

---

9. *Outline of Christian Theology*, 340. [ED.] Italics supplied by Gladden. The correct title is *Christian Theology in Outline*, but the left running head throughout the volume is "Outline of Christian Theology."

teaching of Jesus to the test of life. And by this purely scientific experiment it verifies his claims. It finds that those who open their minds to his teaching and their lives to his spirit, who become identified with him in thought and feeling, do find peace of mind, strength to resist temptation, courage and hope and moral vigor. In short, they find that fellowship with Jesus brings God into their lives, brings into their lives that practical power to help and to deliver which we call God. There is no speculation about this, it is an actual experience.

Not only as individuals, but as social groups, they find that when they receive him into their midst, when they feed upon his truth, when they seek to govern their lives by his law and to live together according to his way, harmony and peace prevail, and the community is the home of welfare and happiness. The historical evidence of this is not so abundant as it ought to be, for this has not been the field in which men have been looking for the proof of the truth of Christianty; it has never been really expected, until very lately (by the majority of Christians), that the religion of Jesus would exert any appreciable influence in transforming human society. That idea is beginning to dawn upon the minds of many Christians, but there are few who have fully grasped it, and there are multitudes yet who scout it as a delusion and a heresy. Their notion is that the work of Christ is to get people safely away from this world to heaven; the idea that this world is being made better or can be made better by spiritual and moral agencies they scoff at, as contrary to Scripture; they say that it is going to wreck and rottenness as fast as it can, and that nothing can be done to arrest its decadence; that our only hope is in the return of Jesus in the flesh to earth to gather out of the wreck the few faithful ones, and take them up into the sky, leaving the rest to sink deeper and deeper into degradation and misery until by and by Christ will come back again and wipe the whole population from the face of the earth in a great conflagration, after which he will set up his throne on the earth. That, they say, is what you ought to mean by the prayer, "Thy kingdom come, thy will be done on earth as it is in heaven." That is the only way his kingdom will ever come.

Such has been the cheerful belief entertained by hosts of Christians in all the centuries. So long as any such notion as this was entertained, all expectation of the Christianization of human society by methods purely moral and spiritual was, of course, very dim. This world, lying in wickedness, was to lie and rot. And therefore, there has been no courageous and hopeful endeavor to apply to human society, in any large way, the transforming power of Christ's gospel. Consequently, the proofs of this transforming power are far less plentiful than they ought to have been, in this twentieth century. Nevertheless, imperfectly as the truth has been applied, there is evidence enough that this renovating power is in it, and that when the Christian people begin to comprehend what their religion is for, and set it to work in a wholehearted way, it will speedily bring heaven to earth. There are facts enough, when they are gathered together, to make it clear, that the social gospel has in it the power of God unto salvation.

This, then, is what the men of the new theology find, when they go directly to Jesus Christ and learn from him what he proposes to do for men. They find, as individuals, that in his fellowship and under his leadership, they are inspired, uplifted, invigorated, filled with the passion of service. They find that the God and Father of our Lord Jesus Christ becomes to them their Almighty Friend and Helper, and they are able to verify the words of Jesus when he said, "If a man love me he will keep my word and my Father will love him and we will come unto him and make our abode with him." They find also in their hearts and in the world about them, reasons for an abiding faith that he who said, "I came not to judge the world but to save the world," is able to do what he said; they are perfectly sure that this present world is to be filled with the light of the knowledge of the glory of God as it shines in the face of Jesus Christ, and they are filled with a great and solemn thankfulness because it is their high privilege to have part with him in this great work and to enter into the joy of their Lord.

Speaking for myself, that is what the new theology has taught me to think about Jesus Christ. That is what it has done for me. I am not ashamed of the gospel of Christ as I understand it, for I know that it is the power of God unto salvation, to every one who will receive it.

What has it done for the church? For a good many it has done nothing, because they are blindly refusing to consider it. But some great gains have come to those who have eyes to see and ears to hear. I am going to let Dr. William Adams Brown tell you something of what has been done for the Christian world by this new approach to Jesus Christ.

First of all, the humanity of Christ has recovered its rightful place in Christian thinking. We are no longer content to assert it as a doctrine; we wish to realize it as a fact. Through the mists of dogma and of tradition, under which he has so long been hidden, the gracious figure of the Man of Galilee begins again to be seen; and as the outlines take on greater and even greater distinctness, we are brought more and more under the spell of his simplicity, his originality, his greatness. We see the environment in which he lived, the quiet home at Nazareth, the simple life in the synagogue and at the carpenter's bench. We reconstruct the conditions of the time, political, social, ecclesiastical. . . . In this human world we see Jesus walking as a man among men; growing in knowledge with growing experience; deepening his sympathies by contact with suffering; winning men by the charm of unexampled frankness and simplicity; clothing his teaching with familiar imagery taken from the scenes of daily life; going at last to a death which was the inevitable result of the clash of two great ideals, only to appear again to the faith and love of his disciples, and to carry on through their devotion a work a thousand-fold greater than it had been given him to do within the narrow limits of his earthly life.

We have a better understanding of the gospel of Jesus. The Fatherhood of God, the brotherhood of man; the worth of the individual human soul, greatness through service, salvation through sacrifice, the kingdom of God as the goal of humanity — these truths, so inexhaustible in their richness and freshness, are seen to be his peculiar contribution to the religious thought of the race. . . . Today, as in each preceding generation, men turn to him with wonder and reverence as the supreme religious teacher of the race. . . .

Greater than his teaching is the character of Jesus. Here, too, Christian thought owes a great debt to modern scholarship. When Christ is conceived from the point of the Absolute, it is impossible to appreciate his moral greatness. But look upon him as a man of like passions and temptations with ourselves, and the full majesty of his character makes itself felt. A man who could live in the world and do what he did is unique. Where did he get his insight? What explains that self-mastery unexampled? This only is clear, that the gospel and the character of Jesus belong together. He could speak of God as he did because he had had experience of God in his own soul and knew whereof he affirmed. . . .

The same causes which have led to a new appreciation of the character of Jesus have given us a new insight into the significance of his claims. Here again a frank recognition of the true humanity of Jesus is the necessary condition of realizing his uniqueness. Humble and lowly as he was, clear-eyed and just in his perception of moral values, frank to recognize the rights of the least of his brethren to the same access to God which he claimed for himself, he was yet conscious of a unique relation to the Father and a unique function in mediating them to men. He recognized in himself the center of human history, and looked for a day when all men should be gathered into the kingdom of which he was the head. This is what the Messiahship of Jesus means, an authority spiritualized, transformed, reborn, but authority none the less. In proclaiming Jesus as Lord, the Christian church has made no departure from the gospel of Jesus.

Thus it is in Jesus Christ, understanding by the term all that we have passed here in review — life, character, authority, gospel — that we find the distinctive mark of Christianity. With his supremacy in the religious life of humanity, its claim to be the final religion stands or falls.[10]

This is a long quotation, but you could not afford to miss any of it. And it seems to show that the present-day theology has found its way to a very large conception of Jesus Christ and his work. But it reached this inspiring conviction by the discovery that the great gulf which the traditional theology had fixed between man and God does not exist; that the human and the divine are not contrasted natures. The fundamental fact is that God is our Father and that we are his children. He is not only the Former of our bodies, he is the Father of our spirits. If anything is clear it is that children must be of the same nature as their Father. Everything that is essentially human is included in the nature of God; everything that is essentially divine is found in the nature of man. Divinity is finite in man; humanity is infinite in God. "Strictly speaking," says Mr. Campbell, "the human and the divine are two categories which shade into and imply each other; humanity is divinity viewed from below, divinity is humanity viewed from above. If any human being could succeed in living a life of perfect love, that is, a life whose energies were directed toward impersonal ends, and which was lived in such a way as to be and do the utmost for the whole, he would show himself divine, for he would have revealed the innermost of God." [11]

Such a life as this Jesus lived. That is the historical fact. By living this life he became the most perfect revelation of God to men that it is possible for us to conceive. The strong saying of one of the early witnesses sets forth the truth. "The Life was manifested, and we have seen and bear witness and declare unto you the Life, the eternal Life which was with the Father and was manifested unto us." The life of God was manifested to men in the life of a man. In no other form of manifestation could it have been so fully revealed. It is through the human nature that the di-

10. *The Essence of Christianity*, 298–301. [ED.] Subtitled *A Study in the History of Definition* (N.Y., 1902).

11. [ED.] Reginald J. Campbell, *The New Theology* (London, 1907), 75. Campbell (1867–1956) was then a liberal Congregationalist, minister of the City Temple in London. He later entered the ministry of the Church of England.

vine nature finds its most perfect expression. Because Jesus was a perfect man he shows us the most and the best that we can know of God.

Thus the present-day theology puts an end to the old dispute about the person of Christ by getting rid of the ancient dualism, which set God and man over against each other as opposite poles of thought. This dualism was not merely the vice of orthodox thinking; the liberals were quite as much addicted to it. In the popular theology the orthodox were always saying, Jesus is divine, and therefore he cannot be human in any proper sense of the word; his humanity is only a temporary attachment or appendage. On the other hand, the liberals were always saying, Jesus is human, and therefore he cannot be in any proper sense divine. When we have once grasped the unitary conception, which unites God and man in the terms of a common nature, that old dispute is ended. If God is the Father of us all, if we are the sons of God, there can be no contrariety between our nature and his. We have got rid of the dualism which insists on putting humanity and deity into two separate categories. And Jesus Christ stands forth not only as the brightness of the Father's glory but as the perfect flower of humanity. The creed-makers try to set forth this faith in metaphysical terms, but the best theologian of them all is the good Quaker poet:

> We may not climb the heavenly steeps
>   To bring the Lord Christ down,
> In vain we search the lowest deeps,
>   For him no depths can drown.
>
> But warm, sweet, tender, even yet
>   A present help is he,
> And faith has still its Olivet,
>   And love its Galilee.
>
> The healing of his seamless dress
>   Is by our beds of pain,
> We touch him in life's throng and press
>   And we are whole again.
>
> Through him the first fond prayers are said,
>   Our lips of childhood frame,
> The last low whispers of our dead
>   Are burdened with his name.
>
> Our Lord and Master of us all,
>   Whate'er our name or sign,

We own thy sway, we hear thy call,
  We test our lives by thine.

To thee our full humanity,
  Its joys and pains belong;
The wrong of man to man on thee
  Inflicts a deeper wrong.

Deep strike thy roots, O heavenly vine
  Within our earthly sod,
Most human and yet most divine,
  The flower of man and God.

O Love! O Life! Our faith and light,
  Thy presence maketh one;
As, through transfigured clouds of white
  We trace the noonday sun,

So, to our mortal eyes subdued,
  Flesh-veiled, but not concealed;
We know in thee the fatherhood
  And heart of God revealed.

We faintly hear, we dimly see,
  In differing phrase we pray,
But, dim or clear, we own in thee
  The Light, the Truth, the Way.

The homage that we render thee
  Is still our Father's own,
No jealous claim or rivalry
  Divides the Cross and Throne.[12]

Thus we have learned what to think about Jesus Christ, not by questioning the philosophers and the dogmatists but by going first directly to him, and opening our lives to the grace which bringeth salvation, and then by believing what he tells us about the Fatherhood of God. One who helps us as he helps us, who gives us the power to rise from selfishness and animalism into newness and fullness of life, is entitled to be believed when he tells us that the Eternal God is his Father and our Father; that he is our Elder Brother; and that he, in his self-sacrificing love, is revealing to us the very heart of God; that as he loves us, so God loves us;

12. [ED.] From "Immortal Love, Forever Full" by John Greenleaf Whittier (1807-92), Quaker journalist, abolitionist, and poet.

that as he shares our burdens of pain and woe, so God suffers with us and for us to save us from our sins.

This is the substance of what I believe about Jesus Christ. I do not know that I care to put any label on my belief; I would rather it should stand on its own logic and shine by its own light. Like Mr. Gilder's heathen in Galilee, in the year 32, I am ready to say:

> If Jesus Christ be a man
> And only a man, I say
> That of all mankind I will cleave to him,
> And to him will I cleave alway.
>
> If Jesus Christ be a God
> And the only God, I swear,
> I will follow him through heaven and hell
> The earth, the sea and the air.[13]

If I have not made his humanity a glorious fact, I have failed in my highest endeavors, but I do not think that any of you will say that I have made him no more than one of ourselves. More he is — so much more that we have no terms in which to express the difference; more, but not *other;* his nature is the same as ours; and toward that glorious perfection we are called to rise; it is the high calling of God in Christ Jesus. "It is impossible," says Reginald Campbell, "to deny the uniqueness of Jesus; history has settled that question for us. If all the theologians and naturalists put together were to set at work tomorrow to try to show that Jesus was just like other people they would not succeed, for the civilized world has already made up its mind on this point and by a right standard recognizes Jesus as the unique standard of human excellence. But this is not to say that we shall never reach that standard, too — quite the contrary. We must reach it in order to fulfill our destiny and crown and complete his work." [14]

The old theology was a theology of contrasts and contrarieties and antagonisms, and therefore it was constrained in estimating the person of Christ to emphasize the theory that in his origin he differed from all the rest of humankind. It has thus made the doctrine of the virgin birth of Jesus an essential doctrine of orthodoxy. It has taught that his life began

13. [ED.] Richard Watson Gilder (1844–1909), poet and editor of *The Century Magazine* (1881–1909), was a close friend of Gladden. The poem, "The Song of a Heathen (Sojourning in Galilee, A.D. 32)," is in his *Five Books of Song* (4th ed., N.Y., 1903), 51–52.

14. [ED.] *The New Theology,* 76.

in a miraculous way; that he had a human mother but no human father. I have never felt inclined to make this a subject of controversy. I am not prepared to dogmatize about it. The beginning of every conscious life is to me a stupendous marvel. I can think of nothing more wonderful than that a free spirit, endowed with thought and affection and volition, should emerge from nothingness into being. There is nothing in biology that explains it. But that marvel constantly appears; it is as much beyond my power of explanation as is the origin of the universe; and since I must accept that, I am not disposed to make any very positive assertions about what can and cannot be in the beginnings of conscious life.

On the other hand the scriptural proofs of the doctrine of the virgin birth are rather dubious. In only two of the New Testament books is it referred to. The gospel of Matthew and the gospel of Luke contain allusions to it. The gospel of Mark, which is, by all, now admitted to be the earliest gospel, and the foundation of both Matthew and Luke, does not mention it. The Gospel of John, which is regarded as the chief proof of Christ's divinity, has not heard of it. The apostle Paul, who is the author of thirteen of the twenty-eight books of the New Testament, never speaks of it. No word of Jesus reported in any of the gospels alludes to it. There are two genealogies of Jesus, in Matthew and Luke, and both of them make Jesus the son of Joseph. The stories of the virgin birth in Matthew and Luke contradict each other at several points. There seems, certainly, to be much justification for the conclusion of many great Christian scholars that the stories in Matthew and Luke are late legendary additions to these gospels.

It is not disputed that the life of Jesus was sustained in the same way that our lives are sustained. Food and drink and sleep and exercise were as needful for him as for us. He claimed no exemption from the common experience of humanity in the maintenance of his life. He would not have been the Saviour that he is, if he had not shared with us all these human experiences — if he had not known what it was to be hungry and cold and weary. And I confess that I should be glad to know that he was one with us in the origin of his life as well as in the maintenance of it. It seems to me that this idea of the virgin birth tends to throw some discredit upon the sacredness of marriage, which is a tendency to be deprecated.

At all events I protest against making any man a heretic because he believes that Mary told the truth when she said to Jesus in the temple, "Thy father and I have sought thee sorrowing." The latest and one of the most staunchly orthodox of books on the Person of Christ, by Dr. Mackintosh, a Scotch Presbyterian, says positively: "For my own part I should not think of regarding an explicit belief in the virgin birth of our Lord as essential to Christian faith; otherwise St. Paul was no Christian," and again, "We cannot imagine Christ himself insisting on acceptance of the birth narratives as a condition or preliminary of personal salvation." [15]

The truth is that nothing is added to the moral greatness of Christ by insisting on this doctrine, and nothing subtracted from his essential divinity by the belief that he entered the world in a way that God has sanctified for all his children; and all disputation about the subject is not only unprofitable but unseemly.

I trust that this discussion may have brought the man Christ Jesus a little closer to your apprehension — may have helped you to see that he is

> No fable old, nor mythic lore,
> Nor dream of bards and seers,
> No dead fact, stranded on the shore
> Of the oblivious years,

but one who is sharing our life, bearing our burdens, feeling in his own soul the shame of our sin, and helping us to escape from it, understanding to the uttermost our needs and our limitations, yet strong to bring to us all the fullness of the divine compassion and invigoration and lift us up to newness and nobleness of life. And I hope that all these studies may be enabling you to see that the men of this generation who are seeking to interpret in more rational terms the great facts of the Christian gospel are not all the enemies of Christ. If I may ask Dr. Brown once more to speak for them, it shall be in these words:

> We have learned from Christ to call [the] Supreme Being Father, and to see in his will the expression of a character like that of Jesus Christ. For the abstract Absolute of philosophy we substitute the God and Father of our Lord Jesus Christ. When we confess his sovereignty we mean that the principles of Jesus are some day to dominate the world. When we speak of the Incarnation we mean that in the life of Jesus of Nazareth, simple, human, brotherly as we have learned to see it, God is revealing to all who have eyes to see what he himself is like, and what he would fain have all men become.[16]

15. [ED.] Hugh Ross Mackintosh (1870–1936) was professor of theology, New College, Edinburgh. Cf. his *The Doctrine of the Person of Jesus Christ* (N.Y., 1912), esp. appendix, "Jesus' Birth of a Virgin," 527–34.

16. [ED.] *The Essence of Christianity*, 313.

Yes, and there has never been a day since Jesus was lifted up on Calvary when this life of Jesus, simple, human, brotherly, held so commanding a place in the thoughts and affections of the human race as it holds today, never a day when he was speaking through so many lips his messages of good will and peace; never a day when it was so plain that the way of Jesus is the way of life for the world.

PART TWO

✤

Richard T. Ely

1854-1943

RICHARD T. ELY

AN INTRODUCTION

RICHARD T. ELY was a distinguished professor of economics who is remembered not so much for contributions to economic theory as for an ability to present complex matters clearly and to popularize the "new," historical-ethical approach to economics as against the older, "classical," laissez-faire views. A teacher of many who later followed brilliant careers (including Woodrow Wilson), he was an indefatigable speaker and writer during a long and active life. For about a decade, Ely played a conspicuous role in the shaping of the social gospel. "There was probably no other man of the period," John R. Everett has written, "who had as much influence on the economic thinking of parsons and the general religious community." [1] His fame as author and teacher lent this layman's work impressive weight in church circles.

Ely, son of a civil engineer and a schoolteacher, was born in Ripley, New York, on April 13, 1854. The next year the Elys moved to a farm a mile and a half northwest of the center of Fredonia, where, like Gladden, the boy became acquainted with the incessant labor necessitated by nineteenth-century farm life. Also like Gladden, Ely had a strict Presbyterian upbringing. Unable to accept the doctrine of predestination, Ely "finally went over to the Protestant Episcopal Church, which I thought offered a fuller and richer life." [2]

In 1872 the young man entered Dartmouth College. When the crisis of 1873 affected the family finances, it looked as though he might have to leave college altogether. Happily for him, he was able to attend Columbia College free of tuition, while living at the home of an uncle in New York.

1. *Religion in Economics: A Study of John Bates Clark, Richard T. Ely, Simon N. Patten* (N.Y., 1946), 75.
2. Ely, *Ground Under Our Feet: An Autobiography* (N.Y., 1938), 16.

By dint of hard work, at his graduation in 1876 Ely won a fellowship in letters, which he used for graduate study in Germany.

His studies abroad began at the University of Halle, where he took up philosophy in search of the "absolute truth." But he soon concluded that "if I was ever to be a great philosopher and make a really worthy contribution, I needed preparation which would take far more money and time than I had." He then chose instead the fields of economics and political science, as they were being developed at Heidelberg. There, in the spring of 1878, he met Karl Knies, and concentrated his work under that scholar's direction.

Knies (1821–98) was one of the founders of the historical school of economic thought. One of the others, the German economist Wilhelm Roscher (1817–94), had been a pioneer in infusing economic inquiry with the historical spirit, though he kept some of the devotion to the abstract that had marked the classical approach to economic theory. Bruno Hildebrand (1812–78), in explicitly rejecting the insistence of classical economists that there are universally valid economic laws, was a more consistent exponent of the historical school. He directed attention to the study of the actual economic experience of various peoples. Knies paid greater attention to methodological issues than the other founders of the school, and became a more determined opponent of the classical position.[3]

Ely quickly appropriated Knies's views, eagerly defending his teacher, who "conceived of economics as belonging neither to the natural nor to the mental sciences, but to the group of historical disciplines which have for their object the study of man in society in terms of its historical growth."[4] With Knies, he challenged the absolutism of theory in economics, and emphasized a doctrine of relativity: a policy good for one time or one country might not apply to another time and place. Correct economic policy for a particular state would have to be based on analysis of its situation, past and present. Following the lead of his German mentor, Ely became deeply interested in the aspirations of the workingmen. The young American student was permanently stamped by the influence of the man he was ever afterward proud to call his master.

3. See Ely, *The Past and the Present of Political Economy* (Baltimore, 1884), 36–49; Erich Roll, *A History of Economic Thought* (N.Y., 1939), 301–309; Joseph Dorfman, *The Economic Mind in American Civilization* (5 vols., N.Y., 1946–59), III, 87–98.

4. *Ground Under Our Feet*, 44.

Ely's diligent study at Heidelberg won him a Ph.D., *summa cum laude.* After a year of further study and private teaching in Berlin, he returned to the United States in the summer of 1880. The next year he began his professional teaching career in the department of political economy at The Johns Hopkins University, whose faculty were experimenting with changes in teaching methods and curriculum, and were among the leaders in organizing American learned societies.

The ambitious young teacher was soon known as a prolific and effective writer. In 1884, in *The Past and the Present of Political Economy* he attacked the classical, individualistic, laissez-faire version of economics, still so strong in America at the time, in favor of the historical approach to economics he had brought from abroad. His next book, which drew heavily on his researches overseas, surveyed dispassionately the various kinds of European socialism, and showed a sympathetic awareness of the growth of internationalism.

> The International Workingmen's Association [he wrote] is one of the many signs which gives us reason to hope for a continued growth of international relations; and this growth may terminate in that longed-for internationalism, which shall lead to the formation of a world organization, guaranteeing to the nations of the earth perpetual peace. There are numerous evidences of this development, of which the following are a few examples; the international postal union, international congresses, international courts of arbitration, and the efforts to establish international factory legislation.[5]

He also displayed sympathy for the mild, evolutionary socialism favored by Christian leaders:

> Professors of political economy, finding themselves forced to abandon every hope of reconciling adverse interests of society without a moral and religious regeneration of the various social classes, turn to Christianity, and appeal to it for cooperation in their endeavors to bring about an era of peace and harmony. Professorial socialism terminates in Christianity. Christian socialism seeks in it a starting point.[6]

His early books provided much information on the development of social and labor movements abroad.

He soon discovered that the American public lacked a clear idea of the labor movement at home, despite the great attention given to it in the

5. *French and German Socialism in Modern Times* (N.Y., 1883), 187.
6. *Ibid.,* 245.

press. The Knights of Labor were then declining, and the American Federation of Labor was in process of formation. Many were confusing the union movement, socialism, and anarchism. Ely felt a call to bring clarity where confusion, ignorance, and alarmism were rife. "There were a great many trees all around, but no one could see the forest for the trees. I plunged in and tried to make a road through the trees and to get a glimpse of the forest," he later recalled. "At the time I was full of enthusiasm and was fired with the thought that I was fulfilling a mission." [7] For this reason he wrote a detailed study of the American labor movement. His concluding chapter, "The Remedies," stated the premises on which he was to base a decade of activity on behalf of the social gospel:

> A wider diffusion of sound ethics is an economic requirement of the times. Christian morality is the only stable basis for a State professedly Christian. An ethical demand of the present age is a clearer perception of the duties of property, intelligence, and social position. It must be recognized that extreme individualism is immoral. . . . The absolute ideal was given two thousand years ago by Christ, who established the most perfect system of ethics the world has ever known.[8]

Looking back on it fifty years later, he declared:

> The struggle between the organized forces of labor and capital which manifested itself in this spectacular crisis of the eighties indicated a conflict which was deep and which would probably be prolonged. A crisis means an opportunity and I saw in this special crisis an unprecedented, unparalleled opportunity for the church to direct the conflicting forces into such fruitful channels that they might have become powerful for the "good of man and the glory of God." [9]

So for some ten years, often as a part of his professional activities, he spoke and wrote and organized on behalf of the social gospel.

Ely's basic world-view grew out of the simple, uncomplicated, non-dogmatic faith of a liberal Christian layman. "It appears quite obvious that Ely worked out his whole social theory from religious assumptions," Everett has explained. "His ultimate questions were answered by the acceptance of Christ as the true revealer of God's will for man." [10] He did not argue the point; to him it was axiomatic. In his book on the American labor movement he declared:

7. *Ground Under Our Feet,* 72.
8. *The Labor Movement in America* (N.Y., 1886), 311–13.
9. *Ground Under Our Feet,* 72.   10. *Religion in Economics,* 97.

Christian ethics — by all acknowledged to be the most perfect system of ethics, regardless of divine origin—contains the principles which should animate the entire labor movement. But how are men to learn these? The masses can acquire such an acquaintance with the data of ethics as to render them a living reality only through some one who is a personal embodiment of them. Abstract ethics have not and never will become a mighty vital power in this world. It is the concrete which moves men. Now, I know only one perfect concrete embodiment of Christian ethics, and that is their Founder. He it is who must become the personal Saviour of this labor movement, if it is ever to accomplish its legitimate end.[11]

As a footnote to the above paragraph, he added, "All this is said entirely apart from my views as a church member. I come to it by an independent route as a social scientist." But his work was all of a piece; his labors as a social Christian and social scientist were rooted in the same ground. In an article entitled "Fundamental Beliefs in My Social Philosophy," Ely affirmed that "Science is not religious revelation but a progressive unfolding of truth."[12] David W. Noble has given this statement a perceptive interpretation:

Here, summed up in brief, is the key to the unconscious and all-important presumptions of Ely's climate of opinion. Proudly, he cut the connection of science from anything like a direct religious control of the facts men knew. Just as proudly, he brought religion back into the scientific world, a religion controlled and upheld by the concrete and unarguable facts of science; it was a religion of a progressive unfolding of truth.[13]

But it was also a religion controlled and upheld by what was for him the concrete and unarguable fact of Jesus Christ. For to him, "it is with satisfaction one turns from the study of social problems to the teachings of Christ, which seem, from a purely scientific standpoint, to contain just what is needed."[14]

His version of Christianity was a simple one. All God's commandments were reduced by Christ to two simple injunctions: love of God and love of one's neighbor. True Christian faith was concerned with this world and its affairs. In an address to the Baptist ministers of New York, he said: "I take this as my thesis: Christianity is primarily concerned with this

11. The Labor Movement in America, 321.
12. The Forum, XVIII (September 1894–February 1895), 173. The article is reprinted below, 210–20.
13. The Paradox of Progressive Thought (Minneapolis, 1958), 166.
14. The Labor Movement in America, 331.

world, and it is the mission of Christianity to bring to pass here a kingdom of righteousness and to rescue from the evil one and redeem all our
social relations." [15] Nearly half a century later, in reflecting on his earlier
efforts to describe what would constitute a kingdom of righteousness and
what should be aimed at in social reform, Ely declared, "The answer I
gave then still applies today." [16] His religion and his social science were
interpenetrated throughout his long career. He believed that the function
of social science was to teach how the second commandment might be
fulfilled, and much of what he did, especially during the period of his
activity for the social gospel, was explicitly directed to that end.

For Ely there was, in principle, no serious tension between church,
state, and science. His book on the labor movement concluded with these
words: "In the harmonious action of state, church, and individual, moving in the light of true science, will be found an escape from present and
future social dangers. Herein is pointed out the path to safe progress;
other there is none." [17] This is predicated on a religious interpretation of
the state: "Now it may rationally be maintained that, if there is anything
divine on this earth, it is the state, the product of the same God-given
instincts which led to the establishment of the church and the family." [18]
Ely found the thought of Canon W. H. Fremantle most congenial, and
wrote an introduction to the American edition of the latter's Bampton
lectures.[19] He also drew upon Elisha Mulford's *The Nation*, in which influences from Hegel and Maurice were commingled.[20] One of Ely's central themes was "social solidarity," the oneness of all human interests.[21]
According to his monistic idealist view of reality, the truths of science
and religion were complementary, and all the institutions of men—
church, state, family, school, industry—should work together to advance
human progress.[22]

15. *Social Aspects of Christianity, and other Essays* (N.Y., 1889), 53. For more
about this book, see below, 184–209.

16. *Ground Under Our Feet*, 77.   17. *Labor Movement in America*, 332.

18. *Ibid.*, 325–26. I am indebted to a participant in my seminars, Mr. John Aber-
nathy Smith, for insights on Ely's view of the state.

19. *The World as the Subject of Redemption: Being an Attempt to set forth the
Functions of the Church as designed to embrace the whole Race of Mankind* (N.Y.,
1892). Fremantle (1831–1916), then a canon of Canterbury, was later dean of Ripon.

20. *The Nation: The Foundations of Civil Order and Political Life in the United
States* (N.Y., 1870). Mulford (1833–85) was an Episcopal clergyman, scholar, and
teacher.

21. See his essay, "Social Solidarity," in *The Social Law of Service* (N.Y., 1896),
reprinted below, 235–41.

22. Ely wrote, "I have always been an idealist in the philosophical sense, firm in
my belief that ideas govern the world" (*Ground Under Our Feet*, 95).

Ely carried these ideas into the circle of professional economists. Just as his colleague at Hopkins, Herbert Baxter Adams, had been instrumental in founding the American Historical Association in 1884, Ely the next year took the lead in the formation of the American Economic Association. Not all of its founders shared Ely's religious attitudes. A modified four-point "statement of principles" prepared by a committee of five that included Ely and Washington Gladden, was finally adopted, but with the stipulation that it was not to be regarded as binding on individual members. Evident in the statement are ideas characteristic of Ely:

1. We regard the state as an agency whose positive assistance is one of the indispensable conditions of human progress.
2. We believe that political economy as a science is still in an early stage of its development. While we appreciate the work of former economists, we look, not so much to speculation as to the historical and statistical study of actual conditions of economic life for the satisfactory accomplishment of that development.
3. We hold that the conflict of labor and capital has brought into prominence a vast number of social problems, whose solution requires the united efforts, each in its own sphere, of the church, of the state, and of science.
4. In the study of the industrial and commercial policy of governments we take no partisan attitude. We believe in a progressive development of economic conditions, which must be met by a corresponding development of legislative policy.[23]

A good many leading exponents of the social gospel were charter members of the new association.[24] Ely served as its first secretary (1885–92), and later as president (1899–1901).

Some of Ely's work was explicitly in the field of religious organization. "My attempts to influence the churches were not confined to my writings alone," he explained. "I used every means within my reach to awaken the conscience of the churches to an appreciation of their obligations, the obligations resting upon them to do their part in bringing about a social order in harmony with the principles of Christianity. I spoke in churches very frequently. I addressed religious gatherings of all sorts, like the Epworth League, St. Andrews Brotherhood, etc." [25] In 1891, members of the Protestant Episcopal Church founded an American branch of the Christian Social Union, an English society. Ely served for several years as its secretary and as a member of the American executive committee. The files of his correspondence show that he worked seriously at this

23. *Ibid.*, 140   24. Hopkins, *Rise of the Social Gospel,* 116–17.
25. *Ground Under Our Feet,* 78.

task; he exchanged many letters with Canon Fremantle and others in England.[26] The work of the union was primarily educational. Ely's books were among those promoted by it. Ely was also a founder in 1893 (with Gladden and others associated with the social gospel) of the short-lived American Institute of Christian Sociology, whose aim was to study how to apply the principles of Christianity to the social and economic problems of the time. He served as its first president.[27] All of this organizational effort Ely saw as part of his work as educator.

Ely's technical works in political economy reflected his basic religious orientation—most often indirectly, but sometimes quite explicitly. One of his basic texts, *Outlines of Economics*, was to go through six major editions (some with co-authors); over a million copies were eventually sold. In its first edition Ely said: "The most modern movement in economics, as it is in part a return to Aristotle, may also be regarded as in part a return to the teaching of Christ, although yet far from the ideal which he placed before men. . . . The doctrine of brotherhood is a powerful economic factor. Let us bear one another's burdens." [28] What was mentioned briefly in his professional writings was articulated in greater detail in the many addresses and essays directly concerned with the social gospel. Like those of Gladden, his works in this field were mostly given first as addresses, then published as magazine articles, and finally incorporated into books. Two of his works were distinct contributions to the social gospel: *Social Aspects of Christianity* and *The Social Law of Service*. During the summers of the 1880's Ely spent much time lecturing at the Chautauqua assembly in New York, and several of his books appeared in Chautauqua editions. He believed that "it was largely through Chautauqua that I was able to exercise my greatest influence." [29]

Ely was a famous man when he was called from Johns Hopkins to become professor of political economy and director of the School of Economics, Political Science, and History at the University of Wisconsin in 1892. His former student, Frederick Jackson Turner, soon to gain fame as the exponent of the "frontier thesis" in American historiography, was largely responsible for arranging the shift to Madison.[30] For more than

26. Ely Papers, State Historical Society of Wisconsin, especially Boxes 6–12.
27. John R. Commons, "American Institute of Christian Sociology," *The Congregationalist*, LXXXVIII (July–December 1893), 32.
28. *Outlines of Economics* (N.Y., 1893), 383. This book grew out of his earlier work, *An Introduction to Political Economy* (N.Y., 1889); after an almost total revision it was given the new title.
29. *Ground Under Our Feet*, 79.
30. The actual negotiations were, of course, with the president of the university,

thirty-five years, Ely remained Wisconsin's most widely known faculty member.

In the summer of 1894 came the event that attracted national attention, and further added to the luster of Ely's name. The Wisconsin superintendent of public instruction, Oliver E. Wells, was an ex officio member of the University's Board of Regents. On July 12, 1894 a letter in which he violently attacked Ely appeared in *The Nation*. Ely was accused of believing in strikes and boycotts, of encouraging and justifying the one and practicing the other. He was further charged with giving moral justification for attacks on life and property, and it was implied that he held socialist and anarchist views. These were serious charges in a country where several years of increasing tension between labor and capital had been climaxed by the terrible Pullman strike of 1894.

Ely seethed under the attack. In a private letter to Amos P. Wilder, editor of the *Wisconsin State Journal*, he asserted that Wells's letter was full of lies, adding, "I believe I have given the strongest refutation of socialism which you can find—all the stronger because I do not call names and do not make misrepresentations." [31] The president of the Board of Regents appointed an investigating committee. Public hearings were held in August 1894. Shortly before the committee met, Ely gave from the

---

Thomas Chrowder Chamberlin, whose letters to Ely are preserved in the Ely Papers, Boxes 7–9. Ely was not always the easiest man to deal with, as his correspondence shows. After the long negotiations had been virtually completed, the news came to Ely that Chamberlin was leaving Wisconsin to head the department of geology at the new University of Chicago. In a letter Ely berated Chamberlin, who replied on June 27, 1892: "Your methods of treating your friends and those of whom you seek aid are the worst I have ever encountered in similar correspondence. In your last letter, as one of many instances, you lash and prod me and then ask me to look you up a house. You distort what I may have said about a possible successor and combine it with your imagination so as to put me in a false attitude and then urge me to bestir myself because of your forlorn condition. This style of treatment, which has run through your correspondence, has only taken away time and strength that I might have given to improving the situation perhaps, and has removed the larger part of the regret that I would otherwise have felt at not being able to inaugurate the important movement which you are to lead and to aid you to the utmost of my power." (Ely Papers, Box 9) The house was important to Ely; he had married Miss Anna Morris Anderson in 1884, and needed space for his growing family.

31. The basic materials concerning this event are in the Ely Papers. A microfilm prepared by the State Historical Society of Wisconsin, "Selections from the Richard T. Ely Papers, John M. Olin Papers, and Theodore Herfurth Papers, 1894–1915," includes Ely's letter to Wilder, dated July 22, 1894. Another microfilm reproduces the "Proceedings before Committee appointed by the Board of Regents to investigate and report concerning charges against Dr. Richard T. Ely." Copies of both microfilms are in the Butler Library of Columbia University.

Chautauqua platform a "personal statement" denying the charges, and calling attention to his published works—especially his unsparing attacks on anarchy. At the hearing, Ely and Wells were both accompanied by attorneys. The first charge concerning strikes and boycotts was soon shown to have been false. At a later session Wells was absent, but sent a letter which once more accused Ely of socialistic views. The defense placed on record many testimonies concerning Ely's opinions, especially on socialism. He was called to the stand, along with witnesses on his behalf.[32] In the end Ely was cleared; *The Nation* withdrew its charges; the Regents censured Wells and approved the investigating committee's report, which included a ringing defense of academic freedom.[33] Ely emerged from the ordeal more popular than ever.

In the later 1890's, Ely largely withdrew from promoting the social gospel to devote himself to professional affairs. He was more and more disturbed by disunity among Protestants, whose many divisions had led to confusion and ineffectiveness in social reform. He turned his attention more and more to the state, as the most inclusive of divine institutions, in which men of all sects participated. The essay on "The State" in *The Social Law of Service* concluded with a glowing assertion of the unity of Christians of all denominations within the state, where all might work together for the establishment of righteousness.[34] Although Ely became almost wholly preoccupied with municipal reform, land economics, co-operation, and related social questions, he had not changed his point of view or his general frame of reference, which remained the same up to his death in 1943. In his late years he still vouched for the Christian social views he had taken as a young man. After he shifted his public work to other channels, his books long remained influential upon those who espoused the social gospel.

On March 19, 1891, the young Walter Rauschenbusch, on leave from his pastorate in New York, wrote Ely from on board the steamship *Servia*, thanking him for his "balanced" and "daring" book, *An Introduc-*

32. Ely had written a great deal on socialism, a movement with which he disagreed, though he took it seriously. He and his defenders in 1894 could and did cite the recently published *Socialism: An Examination of its Nature, Its Strength and Its Weakness, with Suggestions for Social Reform* (N.Y., 1894). Part III dealt with the weaknesses of socialism, and chap. v of that part had the title "Socialism a Menace to Liberty." See below, 217–18.

33. The whole episode is summarized in Merle Curti and Vernon Carstensen, *The University of Wisconsin: A History, 1848–1925* (2 vols., Madison, 1949), I, 508–27.

34. *The Social Law of Service* (N.Y., 1896), 175. The essay in full appears below, 221–34.

tion to Political Economy, and commenting on the appalling conservatism of the churches.[35] He was one of a growing number who were committing themselves to social Christianity and who were greatly influenced by this famous academic advocate of the social gospel.

35. Ely Papers, Box 6.

SOCIAL ASPECTS OF CHRISTIANITY [1]

Editor's introduction. Ely's best-known exposition of the social gospel was originally given as a lay sermon in the Presbyterian Church of Fredonia, New York, his home town. It was later expanded into a series of articles for *The Congregationalist,* and then published as the first (and longest) essay in a book to which it gave the title. Originally published in 1889, the book was later reprinted in a "new and enlarged" edition. As "the first influential effort on the part of a prominent American to state 'the social side of the Church's mission,' " [2] Ely's work was widely noticed and discussed. The essay now seems rambling and uneven, and many of the ideas it presents have long been familiar; but at the time, its coupling of familiar Bible passages with social questions was quite new to many of his readers, and its impact upon them was great.

I. STATEMENT OF FUNDAMENTAL PRINCIPLES

But when the Pharisees had heard that he had put the Sadducees to silence, they were gathered together.
Then one of them, which was a lawyer, asked him a question, tempting him and saying,
Master, which is the great commandment in the law?
Jesus said unto him, Thou shalt love the Lord thy God with all thy heart, and with all thy soul, and with all thy mind.
This is the first and great commandment.
And the second is like unto it, Thou shalt love thy neighbor as thyself.
On these two commandments hang all the law and the prophets.

(Mt. xxii, 34–40)

This is a most remarkable, and at the same time a most daring, summary of the whole duty of man. A human teacher would never have ventured

---

1. *Social Aspects of Christianity, and Other Essays* (new and enlarged ed., N.Y., c1889), 1–48.
2. Hopkins, *The Rise of the Social Gospel,* 106.

to reduce all God's commandments to two simple statements; nor would such a teacher have presumed to exalt man's obligation to love and serve his fellows to an equal plane with his obligations to love his Creator. All other religious systems will be searched in vain for such a classification of human duties. The first and great commandment, "Thou shalt love the Lord thy God with all thy heart, and with all thy soul, and with all thy mind," does not strike us as strange. It is natural that the Supreme Being of the universe should require of us, his creatures, an unconditional and unlimited homage; but — listen! — The second commandment is like unto it — is like unto it — of the same nature: Thou shalt love thy neighbor as thyself — and — on these two commandments — on these two equally — hang all the law and the prophets.

But John, the beloved apostle, the apostle of love — and, as God is love, we may suppose that he understood better than others the nature of Christ — is very bold in his exposition of our duty to love our fellows, making that a test of one's love to God. "If a man say, I love God, and hateth his brother, he is a liar: for he that loveth not his brother whom he hath seen, how can he love God whom he hath not seen?" And in another verse in the same chapter [sic] of his Epistle, John says, "We know that we have passed from death unto life, because — because — we love the brethren." St. Paul, indeed, goes so far as to say, "For all the law is fulfilled, even in this: Thou shalt love thy neighbor as thyself" (Gal. v.14). St. Paul evidently felt that love to neighbor carried with it love to God.

Christ himself has told us the method by which he will at the Last Judgment separate the sheep from the goats. Listen to his words, which must be quoted in full, and every word should receive careful attention:

> When the Son of man shall come in his glory, and all the holy angels with him, then shall he sit upon the throne of his glory:
> And before him shall be gathered all nations: and he shall separate them one from another, as a shepherd divideth his sheep from his goats:
> And he shall set the sheep on his right hand, but the goats on his left.
> Then shall the King say unto them on his right hand, Come, ye blessed of my Father, inherit the kingdom prepared for you from the foundation of the world:
> For I was an hungered, and ye gave me meat: I was thirsty, and ye gave me drink: I was a stranger, and ye took me in;
> Naked, and ye clothed me: I was sick, and ye visited me; I was in prison, and ye came unto me.

Then shall the righteous answer him, saying, Lord, when saw we thee an hungered, and fed thee? or, thirsty, and gave thee drink?

When saw we thee a stranger, and took thee in? naked, and clothed thee?

Or, when saw we thee sick, or in prison, and came unto thee?

And the King shall answer and say unto them, Verily I say unto you, Inasmuch as ye have done it unto one of the least of these my brethren, ye have done it unto me.

Then shall he say also unto them on his left hand, Depart from me, ye cursed, into everlasting fire, prepared for the devil and his angels;

For I was an hungered, and ye gave me no meat: I was thirsty, and ye gave me no drink:

I was a stranger, and ye took me not in; naked, and ye clothed me not; sick, and in prison, and ye visited me not.

Then shall they also answer him, saying, Lord, when saw we thee an hungered, or athirst, or a stranger, or naked, or sick, or in prison, and did not minister unto thee?

Then shall he answer to them, saying, Verily I say unto you, inasmuch as you did it not unto one of the least of these, ye did it not to me.

And those shall go away into everlasting punishment: but the righteous into life eternal. (Mt. xxv, 31–46)

The minds of readers have been so generally absorbed by the awful punishment meted out to the wicked, that terror has not allowed them to notice what is the most marked feature in the narrative; namely, the exquisite beauty of the humanitarianism which it breathes. It is the gospel of humanity, because it is the gospel of the Son of man.

The marks of distinction are perceived. They are not regular attendance at church — not sound notions in regard to the form of baptism or methods of ordination, or apostolic succession, or the nature of the Lord's Supper, or church organization — not any notions whatever as regards the future life — not any subjective feelings in regard to God. These are all, doubtless, important; but these are not the distinctive things by which Christ separates the good from the bad. The performance or non-performance of social duties in the gospel narrative separates the doomed from the blessed: "I was in prison, and ye visited me," etc.

I say this is something new in religious systems. All false systems of religion exalt the love of God above the love due our fellow men, and tell us that we may serve God by injuring our fellows. How many millions of human beings have thought that they did God service by human sacrifice! Not only is this true, but it is furthermore true that, in proportion as believers in the true religion depart from the mind which was in Jesus Christ, they neglect the second commandment. Thus, when Christ dwelt on earth, he found men excusing themselves from duty to their fellows on the plea of higher obligation to Deity. The reader will recall at once one instance. Moses commanded men to honor their fathers and mothers, and included, as a matter of course, the maintenance of father or mother in case of need; but the Hebrew theologians said a man could exempt himself from his duty to support his parents by consecrating his goods to the Lord. "But, ye say" — thus Christ addressed the scribes and Pharisees — "if a man shall say to his father or mother, It is corban, that is to say, a gift (devoted to God), by whatsoever thou mightest be profited by me (by which I might support thee), he shall be free. And ye suffer him no more to do aught for his father or mother." But Christ added, "Ye have made the commandment of God of none effect by your tradition," and he upbraided them by addressing them as "Ye hypocrites."

Nothing is more difficult, nothing more requires divine grace, than the constant manifestation of love to our fellows in all our daily acts, in our buying, selling, getting gain. People still want to substitute all sorts of beliefs and observances in the place of this, for it implies a totally different purpose from that which animates this world. It is when men attempt to regulate their lives seven days in the week by the Golden Rule that they begin to perceive that they cannot serve God and mammon; for the ruling motive of the one service — egotism, selfishness — is the opposite of the ruling motive of the other — altruism, devotion to others, consecration of heart, soul, and intellect to the service of others. Men are still quite willing to make long prayers on Sunday, if on week days they may devour widows' houses; or, as Reverend Mark Guy Pearse said two summers since at Chautauqua, they are ready to offer their prayers and their praise on Sunday, if on Monday they may go into the market place and skin their fellows and sell their hides.[3]

The second commandment, which is like the first, means that in every act and thought and purpose, in our laws and in their administration, in all public as well as private affairs, we — if indeed we profess to be Christians — should seek to confer true benefits upon our fellow men. It means that the man who professes to love God and who attempts to deceive others in regard to the real value of railway stock, or, for that matter, any other property, that he may coax their money into his pockets, is a hypo-

3. [ED.] Mark Guy Pearse (1842–1930) was a British Methodist minister with whom Ely had been favorably impressed when they were both lecturers at Chautauqua.

crite and a liar. It means that the man who oppresses the hireling in his wages is no Christian but a pagan, whatever may be his declarations to the contrary notwithstanding. What does God say of such an one? He says: "I will be a swift witness against those that oppress the hireling in his wages." What does his second commandment mean for those rich men who keep back the hire of their laborers? It means that they "must" weep and howl "for the miseries that shall come upon them." And what does this message mean for monopolists who use their superior advantages of wealth or intellect, or bodily strength or other resources, to crowd out and grind down their fellows according to the methods of modern commercial competition? The prophet Isaiah shall tell us: "Woe unto them that join house to house, that lay field to field, till there be no place, that they may be placed alone in the midst of the earth."

It is needless to enlarge upon this. It must be seen that the arrangements of this world are not in accord with the commandment given to love our neighbor as ourselves. These words may be found in writings previous to Christ, but never before his time had there been a serious attempt to carry this teaching into all the relations of life with all men. Thus it was a true word when Christ said to his disciples: "A *new* commandment I give unto you, That ye love one another; as I have loved you, that ye also love one another."

It is indeed a strange conception that some people have of the gospel of Christ. That gospel which in its highest unity is Love is divided into two parts: the first is theology, the second is sociology — the science of society.

"Theology treats of God and his relations to his creatures, and of the existence, character, and attributes of God, his laws and government, the doctrines we are to believe and the duties we are to practice." Such is the definition of theology found in Webster's dictionary. The first words are sufficient. Theology "is the science of God and his relations to his creatures." But the whole science is simply an elaboration of the first of the two great commandments on which hang all the law and the prophets. It is a proper study for man; especially is it a fitting study for those who are called to serve as ministers in God's church. We all know with what assiduity the study of theology has been pursued. Men of great intellect have by the thousand devoted their entire lives to it, and every clergyman is expected to prepare himself for his sacred office by a training in a theological seminary for several years. This is well so far as it goes. This ought not to be left undone, but this is not enough. What has the church done with the second commandment, which, in its elaboration, becomes social science or sociology?

II. Statement of Fundamental Principles Concluded

The question was asked at the close of the last paragraph: What has the church done in the way of careful research in social science? It is necessary to reply that she has done comparatively little, and next to nothing since the Protestant Reformation. It is necessary to offer a word of explanation. In the earlier ages of the church, social science was cultivated to a greater or less extent by theologians, and there is much in their writings of which note must be taken in any history of that part of social science called political economy. This is particularly the case, it needs scarcely to be said, with the writings of St. Thomas Aquinas in the thirteenth century. Now in later centuries it is doubtless true that the greatest and best thoughts in social science may be traced very generally to Christian inspiration, but they have been an indirect rather than a direct outgrowth of the life of the church. Yet as this social science, which deals with the relation of man to his fellows in what we call society, has for its special province human happiness and well-being, and the underlying conditions of a prosperous, righteous, and progressive state of society, it might naturally be supposed that such a science, above all others, would absorb the attention of men seeking to obey Christ's new commandment to love one another, and to promote the true welfare of their neighbors in all those infinite ways which love suggests.

The church has in recent years, for the most part, contented herself with repeating platitudes and vague generalities which have disturbed no guilty soul, and thus she has allowed the leadership in social science to slip away from her. It can, then, scarcely excite surprise that communism has become infidel, and socialism materialistic. Has she not, indeed, without any careful examination of their claims, hastened to condemn them to please the rich?

The wrong of this is not connected with the fact that socialism and communism are not practicable theories for modern industrial society. It was not a deep penetration into the principles of social science which led the church to take this stand, but subserviency to the powers of this world. I suppose there is nothing which causes the worldly-minded among professing Christians such uneasiness as the narrative of the rich young man who turned away in sorrow when told to sell all that he had and to give to the poor, and those verses in the Acts of the Apostles which tell the simple story of the communism, founded in love, which prevailed among the early Christians.

But do not our fashionable pastors hasten to tell us first that Christ did not really mean the young man to give up his property, but only wanted to try him, which from the context and the nature of the case is a manifest absurdity; second, that this communism of the Christians at Jerusalem was a lamentable failure, which explains their subsequent poverty? I am sure I have frequently seen such statements, and I know with what eagerness these comforting words are received into willing ears; but I know not of the slightest historical foundation for this alleged connection between the communism of the Christians and their poverty, while there is, indeed, reason to attribute it to other causes. Still less can it be claimed that there is any such necessary connection when in the United States we have a single communistic settlement whose property is valued at ten millions of dollars, and several which are in a really prosperous condition.

The ministers of the church repeat often enough the words of the Golden Rule; but the question arises, How am I to show my love for my fellow men? How am I to go to work to elevate them, to make them both happier and better? How am I, as a follower of Christ, to conduct myself in the industrial world? What are my duties as employer, as landlord or tenant, as creditor or debtor? What position should I take on the land question, on the subject of labor organization, and the other aspects of the great labor problems? What force have the regulations of the Old Testament concerning business for me now? What about such a matter as interest on money? To take usury — which, as every one knows, in the Bible means simply interest, not excessive interest as now, but any interest at all — seems to be regarded as a great sin. It was forbidden the Israelites in their dealings with one another; and in case of poverty, it was forbidden to take interest even of strangers. In Leviticus xxv.35-37, we read as follows:

> And if thy brother be waxen poor, and fallen in decay with thee; then thou shalt relieve him: yea, though he be a stranger, or a sojourner; that he may live with thee.
> Take thou no usury of him, or increase: but fear thy God; that thy brother may live with thee.
> Thou shalt not give him thy money upon usury, nor lend him thy victuals for increase.

And the Psalmist answers his own question, "Lord, who shall abide in thy tabernacle, who shall dwell in thy holy hill?" with the words, "He that putteth not out his money to usury."

It was, moreover, long forbidden members of the Christian church to take any interest on money lent; and, while the church is silent now, the laws of many of our States at least limit the rate of interest. Now I do not propose to discuss exhaustively this question of interest, which would require too much space. I simply mention it as one of those questions which a Christian man ought to consider, and which ought not to be ignored by the church. It is, moreover, a question which it seems to me can be easily resolved by a study of the evolution of industrial society. If my opinion is wanted, now that I have raised the question, I can only say, without going into my reasons, that I believe moderate interest is, as a rule, not sinful increase in our days, but that I do think it conduct unbecoming a Christian — to put it very mildly — for a rich man to charge interest on money lent a poor man to relieve him of distress, or to put him on his feet again when he is once down. I do not believe it is right to exact anything more than the return of the principal, nor do I believe that the poor man ought to feel obliged to give more. Rather let him relieve some one else in time of increasing prosperity.

This is, as I take it, the spirit of the old usury laws, for the capitalistic mode of production did not exist when they were promulgated, and loans were made chiefly to relieve personal distress. Now can any one tell why the spirit of the economic and industrial laws of Moses should not be binding on us? Christ said he came to fulfill the law, and those for whom love has abolished the old ceremonial law must feel compelled to do more — not less — for their fellows than the old Mosaic legislation required.

Moses founded a commonwealth which for generations continued free, happy, prosperous, knowing neither pauperism nor excessive wealth; and Moses, viewed merely as a statesman, probably never stood so high in the estimation of scholars as he does today. Yet the church passes over the Mosaic economic legislation as of no consequence, or as of no binding force. The letter of the law would in this case be death, but I believe the spirit would mean life. There is much in the Mosaic legislation which mere "money-makers," whose Christianity is confined to professions, would not like to hear, but there is reason to think that careful study might have adapted some of its provisions to modern life with benefit to all who wish to live righteously.

There is more or less concern on the part of the clergy with the problems of the day; and as they are so largely ethical, they cannot avoid reference to them in sermons and lectures. Their flocks look to them for leadership, but they too often appear like blind leaders of the blind; for they manifestly have never received instruction in sociology, and there has been universal failure to give it that prolonged, concentrated attention which theology has received for hundreds of years. The blame rests by no means exclusively on the clergy and least of all on the present generation of clergymen. The mistake is one of historical growth, and we and our fathers, laity as well as clergy, are responsible.

These questions, upon which I barely touch, are difficult, and require profound thought from truly great minds. Is this discouraging? It undoubtedly proves that the course of action for Christians in modern practical life is a difficult one to discern. It undoubtedly proves that it is not easy to follow the command, Love thy neighbor as thyself. I do not suppose that the Almighty intended it should be easy. I do suppose that — to take one example — he intended that the man who carelessly scatters his alms here and there without reflection should be as likely to do harm as good, and that such is the case the history of charities amply demonstrates.

We cannot love our fellows effectively unless we give them our mind. We must devote ourselves long and carefully to the study of the science of human happiness, social science. This second branch of the gospel of Christ, so long neglected, ought to be pursued with equal earnestness, with equal diligence, by Christians, with theology.

Suppose when we went to church we heard Sunday after Sunday nothing about the nature of God, and our relations to him, save a ceaseless iteration of the first commandment, "Thou shalt love the Lord thy God with all thy heart and with all thy soul and with all thy mind." That contains all of theology; yet we would regard it as absurd for the minister not to develop the thought of that grand, all-inclusive precept. Equally absurd is it for the church not to develop in all its ramifications the second commandment.

What is wanted is not dilettantism with respect to those duties which we owe our fellows, but hard study, pursued with devotion for years. I should say that half of the time of a theological student should be devoted to social science, and theological seminaries should be the chief intellectual centers for sociology.

It is true that we get at the second commandment through the first; and we must first love God, in order to serve as we should our fellow men.

There seems to be little danger, however, that the theoretical truth respecting our duties to God will be overlooked. The real danger is that we will come to think that we can serve God without devoting our lives to our fellow men, without becoming, in the fullest, completest sense of the word, philanthropists.

Did it ever occur to you that a man who claimed to be a Christian, and was not at the same time a philanthropist, was a hypocrite and a liar? Yet, if Christ speaks true, this is undoubted. Select one of the gospels, and read therein the words of Christ, and you will see how Christ comes back again and again to our social duties. The Sermon on the Mount illustrates this, as do also the last three verses of the ninth chapter of St. Matthew's gospel. Christ was "moved with compassion," and he turned the thoughts of the disciples away from themselves to the plenteous harvest, and bid them pray the Lord of the harvest to "send forth laborers into the harvest." But still more striking are verses fifteen to seventeen in the twenty-first chapter of the gospel according to St. John. Christ asks Peter three times if he loves him. "Simon, son of Jonas, lovest thou me more than these?" Peter asserts his love each time; and how is he bidden to show his love? Is it by fasts? or self-torture for sin? or withdrawal from the world? or prayer and meditation? By no means; but by service to his fellow creatures. "Feed my lambs" — "Feed my lambs" — "Feed my sheep." These are the three answers of Jesus.

III. THE SIMPLE GOSPEL OF CHRIST

Now what have been the results of this neglect by the church of the nature of our duties to our fellow men? They have been of the most far-reaching character, and explain the fact that in eighteen hundred years the church has not made greater progress.

The cause of this neglect is sin. Largely, if not chiefly, the sin of concession to the powers of this world, so that they might hear nothing to terrify or alarm them, or even to make them uncomfortable; and the result has been sin, sin, sin, until in the markets of the world you cannot distinguish a Christian from one who professes to live for this world only. Howells says — and I believe truly — that it is a sorrowful comment upon our Christianity that Tolstoy's frank acceptance of the message of

Christ should make him seem to the world as eccentric or mad.[4] What
are you going to do about it?

I notice that, according to Mr. Howells, a radical clergyman replies:
Yes, those are doubtless the teachings of Christ; but the political economy
of Christ was ignorant and mistaken. He says that Christ was a good soul,
but an inferior intellect. You see we have here the old question, What
will you do with Christ? One answer is given, and it reduces him to the
rank of idle dreamers of impossible utopias; a good man, but one of weak
mental capacities. Whether or not Mr. Howells has correctly interpreted
this clergyman, it is, at any rate, but an exact description of a common
form of unbelief, though it rarely finds so frank and outspoken an expression. A clergyman of another denomination recently used these words in
a published article: "If the Bible entirely sustains 'Progress and Poverty,'
then with Mr. Henry George the Bible must stand or fall. For my own
part, if I could be convinced that the Bible did somewhere or other really
affirm the peculiar doctrines of that very popular agitator, that part of the
Bible I should most unhesitatingly reject." And in the same article, after
stating that his first great master in political economy was John Stuart
Mill, for whom he has never lost his reverence, he proceeds to state that
Mill seems to him "to be superseded neither by Moses nor by Karl
Marx." [5] I do not quote this because I believe that Henry George is en-
dorsed by the Bible, any more than I believe that Tolstoy is free from
grave defects, but to show the position into which a considerable portion
of the church has drifted.

Let us look at this matter from a somewhat different standpoint. The
prayer for us all is: "Thy kingdom come, thy will be done on earth." Yet
the church has so failed to instruct us in regard to the will of God in
earthly matters, that professed Christians seem at times to lose all distinction between right and wrong in affairs of this life, and occasionally
one hears it said that Christian ethics have nothing to do with practical

4. [ED.] W. D. Howells (1837–1920) was famous as a novelist of social change in
America, and as editor of the *Atlantic*. He considered Tolstoy (1828–1910) the supreme influence of his life, and in his reviews he helped to introduce the Russian
thinker to America.

5. [ED.] On Henry George, see below, 294. John Stuart Mill (1806–73) was an influential British philosopher and economist, who though ostensibly a defender of the
classical economic school of Ricardo and Malthus, in fact made concessions antici-
patory of the historical school. His eclectic approach permitted him to advocate
the reform of existing institutions, even to the extent of government interference
with the rights of private property.

business. Let us take this matter of gambling in stocks or provisions. I mean merely speculative dealings — not bona fide purchases. Can a Christian do such a thing? If social science had been studied by Christian ministers with as much diligence as the one theological doctrine of baptism, there could be no doubt — it would be needless to ask the question.

What is the essence of theft? I mean from a moral, not a legal point of view. Is it not trying to get something for nothing? Is it not trying to get hold of your neighbor's property by some kind of hocus-pocus, without making him a fair return? Most assuredly; and that is precisely what those do who buy stocks on margin, deal in futures, and the like. I was glad to see, in a village paper published in New York State, so clear a moral perception of the nature of the transactions of a misguided and fallen young man who lost money in wheat speculations, stole money from the bank of which he was president, and fled to Canada. Suppose his wheat speculations had been successful, would that have altered his moral character? Most certainly not. He was all the time engaged in attempts to get hold of the property of others without a return. There is only this difference. In the one case he would have been, morally speaking, a thief; now he is, legally speaking, a thief. This paper to which I have referred then very properly says: "We may look for the cause of this fall to the unholy greed for money, the reckless spirit of gambling and speculation, so common in these last years."

I was also glad to see — and it is a cheerful sign of the times — a powerful article on this very topic in a Presbyterian paper, published in Omaha, I believe, but the name of the journal escapes me.

I do not mean to condemn unreservedly the stock exchange. A considerable part of its business is perfectly legitimate. Nevertheless, it is a great gain when the speculative element in its transactions can be dismissed. Professor Adolf Wagner, of Berlin, counts it as one of the good features which have resulted from the purchase of Prussian private railways by the state, that their stocks can no longer be used as formerly, *merely* for speculative, that is, gambling purposes.[6] I regard this as a strong argument for the nationalization of railways. The idea of the stock exchange is sound, but it is inevitably so fruitful of mischief and all manner of iniquity that we can regard it only as a necessary evil and must rejoice when the field of its operations is curtailed.

Yes, yes; strange conceptions have people of the gospel of Christ! and a

6. [ED.] Adolf Wagner (1835–1917) was a leader in the historical school of German economics, and an exponent of "professorial" socialism.

phrase has been invented, "the simple gospel of Christ," which means an emasculated gospel of Christ, a gospel of Christ with one-half omitted, a gospel which, while teaching us to pray, Thy will be done on earth, yet would keep Christians from concerning themselves with things of this world, so that the will of God may be done — things like temperance, righteous dealing, fair elections, the uprooting of crime and poverty, the elevation of the masses.

Two years ago last winter, in Baltimore, the streetcar employees were working over seventeen hours a day, and rebelled against this monstrous cruelty. A mass meeting was called to favor the passage of a bill for a twelve-hour day — a bill finally passed — and several clergymen attended the meeting and spoke in favor of the measure. One clergyman, Mr. S., took the ground that it was a question of the preservation of that Christian institution, the family; for what kind of a family life can you have where the father is away seventeen hours a day, seven days in the week, and scarcely knows his children by sight? Well, shortly after the event, a Presbyterian minister, Mr. G., was accosted by one of his parishioners with the remark, "I wish your friend, Mr. S., would confine himself to preaching the simple gospel of Christ." "The simple gospel of Christ," replied Mr. G., "the simple gospel of Christ! What is this I hear, my friend? So you own some street-railway stock, do you?" The parishioner looked very uncomfortable, and finally confessed that though he didn't, his wife did.

Two years ago the present autumn we heard of a somewhat similar instance, in what is called Mr. Moody's church in Chicago. Reverend Mr. Goss preached a sermon on the trials and temptations of working girls, and remedies for them, to which some members of his flock objected — not because they took exception to any specific utterance, but because they wanted simple gospel sermons.[7] Simple gospel sermons, indeed! More likely, if we may judge from other instances, because they wanted to serve mammon six days a week, and to atone for it by formal lip service rendered to God on the seventh! If the preacher had hammered away at the sins of the ancient Egyptians, four thousand years ago, or the immoralities of Paris, four thousand miles away, we would hardly have heard objections because the sermon was not a simple gospel sermon.

Once more: some earnest men have formed the American Economic

7. [ED.] Charles F. Goss (b. 1852), a Presbyterian, was pastor of the Moody church in Chicago, 1885–90. That church had grown out of Sunday school work begun by Dwight L. Moody (1837–99) in 1858, before he became internationally famous as a lay evangelist. It was later known as the Moody Memorial Church.

Association, to investigate problems of social science, in order thereby to contribute to human progress. Its aim is to advocate no opinions, but simply to strive to find out the underlying principles of industrial society, and to diffuse information among the working classes and all classes. Briefly stated, its purpose is to study seriously the second of the two great commandments on which hang all the law and the prophets, in all its ramifications, and thus to bring science to the aid of Christianity.

Now you would imagine this something to appeal to every Christian, would you not? Yet it does not. As secretary, it has been my duty to solicit members, and raise the few hundred dollars needed every year for printing its publications and other purposes, and I can assure the reader it seems impossible to induce one in ten Christians, among those who can well afford it, to contribute three dollars a year or twenty-five dollars for a life membership.

It is difficult for them to grasp the idea that this society is a real, legitimate Christian institution. Prizes encourage research. The experience of our best universities with fellowships shows the advantages of prizes, suitable in amount and awarded under satisfactory conditions. Yet any one who will try — as several have done — to raise a few hundred dollars for prizes for the best monographs on subjects like child labor, women wage-earners, the housing of the poor in cities, taxation in American cities, will be surprised at the general apathy and indifference of people asked to contribute, and to find how few they are, comparatively, who seem to care to do anything more for their suffering fellow creatures than to administer some kind of soothing syrup.

Now it must not be supposed that I am pessimistic. Far from it. I see many evidences of better things. To begin with this very association of which I have spoken: we do get sufficient support to live, and no professional class is so largely represented in our membership as clergymen.

The American Economic Association is mentioned, not because it is more important than other societies, but because its history has shown me the feeling of too many Christians with respect to simple philanthropy, unconnected with any sectarian glory, and because it serves as illustration. Illustrations abound on every street corner in every city. As I was waiting one Sunday in a hotel parlor in Toronto, Canada, I heard two ladies discussing the fact that streetcars in that city did not run on Sunday. The decision finally reached was that the only good feature about the arrangement was that it gave the horses a chance to rest! And are not societies for prevention of cruelty to animals stronger than those for prevention of cruelty to children?

Most remarkable is the illustration given of the shortcoming of the church by the hymns of the church. It is said you may know a nation by its songs. We may know the life of the church by its hymns. If the church in her history has been full of love for man, it must be seen in her hymns. Hearts welling up, filled to overflowing with love to our fellows, must seek expression in song. Let the reader take any hymnbook he pleases and read hymn after hymn, and seek for the hymns expressive of burning, all-consuming altruism. He will not find them, though he will find any number which turn the heart in on itself and tend to nourish a selfish, individualistic piety. I and me — I and me — these are the frequently recurring pronouns.

Theological seminaries — would that they might be called gospel seminaries — are beginning to turn at least some serious attention to social science, which, if it be little, is nevertheless a beginning. The Andover, Yale, and Hartford seminaries have courses of lectures on social science, and I see that Bishop Potter of the Episcopal church includes provision for instruction in social science in his plan for a great cathedral in New York.[8]

I would gladly dwell on some conclusions which flow naturally from what has been said, but the shortness of space forbids it, and I can only call attention to a few things which Christianity requires.

First, let us look at the internal arrangements of the church. It goes without saying that these should be thoroughly Christian; but what does that mean? To begin with, certainly an absence of all that fosters the caste spirit — for that separates man from his brother; and a presence of everything which tends to draw man to man, and thus to promote a realizing sense of the brotherhood of man.

We are taught that the strong should bear the burdens of the weak, from which we may conclude that the church should be tender and considerate in all her dealings with the unfortunate, with all those that labor and are heavily laden. Apply this to dress. The attire of Christians should be plain and simple, such as will not divert attention from the word of God.

An entire absence of everything in dress which cultivates worldliness and awakens a desire for perishable riches must be enjoined. Absence of such dress as will awaken envious desires in weak natures is equally a mat-

8. [ED.] Henry C. Potter (1835–1908) was Protestant Episcopal bishop of New York, and a co-worker with Ely in the Christian Social Union. The reference is to what became the Cathedral of St. John the Divine.

ter of course. And this means not merely plain dressing; for the simple dressing so often admired in fashionable churches is frequently more expensive, far more expensive, than the gaudiest dress in poorer churches. Plain and inexpensive dress is what is required. Rich Christians are especially called upon to take the lead in all this. Let the strong bear the burdens of the weak.

Apply Christian principles to the matter of pews. We all know what James says about those who give the back seats to the poor, and the choice seats to those of goodly apparel and gold rings. Yet by our system of rented pews — for we have gone so far as to introduce notions of private property in the house of God — we do not simply occasionally violate the command given by James, but we bring it about that the rich habitually have the best seats.

Now, as I take it, the Christian principle is this: Seat first the guests of the church. The Christian duty of hospitality enjoins upon us to reserve the best for the stranger. Then the poorer people should follow, and the rich and powerful, the strong, should take what is left.

The ordinary arguments in opposition to free churches are "of the earth, earthy." They are said not to be "practical." "It won't work," we are told. What has a Christian to do except to believe that the right is practical, and the only practical thing in the universe? Christ's life itself was not, as the world goes, very practical. One might have told him, "This will not work. You are not practical." And indeed he was rejected and put to death, and his life *appeared* to be a worse failure than a church sold at public auction by the sheriff.

Friendly intercourse between church members is likewise an obvious duty; but I have never yet heard any attendant on a fashionable church exclaim, "How these Christians love one another!"

The injunction of Christ in regard to feasts, I think, ought to be taken literally. A Christian will seek out the neglected, the lonesome, the needy brothers and sisters, and invite those who can never reciprocate with like social courtesies.

IV. The Christian in the World, but not of the World

Besides the exhibition within the church of the spirit of Christian brotherhood, the life of Christians outside of the church, in their dealings with the world, must also conform to Christian principles. Christ calls upon us to choose between him and the world, and he wants no half-hearted followers. Remember the message unto the Laodiceans: "I know thy works, that thou art neither cold nor hot: I would thou wert cold or hot. So then because thou art lukewarm, and neither cold nor hot, I will spew thee out of my mouth. Because thou sayest, I am rich, and increased with goods, and have need of nothing; and knowest not that thou art wretched, and miserable, and poor, and blind, and naked."

Every opportunity to bring to pass righteousness in this world is one that a Christian cannot neglect. There are the working classes needing intellectual and moral enlightenment — and rich people, too, equally needing enlightenment — there are children, little children in factories, ruining body, mind, and soul by excessive toil and dangerous companionship at a tender age, who ought to be rescued; there are women engaged in improper toil away from home; there is intemperance, the curse of liquor, to be fought; there are tenement-house districts to be redeemed — work, work on every hand for Christian men and women, but where are the workers?

Some say we cannot maintain ourselves in the business world if we attempt to carry into our business Christian principles. Very well, then, change the world until Christians can live in it; and in the meanwhile let me remind the reader, with Reverend Mark Guy Pearse, that there was a time when men and women could not be Christians and keep their heads on their shoulders, and that then they died cheerfully as Christians.

It is one of the fundamental principles of Christianity that temporal goods are committed to us in trust, and that we shall be held accountable for our trusteeship. But temporal goods mean more than money. They include time and opportunities, and the idle man is truly a robber — a robber of God's bounty. If we deliberately and persistently fail even to try honestly to administer our property — be it much or little — also our time, talents, and opportunities, according to the principles of altruism — by which I mean simply all-embracing Christian love — we cannot fairly claim to be Christians, and, if the Bible speaks true, pains await us for our disobedience. It is idle to talk about a belief which does not manifest itself in works. A good tree must bring forth good fruit. It is the law of nature. So when a heart is welling over with love to all of God's children, loving action is bound to follow. It comes of itself, just as the trees put forth their leaves in springtime.

How, then, do professing Christians employ their substance? When one visits the leading churches of New York and Boston, when one forms acquaintanceship with their members, with the very best will, it is simply impossible to believe that they are even trying to place the needs of others on a par with their own needs. Self comes first, and there is little apparent effort to obey, in their expenditures of money, the precept that love for others should hold equal place with love for self. The more seriously one reflects upon this, the longer one turns it over in one's mind, the more shocking appears the divergence between profession and practice. The average Christian is "of the world," and is governed by its motives in his expenditures. To get on in life, to enjoy the pleasures of wealth, to be spoken well of by those high in the ranks of fashion — all this is the dominating motive. Consider a case like this: a man spends $1500 on an evening's entertainment to gratify vanity. What could have been done with $1500? Here is one thing: it could have been used to endow a permanent scholarship in the Hampton Normal and Agricultural Institute in Virginia. Let the reader reflect upon that. It means that for all time our colored pupil shall receive education at this most excellent school, where with the training of the head goes the training of the hand — one of the most essential things in the development of the colored race. These Hampton pupils go forth to serve as teachers and preachers, and form the best leaders of their people. The colored youth educated are benefited, and those whom they influence are benefited. This is not only Christian, it is patriotic, for our American institutions depend upon the elevation of the ignorant masses, and how urgent are the appeals for means with which to extend this work! Read these words from the circular of that admirable man, General S. C. Armstrong:

> In the country districts, which contain the majority and the best material of the colored population, the teacher is usually the only fit and available leader. He, and he only, can start Sunday schools and temperance societies, can initiate sound Christian work, and overcome the hostile influence of the "old-time religion" and its votaries. In the earlier stages of a people's progress, the teacher's sphere is in the field, shop, church, and home, as much as in the schoolhouse. In the past eighteen years our army of graduates has done this many-sided work among a benighted people thirsting for knowledge. They have secured the good will of all true men, and peace and progress have followed them.
>
> Is there any sounder policy, any more comprehensive philanthropy, than that which shall firmly establish such schools as Hampton, and enable them to pour into this mass of ignorance an annual stream of self-reliant young men and women whose training has in-

cluded the whole range of practical living? The South calls for over twice as many teachers as can be supplied for its 15,000 Negro schools.[9]

It is within bounds to say that within a comparatively near future a thousand people will be rendered happier and better by a gift of $1500 to the Hampton Institute. Now will a man who spends $1500 for an evening's pleasure, or for any luxury whatsoever — even should the enjoyment of it extend through years — tell me that he is sincerely endeavoring to act with respect to these poor colored people, in accordance with God's command that he should love his neighbor as himself?

It is not my purpose to make a plea for Hampton. This is merely an illustration. I have known $1500 to send one hundred boys from the slums of New York to homes in the West, where the majority — not all, but a large majority — will become honest, industrious, and useful citizens. Reflect on the incalculable amount of good that such an expenditure produces. Yet a professedly Christian woman will sometimes spend $1500 on dress in a year! There is a plea for extravagance with which it is hard to have patience, so obviously is it contradicted by the application of a little common sense. It is said it gives employment to labor — as if every expenditure of money did not do that! It would be hard to name an expenditure of $1500, which would give such a vast amount of employment to labor as the endowment of a Hampton scholarship, or the removal of a hundred boys from the slums of New York. The employment which a feast or a few fashionable dresses give is not to be mentioned in comparison. You, my reader, are bound to employ labor when you spend money, but God gives you a choice. You may employ the labor to work for yourself, or you may give labor such a direction that others will receive benefit therefrom, and you are answerable for that choice. If you spend $200 on a dress, you do it because you prefer your happiness to others. That same money spent for cheaper dresses for old ladies in a home would give quite as much employment.[10]

Now the number of ways in which money can be so spent as to benefit others, not to pauperize others like almsgiving, but to lift up men and women into a higher life, is simply infinite. If one has the wealth of Croesus, every cent of it can be spent advantageously for the good of

9. [ED.] Samuel C. Armstrong (1839–93) had founded the Hampton Institute in 1868.

10. This thought is more amply developed in my *Political Economy*, Chautauqua Press, 1889.

men. Tenement-house reform in the single city of New York could well consume eighteen millions of dollars. Take the grand work going forward at Chautauqua, which only needs comparatively little money to place it upon a firm foundation, but which could use profitably millions. The Chautauqua work in its various ramifications reaches three or four hundred thousand people a year, and all over the length and breadth of the land are scattered isolated households, hamlets, villages, even cities, whose life is richer and fuller by reason of Chautauqua. Baltimore is today a happier and better city because Mr. Enoch Pratt gave over a million dollars to found a magnificent free library with branches all over the city.[11] But in every State there are villages and even large cities without suitable libraries. Playgrounds for children are a need in every city. The love of the beautiful ought to be cultivated by better public art galleries than exist in this country, and by more of them. The money which can be spent in improving elementary instruction, by adding to it physical culture, sewing, cooking, and manual training, is simply unlimited, while even a little can do much for one primary school. Limits of space forbid any extended mention of mission work at home and abroad; but it is safe to say that if Christians were consistent in their use of wealth, the revenues of home and foreign missionary societies would be quadrupled immediately.

A Christian may say, if I love my neighbor as myself, my necessities are as important as his. True, but my comforts are not as important as his necessities, nor are my luxuries and superfluities as important as my neighbor's comforts. Luxury can never be indulged in by a Christian so long as he can minister to the real well-being of others, and supply them with material goods helpful for their development; and this forever renders luxury an impossibility for a Christian.

Luxury is materialistic and selfish; it retards the mental and spiritual development of a people, and tends to impoverish a nation. Luxury breeds luxury, as sin begets sin. One tries to outvie another. Men spend more than they can afford. Speculation is fostered as a means of money-getting, and fraud and embezzlement are the legitimate outcome. Wasted fortunes, blighted careers, broken hearts, boundless opportunities forever lost — these are the end of which the beginning is self-indulgence.

It is impossible for a Christian carefully to examine the nature of industrial society, or even to look a very little way into social science, without drawing a very close line around personal expenditures which are not sin-

11. [ED.] Enoch Pratt (1808–96) was a business executive and philanthropist who gave generously to various public and educational causes.

ful. This looks very much like cross-bearing, and it seems to me that we modern Christians have well-nigh forgotten the existence of a cross. Christ meant that we should lead a life of renunciation. He said we must take up our cross. What he did say was this: "My yoke is easy, and my burden is light." Why? Because love renders sacrifice easy; and if we love our neighbor as Christ loved us, we will rejoice that it is permitted us to give our goods, our lives, and all that we have, for others, and we will account the renunciation of pleasures in which this world delights as but an easy yoke and a light burden.

V. The Alienation of Wage-Workers from the Church

There are those who deny that wage-workers are alienated from the church, and I have carefully considered their arguments; but after years of observation and reflection I have been forced to the conclusion that there is a clear alienation of thinking wage-workers from the church which, on the whole, is growing. I do not say this with any other feeling than one of profound regret; but as it appears to me a fact which can be denied only by those who are ignorant of the actual situation, I hold it to be well that it should be known.

I could give evidence which would fill pages of this book; but as there are other things to be said, I can only leave my readers to look carefully into the matter, and by a perusal of the labor press, and by conversation with representative wage-earners, to form an opinion for themselves. I think, however, I can safely say that I have had unusually favorable opportunities for getting at the facts, as I have followed the labor movement with interest, and have enjoyed the confidence of representative workingmen to a great extent.

This alienation sometimes amounts to positive hostility, as I think is quite generally the case in New York and Chicago. In other places, as in Baltimore, there is little aggressive opposition, but simply widespread indifference. I will quote a few sentences from a labor paper, published in Chicago, by men who are inclined to be comparatively conservative, and who resist all proposals of violence and anarchy as stoutly as any so-called "capitalistic" newspaper. These words, I think, represent fairly the honest opinion of a large class of our best wage-workers:

> On Thursday evening the Reverend C. F. Goss addressed a meeting called under the auspices of the Brotherhood of Carpenters. . . . In order to get an expression of opinion from his audience, he asked

those who had ceased to sympathize with the churches to hold up their hand. It is needless to say the number of hands that were uplifted caused a pang of regret to the speaker.

A question that we would like to propound to the ministers of Chicago is: Have the working classes fallen away from the churches, or have the churches fallen away from the working classes? We know hundreds and thousands of workingmen who have the utmost respect, admiration, and even love for the pure and simple teachings of the gospel, and the beneficent and exalted character of Jesus Christ, and yet they scarcely ever put their feet inside the church that "is called" his. Not because they love the church less, but because they love their self-respect more. They realize that there is no place in the average Chicago church for the poor man unless it is in the position of janitor, certainly not in the cushioned pews surrounded by individuals who not only regard poverty as a disgrace, but by their vulgar display endeavor to perpetually remind the poor man of his poverty. . . . While there are noble and notable exceptions, it must be confessed that but few of the average Chicago preachers go out of their way to "preach the gospel to the poor" — of course "good" people who are "rich" establish mission schools for "bad" people who are "poor," and they occasionally succeed in bringing within the fold a few women and children who are not sufficiently intelligent to realize that a mission school is a sort of a religious soup-house, where the gospel is distributed as charity.

One reason why wage-workers do not love the church is not peculiar. The wickedness of men's hearts leads them to resist the gospel. Workingmen are like others in this respect, although certain temptations, as pride, and arrogance, and absorption by concerns of this world, are not so powerful in their case. We must remember that Christ said it was hard for a rich man to enter the kingdom of heaven, and never alluded to any special difficulties in the way of the poor as a class. We are also told that time was when the common people heard Christ gladly. These, however, are general considerations. What is now desired is to know the peculiar cause which alienates wage-workers as a class of industrial society from the church, and this may be stated in a single sentence.

The leaders of the church, the representative men and women in the church, profess to love the working classes, but as a matter of fact, they do not love them, and this wide divergence between profession and practice is keenly felt. I here state a grave charge, but who among my readers will deny it? Before any one does, let him examine his own conscience.

How do I know that churchgoers do not love the day laborer? How do I know that my wife loves me? There is a conduct suitable to love; a conduct not prescribed by law, but which is the natural, spontaneous outcome of love. Now the consequences which would inevitably follow did the representative men and women of the church love the breadwinners of the United States are sadly missing. I will give a few specifications.

First, these church leaders are so far away from the toiling masses that they fail to understand their desires, and the motives of their action. I meet few clergymen who, even when they want to be friendly, can give an intelligent statement of the side of labor in any of its many controversies with capital. They rarely converse with leaders of the workingmen, and perhaps more rarely read any labor paper. If they loved the masses, they would instinctively draw near enough to know their aims and motives. Christ moved among the masses and understood them, and today the poorest laborer and the most obstinate trades unionist, yes, even the despised walking delegate, will feel a strange attraction for that wonderful Being who spoke words which go straight to the heart. Did not an assembly of workingmen in these United States not long ago greet the name of Christ with applause, and the mention of the church with hisses?

Second, the failure to rebuke wickedness in high places is noticed. When you go into a church on Fifth Avenue in New York, rarely, if ever, do you hear the corrupt methods by which the masses have been robbed, and prominent people made millionaires, described and denounced with righteous indignation. When not a workingman is present, the wicked labor agitators are lashed with fury. Why this? Is there any danger that a wealthy congregation in one of our cities will be carried away by the pleadings of the agitator? None at all. Those who sit in the pews have a sufficient appreciation of the wickedness of Knights of Labor and socialists. If the aim were to draw men together, those who minister to congregations made up of employers would so put the case of their employees that it could be understood, and would say everything favorable which could be said in their behalf.[12]

More ought to be said about the duties of property, for we Americans have a sufficiently keen appreciation of the rights of property. Could the idea be conveyed to the supporters of our churches that property exists for the sake of man, and not man for the sake of property, incalculable good would follow.

12. I readily admit that the clergy are better than the laity, take them as a whole. The minister of a fashionable church who tries to do his duty has indeed a hard time, and recent experiences of conscientious and fearless ministers are truly pathetic.

Third, the negative attitude of the church with respect to every proposed reform discourages, disgusts, and even angers, workingmen. The religious press is concerned with the "errors of socialism," "the errors of Henry George," and, in short, the errors of any one who proposes anything positive. "The errors of socialism!" Why talk about them? Are they a living issue? Is there the slightest danger that they will not be sufficiently discussed? There is about as much prospect of a realization of the socialist's dream, in our day, as there is that New Hampshire farmers will harvest their grain in January. If we could hear something about the "truths of socialism" and "the truths of Henry George," it would be far more to the point.

Workingmen — I am talking all the time about the thinking workingmen — instinctively feel that if the church were animated by love, she would be more anxious to discover truths than errors in the plans of those who are working for the elevation of the masses.

Nothing so disheartens one as the failure of Christians to engage in positive work for the masses. One would at least suppose that such a question as freedom from toil on Sunday would concern the clergy. Yet it does not seem to. Scarcely a question is more alive today among all labor organizations than compulsory Sunday work. All over the country, when laboring men meet, they pass resolutions on this subject, and appeal to the public to help them to secure one day in seven for rest. Yet the pulpit is silent. The bakers in New York recently sent petitions to the clergymen of New York and Brooklyn to preach on the subject, and to help them to abolish Sunday work. What came of it? I wrote to the secretary of their national organization to tell me, and here are extracts from his letter: "The Sunday law was not even presented to that legislature. . . . Relying on what the clergy will ever do to assist in enforcing Sabbath laws is equal to relying on a rain of manna that may make labor superfluous. . . . These gentlemen are more interested in the movement of boodle than in the movement of labor. . . . I consented to convince our men that I was right. They are convinced today. Out of five hundred circulars sent to the clergy of New York and Brooklyn, half a dozen answered. You will have a hard time, Professor, to convince the toilers of this country that the clergy will ever do anything for them. There is no money in it, you know."

When the clergy of one denomination in Pittsburgh, Pennsylvania, learned that a gentleman had given money for public conservatories on condition that they should be kept open on Sunday, they denounced the man, and passed formal resolutions against the acceptance of the gift. What kind of effect must that produce on the workingmen of Pittsburgh, who never received aid from these clergymen in attempts to abolish Sunday work? A prominent Presbyterian clergyman of Baltimore called on me recently, and wanted to know why the church failed to get a hold on the workingmen of our city. Had he gone with me to listen to one of his eloquent friends the following Sunday, he would have heard some sound doctrine on Sabbath-keeping, and some courageous utterances on the subject of Sunday festivities in homes of the wealthy in Baltimore. A workingman would have reflected that not a word was said about those who must toil seven days a week. The bakers in Baltimore might have been favorably impressed by something on that topic. And a word to stockholders in street railways would not have been out of place, for shortly after the sermon one of the conductors remarked to me, incidentally, that he had had only one Sunday "off" in twenty-two months.

Anarchistic workingmen contribute, from their scanty earnings, money to disseminate their pernicious doctrines, and wage-workers can at least ask the question, Why do not Christians who profess to love us manifest the same zeal for the dissemination of true doctrines on social and economic topics, if these things which we hear are so bad? The Economic Association published a monograph by Dr. Albert Shaw of the Minneapolis *Tribune,* on cooperation, which was most instructive and wholesome in tone. It did not advocate any rash measures, but told the story of some successful enterprises in Minneapolis. Many workingmen are engaged in like enterprises, and it is safe to say so practical a treatise would save them $100,000 a year. Five hundred dollars would be ample to print 10,000 copies to advertise them, and to sell them for a small sum, say ten cents, whereas the monograph in its original form cost seventy-five cents. The New York *Tribune* reviewed it favorably, and expressed the hope that a cheap reprint might appear for wide circulation. Hon. Andrew D. White wrote to me, and urged that it be reprinted for workingmen. Reverend Dr. Thwing of Minneapolis wrote a similar letter.[13] I tried to raise the money, but my appeals to Christians of means were of

13. [ED.] Albert Shaw (1857–1947) received his Ph.D. from Johns Hopkins in 1884, and had been one of Ely's students. He later was editor of *The Review of Reviews* (1891–1937). Andrew D. White (1832–1918), educator and diplomat, first president of Cornell University, befriended Ely while the latter was a student in Germany and he was minister to that country (1879–81). Charles F. Thwing (1853–1937) was then a Congregational pastor, later a college president.

no avail. I might as well have addressed the ocean. How can men full of love be so careless and indifferent?

Then there is the question of the rights of the masses. What safety is there for the property of the masses, for public property, in the fact that our cities are full of churches? I visited Montreal last summer, and when I saw the many churches I asked myself this question: Are the rights of the people better protected here than elsewhere? Afterwards I learned that the franchise for street railways had been extended for twenty-one years without any compensation to the public. This was public robbery; for had the franchise been put up at auction, it would have brought a large sum to the relief of the taxpayers; or lower fares might have been established, a blessing to workingmen and workingwomen. In Baltimore I fear public property is about to be sacrificed similarly. Many churches exist, but the forgotten millions are still the forgotten, plundered millions.

This is not exhaustive, but my essay is too long. I trust that it may start useful trains of thought in my readers, and arouse more than one conscience to a keener sense of duty. It is not pleasant to write a paper like this, but I believe it is time some one should speak plainly. Some say the condition of the church is hopeless. This I do not believe.

There is in the church a conscience which can be pricked, and it is probably as sensitive today as it has been in centuries gone by. There is a power back of the church, in her divine Master, which makes for righteousness, and which urges her on to a higher life. What is needed is to go back to Christ and learn of him.

FUNDAMENTAL BELIEFS
IN MY SOCIAL PHILOSOPHY [1]

Editor's introduction. On August 20, 1894 — the day that the hearings concerning Wells's charges against Ely were scheduled to begin — Walter Hines Page, then editor of *The Forum,* wrote to request a statement of Ely's "economic creed" for the October issue. As a social scientist, Ely believed he had no creed, but he quickly dispatched a statement of some of his opinions. Page thanked Ely for the manuscript, but requested that it be enlarged a little concerning the functions of the state.[2]

The article appeared while public interest in Ely was at its height. He had been accused of justifying strikes and of supporting socialist and anarchist views. Though he had been cleared officially, he was anxious to set forth his views on these matters accurately to as wide a public as possible. He also vigorously defended a position taken in many of his books, favoring the socialization of natural monopolies. Yet he did not even mention social Christianity as such. As a social scientist and as a member of the historical school of economics, he was convinced his work was based on the progressive unfolding of scientific truth. Though Christian premises informed him deeply, perhaps more deeply than he recognized, his advocacy of the social gospel was one phase — and as it proved, a temporary one — of his busy career.

A scientific person dislikes creeds. Science is not religious revelation but a progressive unfolding of truth. When I am asked, "What is your social creed?" I naturally reply, "I have no creed." When the editor of *The Forum* asks me for an article on my creed, I am obliged to answer

1. *The Forum,* XVIII (September 1894–February 1895), 173–83.
2. Page to Ely, August 20 and 30, 1894, in "Selections from the Richard T. Ely Papers, John M. Olin Papers, and Theodore Herfurth Papers, 1894–1915," microfilm by the State Historical Society of Wisconsin.

that I have none. What have I to do with a creed in economics or, more strictly speaking, general sociology? For it is in reality a sociological creed that is wanted.

Yet more mature thought reveals to the man of science that he may after all go too far in his opposition to a statement of his opinions. As the result of his studies, and, in a case like the present, also of his experiences in life, he may have reached certain conclusions of value to others. There may be no impropriety in a statement of these conclusions, provided it is understood that he reserves the right to change his opinions if longer investigation and riper experience reveal mistakes. It is in this spirit that I consent to state briefly my views concerning some of the most fundamental problems presented by modern society in the United States.

No economic topic of a practical nature occupies a more prominent position in the public mind, at the present moment, than strikes. What do I think about strikes? When we review industrial history it is scarcely possible to avoid the conclusion that strikes have been a necessary evil. They are a species of warfare, and must be viewed somewhat in the same light in which we look at war in general. War has been a terrible scourge to the human race and has brought in its train more misfortunes, both to victors and vanquished, than people generally understand. At the same time it has frequently happened that war has been preferable to other evils, and no historian could be found who would deny that it has produced, along with vast wretchedness and misery, some good results. Not all strikes have been failures, and it has happened before this that the firm resistance of employees to wrong and oppression has been productive of results valuable alike to themselves and their employers. An orderly, well-conducted strike implies labor organizations, and labor organizations in their earlier period find their chief activity in industrial warfare and in the preparations for such warfare. The older trades union was largely an organization of men bound together to accomplish their purposes by means of actual strikes or threats of strikes. I say "largely" because other purposes, and very important ones, have always been connected with labor organizations of any importance.

But conditions have changed. Formerly the trades and occupations of wage-earners were so distinct and separate that those employed in any one craft need have little reference in their struggles to wage-earners outside of their own ranks. Machinery has changed all that, and broken down the barriers between the various occupations of wage-earning men and women. When the shoemakers in the great shops in Massachusetts have struck, they have been replaced with comparatively little difficulty by farmers' sons and daughters never before in a manufacturing establishment; and in a few months, if not indeed in a few weeks, the employers have been able to carry on their work as well as before. It seems clear, then, that the very foundation on which old-fashioned striking trades unions rested has given way. The field of their operations seems to be a more restricted one than has been supposed by those who have considered merely older conditions. Labor organizations are a necessity, but they should change their methods to correspond to our present economic life, making more of other features than heretofore and less of strikes.

When we come to certain primary institutions like railways, telegraphs, gas-works, and the like, upon the continuous operation of which the general welfare is dependent in marked degree, the public interest becomes paramount; and public authority, if it discharge its functions, will not tolerate strikes. Anarchy means no government, and it is genuine anarchy for a great community to stand quietly by while undertakings of fundamental importance are paralyzed by the strife of different parties engaged in their operation. There is every reason why society should not tolerate such suffering as this involves. What we have recently witnessed in railway strikes is barbarism and not civilization. We should not, in this matter, allow a discussion of abstract rights to interfere with determined action which will prevent the recurrence of events like those referred to, which are nothing less than a national disgrace and humiliation. Some way or another, these peculiarly public industries must be kept in continuous operation, and this must be effected while ample protection is afforded to all interests involved. If wrong and injustice are done to employees, effective means must be discovered to remedy them without a disturbance of domestic peace.

But this statement of the problem — that is to say, continuous operation of the industries in question and justice to all interests involved, capital and labor alike — calls to mind practical difficulties which industrial civilization in general, but especially in our own country, has met, and which we have to overcome. Let us always remember that we are Americans and dealing with American conditions. A solution of the problem which in the case under consideration might perhaps be found in England or Germany, may be no solution at all in the United States. Without sharing in any anti-English sentiment, it seems to me that our writers on economic topics, especially our writers of textbooks, have forgotten the elementary fact just stated, and have been too exclusively under the influence of English thought; and that they have not supplemented what they have learned from English masters by a large and varied American experience. The conduct of some of our writers resembles that of an inventor who, having constructed a large and expensive machine, should become enraged because it would not perform the purpose which called it into being. The inventor says: "It ought to work. It conforms to the principles of the books. It is a shame and an outrage that it does not work as it should." But we reply: "My dear fellow, all your talk and all your rage do not alter the main fact. You have overlooked either some principle or some peculiarity in your material. We do not want your machine." Writers and speakers are filled with indignant amazement because the ordinary rules which govern the relations between employed and employers, and between both and the general public, do not hold in the case of these industries with which we are dealing. Is not the reason because we have overlooked fundamental principles and fundamental facts? Let us see.

The peculiarly public industries with which we are dealing are the so-called natural monopolies. Two or three are national in the scope of their operation, some are chiefly local in their activity, while a few are too extensive to be called local, but are not nevertheless strictly national in character. Roughly, they correspond to our three chief political units, the nation, the commonwealth, and the town or city. These undertakings are: streets and highways of all sorts, the means of communication and transportation, and lighting plants. Every one thinks, of course, of railways, telegraphs, telephones, harbors, canals, streetcars, elevated urban railways, gas-works, electric lighting plants. These are monopolies because they can be managed as a unit, and competition is so partial that it does not afford adequate protection to the public. All rivalry and emulation are by no means excluded. Monopoly does not mean that, but it does mean an absence of adequate protection to important public interests. Moreover, reference is had to these industries in their maturity, not in their early stages of development. Railways, in our country, give difficulty to those who do not grasp the principles of monopoly, because our railway systems are not yet fully developed, although every fair-minded person will admit that even now they are not regulated by normal competition, which excludes destructive industrial war as well as combination. Naturally we cannot enter upon the very difficult theory of monopoly, and attempt to elaborate it. Much work remains to be done before we have a complete theory of monopoly, and the treatment of this subject would require a large work if it approached exhaustiveness. Nevertheless some things have been made clear.

Experience in the United States has demonstrated that there are two — and only two — ways of dealing with monopolies. We have, in the main, a choice only between private ownership and operation with control by government, and government ownership and operation. One or the other, our courts and our legislatures have decided, we must have; and their decision has been wise, as it has been forced on them by hard facts. Waterworks in our cities very generally illustrate government ownership and operation, whereas our railways afford illustration of control by government united with private ownership and operation. Government control simply takes the place of the regulation by competition which obtains in agriculture, manufactures, and commerce. This control is, by the necessities of the case, pushed further and further every day. It has not yet included labor; but as the principles of monopoly must in time make themselves fully felt in the relation of the industries in question to labor, and as public interests are paramount, as already indicated, it can be only a question of time when what we have seen in the efforts of the courts to keep our railways in operation will be further developed. Whatever we otherwise think of the injunctions recently issued by the courts, we must acknowledge that they are a step in the right direction. The force operating to bring under the control of government the relations between employed and employers in the case of monopolistic undertakings is like a law of nature which will override all opposition.

The question we have to answer is this: Which is better, government ownership and operation, with the control naturally and spontaneously resulting therefrom, or private ownership and operation, with government control forced on the owners and managers? The question is complex, and the answer is a difficult one, in regard to which men may well differ; but it should receive the careful and conscientious attention of all who have any qualifications calculated to help them to throw light on the problems involved, and above all things it should be considered dispassionately. Whichever alternative we choose, we have complicated problems without end to solve; and this simply calls again to mind the fact that modern civilization is at best an arduous process.

It has seemed to me that the difficulties inherent in minute and detailed public control of private property, especially under American conditions, have been too generally underestimated. First of all, we must remember that private property naturally carries with it the right of exclusive control over the objects of property. A large part of the benefits of private property results from this exclusive control. The farmer exerts himself with diligence and reaps reward or bears loss according to the wisdom with which he exercises his control over his own operations. The anomalous condition of public control over private property is that we ask men to take the responsibilities of private property without its prerogatives; and protests from managers of railways and other similar enterprises are not surprising. Now what are the managers of such property going to say, if, having taken away from them the right to control their relations to the general public, we take from them the right to control the labor they employ? Will not the present friction, already disastrous, between government and powerful private interests, be increased many fold? Were any suggestions thrown out during the recent strike investigation in Chicago which would lead us to think otherwise? Already, at least one railway president insists that the government should purchase railway property if it assumes the right to control it. What may we expect will be the attitude of railway managers if we continue our policy of perpetual interference with private railway property?

But we have difficulties in the way of control which are seldom alluded to. Of necessity, the special expert knowledge must for the most part be on the side of those over whom it is designed to exercise this control. Is this a promising experiment? Can ignorance control knowledge? — inexperience, experience? A German professor, with experience in public life in his own country, tells me how successfully in some instances this control has been exercised in Germany; but I reply: "America is not Germany. Can you, with American conditions, expect similar results? If you do, it seems to me you do not know our country. We have to deal with American farmers and American workingmen. Whatever you may think of them, they are facts, very real, very important."

But we have further to notice the immense power which these natural monopolies inevitably wield. When towns and cities contend with them, we have the spectacle of weakness attempting to exercise control over strength. What must we expect? Let us freely admit that in their moral qualities railway owners and managers are quite equal to the rest of the community, while wiser and stronger than most of their fellow citizens: can we, then, expect beneficial results? If the federal government is stronger than the natural monopolies it seeks to control, can they not treat with it almost as a coordinate power? — and is this beneficial?

Now let us take the question of corruption in public life, and let us freely admit the share of this corruption connected with the control in question, for which public authorities must bear the blame; let us take the view most favorable to the private parties controlled, and must we not admit that, with our American conditions, this corruption is to a great extent an inevitable result of the conflict of interest produced by the American policy? Not only must we protest against solving this question by considerations which hold in England and Germany, but we must likewise protest against a solution based merely upon the facts of life in New England and the Middle States.

The difficulties in the way of public ownership and management are vast. Such ownership and management imply changes and readjustments in our political conditions. Additional safeguards against undue centralization may possibly be necessary, for local self-government needs to be further developed rather than restricted. No danger must be suffered to threaten the American commonwealth. The civil service must be developed far beyond what we have as yet seriously considered, for it would be folly indeed to think of the enlargement of the functions of government mentioned, with our present civil service. Every one, however, will admit that, were it necessary, we could maintain a military service of one million men. Is it true that, should we set about it, we could not devise measures to maintain a civil service of one million men?

The acquisition by the public of the private property involved, without wrong to any one, suggests numerous difficulties. All these difficulties and obstacles in the way of the socialization of natural monopolies deserve most careful consideration; but, after all, which alternative suggests the greater difficulties? Which course promises most for the future?

Should it be decided that government ownership, immense as are its difficulties, is on the whole preferable, it will then be necessary to pass on to details; but it does not seem likely that such a decision will be reached except for some local monopolies, and perhaps the telegraph and telephone, in any near future. It may be one generation — it may be two generations — hence, before the public will be fully persuaded; and in such matters prediction is extremely unsafe. The change may never come, while it is possible that it may come sooner than I have anticipated. It is well for us, however, to have clear ideas in regard to the goal which it would be desirable to reach, could we attain it, in order that we may approximate as nearly to it as possible.

It should, however, be distinctly understood that a belief in the policy of socialization of national monopolies does not involve endorsement of every scheme for carrying into effect this policy. If a party arises which demands the socialization of natural monopolies, we may well ask ourselves what kind of leadership has this party. Has it in its leadership such mental capacity and such moral qualifications that it would be expedient to turn over the government to it, especially when so doing involves grave changes, requiring the best brains and ripest experience of the nation to effect them with safety? Furthermore, we may ask, what else does this party couple with the demand for the socialization of monopoly? Has this party ideas which seem to us wildly impracticable in regard to money and public finance? If so, we may conclude that adherence to older parties is preferable to support of a party deficient in leadership, and which couples unsound planks with one which, differently brought forward, might command our support.

Furthermore, it should be clearly understood that the policy of socialization of natural monopolies does not carry with it any idea of spoliation. Whatever we think about that policy, we should all, it seems to me, insist on full payment for all property taken from private owners.

A still more fundamental question is that suggested by the word "socialism," which is something so radically different from my general thought, that the competitive field of industry — that is, in the main, agriculture, manufactures, and commerce — is suitable for private effort, and the field of monopoly for public activity, that only shallow thinkers can confound the two. Socialism, however, is not so much a single question as a series of questions, vast and intricate. Socialism is indeed a philosophy of society supported by many very able men. I have held, and still hold, that the study of socialism is most useful, and that on several accounts. First of all it gives us a standpoint from which to survey existing institutions, and enables us to understand them and weigh in the balance their merits and demerits. It is general principle that indirect methods, both in science and industry, are speedier and more effective than direct methods. A critical study of socialism not only interests a student in the study of present society, but gives an aid in this study which it is difficult to find elsewhere. This is a position which was taken long ago by John Stuart Mill, and subsequent experience has only confirmed what he stated when he expressed the opinion "that the intellectual and moral grounds of socialism deserve the most attentive study, as affording in many cases the guiding principles of the improvements necessary to give the present economic system of society its best chance."

Socialism has also been a force which has stimulated the consciences of many and transformed beneficially the lives of not a few. Again, socialism has furnished a needed corrective to certain anarchistic tendencies in our life.

On the other hand, the agitation of socialism as it has been too frequently conducted has tended to an undue exaltation of manual toil, a depreciation of the brain work which alone can render mere physical exertion fruitful, and to class separation and hatred, and has at times turned away the attention of the masses from true remedies for evils which afflict them. The difficulties in the way of socialism seem to me to be insuperable. First of all there is the difficulty in the way of the organization of agriculture, which has never yet been squarely faced by socialists. Then, socialism once organized, there remains difficulty in securing that distribution of annual income which would give general satisfaction and at the same time promote progress. There is reason to apprehend that under socialism those pursuits upon which the progress of civilization depends would not be amply supported, and that the result of socialism would thus be a non-progressive society. If this is true, then the masses would ultimately suffer, even if we admit that their condition at first would be improved.

Finally, it is my opinion that the concentration of dissatisfaction under socialism would be revolutionary in character. As I have stated in my recent work on socialism and social reform, "The outcome of socialism then, it is to be apprehended, would be such an amount of dissatisfaction that one of two things would happen: either socialism would result in a series of revolutions, reducing countries like England and the United States to the condition of the South American republics, and rendering progress impossible; or the dissatisfaction would cause a complete overthrow of socialism and a return to the discredited social order." [3]

I have stated my views in regard to anarchy so often and so emphatically that it is difficult for me to do more than to repeat what I have said elsewhere. Anarchy comprises the sum and substance of all evils of a social nature. Every step in the direction of anarchy is a calamity. The propaganda of anarchy is a terrible evil, leading to disturbance and insurrection. The evils which flow from anarchy or even the propaganda of anarchy are not incidental, but proceed from the very nature of the doctrine. Progress depends upon obedience to law and constituted authori-

3. [ED.] This, the passage several times cited in Ely's defense at the hearing, is from *Socialism: An Examination of Its Nature, Its Strength and Its Weakness, with Suggestions for Social Reform* (N.Y., 1894), 204.

ties, and anarchy in its very nature is rebellion. Anarchy is lawlessness elaborated into a social philosophy, and anything more diametrically opposed to my own social philosophy is to me scarcely conceivable.

But this consideration of anarchy raises the question, Upon precisely what foundation does the opposition to anarchy rest? Anarchy is the negation of the state. What is the source and sanction of the authority of the state? Is the state a mere aggregate of individuals accomplishing their purpose simply by brute force? Does might make right? If it does, then is not the question between anarchy and its opponents simply a question of superior force? But if might does not make right, what does make right? Has the state an ethical nature? If the state is itself non-ethical, can the power which it exercises have an ethical element? But if it is devoid of an ethical element, can it rest upon anything less than mere brute force? The doctrine of the Christian church has been from time immemorial that the state is a divine institution and that its authority comes from God. If this is true, then we have a ground of opposition to anarchy which appeals alike to intellect and heart. Is this a true doctrine or is it not? Is it a doctrine which science can recognize? If science does not recognize it, what does science put in its place? I do not attempt to answer these questions, although I think a sufficiently clear answer can be found in my various writings; but I commend them to the careful consideration of the readers of the present article.

Finally, if my views have, as the editor of *The Forum* thinks, a public interest, probably it may be well for me to say a few words about the future progress of society. No sane man can claim that in our social arrangements we have as yet reached perfection. Every one acknowledges that there is room for improvement in literature, art, religion; but, strangely enough, some seem inclined to resist the conclusion which follows from the nature of man and the conditions which surround him, that there is room for improvement and possibility of improvement in our industrial relations. We have made advance in the past, and we shall certainly make progress in the future. It is inconceivable that industrial society two hundred years from now will be like the industrial society of today. It is eminently desirable that right-minded and intelligent persons should work for improvement and endeavor to render change — which must come in some way or another — as little injurious and as beneficial as possible.

First of all, the necessity is suggested of careful, conscientious study. The importance of study is generally felt, and the educational institutions of the land are moving in the right direction in the development which they are giving to all branches of social and political science. We need trained men in the pulpit and the press, and especially in legislative halls. Careful, impartial, thoroughly scientific study of the actual facts of life is today one of the most striking needs of the civilized world.

Such study and observation as have been already made show clearly that there is no panacea for individual and social ills. There is no royal road to a happy condition of society, but the road is long, arduous, and often painful. There is no possibility of escape from toil and suffering. Mitigation and gradual improvement are the utmost which we can hope for, and it is a duty of all those who have the ear of the masses to tell them this plain truth even if it be not altogether palatable. To arouse false hopes and to cultivate illusions result only in increased suffering. At the same time there is enough which can be accomplished, to stimulate all to put forward their best efforts, and to give encouragement in the midst of the weary struggle for better social conditions.

The eighteenth-century doctrine of essential equality among men is, in my opinion, pernicious. It seems to me that it has been a most fruitful cause of misfortune and misdirected social effort. It nourishes false hopes and turns attention away from facts of the utmost moment. There is no more marked social fact, no one more momentous in its consequences, than the essential inequality of men. Men are unequal in power, capacity, requirements; and the more one thinks about it the more marvelous do all these inequalities appear. Any social action based upon an assumption of equality is mischievous. It is especially the feebler members of the community who suffer under the doctrine of essential equality, because, as has been well said by a jurist, "Nothing is more unequal than the equal treatment of unequals." The doctrine of equality also weakens the feeling of responsibility on the part of those who are superior to their fellows either in their persons or their fortunes, whereas a frank recognition of inequalities and of the favored position of a few must tend to awaken in them a feeling of responsibility.

As far as my general social philosophy is concerned, I may then say that I am a conservative rather than a radical, and in the strict sense of the term an aristocrat rather than a democrat; but when I use the word "aristocrat," I have in mind of course not a legal aristocracy, but a natural aristocracy; not an aristocracy born for the enjoyment of special privilege, but an aristocracy which lives for the fulfillment of special service.

THE SOCIAL LAW OF SERVICE [1]

Editor's introduction. The essays that make up *The Social Law of Service* deal with theology, ethics, and economics. "While the author's aim," declared Ely, "has been to write a work which the young person of high school attainments may read with profit, possibly even the more mature reader will not in one perusal exhaust all the meaning which has been put into it." [2] Through the efforts of his friend Bishop John H. Vincent (1832–1920), the founder of Chautauqua, the book was given wide use by the Epworth League, the youth organization of the Methodist Episcopal Church. In his later years, Ely regarded this book as one of the best things he had written. "Because I am convinced, today more than ever," he wrote in the 1930's, "that this book contains much that is wise, because I humbly believe it to be one of the few inspired things I have ever done, I am profoundly grateful that its contents were made available to at least a portion of the youth of this country." [3]

The fourth essay, which gave the book its title, emphasizes a theme frequently stressed by the earlier advocates of the social gospel in particular — the sacrifice of self for the good of humanity.

❖ ❖ ❖ ❖

We all crave happiness. Happiness is an end of life which is worthy of effort, but it is an end which must be subordinated to another end if it is to be pursued successfully; and this other end is service. But service means sacrifice; apparently the opposite of happiness. We reach this paradox then: Happiness is a worthy end of our efforts; but if we place it before ourselves as the direct and immediate end to be striven for, we cannot reach it. It will elude us. It will be to us like the water all about Tantalus, the cold flood welling ever to his chin, yet always retreating from his fiery lips; like the fruit over his head which the winds whirled skyward through the air:

1. *The Social Law of Service* (N.Y., 1896), chap. IV, 77–102. 2. *Ibid.*, 7.
3. *Ground Under Our Feet*, 87.

221

> Whensoe'er
> The old man, fain to cool his burning tongue,
> Clutched with his fingers at the branches fair.

Individual lives repeat the race-history. If you would attain to happiness seek something else. Poets, philosophers, and prophets all tell us this, for to all it comes as the result of the deepest insight and the ripest experience. But all go further. You must cast aside the thought of happiness as a chief aim. You may not keep it concealed in a corner of your mind and heart as after all the main thing, but a thing to be reached in a roundabout way. You cannot successfully juggle with yourself. You must in very truth renounce yourself to find yourself, and give up yourself to save yourself.

To the author's mind there are few more interesting, more instructive, and withal pathetic life histories than that of John Stuart Mill, penned by himself. It is the story of a rarely gifted, noble nature, purposely brought up outside of the pale of Christianity and taught to look upon all religions as so many forms of superstition, yet gradually approaching the light as the years passed by. Mill tells us that in his early life his object was to be a reformer of the world, and that his conception of his own happiness was entirely identified with this object. He thought he had the certainty of a happy life, because he had placed his happiness in something durable and distant; in a goal toward which approach could always be made although it could never be reached. But Mill found that even so noble a pursuit could not give permanent happiness when happiness was the end sought. He reached a period when existence seemed almost an intolerable burden; a burden which he himself said was well described by Coleridge's lines on "Dejection":

> A grief without a pang, void, dark, and drear,
> A drowsy, stifled, unimpassioned grief,
> Which finds no natural outlet or relief,
> In word, or sigh, or tear.

When a moderate happiness returned he discovered that "those only are happy who have their mind fixed on some object other than their own happiness; as, the happiness of others, on the improvement of mankind, even on some art or pursuit, followed not as a means, but as itself an ideal end. Aiming thus at something else they find happiness by the way."

We have in these words of Mill a partial statement, at least, of the great ethical *law of indirectness*. We reach ethical ends only indirectly. Resolving to be good will in itself never make us good.

But shall we heap paradox on paradox? We have already found that while the craving for happiness is natural and the desire for happiness is legitimate, we shall lose it if we seek it. We have discovered that the secret of life is renunciation. We must sacrifice our life to receive it in fullness. "Surely, then, self-sacrifice is an end," we may be told. By no means. Self-sacrifice in itself is no virtue, and may not be made an end in itself. Self-sacrifice pursued as an end leads to a gloomy asceticism which would have us refuse the joy of life as something bad and hateful to the Giver of all good things. Self-sacrifice bears its fruit of peace and happiness and life only when it is pursued indirectly.

Self-sacrifice itself falls under the law of indirectness. Let us listen to wise words of Bishop Boyd Carpenter: "A man cannot perfect himself in anything if he seek perfection directly; for, if he does, the shadow of himself intervenes and spoils his work. Sacrifice, when it is sought as a sacrifice, has a self-consciousness which mars its simplicity and spoils its moral force. When men preach self-sacrifice — self-sacrifice as the moral force which can regenerate mankind — they forget that self-forgetfulness is essential to perfect sacrifice; a sacrifice, undertaken because sacrifice is noble, is alloyed with that self-regarding look which mars its beauty in the view of the soul itself. Sacrifice which knows itself as such is not pure sacrifice." [4]

Have we not seen this in those who have found the secret of life? Have we not noticed how those whose life is wholly given to others — perhaps in some far-away land, deprived of almost everything which we hold dear — speak of their privileges? Have we never heard a noble woman, wholly given to good works in a dreary slum of a great city, and who in the opinion of a host of admiring friends is almost ready for canonization, resent the thought that her life was one of self-sacrifice? Undoubtedly. And there is one word that gives the key to these paradoxes. What is it? We know what it is: Love — love, the secret of the universe. Sacrifice is not an end in itself, but sacrifice is the condition of service. The law of society is service. This is the supreme law of society, from which no one can escape with impunity. Ethical teachers now approach unanimity in the assertion that the criterion of right conduct is social well-being. The

4. *The Permanent Elements of Religion*, 36, 37. [ED.] The Rt. Rev. W. Boyd Carpenter (1841–1918) gave the Bampton lectures at Oxford in 1887; they were published under this title (London, 1889).

welfare of society is the test of conduct in the individual. It would be interesting to take four great writers — a theologian, a jurist, a professor of natural science, and a student of society — and to discover their entire and complete harmony in the view that the purpose of the rules of right individual conduct is the welfare of society.

There is one law, and only one, taught by the Christian religion and on its manward side; that is, the law of love, which finds expression in the social law of service. Christianity and ethical science agree perfectly. Social welfare is the test of right conduct. All right laws which regulate human relations have in view the well-being of society, and they are all one. Thus it is true that he who breaks any one law breaks all, for they all have one source and one purpose. The thief and the undutiful child, the murderer and the slothful person, all alike have violated the social law of service. When you utter unkind words, when you neglect an opportunity to lend a helping hand, when you spend material wealth to gratify whim, caprice, vanity, instead of to accomplish worthy ends, you have broken the same law which has been violated by the criminal classes in our prisons and penitentiaries.

This may seem like a hard saying, but the more we ponder it, the more meaning it will have for us. And the message which it conveys to us is one which is needed in these days of great wealth and easygoing self-indulgence, if it ever was needed.

It will be well for us to contrast at some length Christian self-sacrifice, the condition of social service, with asceticism, which is its perversion. The two following quotations will be so helpful to us that we take them as a text in our treatment of the entire subject of Christian self-sacrifice versus asceticism:

> Then said Jesus unto his disciples, If any man will come after me, let him deny himself, and take up his cross, and follow me.
> For whosoever will save his life shall lose it: and whosoever will lose his life for my sake shall find it.[5]
> The first condition of all really great moral excellence is a spirit of genuine self-sacrifice and self-renunciation.[6]

An enduring truth is expressed in these quotations. The first is one of those pregnant sayings of Christ which have been bearing fruit for nearly two thousand years, and which are as vital today in Christendom as ever before. They have, indeed, but begun to do their work, because they contain lessons founded on the fundamental principles of man's nature. They

5. Matthew XVI, 24, 25.   6. Lecky, *History of European Morals*, II, 155.

belong to no age and to no country. They reveal that marvelous insight, not merely into human nature, but into the depths of moral and spiritual truth, which again and again has provoked from men the spontaneous and surprised exclamation: "Never man spake like this man." [7] What Emerson says — with some exaggeration, perhaps — of Plato, is fully true of Christ in the sense in which Emerson uses the words: "The citizen of an Eastern [Greek] town, but no villager nor patriot." Christ was one of those who, in the best sense of the word, are cosmopolitan — belonging to the world — laying the foundations of a true patriotism, yet not patriotic in a narrow and exclusive sense, because transcending all national bounds.

The second quotation, taken from Lecky's *History of European Morals*, is the author's profound reflection after his admirable study of Christian asceticism, and is, perhaps, all the more significant because the author reaches his conclusions as a result not of religious experiences, but of independent investigations and historical researches. [8]

What is the difference between Christian self-sacrifice and asceticism? Certainly it is not in the degree of self-renunciation. What asceticism has exacted from those who have thought to find in it the way of life, we may read in the painful narrative of Lecky. Wife, husband, children, the blessings of civilization enjoyed in the midst of abundant comfort, pleasures of every sort, all have been exchanged gladly for the hermit's cell, often a wild beast's den in the desert, for rags and filth, for the scantiest diet, for long vigils, for castigations, for privations and sufferings, which have cut short thousands of lives. St. Simeon Stylites on his pillar, bidding his attendant replace the worms which fed on his flesh, as they fell from the sickening sores of his disgusting body, saying to the worms, "Eat what God has given you," is a well-known type of the ascetic. Blaise Pascal is one of the higher types of the ascetic, and his self-inflicted tortures are described in these words:

> To avoid wandering and worldly thoughts when engaged in conversation, he took an iron girdle full of sharp points, which he placed next to his flesh, and when conscious of an impulse to vanity, or even a feeling of pleasure in the place where he happened to be, he struck the girdle with his elbow in order to increase the pain of the punc-

7. John VII, 46.

8. [ED.] The classic work by the famous English historian and philosopher of history, W. E. H. Lecky (1838–1903), *History of European Morals from Augustus to Charlemagne* (2 vols., 3rd ed. rev.; N.Y., 1879), has been reprinted as recently as 1955.

tures. He ate a certain regulated quantity of food whether hungry or not, never exceeding it, however good his appetite, and never eating less, however great his loathing; and this on the ground that taking food was a duty, which was never to be accompanied by any sensual pleasure. . . . He mortified his affections not less than his body, and said that we should never allow anyone to love us with fondness; in fostering such attachments we occupied hearts which ought to be given solely to God; that it was robbing him of that on which he set most store. "It is not right that others should attach themselves to me, even if they do it willingly and with pleasure. I should deceive those in whom I excited such a feeling. Am I not about to die? The object of their love will then perish. As I should warn people against believing a falsehood, however profitable to me, I should warn them not to attach themselves to me; for their duty is to spend their lives in striving to please God, or in seeking him.[9]

Yet the sufferings of the ascetic were not more severe than those which Christ invited his followers to endure. How strange the allurements held out to men to join the Christian ranks in the time of Christ and his apostles! The birds of the air have their nests, the beasts of the field have their holes, but I, the Christ, have nowhere to lay my head, yet follow me. I am not to receive earthly honors, as has been vainly supposed — I shall be despised and rejected, persecuted to the death, hung upon the shameful cross to die an ignominious death; yet follow me and see the things which I must suffer. Do not think, however, that you will fare better than I! Far from it. If they have called me Beelzebub, how much more shall they call you the children of hell! If I have been maltreated, so shall you also be scourged, imprisoned, crucified. Follow me and I will show you how great things you must suffer for me! Did ever captain draw his hosts about him with such promise of reward? Yet a response to the call of Christ has never been lacking. From the time of Christ to this day, an interesting multitude of believers have accepted the call to suffer for Christ, and accepted it not only without reservation but with joy. Remember the conversion of St. Paul. The disciple of Christ who hesitated to receive the persecuting Saul is reassured with these words: "He is a chosen vessel unto me, . . . for I will show him how great things he must suffer for my name's sake." And St. Paul entered on his work not with assurances of great success in a large field of usefulness, not with promises of large victories as a result of battles with the enemies of Christ, but with the knowledge that he must bear unusual cruelties. This

9. J. C. Morison, *Service of Man,* 211, 212. [ED.] A book published in London in 1887.

was his incitement, this was the inducement held out for an alliance with a despised sect. Yet gladly did St. Paul accept the proffer, and before the end of his sufferings we find him describing with a certain feeling of exultation his experiences as a follower of the Nazarene: "Of the Jews five times received I forty stripes save one. Thrice was I beaten with rods, once was I stoned, thrice I suffered shipwreck, a night and a day I have been in the deep; in journeyings often, in perils of waters, in perils of robbers, in perils by mine own countrymen, in perils by the heathen, in perils in the city, in perils in the wilderness, in perils in the sea, in perils among false brethren; in weariness and painfulness, in watchings often, in hunger and thirst, in fastings often, in cold and nakedness; besides those things that are without, there is that which presseth upon me daily, anxiety for all the churches." [10]

Nevertheless there is a marked difference between the exhortations of Christ and the entreaties of the preachers of asceticism and self-renunciation. Asceticism is self-denial for its own sake, and Christ never urged that upon his followers. What the world offers is in itself good and to be enjoyed with thanksgiving. The flowers of the field have been clothed by God with a beauty of which Solomon could not boast, to rejoice the eye of man. The beasts and fields produce food and raiment in abundance, and all innocent enjoyment is a positive duty rather than a sin. Rejoice and be exceeding glad for the gifts of your heavenly Father; this is the spirit of Christ.

We may, indeed, rejoice that we have been emancipated from the bonds of a gloomy asceticism which made a virtue of sacrifice and suffering in themselves. Suffering goes with sin; joy with righteousness. Christ came to make this world a happy world, and as his purposes approach completion, happiness of the highest sort must increase. This world will become a happier and happier world as time goes on, for the coming of the kingdom means the subjugation of the entire world to Christ. And by the entire world we understand not only man, but external physical forces. This thought is clearly revealed in the prophecies of the Old Testament, especially in Isaiah: "Instead of the thorn shall come up the fir tree, and instead of the brier shall come up the myrtle tree." [11] This signifies the subjugation of the forces of nature; but nature includes man's

10. 2 Corinthians XI, 24–28. The author wishes to acknowledge at this point the valuable assistance received from Bishop Boyd Carpenter's *Permanent Element of Religion*, from which book this illustration and some other quotations are taken.

11. Isaiah LV, 13.

physical body, and that, too, in a righteous state, will have long life gradually, peacefully, fading away at last. "And I will rejoice in Jerusalem,
and joy in my people: and the voice of weeping shall be no more heard in
her, nor the voice of crying. There shall be no more thence an infant of
days, nor an old man that hath not filled his days: for the child shall die
an hundred years old. . . . They shall build houses, and inhabit them; and
they shall plant vineyards, and eat the fruit of them. . . . For as the days
of a tree are the days of my people, and mine elect shall long enjoy the
work of their hands." [12]

The miracles of Christ have this same significance. The Son of man
must show himself Lord of the external physical world in order to bring
out its significance and the ultimate domination of man. The miracles
puzzle many, but when we think about it in this light we must see that
the life of the Messiah would have been strangely incomplete without
them. This must be felt by all who think deeply on social righteousness
and its results. The teachings of the French socialist Fourier are instructive at this point. These teachings are wild and erratic in many particulars. They contain much chaff, but in the chaff we find valuable grains of
wheat. Fourier predicted a happy social state to continue long in the
future, and he prophesied that in this state lions should become servitors
of man, drawing his chariot hundreds of miles in a single day, that whales
should draw his ships across the great deep, while the ocean itself would
become a delightful beverage.[13]

We laugh at these crude fantasies, yet there is in them the sound
thought indicated.

But we have in all this only the teachings of history and the revelations
of natural science. National wickedness has repeatedly turned fruitful
plains into deserts, and social righteousness is capable of turning barren
wastes once more into smiling gardens.

Yet there is the great fact of self-denial and self-renunciation — "the
first condition of all really great moral excellence." And this fact, stern
and unrelenting, so far from anywhere in the New Testament being concealed, is thrust — at times it would seem almost with unnatural violence
— into the foreground of the entire gospel message.

12. Isaiah LXV, 19–22.
13. Ely, *French and German Socialism*, 88, 89. [ED.] Ely devoted chap. v of this
book to Charles Fourier (1772–1837) and his utopian proposals. More than thirty
communal experiments along Fourieristic lines were undertaken in the United States,
including the famous Brook Farm.

Why did Christ himself suffer? Why was he, although keenly appreciative of the beauties of nature and social in his disposition, loving to eat and drink with his friends — why was he "a man of sorrows and acquainted with grief"? [14] These words contain the explanation: "And I, if I be lifted up, will draw all men unto me." Ah, the sacrifice of Christ had an object outside of himself. It was not sacrifice for sacrifice's sake, but sacrifice for others' sake. Because Christ loved men with an infinite yearning love, he died for men. Love was the ground of sacrifice. "God is love." This is the secret of Christian self-denial, and asceticism, whatever its external resemblance, is its perversion. It is like the perversion of charity, in the lower sense of the word charity; that is to say, almsgiving. Men first gave to benefit their fellows, then later, in the time of the perversion, to benefit themselves by accumulating thereby, as it was supposed, heavenly treasures; but when the true end of charity was lost sight of, it became a curse and not a blessing to the world. It is not said that a proper motive in giving is not the benefit which may come to one's character, but a true saint will scarcely think of this, but only of those to whom he hopes to minister, because he loves them as children of a common Father.[15] The self-motive is altogether subordinate. Likewise it is not claimed that self-denial should not be practiced for the sake of character-culture, and we may admit an educational value in asceticism, though we claim the same end can otherwise be reached and that by methods more in harmony with the teachings of Christ.

Asceticism, indeed, often grows out of self-sacrifice. Men go without for the sake of others; then, later, they lose their love for others and continue their self-denial as if there were virtue in that of itself. The spirit is gone, the lifeless form alone remains. Thus asceticism has often displaced love to others and become intensely cruel.

Love leads to self-sacrifice of necessity, as we see in the lives of those who have manifested in a marked degree generous love for men. The biography of the seventh Earl of Shaftesbury shows us this; also, the biography of two American women, the Grimké sisters.[16] These sisters

14. Those persons who think they imitate Christ in merely wearing long faces, miss the mark widely. It was the intense sympathy of Christ which made him sad.

15. [ED.] The syntax here appears to be faulty; probably the first "not" should be omitted.

16. *The Sisters Grimké, a Biography,* by Catherine H. Birney. [ED] Angelina (1805–79) and Sarah (1792–1873) Grimké, daughters of a South Carolina judge, John F. Grimké (1752–1819), were prominent leaders of the anti-slavery movement. Angelina married Theodore Dwight Weld (1803–95) in 1838. Cf. Gilbert H. Barnes

illustrated the motto on the title page of the book in which is recorded the story of their lives: "The glory of all glories is the glory of self-sacrifice." At first sacrifice with them found a basis in asceticism. It was thought well pleasing to God that they should deny themselves without any human motive or aim external to themselves. This early period of their history finds expression in many passages in the book. Sarah Grimké writes: "I went to meeting, and it being a rainy day I took a large, handsome umbrella which I had accepted from brother Henry, accepted doubtfully, therefore wrongfully, and have never felt quite easy to use it, which, however, I have done a few times. After I was in meeting I was much tried by a wandering mind, and every now and then the umbrella would come before me, so that I sat trying to wait on my God, and he showed me that I must not only give up this little thing, but return it to my brother." After other reflections she adds, in a note: "This little sacrifice was made. I sent the umbrella with an affectionate note to brother, and believe it gave him no offense to have it returned, and sweet has been the recompense, even peace."

Angelina says: "A great deal of my finery, too, I have put beyond the reach of anyone." She had put into a cushion two handsome lace veils, a lace flounce, and other laces. This was done, as she wrote on a slip of paper sewed up in the cushion, "under feelings of duty, believing that as we are called with a high and holy calling, and forbidden to adorn these bodies, but to wear the ornament of a meek and quiet spirit, as we have ourselves laid (in this cushion) these superfluities of naughtiness, so we should not in any measure contribute to the destroying of others"; that is, by allowing others to wear all this finery. The sisters wanted at this time by such means to separate themselves from the world and condemn it. Angelina was troubled by a cashmere mantle which had cost a sum which then seemed large to her, and cut the trimming off; but this did not suit her, and she finally decided never to wear it again although she had at the time no money to replace it with anything else.

Soon, however, we perceive other motives, motives of an altruistic nature, appearing as the ground of self-sacrifice. Angelina writes in her diary at a somewhat later date than the time of the last quotation: "It is not only the food I eat at mother's, but the whole style of living is a direct departure from the simplicity that is in Christ. The Lord's poor tell me that they do not like to come to such a fine house to see me; and if they come, instead of reading a lesson of frugality and deadness to the

and Dwight L. Dumond, eds., *Letters of Theodore Dwight Weld, Angelina Grimké Weld, and Sarah Grimké, 1822–1844* (2 vols., N.Y., 1934).

world, they must go away lamenting the inconsistency of a sister professor. One thing is very hard to bear. I feel obliged to pay five dollars a week for board (then a much larger sum than now), though I disapprove of this extravagance, and am actually accessory in maintaining this style of living, and am therefore prevented from giving to the poor as liberally as I would like."

It was not, however, until these sisters were aroused to the wrong of slavery, and began to take a part in the abolition movement, that the full measure of their capabilities for self-sacrifice appeared, and then self-sacrifice found its true basis in love for others. They lived a life of self-sacrifice then because, loving others and perceiving the needs of others, they could not do otherwise. They with all their resources were dedicated to what they deemed a holy cause, and every cent saved from personal expenditure was a cent to be used to help others. They had, indeed, a "love-purse," as it was called, into which such savings were dropped. These sisters Grimké were the daughters of Judge Grimké of Charleston, South Carolina, and were brought up like young ladies in the best Southern social circles. Only those who know what this means can appreciate the self-sacrifice in them when they lived in a rude little cottage in New Jersey, across the Hudson from New York, and did their own housework, dressing simply, while the husband of one of the sisters, Theodore Weld, wore noticeably coarse clothing, which he thought might have cost him nearly one hundred dollars one year, when he was traveling and lecturing, and the whole of one suit and part of another were destroyed by mobs. Listen to a few quotations from letters. Sarah writes: "We can make good bread, and this with milk is an excellent meal. This week I am cook, and am writing this while my beans are boiling and pears stewing for dinner." Angelina writes at another time: "As to how I have made out with cooking, it so happens that labor (planting a garden) gives Theodore such an appetite that everything is sweet to him, so that my rice and asparagus, potatoes, mush, and Indian bread, all taste well, though some might not think them fit to eat." Shortly after her marriage to Mr. Weld, Angelina wrote: "We ordered our furniture to be made of cherry, and quite enjoy the cheapness of our outfit, for the less we spend the less the Anti-slavery Society will have to pay my Theodore for his labors."

Does it not become apparent that this represents the spirit which must of necessity animate all Christians? No one can love his fellows truly and waste any resources.

Now this parallel between charity and asceticism, to which allusion has

already been made, is instructive in another sense. Men saw the evils connected with perverted charity, and said: "Charity is a bad thing. Gifts are
bad things. One may sell things, but may not without injury give them
away. Self-seeking is a beneficent social law." Thus men substitute the
teachings of Satan for the commands of Christ. Without love we may
not, it is true, give to our fellows and benefit them.

Likewise in our day men, perceiving the excesses of asceticism, and the
cruel selfishness which has too often accompanied it, and even been a part
of it, have acquiesced silently or openly in self-indulgence. Give nothing
without a valuable equivalent, and enjoy all that your resources permit
you to enjoy — this is the logical conclusion of much that passes for
Christian teaching.

No earnest man is today satisfied with the influence of the Christian
church. Its members are not leading the life which is expected of them. It
may or may not be true that they are better than they have been in
former ages, but we are still sadly far behind the mark. Under present
circumstances what is particularly needed is for us to take home to ourselves the doctrine of Christian self-sacrifice. To renounce "the devil and
all his works, the vain pomp and glory of the world, with all covetous
desires of the same, and the sinful desires of the flesh, so as not to follow
or be led by them," is a very real thing and a very great sacrifice. It is a
cross which only the love of Christ can make an easy burden. Our resources of every sort, time, strength of body and mind, and our economic
resources, are all limited, and, however great they may be, love will show
us how we can use all to the last minute of time and the last farthing of
money for the promotion of the welfare of humanity.

Let us consider a few quotations from great thinkers who are strongly
impressed with the necessity of self-sacrifice, and the testimony for
present purposes is perhaps all the more valuable because so many of them
profess slight allegiance to Christianity. Says Carlyle: "It is only with
renunciations that life properly speaking can be said to begin." [17] . . .

"In a valiant suffering for others, not in a slothful making others suffer
for us, did nobleness ever lie." [18]

George Sand uses these words: "There is only one sole virtue in the
world — the eternal sacrifice of self."

George Eliot sings:

17. *Sartor Resartus*, quoted by Bishop Boyd Carpenter in his *Permanent Elements
of Religion*, 350, 351. [ED.] The three quotations that follow are from Boyd-Car-
penter's work.
18. *Past and Present*.

> May I reach
> That purest heaven; be to other souls
> The cup of strength in some great agony.
>
> .   .   .   .   .   .
>
> So shall I join the choir invisible,
> Whose music is the gladness of the world.

Another writer [19] expresses himself as follows: "You talk of self as the motive to exertion; I tell you it is the abnegation of self which has wrought out all that is noble, all that is good, all that is useful, nearly all that is ornamental, in the world."

Our American philosopher, Emerson, says: "A man was born, not for prosperity, but to suffer for the benefit of others, like the noble rock-maple, which all round our villages bleeds for the service of man." [20]

Let us hear the great German, the poet Goethe: "Everything cries out to us that we must renounce. Thou must go without, go without! That is the everlasting song which every hour, all our life through, hoarsely sings to us: Die, and come to life; for so long as this is not accomplished thou art but a troubled guest upon an earth of gloom." [21]

Matthew Arnold, from whom these last quotations are taken, expounds these words of Jesus: "He that loveth his life shall lose it; and he that hateth his life in this world shall keep it unto life eternal." "Whosoever will come after me, let him renounce himself, and take up his cross daily, and follow me." He tells us that these words contain the secret of Jesus, and says: "Perhaps there is no other maxim of Jesus which has such a combined stress of evidence for it, and may be taken as so eminently his." This is the secret by which his gospel, says Arnold, brought life and immortality to light, and it is repeated by each one of the four gospel writers.

The writer has often thought of a remark made by a principal of a normal school in a New England State. This principal was a lady who had been brought up in the strict ways of a religious denomination which in her childhood was inclined to be severe in many of its requirements, but she had changed with the change of her church and had become liberal in her views. She asked one day, "Why is it that when I want a faithful teacher in my school, I seek a young woman brought up in the old strict ways in which I myself no longer believe?"

Do we not come, in what has been said, to the root of the difficulty? It

---

19. Whyte Melville, *Bones and I.*   20. Emerson, *Method of Nature.*
21. M. Arnold, *Literature and Dogma*, 186, 187.

is better for men to be called upon even by superstition and false religion to make self-sacrifice, than to lead a life of self-indulgence; and a certain so-called liberalizing tendency in all the churches has been over-inclined to say simply: Thou mayest do this, thou mayest do that; go to the theater, dance, play cards, enjoy a good horse race, etc. Now, if this teaching be true, it is only half of the truth. We need not now enter into the question of dancing, card-playing, etc. If the reader objects to these, he will see an argument in what has been said for his convictions. If the reader regards these as innocent recreations, then he will, perhaps, be more keenly aware than before how near to their use is their abuse. If the old restrictions are removed, new ones equally, nay, more severe, are raised by the duty to love and serve our fellows, and to make of the earth God's kingdom.

A young lad, full of the enthusiasm of humanity and eager for self-sacrifice, once said: "Father, I almost feel sorry that slavery has been abolished, and that I can have no part in that struggle." Alas! evils still exist, evils as bad as slavery, and those who fight the world, the flesh, and the devil will still have opportunity to suffer. Frequently men will not speak well of them, but will turn them the cold shoulder, will malign, slander, and persecute them. Christ said to the men of his day: "Woe unto you! for ye build the sepulchers of the prophets, and your fathers killed them." [22] These words express a permanent historical truth. We are all brave with respect to the struggles of the past, and we honor the memory of those we would have helped to persecute had we lived in their day. When the twentieth century is well advanced, it may be found that we have been stoning those to whom our children will then be erecting monuments. The world advances, true, and in some respects it is easier to do good than before, but there is still no lack of opportunity to suffer. The cross is still a reality.

The Roman Catholic Church provides opportunities for self-renunciation the most complete. To Protestants this often appears worse than useless; but it is, nevertheless, one source of its strength. May not our own Protestant churches return from one of the mistakes of Protestantism, and in orders of deaconesses, brotherhoods, sisterhoods, and associations of lay worshipers provide a fruitful channel into which self-sacrificing efforts can flow to the glory of God and the good of our fellow men? Let us, at any rate, see to it that for us religion is something more than a "graceful and pleasing appendix to life."

22. Luke XI, 47.

SOCIAL SOLIDARITY [1]

Editor's introduction. During his days as a graduate student in Germany, Ely "was most impressed with the idea of social solidarity. He felt that Knies had the truth when he informed his classes that there was no such thing as a science of political economy apart from the rest of society." [2] He became convinced that no aspect of human existence could be abstracted from the rest, for life was a complex of interacting and interrelated forces.

The concept remained basic to his later work. Indeed, he later summed up his services to social Christianity under the heading, "I Preach Social Solidarity." [3] He referred to the section on social solidarity as the central concept of *The Social Law of Service.* In Chapter vi of that work he shows how the idea of social solidarity is emphasized in true religion, literature, science, politics, and economics.

❖ ❖ ❖ ❖

Nothing in that associated life of man which we call society is more remarkable than social solidarity. Social solidarity is a principle which underlies a large proportion of all social facts, but one which has received comparatively little attention, and which is probably grasped in its full import by no one. It means so much, and reaches out in so many directions into the social life of men, that it is difficult to give anything like an adequate idea of its true significance. Doubtless we must know more about social solidarity than we do before it will be possible to frame a perfect definition of this principle, which is at the same time a mighty social force. However, there are some things we may say about it.

Social solidarity means the oneness of human interests; it signifies the dependence of man upon man, both in good things and in evil things. Social solidarity means that our true welfare is not an individual matter purely, but likewise a social affair: our weal is common weal; we thrive

1. *The Social Law of Service,* chap. vi, 127–40.
2. Everett, *Religion in Economics,* 79.   3. *Ground Under Our Feet,* 87.

235

only in a commonwealth; our exaltation is the exaltation of our fellows, their elevation is our enlargement. Social solidarity implies not only fellowship in interests and responsibilities, but that unity in nature which is brought before us by the expression "human brotherhood." Social solidarity signifies not only that man needs association with his fellow men, but that he shares with them their sins and their sufferings. Our sin is sin for others; their sin is our sin. There is no such thing either as purely individual sin, or a purely individual righteousness.

Although social philosophy and natural science are just beginning to get a glimmering of the grand truths of social solidarity, the doctrine itself is a very old one. No one has ever given clearer expression to it in its ethical and religious bearings than the apostle Paul. Human sin comes to us through the human race. The unity of the race is shown in its sin-taint. We are one in our evil character, and in our wrongdoing in which this evil character terminates. This is what is meant in the statement that in Adam we have all sinned. The sin of Adam is not imputed to us in any mechanical fashion, but we have the nature of Adam; that is, the race-nature. "By one man sin entered into the world, and death by sin; and so death passed upon all men, in that all have sinned." "In Adam all die." This states the law of social solidarity on its passive side; but it is stated with equal plainness in its active aspects: "For as by one man's disobedience many were made sinners, so by the obedience of one shall many be made righteous." "For as in Adam all die, even so in Christ shall all be made alive."

The doctrine of social solidarity is brought forward again and again throughout the entire Bible, from Genesis to Revelation, and is, indeed, one of the most remarkable features of this wonderful book. It is clearly expressed in that part of the Bible which deals with the human race before the time of Abraham; and the entire history of the Jews, both in their internal relations and their relations to foreign nations, emphasizes social solidarity. The nation rejoices together and suffers together; the nation partakes of the benefits of the righteousness of the righteous, and is punished on account of the wrongdoings of the wicked. The active power of a few righteous men is told us in the history of Abraham's pleading for Sodom, the city of Lot. The Lord promised that should but ten righteous men be found in the city, it would not be destroyed for the ten's sake. But when Israel departs from God and no longer maintains righteous relations among men, and when the rich oppress the poor and the strong make a prey of the feeble, then the nation is led away into cap-

tivity. And this is all easily enough understood. It is the legitimate outcome of natural laws established by God. And these laws are still opera-
tive, and their working in the history of Israel is written for our
admonition.

When we come to the New Testament we have [sic] taught, with even
greater force, the law of social solidarity. But there is that difference
which has been pointed out in general between the Old and the New
Testaments. The law is not merely national but universal, and it becomes
more intensive. If we collectively, as well as individually, seek the kingdom of God, all material blessings will be added unto us. Let it not be
forgotten that it is the kingdom which we are to seek, and a kingdom is a
social state. Many a theologian interprets the passage as if it read, individual salvation, and not the kingdom of God. The few may prosper materi-
ally through unrighteous social relations, but is only through right social
relations that the many can thrive. "Righteousness exalteth a nation." So
long as wrong relations exist among men, the righteous man, the man who
seeks the kingdom of God, may suffer in material things on account of his
righteousness. A mistake is often made by a too narrow interpretation of
Christ's words. When we forget that Christ spoke of the coming of his
kingdom continually, and always had this kingdom in his mind, we are
apt to interpret individually what he intended should be taken as applicable to society. When a condition of things exists like that found in Jerusalem in Christ's time, a man may seek the kingdom of God, and yet may
be persecuted even unto death. In the Epistle to the Hebrews we read of
the prophets who subdued kingdoms and did many wonderful works, and
of whom the world was not worthy; that they were stoned and sawn
asunder; that "they wandered about in sheepskins and goatskins; being
destitute, afflicted, and tormented."

This oneness of men was peculiarly close among the followers of
Christ, for they are spoken of again and again as "one body." "We are
one body in Christ, and everyone members one of another." In another
place it is said we are members of Christ's body, "of his flesh and of his
bones." Christ ardently longed for a more perfect union with his disciples
than that which existed, and he prayed for his disciples that remarkable
prayer recorded in the seventeenth chapter of the gospel according to St.
John, containing these words: "Neither pray I for these alone, but for
them also which shall believe on me through their word; that they all may
be one; as thou, Father, art in me, and I in thee, that they also may be one
in us: that the world may believe that thou hast sent me. And the glory

which thou gavest me I have given them; that they may be one, even as we are one."

If we read the words of Christ in the light of this doctrine of social solidarity, we shall find in them a meaning which probably has escaped most of us. This doctrine does not take away anything from what we have rightly held dear, but it adds new fullness and depth to Christ's teachings. We find Christ again and again rebuking those who would separate themselves from their fellows, who thought they could exalt themselves above their fellows, and believed that they were free from the wrongs which prevailed all about them. Again and again Christ convicts those self-righteous people of their iniquities. One of the most remarkable instances is given in the narrative of the woman taken in the very act of sin. She was brought to Christ, and he was reminded of the law of Moses that such a woman should suffer death. He was asked what should be done with her. Christ commanded that he who was without sin should cast the first stone, and "they which heard it went out one by one, beginning at the eldest, even unto the last." This by no means signifies that each one of those Pharisees had been guilty of this very act, but that they all shared in the common guilt, for they had not done what might have been done to banish sin and to restore men to righteousness. They neglected sinners and did not seek to save the lost.

Social solidarity relieves the weak and erring, it is very true, of a part of their individual guilt; and for this reason doubtless Christ was so gentle with this class, but on the whole it increases individual responsibility immensely. This is unconsciously admitted in the very general desire to escape social responsibility. We are responsible to a certain extent for all the poverty and sin and suffering about us. An entire city is guilty on account of the murder which occurs in some alley in a slum; yet whoever utters a word publicly which tends to separate men out from the common lot of their fellows, and to assist them in an evasion of their share of social responsibility, is a speaker sure of a warm welcome, and what he says will pass readily from newspaper to newspaper throughout the entire length and breadth of the land.

Writers of deep insight have given frequent expression to the great truths of social solidarity. Hawthorne says: "While there is a single guilty person in the universe, each innocent one must feel his innocence tortured by that guilt." Margaret Fuller utters a similar thought in these words: "While one man remains base, no man can be altogether great and noble." Matthew Arnold expresses the principle of social solidarity in these words: "Culture, or the study of perfection, leads us to conceive of no perfection as being real which is not a general perfection, embracing all our fellow men with whom we have to do. Such is the sympathy which binds humanity together that we are, indeed, as our religion says, 'members of one body,' and if 'one member suffer, all the members suffer with it.' Individual perfection is impossible so long as the rest of mankind are not perfected along with us."

Man is the son of man, the blood of the race flows in his veins. If we trace back our ancestry we find that the lines of our descent cross and recross almost to infinity. Thus it is a true saying that "society gives us ancestors." Recent interest in families awakened by organizations like the Daughters of the Revolution, shows how all the old New England families and all the old Virginia families are related, and closer research gives an immense network embracing both sections. The lines in reality extend much farther than anyone thinks, because in certain directions these lines are not pleasing and consequently not followed out. We lose the threads which would enable us to trace back our ancestry very soon, but we can go far enough to furnish at least strong evidences of a unity of considerable proportion of the race, and science can carry the proof much farther. There is a race-blood given as our inheritance, carrying with it tendencies and capacities. Man is born into a moral atmosphere; he breathes it in and shares in its guilt and in its excellence. At first the moral quality is given, and the early development of personality takes place on the basis of what is given. Responsibility of the individual increases with age. The individual is first a result, but later becomes a cause. Early individual irresponsibility is recognized by the courts of all civilized lands, equally with growing responsibility.

Investigations into causes of physical infirmities, like deafness and blindness, show very generally wrongdoing on the part of some ancestor. Quite frequently this wrongdoing takes the form indicated by alcoholism. The child suffers for sins committed before his birth. Investigations into causes of crime and pauperism show us a network of evil forces indicated by the two words "heredity" and "environment," surrounding thousands and hundreds of thousands at their very birth. Those more fortunate ones, well born physically, mentally, and morally, are apt to turn away in scorn from the unfortunate and degenerate classes, and to neglect the opportunities which are abundant to improve the conditions under which they live. It was to such as these that Christ gave warning that those upon whom the tower in Siloam fell were not guilty above all the other dwellers at Jerusalem, but that unless they repented they should likewise perish. So it is with us; wretchedness and disease travel from class to class and from individual to individual.

We may trace social solidarity into every department of our common life. If we take it on its physiological side, we find that physically we suffer together: "The whole creation groaneth and travaileth in pain together until now." This was understood in a general way long ago, but in the modern study of disease it has received scientific demonstration. The whole world is bound together in the chains of disease. Mohammedans gather together in multitudes in a city in Persia at a time of unusual drought, and cholera begins to make its way round the world. There is a crop failure in five provinces of Russia, and during the ensuing famine Russian peasants die by the thousand. In this suffering region we find the origin of the grippe, which has carried away hundreds of thousands in Europe and the United States. Still more closely are all parts of one country, and more especially of one city, connected together in health and disease. Says Dr. Cyrus Edson in a remarkable article on the subject: "While the communities have, through their Boards of Health, prepared for the battle with contagious diseases, and while they can trust with perfect confidence to their defenses, the work of the men employed in these boards reveals to them more clearly day by day the close connection which exists between the health interests of all members of the community, be these rich or poor; the microbe of disease is no respecter of persons; it cannot be guarded against by any bank account, however large." Nevertheless, it is true that a bank account is a help, although no sure guarantee. Persons of wealth live much longer than the poor, but in so far as they escape the common consequences of disease their moral responsibility increases, and morally they are the more guilty if they do not use their larger resources to establish conditions of health for all.

Social solidarity may also be traced in things intellectual. Our intellectual products are peculiarly individual, and yet they are all dependent upon conditions which no one man has established or could establish. A Shakespeare could not arise in the heart of Africa, nor could we find a Tennyson today in China. Man has achieved his greatest and best in intellectual efforts of every sort when surrounded by a large life. When man speaks nobly the race speaks through him and he speaks for the race. Witness the great eras of literature and art in Greece, in Rome, in England.

Political solidarity is something so old and so familiar that we need scarcely more than mention it. We are all responsible for the political acts of our country, both with our persons and with our property. If those who manage the affairs of the nation act foolishly, we may lose both our goods and our lives. Punishment for the sins of the rulers is a fact as old as history, yet the rulers of nations do not stand alone. As John Wesley says, "God frequently punishes a people for the sins of their rulers, because they are generally partakers of their sins in one kind or other."

It is a peculiar fact that social solidarity grows with the growth of civilization; men come closer and closer together and the unity of the race becomes more and more intensive. This is best of all illustrated in that department of life in which it is most marked, namely economics. To a greater and greater extent we are dependent on others for the conditions of our own prosperity. It has been pointed out in modern society that man is dependent for his economic well-being, first upon what he himself produces; second, upon the exertions of others who produce the things which he wants in exchange for his own products; third, upon the efforts of others who produce the same things which he produces, giving us competition among sellers; fourth, upon the efforts of those who want the things that he wants, giving us competition among purchasers. Along one line, then, man is dependent upon himself; along three lines, he is dependent upon the efforts of others. The man who produces only shoes would starve to death did not others work for him, while he works for them. As the division of labor is carried farther and farther, economic dependence increases, and thus social solidarity grows.

The author has a friend connected with a hospital whose experience shows what an awful thing it is for a man to get out of human relations, either because he has sundered the essential ties of humanity, or because they have been sundered for him by others, or because, for him, perchance, they have never existed. The waifs, the strays, the morally abandoned, frequently have no special tie binding them to anyone. This friend of the author makes inquiry into the personal relations of those coming to the hospital; he asks especially, in case of possible death, "Who cares for you, what relative have you?" and like questions. Frequently the reply is, "No one." To upbuild human character in men you must establish for them right social relations. On the other hand, we fulfill our own mission and develop our own true individuality, not in isolation, but in society, and by bringing ourselves in body and mind into harmony with the laws of social solidarity.

THE STATE[1]

Editor's introduction. Ely was convinced that in modern society the role of the state, broadly conceived, was bound to increase in certain areas. Those steeped in the individualism so strong in certain parts of America frequently criticized this aspect of his work; for them the increase of state activity was "unnatural." Many of Ely's writings took issue with them. In his widely used *Outlines*, for example, he declared:

We have noted a tendency to increase public activities as civilization develops. . . . *As men come into closer and more vital contact with each other their activities tend to become social, conscious, and ethical.* By no means all of this tendency culminates in governmental action, but much of it does so, and whatever we may conclude as to the wisdom of such action we must not beg the question by calling it unnatural.

Ely firmly believed in private property and private industry; indeed, as he saw it, part of the state's task was to protect them. His rule was, *"Public industry in the monopolistic and private industry in the competitive field seems to be the only feasible or natural law."* [2]

As in most of his work, religious and social views informed each other; his interpretation of Christianity contributed to his positive assessment of the state. Rarely did he put it more strongly than in his introduction to the American edition of Canon W. H. Fremantle's Bampton lectures: "The legislator in city, state, or nation is likewise a minister in Christ's church, and he is guilty of violation of a sacred trust if he does not endeavor to bring to pass the kingdom of God in his sphere." [3] The full expression of his religious views of the state emerged in the essay that follows. The concluding paragraph was significant; henceforth he turned his attention to working with "men of all denominations . . . in the administrative, legislative, and judicial branches of government for the estab-

1. *The Social Law of Service,* chap. VIII, 161–75.
2. *Outlines of Economics* (N.Y., 1893), 253, 304.
3. *The World as the Subject of Redemption,* ii.

lishment of righteousness." As educator and economist, he turned to the public sphere, and his avocation as a spokesman for the social gospel dropped into the background.

❖ ❖ ❖ ❖

The word State is, in the United States especially, liable to be misunderstood, when it is used in its generic sense. Our United States is made up of forty-five commonwealths, and these are called states. But State in its most general sense is not equivalent to state in the sense of the American commonwealth. The State means the entire American nation, politically organized. The American State embraces the American in all his political relations, as the German State embraces the German in all his political relations. The English State and the French State similarly embrace the Englishmen and Frenchmen respectively in all their political relations. The Americans, however, like the Germans, have a federal State, while the English and the French have a unitary State. We might therefore, in the present chapter, when speaking of Americans, substitute for State "the nation and the commonwealth," because both make up our State; but the substitution would be objectionable, first, because it would involve the use of three words where one is sufficient, and this would frequently be awkward; second, because it is desirable that we should become accustomed to the use of the word State in its generic sense and remember our relations to nation and commonwealth alike.

Commonwealth is often used as equivalent of State, as later in this chapter. If a commonwealth has full and complete sovereignty, it is of course a State in its complete sense. In the United States, the nation and commonwealth must be taken together to give complete sovereignty. The word State is used in this broad sense both in John Wesley's "Sunday Service" and in the revised book of Common Prayer of the Protestant Episcopal Church in the petition, "O Lord, save the State."

Family, Church, and State are frequently mentioned together as the three pre-eminently divine institutions known to man. It is claimed by some that the State is the chief institution of these three, and that if we select one institution as above all others divine it must be the State. Such a comparison manifestly cannot be understood too literally. If several institutions are established by God, it can hardly be strictly true that one is more divine than another. What is meant is this: That God works through the State in carrying out his purposes more universally than through any other institution; that it takes the first place among his instrumentalities.

The family is clearly a divine institution. The Bible leaves no doubt about this in the mind of anyone who accepts the Bible as true. Destroy the family and you destroy one of the fundamental conditions of that righteousness which God desires to establish. Yet the family is not inclusive of all men, like the State. Most men are undoubtedly born into this world as members of a family, and not to be included in a family at one's birth is abnormal and most unfortunate. Yet as men grow up they must leave the family, if, as not infrequently happens, death has not already destroyed it. Many of those scattered elements of former families unite and form new families; yet there are always large numbers living isolated lives, forming no part of any family. Not only has this always been the case, but it always must be; and there is some reason to believe that it will be the case to even a greater extent in the future than at present. There are physical reasons why many men and women should not marry and establish families, and there are economic reasons. Men otherwise amiable and intelligent occasionally lack the capacity to support a family according to the standard of life suitable to their station. Physical and economic reasons for a single life will be more appreciated, as men become more conscientious about assuming responsibilities toward others. Disparity between the number of men and the number of women in most parts of the earth is a cause of singleness. It is not to the point to reply that the whole number of men in the world is nearly equal to the number of women, provided they are not evenly distributed. A bachelor in Montana cannot marry a spinster in Germany. The more dangerous avocations of men tend to reduce the supply of available husbands. Again there are humanitarian and religious motives which keep men and women from marrying. Christ ranked such motives very high, and promises great rewards to those who for his sake give up husband or wife. Much more might be said about the family and its limitations, but space will not admit of it. The State includes now and always has included within its embrace all civilized men and women, but only some of these, and not all, belong to distinct families or households.

The Church, as we understand it, began to exist less than two thousand years ago; but long before the apostles of Christ established the Church, God worked in the world, and the institution through which he worked above all others was the State. His chosen people, the Jews, constituted a commonwealth established, we are told, by God. The revelation of God to the Jews, and through the Jews to the rest of the world, is found in the laws and in the life of the Hebrew State. These laws and this life were an inspiration to David and the other poets of Israel, and they were the prime object of solicitude to the prophets. The prophets, in fact, were statesmen, or, if you will, politicians, in the nobler sense of the word. When Christ came his mind was full of the kingdom or commonwealth in which righteousness should prevail. The coming of the kingdom was proclaimed by Christ, and it was his followers who began to talk about a Church as distinct from the State. The Church was early established, and it has increased in numbers and in power, but it has never embraced more than a minority of civilized human beings. There have always been followers of God who have not been adherents of any visible Church, any regularly established ecclesiastical organization, but these are all embraced within the State, and the State also includes those outside sinners, those unregenerate persons who do not love God and man, and do not seek righteousness, among whom the Church works.

We must ever remember that Christ and his apostles always recognized the authority of the State as divine in character even under most trying and perplexing circumstances. Christ counseled obedience to the Roman emperor, and St. Paul uses well-known words which could scarcely be more explicit:

For there is no power but of God: the powers that be are ordained of God.

Whosoever therefore resisteth the power, resisteth the ordinance of God. . . .

For rulers are not a terror to good works, but to the evil. Wilt thou then not be afraid of the power? do that which is good, and thou shalt have praise of the same:

For he is the minister of God to thee for good. But if thou do that which is evil, be afraid; for he beareth not the sword in vain: for he is the minister of God. . . .

For this cause pay ye tribute also. . . .

Render therefore to all their dues: tribute to whom tribute is due; custom to whom custom; fear to whom fear; honor to whom honor.[4]

It has also been pointed out that while Christ manifested no respect for mere wealth or assumed titles, he never failed to show obedience and honor to the regularly constituted public authorities.[5]

So essential is the State to the work of God in this world, that if

4. Romans XIII, 1–7.
5. By Rev. F. W. Robertson in his sermon, "The Message of the Church to Men of Wealth," in the volume of his *Sermons*.

missionaries penetrate into a stateless region, say, the heart of Africa, and convert men to Christianity, those men will at once form a new State, or become incorporated as part of an old State. All great and glorious deeds of men have taken place within a State, and the highest achievements of the mind of man have been preceded or accompanied by a large and expanding national life.

The State has been described as a continuous, conscious organism, and a moral personality, which has its foundations laid in the nature of man. It is not the product of the will of man. Men have never come together in a state of nature, and then by the formation of a State passed out of a condition of nature into an organized political existence. The State grows up naturally, spontaneously, and men are born into the State, and the State is one of the forces making them what they are. The basis of the State is human nature, and the State is the natural condition of men. Some would have us to go to savages to find out what is natural, but Aristotle has taught us that it is the perfect man, and not the imperfect man, who can reveal to us what is natural, just as we look at a perfect and not an imperfect specimen of fruit to understand the nature of the fruit.

Aristotle described an order of development when he said the State was formed for the sake of life, but that it was continued for the sake of the good life. This means that the State is necessary in order that man may live at all. Its first purpose was the provision of material resources for the nourishment of the animal life, but the higher, nobler purpose of the State is not the material life, but the soul and mind of man. As soon as the means of life are provided, we must aspire to the good life. The ignoble doctrine that the State is a necessary evil was as far from Aristotle as it has been from all great political thinkers. The State was to him not only a necessary good, but the highest and noblest of all good.

For a long time previous to the Protestant Reformation, false notions concerning the Church obscured the idea of the State. It was held by leaders in the Church that the Church was noble because it was concerned with spiritual things, and that the State was base because it was concerned with temporal things. Consequently it was maintained that the Church should dominate the State, as the spirit ought to rule the body. The rulers of the State were to be the servants of priests, humbly doing their bidding. The Protestant Reformation meant the exaltation of the State. The truth was proclaimed with emphasis that the work which God intended his people to do while on earth was to concern themselves with the things of the world, and to establish here on earth righteous relations among men. The wide separation between things secular and things sacred was denied. The whole earth was held sacred. Nothing was secular in any bad sense of the word except sin, and the purpose of Christians was to combat it. As soon as it was recognized that the work given to Christians was the establishment of righteousness, the function of the magistrate became as sacred as that of the priest. One of the reformers uses these words, expressing a belief of early Protestantism: "The distinction of ecclesiastical and profane laws can find no place among Christians. The magistrate himself is holy and not profane, his powers and laws holy, his sword holy." This exalted idea of the State was followed by most momentous practical consequences. The State began to concern itself with education, and schools and universities became State institutions, and the educational work of the State continued until in the most enlightened Protestant nations every child was guaranteed at least a minimum amount of education. The cry of the poor became a matter of concern to the civil authorities, and in Protestant Teutonic countries the right of man to at least a bare livelihood was guaranteed by the Poor Laws. The obligation to maintain the poor was for the first time assumed by civil society in the sixteenth century, after the Protestant Reformation. Another consequence of the exaltation of the State was the curtailment of the functions of ecclesiastical courts and the extension of the function of the civil courts, to which all alike, clergy included, ultimately became subject. If the civil sword was holy and civil justice divine, why should there exist a separate ecclesiastical jurisdiction arrogating superiority to itself?[6]

The only limit to the functions of the State is that laid down by Aristotle; the general principle cannot be stated better than he stated it: "It is the duty of the State to do whatever is in its power to promote the good life." Any other limitation is false to the fundamental principles of Protestantism, both ancient and modern. The venerable Hooker repudiated with these vigorous words the doctrine that the State existed only for the sake of material goods: "A gross error it is to think that regal power ought to serve for the good of the body, and not for the good of the soul; for men's temporal peace, and not their eternal safety; and if

6. The author does not understand that there is anything in this paragraph which a Roman Catholic must of necessity reject. Every enlightened Roman Catholic acknowledges that those claiming to speak and act for the Church have made many mistakes. The writer, however, speaks from the Protestant point of view, but can only rejoice if Roman Catholics also can accept what is here stated, as he is convinced many of them can.

God had ordained kings for no other end and purpose but only to fat up men like hogs and see that they have their mast?" [7]

The imperfect political life of our time, especially in our own country, may be thought by some to be antagonistic to the doctrine of the divinity of the State. The divinity of an institution, however, does not mean its perfection in its actual existence, but only in its idea. God has given us the idea, and we have carried it out poorly. The State is, alas, corrupt and degraded; but so have been also the Church and the family at many times and in many places. The polygamy of the Mormons no more militates against the divine idea of the family than the corruption of New York politics against the divine idea of the State. Government is divine in idea and purpose, but those in New York City who administer government are too generally unworthy of their high trust. One reason why political life in the United States is so unworthy is because the true idea of the State has become so obscured. The nature of offenses against the purity of political life as offenses directly against God has not in recent years been adequately emphasized. Yet we may feel encouraged when we compare American political life with the life of the Church in the period preceding the Protestant Reformation. How could a President of the United States be conceived as living a life so debased as that of some of the popes, or others who have held high positions in the Church?

Church and State are much alike in their nature and in their purposes, and it is because they are so much alike that there has been so much conflict between them — conflict of which we shall hear more in the United States in future years than we have in the past. It has been held by some Protestants, like the Lutheran Rothe,[8] that the State in idea is the Church, and that when the perfect State comes it will be the Church. He of course speaks of an idea to be realized in a distant future, but he distinctly states

7. Hooker, *Ecclesiastical Polity*. This is a reprint of the text, but it appears to be corrupt or incomplete, although the meaning is clear enough. [ED.] Richard Hooker (1553?–1600) prepared his *Laws of Ecclesiastical Polity* (1594–97) as a defense of the Church of England against Puritan claims on the one hand, and those of Roman Catholicism on the other. The several modern editions of the work are of varying quality. On some of the problems of modernizing the original text, see, e.g., the introduction by R. W. Church to his edition of Book I (1876).

8. [ED.] Richard Rothe (1799–1867) taught at the theological seminary of Wittenberg, and at the universities of Heidelberg and Bonn. He worked first in the fields of biblical exegesis and church history, and then in systematic and speculative theology. He believed that the task of Protestantism was gradually to emancipate Christianity from the ecclesiastical form to the ethical-humane form, and that redemption through the kingdom of God was finally to be fulfilled in the organism of Christian State.

that the Church must decrease and the State increase. This doctrine cannot be elaborated in this place, but it may be asked what need there is of a separate institution for righteousness when the whole of social and individual life and all institutions are permeated with the Christian spirit. We are told, indeed, that there shall be no temple in the New Jerusalem. But certainly we are yet far from this New Jerusalem, and we must work for the extension of the Church, while we at the same time endeavor to instill Christian principles into our entire public as well as private life.

It is true that the main purpose of the State is the religious purpose. Religious laws are the only laws which ought to be enacted. But what are religious laws? Certainly not in the United States laws establishing any particular sectarian views or any theological tenets, in regard to which there may be diversity of opinion, but laws designed to promote the good life. Factory acts, educational laws, laws for the establishment of parks and of playgrounds for children, laws securing honest administration of justice, laws rendering the courts accessible to the poor as well as the rich—all these are religious laws in the truest sense of the word. The Church can go in many respects far beyond the State. It can place ideals ahead of the State to which the State must gradually approach; it can rebuke and inspire the State; it can quicken the consciences of men, of those who rule and of those who obey. The Church always has the opportunity of doing work neglected by the State, and in particular the dogmas of religion are committed to the Church. Theology in the narrow sense of the term belongs to the Church and not to the modern State. On the other hand, let the Church see to it that all her actions and teachings strengthen and purify the State. Let all Christians see to it that they put as much as possible, not of doctrine or creed into the State constitution, but of Christian life and practice into the activity of the State, working, to be sure, to change the constitution in so far as this may stand in the way of righteousness. The nation must be recognized fully as a Christian nation.

Love of country must show itself in service, in the upbuilding of the institutions of the country. The schools of the country must be nourished. If they lack religious instruction, let the churches supplement the schools on this side. If the conversion of the world is our object, we will not attempt to pull a few out of the world, nor will we so much endeavor to separate our children from the public schools as to make these public schools what they should be. We will establish our centers of religious influences at the seat of State universities and reap the harvest in them which awaits Christian effort. If we have our own separate denominational schools we will see to it that they minister to the entire life of the State, and help, not hinder, public effort.

This serves as illustration, and illustration may be continued indefinitely, but one more illustration may be given to emphasize the thought that real patriotism finds expression in acts, not merely words. The matter of tax-payment is one which in its ethical bearing a Christian cannot neglect. The apostle Paul commanded Christians to pay tribute, which was a sign of subjugation; only conquered nations pay tribute. How much more should Christians pay their full share of self-imposed taxes, common contributions for common purposes! And remember, he who neglects to pay his fair share places a heavier burden on some one else, presumably one of the weaker elements in society, as widow or orphan. What would Christ say of tax-dodging coupled with hurrahs for the stars and stripes on the Fourth of July? That is a sort of patriotism to be spewed out of one's mouth.

What in short we especially need, and what the Christian standpoint necessarily carries with it, is emphasis on duties rather than rights. This is a first condition of civic regeneration.

There are now hundreds of various religious sects, and the unity of the various denominations seems remote, even with the best and most earnest efforts. One sort of unity of Christians, however, is found in the State. Men of all denominations act together in the administrative, legislative, and judicial branches of government for the establishment of righteousness. Let this unity be valued at its true worth, let it be cultivated and as much meaning put into it as at any time the circumstances will admit!

PART THREE

❖

Walter Rauschenbusch

1861-1918

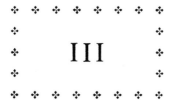

WALTER RAUSCHENBUSCH

AN INTRODUCTION

WALTER RAUSCHENBUSCH, called by Reinhold Niebuhr [1] the "most brilliant and generally satisfying exponent" of social Christianity, came into national prominence after 1907 with the unexpected popularity of his *Christianity and the Social Crisis.* From then until his death in 1918 he produced six more books, two of them major ones, and became America's best-known Christian social prophet. His career as a social gospel advocate had in fact begun some twenty years before he became famous.

He was born in Rochester, New York, on October 4, 1861. His father, Karl August Rauschenbusch, had come to the United States fifteen years earlier as a Lutheran missionary, but had subsequently been won over to Baptist views; in 1858 he had become a professor in the German department of the Rochester Theological Seminary.[2] Reared in a pietistic German Baptist environment, Walter actually began his formal education in Germany, where he lived during the later 1860's, and continued it in Rochester for ten years after his return. In 1879 a conversion experience led to his baptism on confession of faith. Though his theological interpretation of the event later became "liberalized," he always appreciated the value of this "tender, mysterious experience." [3] In that same year he went again to Germany, where he studied at the Gymnasium at Gütersloh. After graduating in 1883 with first honors in classical studies, he traveled in Germany and studied briefly at the University of Berlin. He had decided to enter the ministry, and on his return to the United States was

1. *An Interpretation of Christian Ethics* (N.Y., 1935), preface.
2. See Carl E. Schneider, "Americanization of Karl August Rauschenbusch, 1826–1899," *Church History,* XXIV (1955), 3–14; Walter Rauschenbusch, *Leben und Wirken von August Rauschenbusch* (Cleveland, 1901).
3. For a brief "spiritual autobiography," see "The Kingdom of God," reproduced below, 264–67.

allowed simultaneously to complete his senior year at the University of
Rochester and begin his studies at the Rochester Theological Seminary.
Like many another theological student, he was torn between a teaching
and a preaching ministry, until a summer pastorate in Louisville resolved
the issue. Then he wrote, "It is now no longer my fond hope to be a
learned theologian and write big books; I want to be a pastor, powerful
with men, preaching to them Christ as the man in whom their affections
and energies can find the satisfaction for which mankind is groaning." [4]

After graduating from the German department of the seminary in 1885
and from the regular course the following year, he accepted his first regular pastorate, the Second German Baptist Church in New York City. Its
location on West 45th Street (a new building erected in 1889 on West
43rd is still standing) was at the edge of a depressed area known as Hell's
Kitchen. Here the young pastor, schooled in individualistic conservatism,
was confronted directly by the pressing social problems of the times—the
terrible human effects of insecurity, unemployment, poverty, wretched
housing, malnutrition, disease, ignorance, and crime. He supported Henry
George, author of *Progress and Poverty* and advocate of the single tax, in
his campaign for mayor. Rauschenbusch later wrote, "I owe my first
awakening to the world of social problems to the agitation of Henry
George in 1886, and wish here to record my lifelong debt to this single-
minded apostle of a great truth." [5] During this period he began to read
widely in the literature of social analysis and reform, and to participate in
movements for social betterment. In 1889 he became a founder and editor
of *For the Right,* a short-lived paper intended for working people.

When Rauschenbusch first arrived in New York, his only idea had

4. Quoted by Dores R. Sharpe, *Walter Rauschenbusch* (N.Y., 1942), 54.
5. *Christianizing the Social Order* (N.Y., 1912), 394. Henry George (1839-97) had
a firsthand acquaintance with poverty. He dropped out of high school early, and
worked at many jobs. Walking the streets of New York at the age of thirty, he was
shocked by the contrast between the brilliance of its wealth and the bleakness of its
slums into a resolve to devote himself to a career of reform. Within a decade he had
worked out a social philosophy founded on the belief that men must be given equal
opportunity not only legally but economically as well. Convinced that poverty must
accompany progress so long as increasing land values forced those who worked the
land to pay more and more for the privilege of doing so, he proposed in *Progress
and Poverty* (1879) — which eventually became a best-seller — that the state should
appropriate the unearned increment in the value of land by imposing a "single tax"
upon it. Besides those who accepted his panacea, many others who, like Rauschenbusch, respected his insistence that man can be a social creator and can use the state
as a beneficent instrument, were influenced by him. See George R. Geiger, *The
Social Philosophy of Henry George* (N.Y., 1933).

been "to save souls in the ordinarily accepted religious sense." His social concern came less from within the church than from a confrontation with the condition of working people and with the secular reform movement. But how was he to relate the old evangelical passion with the new one for social action? "When I had begun to apply my previous religious ideas to the conditions I found, I discovered that they didn't fit," he later explained. His friends were soon urging him to give up his social work for "Christian work"; but feeling deeply that "the work was Christ's work, . . . I went ahead, although I had to set myself against all that I had previously been taught. I had to go back to the Bible to find out whether I or my friends were right. I had to revise my whole study of the Bible. . . . All my scientific studying of the Bible was undertaken to find a basis for the Christian teaching of a social gospel." [6] He found that basis in the doctrine of the kingdom of God, which brought together his evangelical concern for individuals and his social vision of a redeemed society.

The tragedy of partial deafness, which overtook him in 1888 when he left a sickbed too soon, had the indirect benefit of giving him an opportunity to concentrate on theological questions. He took a leave from his parish in 1891 for a study of social movements in England and of the New Testament in Germany. Thereafter his theology grew more and more distinctly liberal; he adopted critical approaches to the Bible and to the history of Christianity, and identified himself with the names of Schleiermacher, Bushnell, Ritschl, Wellhausen, and Harnack.[7] His work reflected the romantic, monistic idealism that pervaded much of liberal theology. He had a passion for unity, and sought to establish a coherent relation between religion and science, faith and history, Christianity and secular culture, theology and sociology. The kingdom of God became for him the unifying force which would bind all these things together. As he explained the great change that took place in him in 1891,

So Christ's conception of the kingdom of God came to me as a new revelation. Here was the idea and purpose that had dominated the mind of the Master himself. All his teachings center about it. His life was given to it. His death was suffered for it. . . .
When the kingdom of God dominated our landscape, the perspec-

6. "The Genesis of 'Christianity and the Social Crisis,'" *Rochester Theological Seminary Bulletin* (November 1918), 51–52.
7. See *ibid.*, 54–63, for a popular exposition of his approach to biblical interpretation in his addresses to a Y.W.C.A. convention in 1915 on "The Social Background, Spirit, and Message of the Bible."

tive of life shifted into a new alignment. I felt a new security in my
social impulses. The spiritual authority of Jesus Christ would have
been sufficient to offset the weight of all the doctors, and now I
knew that I had history on my side. But in addition I found that
this new conception of the purpose of Christianity was strangely
satisfying. It responded to all the old and all the new elements of
my religious life. The saving of the lost, the teaching of the young,
the pastoral care of the poor and frail, the quickening of starved intellects, the study of the Bible, church union, political reform, the
reorganization of the industrial system, international peace — it was
all covered by the one aim of the reign of God on earth.[8]

This new revelation of the kingdom that came to him then did not lose its
freshness, but continued through the years to inform his understanding of
both religion and society. "The kingdom of God is the first and most
essential dogma of the Christian faith," he insisted years later. "It is also
the lost social ideal of Christendom. No man is a Christian in the full sense
of original discipleship until he has made the kingdom of God the controlling purpose of his life, and no man is intellectually prepared to understand Jesus Christ until he has understood the meaning of the kingdom
of God." [9]

This idea of the kingdom gave to Rauschenbusch a glowing vision of a
regenerated world, to which he gave an arresting presentation. In the eyes
of later generations his views have appeared idealistic, utopian, and
strongly tinged with the middle-class, moralistic flavor of nineteenth-
century Protestantism. But his aim was to provide a coherent view of the
world, and to state a practical philosophy for personal and social behavior. His doctrine of the kingdom was both a religious and a social one.
He believed that "the kingdom of God is divine in its origin, progress and
consummation," that it "is miraculous all the way, and is the continuous
revelation of the power, the righteousness, and the love of God." The
kingdom was "always both present and future . . . always coming, always pressing in on the present, always big with possibility, and always

8. *Christianizing the Social Order*, 93. A manuscript dated 1892, and recently discovered by Max L. Stackhouse in the Rauschenbusch Papers, entitled "The Righteousness of the Kingdom," is evidently a draft for a book (never actually completed)
by Rauschenbusch and Nathaniel Schmidt (1862–1939), a professor of Semitic languages at Colgate and later at Cornell. See Stackhouse, "Eschatology and Ethical
Method: A Structural Analysis of Contemporary Christian Social Ethics in America
with primary reference to Walter Rauschenbusch and Reinhold Niebuhr" (typed
Ph.D. thesis, Harvard University, 1964).
9. *Christianizing the Social Order*, 49.

inviting immediate action." It tended toward the progressive unity of mankind, it was "humanity organized according to the will of God," it was the purpose for which the church existed.[10] The kingdom was not a utopia — Rauschenbusch insisted that there could be no perfection on earth, but only a continual growth toward perfection. His authority for these beliefs was the teaching of Jesus concerning the kingdom, interpreted in developmental terms.

Rauschenbusch's Christology was decisively shaped by the quest for the historical Jesus. Scientific biblical study, he believed, had brought the Master out of the past into ever sharper detail. He understood Jesus as one who lived close to the Father, who was the perfect religious personality, who taught the highest ethics — the first real man, the inaugurator of a new humanity, the initiator of the kingdom.[11] Rauschenbusch's estimate of man was clearly optimistic. He saw mankind as moving upward toward the kingdom as it gained in resilience and in the capacity for change. "The swiftness of evolution in our own country," he wrote, "proves the immense latent perfectibility in human nature." [12]

After the trip abroad that led to this decisive turn of thought in 1891, Rauschenbusch returned to New York, where he became a leader in the developing social gospel.[13] He made speeches and wrote articles on social issues. To the Baptist Congress, in which for years he played a central role, he presented papers which often dealt with ethical and economic issues. In the early 1890's, he joined with other younger Baptist ministers in the formation of the Brotherhood of the Kingdom, a group that met annually for more than two decades. It became increasingly interdenominational as time went on, involving many of the nation's leaders in the

10. See "The Kingdom of God," 267. For the full development of Rauschenbusch's thought on the subject, see especially chap. XIII, "The Kingdom of God," in *A Theology for the Social Gospel* (N.Y., 1917), 131–45, from which the phrases in this paragraph are taken.

11. For the full development of his Christological thought, see chap. II, "The Social Aims of Jesus," *Christianity and the Social Crisis*, 44–92; chap. II, "The Social Christianity of Jesus," *Christianizing the Social Order*, 48–68; and chap. XIV, "The Initiator of the Kingdom of God," *A Theology for the Social Gospel*, 146–66. See also *The Social Principles of Jesus* (N.Y., 1916), a selection from which appears below. 371–77.

12. *Christianity and the Social Crisis*, 422. For the context of this sentence, see below, 336. Though he worked in the context of evolutionary thought, he was not an exponent of "inevitable" or "automatic" progress. For a discussion of this in an early article of his, see below, 271–72.

13. In 1893 he was married to Miss Pauline E. Rother, a Milwaukee schoolteacher. Five children were born of the union.

social Christian movement. Many of Rauschenbusch's ideas were first presented at gatherings of the Brotherhood.[14]

In 1897 Rochester Theological Seminary called back its able graduate as a teacher in its German department. In 1902 he became professor of church history on the regular faculty of the seminary. His history classes were popular; and though most of his writings dealt with contemporary social concerns, a historical sense informs much of his work. His approach to understanding the Bible, the kingdom of God, the church, and the social situation, was characteristically historical. He was well acquainted with the critical historical treatments of Christian origins and development. He dealt historically with the disappearance from the church of her early social vision, and offered a developmental theory of how that vision could be recovered:

> Translate the evolutionary theories into religious faith, and you have the doctrine of the kingdom of God. This combination with scientific evolutionary thought has freed the kingdom ideal of its catastrophic setting and its background of demonism, and so adapted it to the climate of the modern world.[15]

These ideas, so much in tune with the progressivism of the first decade of the twentieth century, contributed to his great popularity.

Rauschenbusch wrote *Christianity and the Social Crisis*, a book "on social questions for the Lord Christ and the people," to discharge a debt to the working people among whom he had labored for eleven years. Knowing that he was dealing with controversial matters, he was prepared for a storm of criticism—even for dismissal—when he returned from a 1907–1908 sabbatical in Germany. But the book proved to have been well timed. It went through a half a dozen editions in two years. Coming at a time when the progressive movement was rising in popularity and affecting national legislation, it touched a public which recognized the need for social changes. It came in a period when liberal theology was winning a substantial following in many churches. It was ably written, by a mature and sensitive man who had mastered the short, clear sentence and the telling metaphor. Its appeal to both religious and social sympathies awakened a response in many readers. To be sure, its interpretation of history was too sweeping and oversimplified, especially in dealing with the medieval period. Robert D. Cross has said of Rauschenbusch that "his account of

14. See C. Howard Hopkins, "Walter Rauschenbusch and the Brotherhood of the Kingdom," *Church History*, VII (1938), 138–56. Concerning his work with the Baptist Congress, see below, 290–99.
15. *Christianizing the Social Order*, 90.

the development of asceticism, of sacramentalism, of hierarchy, of dogma, reads today as virtually a parody of the extreme Protestant critique on Catholicism." [16] But such a position was quite congenial to the strongly Protestant and progressive feelings of the early twentieth century. The persuasively offered ideal of the kingdom of God on earth opened new horizons to a generation troubled by social questions. Nor was the appeal of the book limited to its own day. It has continued to stimulate and inform Christian thought. Nearly half a century after it was written, Martin Luther King, Jr., reported that the book had

> left an indelible imprint on my thinking. Of course there were points at which I differed with Rauschenbusch. I felt that he had fallen victim to the nineteenth-century "cult of inevitable progress," which led him to an unwarranted optimism concerning human nature. Moreover, he came perilously close to identifying the kingdom of God with a particular social and economic system — a temptation which the church should never give in to. But in spite of these shortcomings Rauschenbusch gave to American Protestantism a sense of social responsibility that it should never lose.[17]

Thrust into the forefront of a growing movement by the success of his book, Rauschenbusch responded unstintingly to the many calls that came to him. He accepted many invitations to preach and lecture. At a joint meeting of Baptist and Congregational leaders in Boston in 1908, he heard Washington Gladden quote from his "epoch-making book" in an address on "The Church and the Social Crisis." [18] He wrote two other major books — *Christianizing the Social Order* and *A Theology for the Social Gospel* — as well as a number of shorter ones. The depths of his own religious piety are glimpsed in a book of prayers which has been widely

16. In his introduction to a reprint of *Christianity and the Social Crisis* (N.Y., Harper Torchbooks, 1964), xiv.

17. "Pilgrimage to Nonviolence," *The Christian Century*, LXXVII (April 13, 1960), 439.

18. The text of Gladden's lecture is presented in the Gladden Papers, Box 56. Rauschenbusch wrote to Gladden on December 2, 1908: "It has been a great satisfaction to meet you thus, and to stand by your side for an hour, for, as I said at the meeting, to me you are one of the veterans who made it easier for us of the next generation to see our way and to get a hearing. You have done a noble day's work and have lived to see the reapers going out to the harvest which you helped to sow." (*Ibid.*, Box 16.) Later Rauschenbusch wrote: "I want to pay the tribute of honor to three men who were pioneers of Christian social thought in America twenty-five years ago: Washington Gladden, Josiah Strong, and Richard T. Ely. These men had matured their thought when the rest of us were young men, and they had a spirit in them which kindled and compelled us." (*Christianizing the Social Order*, 9.)

used.[19] His characteristic combination of evangelical and social themes appears in a small book for social workers, and again in a brief commentary on 1 Corinthians 13.[20] His most widely circulated work was a hand book entitled *The Social Principles of Jesus*.[21]

In all his work, Rauschenbusch set forth a fairly coherent pattern of social and ethical thought. Its sources have been examined in detail by Donovan E. Smucker, who traces four main influences: pietism, sectarianism, liberalism, and transformationism. Initially, his faith was expressed in pietist terms. Though he moved beyond this frame of reference, the sincere personal piety and evangelical concern remained. The sectarian influences came through his interest in Anabaptist history and his loyalty to the Baptist tradition.

It was liberalism, Smucker argues, that largely provided the content of his theology. The theologian most influential upon him was Albrecht Ritschl (1822–89), who taught first at Bonn and then, from 1864 until his death, at Göttingen. During Rauschenbusch's ministry, Ritschlianism was the dominant influence upon liberal theology in Germany, Britain, and America. Ritschl's concept of Christianity as an ellipse with two foci, the kingdom of God on the one hand and redemption through Jesus Christ on the other, is implicit in Rauschenbusch's own theological emphases. Many Ritschlians gave more weight to religious experience than to doctrine; Rauschenbusch insisted, rather more than some other advocates of the social gospel, on the importance of doctrine, though like Ritschl's his theology was ethical rather than metaphysical. Rauschenbusch quoted from Ritschl's most important work, *The Christian Doctrine of Justification and Reconciliation*, in crucial passages of his own works.[22] The Ritschlian influence was also strong in such American theologians as William Newton Clarke and William Adams Brown, whom Rauschenbusch likewise read and quoted.

Rauschenbusch's mature position also showed the influence of the transformationists, who envisioned the turning of man and his culture from man-centeredness to Christ-centeredness. Their hopeful attitude toward culture was based on a concept of the unity of creation and redemption. Transformationist ideas were expressed in the writings of

19. *For God and the People: Prayers of the Social Awakening* (Boston, 1910).
20. *"Unto Me"* (Boston, 1912); *Dare We Be Christians?* (Boston, 1914).
21. For more about this book, and a selection from it, see below, 371–77.
22. E.g., see below, 389. Cf. A. Durwood Foster, "Albrecht Ritschl," in Dean G. Peerman and Martin E. Marty, eds., *A Handbook of Christian Theologians* (Cleveland, 1965), 49–67.

such men as F. D. Maurice and Charles Kingsley in England, and of Hermann Kutter and Leonhard Ragaz in Switzerland, to all of whom Rauschenbusch made reference in his own work. Yet he drew upon them in a free and often quite original way.[23]

A man who loved Germany and was much at home there, Rauschenbusch was deeply troubled in spirit by the outbreak of World War I. Like Gladden, he hated militarism and had pacifist inclinations. To him war seemed to be the negation of both Christianity and social advance. He hoped America might remain neutral. In the revulsion against things German, his popularity somewhat declined. A few even questioned his loyalty, though without any foundation. In April 1917 he delivered the Taylor lectures at Yale; they were published later that year as his last book, *A Theology for the Social Gospel*. Early in 1918 he became seriously ill. During that spring he wrote a poem, "The Postern Gate," which begins:

> In the castle of my soul
> Is a little postern gate,
> Whereat, when I enter,
> I am in the presence of God.
> In a moment, in the turning of a thought,
> I am where God is.
> This is a fact.

He died of cancer in his native Rochester on July 25, 1918.

After the war, the social gospel moved in several divergent directions, none of which would probably have had Rauschenbusch's entire approval. As the synthesis of personal religion and social concern, which had been so important to him, proved more and more difficult to maintain, the tendency of the social gospel (along with much liberal theology in the 1920's) was toward humanism. In the 1930's, under the intensifying strain of international and domestic problems, realistic and neo-orthodox theologians sharply attacked the positions for which Rauschenbusch had stood. His doctrines of Christ, of the kingdom, and of man were all forcefully criticized. No doubt Rauschenbusch had read too much of his own progressive and evolutionary views into his interpretation of Jesus' teachings, especially about the kingdom of God. In his great emphasis on the kingdom, Rauschenbusch was inclined to minimize the importance of the church in history and theology. His understanding of the church was

23. Smucker, "The Origins of Walter Rauschenbusch's Social Ethics" (typed Ph.D. thesis, University of Chicago, June 1957), and "Multiple Motifs in the Thought of Rauschenbusch: A Study in the Origins of the Social Gospel," *Encounter*, XIX (1958), 14–20.

based largely on free-church concepts; he had little feeling for classical doctrines of the church, either Catholic or Reformed. With most of the liberal theologians of his time, he so dwelt on the immanence as to neglect the transcendence and the sovereignty of God. Though he gave much more attention to man's sinfulness than many who preached the social gospel,[24] his definition of sin as essentially selfishness ignored the historic Christian doctrines of sin as pride and rebellion against God. He was far too optimistic concerning the degree to which the nation and its institutions had been Christianized.[25]

As a reformer, Rauschenbusch probably relied too naïvely on the power of the press and platform, and was not realistic enough in facing the political aspects of social change. Yet he was clearly ahead of the social gospel generally in this respect. Donald A. Meyer, reviewing the contributions of the social gospel, has said, "But it was Rauschenbusch who stood foremost, and although Rauschenbusch was hailed for many things, what stamps him most sharply in retrospect is his estimate of tactics, the first clear, concrete estimate in the annals of the social passion." [26] Max L. Stackhouse, in his treatment of Rauschenbusch's social theory, has analyzed this matter with some care. He concludes, "Rauschenbusch is dated; but he is dated for a good reason. Rauschenbusch's analysis, his suggestions, his criticisms were timely and concretely specified actions for a given era." [27] His method was to begin with the descriptive and the comparative, studying past and present by means of historical and sociological tools, and then to move on to the prescriptive and comparative function, both as a social prophet and as a herald of the coming kingdom. In calling for concrete action, Rauschenbusch drew heavily on the progressive, reformist, and socialistic thinking of his time. He was willing to be labeled a Christian socialist; but his socialism was evolutionary, non-doctrinaire, and in fact non-political. Distrusting the materialistic philosophy and the moral laxity of the movement, he never became a party member. [28]

Though his limitations have been pointed out and his essential position has been criticized, Rauschenbusch still towers above the other advocates of the social gospel. His religious and social insights, and especially his

24. See the discussion and a selection concerning this from *A Theology for the Social Gospel*, below, 378–89.
25. For a famous passage on this subject, see below, 361.
26. *The Protestant Search for Political Realism*, 88.
27. "Eschatology and Ethical Method," 121.
28. On Rauschenbusch's attitude toward socialism, see below, 291–92, 308–22.

sense of their interconnection, continues to excite interest and to stimulate reflection. His is the central place in an important chapter in American church history.

Since Rauschenbusch's major works are easily available — two of them in recent paperbound reprints — the selections from his work cover a wide range, including the period before he became internationally famous, but when he was already becoming well known in reform circles.[29] Many of his lectures and articles state a position concisely, or take up matters of importance which are not dealt with in his longer works. As he often said, he had plans for more books than he ever had time to write.

29. The very slight overlap with *A Rauschenbusch Reader: The Kingdom of God and the Social Gospel*, compiled by Benson Y. Landis (N.Y., 1957), occurs only when adequate coverage seems to require it.

❖ ❖ ❖ ❖ ❖ ❖ ❖ ❖

THE KINGDOM OF GOD [1]

Editor's introduction. On January 2, 1913, at the Central Y.M.C.A. in Cleveland, Rauschenbusch spoke very simply of his own religious life and development. Extracts from these autobiographical remarks were transcribed and published in the little bulletin of the Cleveland association. Though the address was given when Rauschenbusch was at the zenith of his career, it concerns the formative experiences of his early ministry. The burning urge to unify his religious and social concerns, and its fulfillment in working toward the kingdom of God, are vividly described in these informal reminiscences.

❖ ❖ ❖ ❖

I was brought up in a very religious family, and I thank God for it. We had household religious service every day, and from childhood I was taught to pray, read the Bible, go to Sunday school, to be in church often, and all those things I have no doubt trickled down into my mind and did their work there. But I was not very much aware of it, and I do not think other people were much aware of it, either. I ran with a gang; for a time I tried very hard to become their leader in swearing, but I never could. I think, however, that other people who observed me thought I was on the road to the devil. And then, physically, came the time of awakening for me, when young manhood was coming on and I began to feel the stirring of human ambition within me; and what I said to myself was: "I want to become a man; I want to be respected; and if I go on like this, I cannot have the respect of men." This was my way of saying: "I am out in the far country, and I want to get home to my country, and I don't want to tend the hogs any longer." And so I came to my Father, and I began to pray for help and got it. And I got my own religious experience.

Now, that religious experience was a very true one, although I have no doubt there was a great deal in it that was foolish, that I had to get away

1. "The Kingdom of God," *Cleveland's Young Men*, XXVII (January 9, 1813).

from, and that was untrue. And yet, such as it was, it was of everlasting value to me. It turned me permanently, and I thank God with all my heart for it. It was a tender, mysterious experience. It influenced my soul down to its depths. Yet, there was a great deal in it that was not really true.

A great deal was said about dying in those days. I used to like to talk a lot about dying, and think about it a great deal, probably because there was no present prospect that I would die. Nowadays, when I am considerably nearer to death than I was at that time, I prefer not to think about it quite so much. But youth can afford to play and deal with death. And we used to think about it, and sing about it, and talk about it. That was part of our religious life.

Now, I would not in any way depreciate these religious experiences. Indeed, I think that one of the reasons for our national strength has been that so many thousands and thousands of our people have been placed face to face with such experiences, and have at some time or other come under the conscious control of religion, and from that time on they lay open to all the fine moral impulses of right living, and of good citizenship, in our topsy-turvy political conditions here. Ruinous and sinful and immoral conditions have been improved wonderfully from the fact that we have so many men of religious experience; otherwise, it would have gone to the bad long ago. And of that religious experience that I had, this is the social note.

Very soon the idea came to me that I ought to be a preacher, and help to save souls. I wanted to go out as a foreign missionary—I wanted to do hard work for God. Indeed, one of the great thoughts that came upon me was that I ought to follow Jesus Christ in my personal life, and live over again his life, and die over again his death. I felt that every Christian ought to in some way or other participate in the dying of the Lord Jesus Christ, and in that way help to redeem humanity. And it was that thought that gave my life its fundamental direction in the doing of Christian work.

But there was another social note in it. Not until I was about twenty-five years old did that come, and then it did not come from the church. It came from outside. It came through personal contact with poverty, and when I saw how men toiled all their life long, hard, toilsome lives, and at the end had almost nothing to show for it; how strong men begged for work and could not get it in the hard times; how little children died — oh, the children's funerals! they gripped my heart — that was one of the things I always went away thinking about — why did the children have to die?

I did not have anything unusual there. I had only the same kind of human information, the same human experiences, you all have — or can have. Why, a single little human incident of that sort is enough to set a great beacon fire burning, and to light up the whole world for you — if you only have the right mind in you. And in that way, gradually, social information and social passion came to me. But, as I say, it did not come through the church. Indeed, I have to say, frankly, that for years the influence was rather against it from the church. This is one of the saddest things that I can say, but I cannot get it out of my mind. The church held down the social interest in me. It contradicted it; it opposed it; it held it down as far as it could; and when it was a question about giving me position or preferment, the fact that I was interested in the workingman was actually against me — not for me. They did not say: "Now here is a young man who loves the workingman, and has some thoughts about him — let us put him into a theological professorship." No! "The fact is, this young man thinks like the workingman, but works against [sic] improvement too much, therefore, he ought not to be a theological professor." That is the way they looked at me.

Now for a time, as these things got into my mind, the necessity came to me of combining this with the religious life that was so strong in me. I had personal religion. I now had that large social outlook, and how was I to combine the two things? I needed a unity of life — faith. A real religion always wanted unity. It wants to bring the whole world into one great conception that can inspire and fill the soul. It sees one God, it wants one world, and it wants one redemption. That is faith. No faith is really complete that cuts life up into sections, and applies only to a little bit of it. We want faith always as a whole thing.

And so my desire was always for a faith that would cover my whole life. And where was I to find it? The ordinary religious conception seemed to cover only some part of it. "Christ died for a sinner. He can be saved again by justification. He can be regenerated. After that, he can be sanctified. Finally, he will die and go to heaven." Yes, but where does the social question come in? Where does the matter come in of saving the world? That does not seem to have any place there, does it? And that was the real difficulty in my thought all the time — how to find a place, under the old religious conceptions, for this great task of changing the world and making it righteous; making it habitable; making it merciful; making it brotherly. Somehow, I knew in my soul that that was God's work. Nobody could wrest that from me. Jesus Christ had spoken too plainly to my soul about that. I knew that he was on the side of righteousness, and on the side of his poor brother. But where could I get it in with my old Christianity — with my old religion?

Now that is the way the matter presented itself to me as a personal problem. And then the idea of the kingdom of God offered itself as the real solution for that problem. Here was a religious conception that embraced it all. Here was something so big that absolutely nothing that interested me was excluded from it. Was it a matter of personal religion? Why, the kingdom of God begins with that! The powers of the kingdom of God well up in the individual soul; that is where they are born, and that is where the starting point necessarily must be. Was it a matter of world-wide missions? Why, that is the kingdom of God, isn't it — carrying it out to the boundaries of the earth. Was it a matter of getting justice for the workingman? Is not justice part of the kingdom of God? Does not the kingdom of God simply consist of this — that God's will shall be done on earth, even as it is now in heaven? And so, wherever I touched, there was the kingdom of God. That was the brilliancy, the splendor of that conception — it touches everything with religion. It carries God into everything that you do, and there is nothing else that does it in the same way.

And then, besides that, you have the authority of the Lord Jesus Christ in it. That was his idea. That is what he came and died for. The kingdom of God, my friend, is a social conception. It is a conception for this life here of ours, because Jesus says: "Thy kingdom come, thy will be done" here. It is something that is here on this earth; that quietly pervades all humanity; that is always working toward the perfect life of God. It cannot be lived out by you alone — you have to live it out with me, and with that brother sitting next to you. We together have to work it out. It is a matter of community life. The perfect community of men — that would be the kingdom of God! With God above them; with their brother next to them — clasping hands in fraternity, doing the work of justice — that is the kingdom of God!

❖ ❖ ❖ ❖ ❖ ❖ ❖ ❖

CONCEPTIONS OF MISSIONS [1]

Editor's introduction. Because of his intense concern for the social question, Rauschenbusch's continuing interest in missions has often been overlooked. He had volunteered for the mission field at the time of his graduation from seminary, but was told that he should have pastoral experience first.[2] The "evangelical conception of missions" set forth in the following article remained constant in his lifelong ministry. He believed that the source of Christian power lay in faith in the crucified and risen Christ, and that the very important work of education and reformation must be built on this foundation. As he explains here, by the early 1890's Rauschenbusch had rejected any comforting view of automatic progress, and was declaring that salvation could come only by the presence of the spirit of the risen Christ, transforming individuals and fusing them into a new society.

❖ ❖ ❖ ❖

I

There is need for emphasizing the evangelical conception of missions. There are so many things that call themselves missions nowadays. It is one proof that the missionary idea is victorious. Any effort to reach out beyond an established circle in the spread of ideas or in the extension of practical help is called a mission.

This is well. It is well that all unselfish impulses in humanity should range themselves under the missionary banner of Christ and obey his command to "go." It is well that the missionary impulse to save humanity is branching out in many directions. If a field is to be irrigated, it will

1. "Conceptions of Missions," *The Watchman*, November 24, 1892, 1, and December 1, 1892, 1.
2. Dores R. Sharpe (*Rauschenbusch*, 58) explains that Rauschenbusch was being considered for the presidency of the Telegu Theological Seminary at Ramapatnam in India, but the objections of one of his professors to his liberal views of the Old Testament blocked the appointment.

have to be done by a multitude of tiny channels and noiseless rivulets. And if the whole of human life is to be penetrated by the saving health of Christianity, it will have to be done by a multitude of movements and a variety of endeavors.

The danger is that in the minor aims, the central aim is forgotten; that in designing the ornaments for the front of the edifice the architects are forgetting to lay a solid foundation; that in seeking the applications of the power of Christianity, the source of that power is neglected. Hence I wish to lay stress on the evangelical conception of missions, as distinguished from secondary conceptions.

By secondary conceptions of missions I mean especially the work of secular education, of philanthropic effort, and of denominational propaganda.

Christian people are taking an interest in the spread of education for its own sake. Our interest in Zenana work and in the school of the Pandita Ramabai is based not so much on the hope of seeing individuals converted, as in the hope that the crippled intellect of Hindu women will be straightened to healthy life, their horizon extended, and the heritage of humanity be secured for them.[3] We feel that the light of intellectual knowledge and the zest of mental activity are blessings in themselves, and that it is really missionary work to pass the torch of knowledge on to those who sit in intellectual darkness. We take a keen interest in the educational movements of Japan and China. The intellectual life of the West is touching these nations with a quickening touch. The laborious erudition of the learned classes in China, their fruitless studiousness and slavish subjection to the classics of their past, are exactly like the learning of Europe in the age of scholasticism and of the undisputed reign of a supposed Aristotelian philosophy. Something is going on there similar to the revival of learning in the fifteenth century through the rediscovery of Greek literature. Now we who live an intellectual life ourselves, and appreciate the blessings of virile and unhampered thought, cannot help being deeply interested in what is going on there, and we justly regard any effort to hasten the incoming of intellectual light as truly a missionary effort.

3. [ED.] Zenana missionary work was carried on in the homes of secluded high-caste women in India. Pandita Ramabai, a woman convert to Christianity, worked as a missionary among girls of low caste in South India. See Robert G. Torbet, *Venture of Faith: The Story of the American Baptist Foreign Mission Society and the Women's American Baptist Foreign Mission Society, 1814-1954* (Philadelphia, 1955), 200, 273.

We have the same feeling about the growth of philanthropic work among the heathen. Here at home there is a growing effort in the direction of practical philanthropy. We are becoming more and more sensible that social misery lies as guilt at the door of the churches. We are responding to the pressure exerted by the growth of the social movement. All this makes every effort for the alleviation of pain and the abolition of wrong very important and very dear to us. We take a lively interest in the abolition of the C.D. [civil disobedience] Acts, in the raising of the age of marriage in India, in the undermining of the caste system by railroad travel and the commercial mingling of the people, in the spread of humane sentiments and the awakening of social compunction in the higher classes of the Orient, in Lady Dufferin's fund for extending medical aid to the women of India, in the first dawn of parliamentary representation for the people of Japan.[4] In the last ten years, there has been a new factor in our home mission work. We have felt as never before the greatness of the disintegrating forces at work in our national life and the need of a quickened and effective Christian life, if our country is to be saved. The remarkable sale of Dr. Strong's little book on *Our Country* has been both a symptom and a cause of the spread of these ideas. This element in home missions has made us more hospitable to similar ideas on the foreign field.

A third conception which even more emphatically deserves the name of secondary, is the conception of missions as a propaganda of our denomination. We all would probably repudiate the insinuation if it were charged that we considered the extension of our own denomination as important for its own sake. We should insist that we love our denomination because it stands for certain truths and principles, and we desire its extension only because we desire the extension of the truths with which it is identified. But let us be candid. Human nature seems to be built on a very finite model. We have a special love for our own family, our own profession, our own political party, our own denomination, which we do not give to the whole of humanity. These enlarged egotisms are perhaps necessary and inevitable, but they ought not to be elevated to the dignity of a principle to be acknowledged and deferred to. We ought not to grow enthusiastic in outstripping some other denomination, while we remain apathetic in saving men. It ought not to be the clinching argument

4. [ED.] Lady Dufferin, wife of the viceroy of India, invited missionary doctors to take charge of the government hospital and nurses' training school in Rangoon (*ibid.*, 197).

with the givers among us that, if *we* do not do such and such a thing, the other fellows will. The welfare of our denomination may be important, but our denominational principles are more important far. And something else is more important than our denominational principles. And what is that? The fact and power of Christianity. The tendency of the natural man is toward denominationalism. We should direct our efforts to lift up the interest in Christianity, and to keep down the interest in the denomination. If we do not, the latter will come up like the lean kine of Pharaoh and swallow everything, and God will not like it.

First of all, and above everything, comes evangelical Christianity. And what do I mean by that? I mean by that not any particular type of doctrine, but the extension of faith in the crucified and risen Christ, who imparts his spirit to those who believe in him and thereby redeems them from the domination of the flesh and the world and their corruption, and transforms them into spiritual beings, conformed to his likeness and partaking of his life. That is the primary aim of Christian missions, first in the order of importance, first also in the order of time.

It is first in order of importance because nothing can exceed in value the regeneration of individual souls who shall become dwelling places and instruments of the Holy Spirit on earth, and here and hereafter members of the eternal kingdom of God. To save men from sin and death and see them become brethren of Jesus Christ must ever remain the first and mightiest motive of Christian missions.

II

And this conception of missions is also the first in order of time, because it is the only solid and trustworthy basis on which to build up all the secondary work of education and reformation.

We are inclined to forget this. One reason why we forget it, is because many of us, through ease of life and the exceeding pleasantness of this present world, are prone to sag down from evangelical religion to humanitarian morality, from spiritual fervor to altruistic earnestness. Another reason is that the spread of the idea of evolution has created an optimism among us which is not warranted by the facts. We have heard so much about the progress of civilization, that a serene faith has come over us that the cart is slowly but surely rolling up the hill, and that all that is necessary is to clear away obstacles by education and reform, and leave play to the inherent upward forces of humanity. I was myself once of this opinion and found it comforting. Observation and the study of history have compelled me to part with it sadly. However evolution may work in the rest of creation, a new element enters in when it reaches the ethical nature of man. Ethically man sags downward by nature. It is ever easy to follow temptation and hard to resist it. The way that leads to destruction is always broad, and its asphalt pavement is kept in perfect order, with toboggan slides at either side for those who prefer a steeper grade. The way to life is always a climb, and every toiling traveler on it feels that asthma clogs his lungs. Moral gravitation is downward. It is accelerated in us by years of sin and by the swirling rush of centuries of wrong which pushes us from behind. Let us not be beguiled by that seductive devil who tells us that man will walk into the millennium, if only you will point out to him where the millennium is, and clear away the worst obstacles for him. Man was never built that way. If he is to get in, he will have to be lifted in. There will have to be a force from above strong enough to overcome all the downward gravitation of flesh and world, and to conquer the devil in addition. It is this force on which the evangelical conception of missions insists, and which evangelical Christianity transmits.

Education has not brought salvation. There was intellectual keenness and light enough among the ancient Greeks, but they rotted just the same. Their wisdom degenerated into hair-splitting and their philosophy into the building of inverted pyramids. There is education and culture enough in France. What a refinement of taste, what an exquisite delicacy of workmanship in the products of their intellectual work. And how that nation is rotting. It is the same thing with political and social changes to some extent, and with the works of philanthropy. It is all a shifting about of what is already in society, and not the introduction of a new force into it. And yet a new force is needed. Salvation came by the coming of the Son of God into humanity, initiating the new humanity with a force not previously among us. It came by the coming of the spirit of the risen Christ, transforming individuals, fusing them into a new society, inspiring new thoughts, impelling to new undertakings, making all things new. They became the salt that stopped the putrefaction of society. They became the bits of leaven mixed into the flat lump of humanity. They furnished the basis for every work of education and reform. To attempt the salvation of heathen nations without that basis to build upon, is to mold statues of soft butter; to build houses with untempered mortar. It is an attempt foredoomed to failure. Such an edifice will slump together, as soon as it is to bear any serious pressure.

The secondary conceptions of missions are just and necessary. We *must* educate. The Christ-life is incompatible with darkness of any sort. Any religion, be it Romanist or evangelical, which does not tend to enlightenment in all things, is to that extent not of the Christ. It is a most significant fact to me that the man who is confessedly the greatest evangelist of the East today, our own Dr. Clough, is also the one who has labored to get the endowment for the seminary at Ramapatnam, and to build the high school at Ongole, and who is now — and in my judgment not a day too soon — endeavoring to found the college there.[5] We must also seek the transformation of political and social life. To be indifferent about any question of justice and love is to fall under the condemnation of Christ. Where his saving health comes, all proud flesh will have to be cut down and all withered muscles will have to distend with a new current of life-blood.

All these things are good, just, indispensable. But spirituality is first. Without it, education will turn into a striving after a wind, culture into lasciviousness, social reformation into social unrest, philanthropy into a sprinkling of rose-water over the carcass.

What was Paul's conception of missions? He believed that God had in Jesus Christ worked a great deed of salvation whereby remission of sins and a life of grace was possible. He believed that the risen Christ was enthroned as the Son of God with power, and that his spirit was indwelling in the hearts of believers, transforming them, neutralizing and turning back the power of sin and death in man and in humanity, and overcoming every spiritual power working in a contrary direction. Faith in the power of the risen Christ — that I take to be the central conviction of the evangelical conception of missions. And on that foundation it will be well for us to build whatever edifice Christ has called us to erect in this generation.

5. [ED.] John E. Clough (1836–1910) began an effective mission among the Telegus in South India in 1866, with headquarters at Ongole. The college was soon founded. In 1894 Rauschenbusch's sister Emma became Clough's second wife. See Clough, *Social Christianity in the Orient* (N.Y., 1914); Torbet, *Venture of Faith*, 257–70.

❖ ❖ ❖ ❖ ❖ ❖ ❖ ❖

THE IDEALS OF SOCIAL REFORMERS [1]

Editor's introduction. An editorial note accompanying this article explained, "The author is corresponding secretary of 'The Brotherhood of the Kingdom,' and this paper is written from the viewpoint of that organization." Much of Rauschenbusch's writing was connected with the organizations with which he worked closely, especially the Brotherhood of the Kingdom and the Baptist Congress. Many of his ideas were hammered out in conversation with his co-workers, yet his writing had its own distinctive stamp and style. What he here called the special task of his generation, that of wedding Christianity and the social movement, was one to which he felt especially drawn. Here he outlined a program of reform at which he was to work faithfully for the rest of his life, as a demonstration that there were those within the churches who took seriously the writings and programs of social philosophers and reformers. The larger significance of this article is that it showed that there were Protestant leaders who were ready to criticize responsibly and to work with the general social reform movement.

❖ ❖ ❖ ❖

One of the special tasks of our generation is the work of wedding Christianity and the social movement. They are divorced now. The bulk of our church members is either ignorant and indifferent in regard to the social movement, or else suspicious of it. The majority of social reform workers, at least if we include Europe, fluctuates somewhere between contempt and avowed hostility toward the church and spiritual religion. We of "The Brotherhood of the Kingdom" believe that such a separation is unnecessary, unwise, and undesirable, detrimental to the full success of both parties concerned, and perilous to the future of humanity.

We believe in the spiritual life, in the fact of sin and corruption, in the need and possibility of salvation, in holiness and eternal life. We have no

1. "The Ideals of Social Reformers," *The American Journal of Sociology,* II (July 1896–May 1897), 202–19.

desire to see evangelical Christianity bled to death; to see the church of Christ turned into a reform club; to see the hidden life of the believer toned down to a mild and sapless altruism; and to have Christian theology changed into a modern gnosticism, into a system of evolutionary philosophy, with a place for Christ as one of the evolutionary forces. On the contrary, we find fault with modern Christianity because it is not Christian enough. We desire a completer surrender to the Spirit of God, a fuller life of trust, and a more ardent zeal for all missionary work, and for the universal reign of King Jesus. But, on the other hand, we also believe in the social movement of the nineteenth century. We refuse to regard it as a red-hot lava eruption from the crater of hell. We hold that it is a river flowing from the throne of God, sent by the Ruler of history for the purification of the nations. We see God's hand in it; we see Christ's blood in it; we see the creative energies of the Spirit in it, bringing out of its chaos the beauties of a new world.

We have this two-sided faith. But our faith is not yet supported on all sides by knowledge. The two chemical elements have not yet completed their union in us. A long and earnest process of thought is necessary. We must overhaul all the departments of our thought, and work out that social Christianity which will be immeasurably more powerful and more valuable to the world than either an unsocial Christianity or an un-Christian socialism. After the process of union is in a measure completed in ourselves, we can become mediators for others, breaking down the middle wall of partition between Christianity and the social movement, bringing them into their just and natural relation to each other, infusing the exalted fervor and power of religion into the social movement, and helping religion to find its ethical outcome in the transformation of social conditions.

In examining the ideals of social reformers I shall try to take up the great ideals that are common to the whole social movement, rather than isolated schemes and measures. I shall first set forth the elements and tendencies in which we can heartily concur, and then the points where the dangers of the social movement seem to me to lie.

The starting point of the social movement is the conviction of the inherent worth of a human being. Its goal is to secure the recognition of that worth in all departments of life. The mention of a few facts will help us to realize that this feeling, that human life is a precious thing, is the hydraulic force in the social uplift.

We view with pity and indignation singly concrete cases of suffering or wrong. Last summer the case of Maria Barberi agitated the people of New York.[2] The pity may have been foolishly betowed in this case; I pass no judgment on that; but the pity was there; thousands of people took thought for it that a single human life, one among two millions, was to be ended. Remember also the public resentment when wrongs done to a whole class are brought to light. Remember how the common people of Brooklyn sympathized with the trolley strikers, in spite of the discomfort the strike inflicted on the city. Think how we are aroused by news of oppression even in foreign countries. The indignation aroused by the Bulgarian atrocities, by the Armenian outrages, by George Kennan's accounts of the Russian prisoners, are cases known to all.[3] Of course, those who espouse a movement of that sort feel that the public conscience is very sluggish and easily goes to sleep again, and that is true, too. But, after all, is it not a remarkable thing that in this great crowded globe, where men are suffering and dying every second, and where most of us need all our strength to provide bread for our own stomachs and to fight off others who are trying to step on us, there should be any interest at all in a lot of foreigners whom none of us has ever seen? Remember, too, how we winced when the heathen at the Parliament of Religions pointed out the poverty in our own cities. All this pity, indignation, and shame are based on the sense of humanity. They are human beings who suffer, and human beings are too good to suffer thus. The argument of the political economist who says that this is the struggle for existence, and that this suffering works out the greatest good in the end; the pious sigh of the Christian Pharisee who assures us that we shall have the poor with us always and that things can't be changed till Christ comes; and the shrug of selfish over-culture which assures us that these people are very low and sordid and desire nothing better; they are all swept away like chaff before the feeling that a man's a man for all that, and the knowledge that human tears are scalding hot and hurt when they fall on our hearts.

Another evidence of the power which this sense of humanity has already acquired over us may be found in the attitude taken by the artistic interpreters of our thoughts. Consider the change which has come over literature since Horace wrote his "Odi profanum vulgus et arceo." [4]

2. [ED.] On July 15, 1895, Maria Barberi was convicted of murder in the first degree for the razor killing of her seducer. It was widely believed that the first-degree conviction was wrong; the case was appealed and a new trial granted.

3. [ED.] In 1885–86 George Kennan (1845–1923), author and lecturer, had investigated the exile system in Siberia.

4. [ED.] "I hate the common rabble and keep it at a distance."

What modern poet would care to write like that? Compare with that the lesson of Sir Launfal's search for the Holy Grail, or these lines of Lowell:

> In a hovel rude,
>   With naught to fence the weather from his head,
> The King I sought for, meekly stood;
>   A naked, hungry child
> Clung round his gracious knee
>   And a poor hunted slave looked up and smiled
> To bless the smile that set him free;
>   New miracles I saw his presence do . . .
> No more I knew the hovel bare and poor,
>   The gathered chips into a woodpile grew,
> The broken morsel swelled to goodly store;
>   I knelt and wept: my Christ no more I seek,
> His throne is with the outcast and the weak.

While not all of our modern poets are such prophets of Christian democracy as Lowell, yet with singular unanimity the greatest novelists of the Christian nations are full of reverence for plain suffering humanity, and full of scorn for the polished selfishness of the upper classes who used to absorb the attention of older novelists. In religious literature we look almost in vain for any honest dealing with the text about the camel and the needle's eye; but one can find quite wonderful expositions of it in Tolstoy's *War and Peace*, Bourget's *Cosmopolis*, Charles Dudley Warner's *A Little Journey in the World*, Franzos' *Ein Kampf ums Recht*, and many others.

In pictorial art it is the same. Compare Watteau's well-finished pictures of well-clipped parks, full of well-dressed ladies exchanging compliments with well-behaved gentlemen, with Uhde's pictures of the Christ in the village school, or Christ at the peasant's table, and feel the difference of spirit, and the sense of the sacredness of life in its lowliest forms, which glorifies the latter. At the International Art Exhibition at Berlin I saw among the statuary the figure of an old man sitting on the ground, his clothes ragged, his shoulders bent, his face dull and weary, a broken potsherd of humanity. Underneath was the simple legend: "Proximus tuus." [5] Modern art is full of such prophetic sermons in oil and marble; but where do we see anything like it in older periods of art? In one of the most popular paintings of our time, Millet's "Angelus," the artist has simply

5. [ED.] "Very near to thee."

tried to show us the beauty and dignity of the humblest life and labor, by surrounding it with the halo of God's sunset and glory of piety.

I have tried with a few touches to bring before our recollection and imagination the strength of that humane sentiment which pervades Christian civilization in spite of its mammonism and greed of pleasure. That sentiment is the nerve of the social movement; the rest is muscle. If that nerve were dead or paralyzed there would be no social movement. There is, in fact, no social movement outside of the Christian nations.

Now that sentiment seeks embodiment. It seeks to stop that which offends it; it seeks to create conditions which it can accept. It has already sought to give even the children of the poor their share in our intellectual heritage by providing universal elementary education, guarding the intellectual rights of the child even against its parents by some measure of compulsion. It has provided night schools, free lectures, free libraries and museums, and many aids to secure even a higher education for those who desire it. In the political domain it has gone a long way toward endowing the lower classes with a voice, by the extension of the suffrage, and is constantly laboring to secure that right against bribery or intimidation by devising better methods of voting, and to make the will of the people act more surely on legislation by planning systems of minority representation and direct legislation. It has abolished many remnants of feudal privileges and made men more equal before the law. It has compelled the state, in the face of traditional political economy, to assume a certain guardianship over women and children and to limit their exploitation in industry. It has granted woman very nearly all that she has really been serious in asking. In religious life there has been a decline of priestly prerogative, a growing recognition of the universal priesthood of believers, an increase of lay activity fostered especially in the young people's movement, and a reaching forward to save the lost classes. The Salvation Army is penetrated with the social spirit.

Here then we have a great movement actuated by the conviction that a human life is precious, and seeking to give every man an opportunity to live his life worthily. What attitude shall the Christian disciple take to this movement? Who ever felt the worth of a soul more deeply that Jesus? Who felt intenser pity for bodily disablement than he who touched the leper and quieted the demoniac's stormy soul? Who had more of the spirit of real democracy than he who shared the fisherman's food, rebuked with dignity the haughty Pharisee who had failed in the common duties of hospitality, exalted the mite of the widow, and made his royal entry into the city of David on the back of a donkey, with boughs scattered by peasants as a carpet on the way? Whose eye was ever quicker to detect the divine glory of a human heart beneath the rust and foulness of sin and social ostracism, than his who made friends with the publicans, and championed the repentant harlot at a dinner table of gentlemen who were his social superiors? We cannot help feeling that the social movement was in Christ, and that Christ is now in the social movement. The disciple of Jesus must follow his master, and he cannot follow him unless he goes in the same direction. By their attitude to this movement, more than by assent to formulated truths, will the men of our generation be judged before God.

> Once to every man and nation comes the moment to decide,
> In the strife 'twixt truth and falsehood, for the good or evil side;
> Some great cause, God's new Messiah, deals to each the bloom
>   or blight,
> Parts the goats upon the left hand and the sheep upon the right,
> And the choice goes by forever 'twixt that darkness and
>   that light.[6]

I have spoken mainly of the effort to secure for the poor and oppressed of our own nation the chance to live a worthy life. But the sense of humanity works horizontally sideways, as well as perpendicularly downwards. It quickens the feeling of interest and kinship between nations and races. The student of history knows what barriers the difference of nationality and religion has drawn between man and man in the past. In Latin the word for stranger and the word for enemy were the same. The barrier is still broad. Of course the increase of commerce and travel has worn away many prejudices, but it has not produced much love as yet. Commerce with uncivilized nations is ruthless and often almost devilish in selfishness and cruelty. I know of only two forces that are really making for international fellowship with fairly unselfish motives. The one is the social movement. It is international in its tendencies. Karl Marx taught European workingmen the cry, "Proletarians of all nations, unite." The tendency to international solidarity is as yet but rudimentary, but it has been strong enough to send many thousands of dollars across the seas to aid in social struggles. It has been powerful enough to alarm thoroughly the governments whose interests lie in an exclusive patriotism. The other force making in the same direction is foreign missions. Foreign missions

6. [ED.] These, as well as the previously quoted lines of verse, are by James Russell Lowell (1819–91); set to music, they became a favorite social-gospel hymn.

have come in for many hard blows from humanitarians, but after all has been said, they are the only case of anybody expending capital on uncivilized peoples without expecting to get anything back. No one has ever charged Christian missionary societies with trying to make more money out of the natives than they spend for them. Scientists go among savages to bring back knowledge; merchants to bring back wealth; explorers to bring back fame and trophies; but the missionary is the only one that makes even a pretense of going for the sake of the people.

Here again we see the confluence of the two streams. The social movement has developed international tendencies and promoted the fraternization of the nations engaged in it. Christianity from the very outset has been international in its character; it has been remiss in fulfilling its missionary obligations, but it has never repudiated its international character, and has always boasted of whatever broadness it could prove.

A second great ideal at work in the social movement lies in the principle of association. Suppose men are politically free and starting in life with equal opportunities; it still remains to be seen what they will do with their freedom and equality. Will they fight or unite? The development since the French Revolution, or rather since the Protestant Reformation, has been toward the enfranchisement of the individual. The victory of personal liberty as a principle is complete in the leading nations; the practical application of the principle is also nearing its completion. The next great word, as Mazzini says, is *association*.[7]

The process of enfranchisement has unfettered immense forces, but it has also resulted in disorganizing society. The old feudal bonds have been dissolved, but new bonds have not taken their place. The peasants of Europe are no longer bound to the soil or to its lord. They are free to go where they like. As a result many of them are torn loose from the sheltering and restraining ties of kinship and neighborhood, and are swept like human flotsam and jetsam into the great cities where none knows them or cares for them. Is it a clear gain to them? The same process comes close home to us in the Negro population of the South. They are free now, under nobody's ownership, but also under nobody's care. It is probably fair to say that the benefits resulting from their emancipation have not been as great as had been hoped. In Germany improved agriculture has

7. [ED.] Giuseppe Mazzini (1805–72), prophet of a united Italy and leading spokesman of liberal republicanism and nationalism, was much admired by many social gospel leaders. Cf. Robert T. Handy, "The Influence of Mazzini on the American Social Gospel," *The Journal of Religion*, XXIX (1949), 114–23.

shortened the harvest season; as a result, large bodies of men and women migrate from place to place, hiring out as laborers; they move like the tide, and one section is swept bare of its youthful population, while other sections are inundated with a crowd of strangers. It is easy to imagine that this migratory life does not tend to stable habits, family affection, or clean morals.

With the city population things are similar. The guilds are gone. The relation of master, journeyman, and apprentice has given place to that of employers and hands. The human interest and relation between them has dwindled away; the money relation is the sole bond. The old feudal relations were often unjust and dwarfing, but they gave a certain security and a definite place in which a man could live and move. Now men are free, but it is often the freedom of grains of sand that are whirled up in a cloud and then dropped in a heap, but neither cloud nor sand-heap have any coherence. This condition is not a final one. New forms of association must be created. Our disorganized competitive life must pass into an organic cooperative life. We all know that this is one of the great ideas of the social movement. The socializing tendency is the dominating tendency in sociological thought, and is bound to become the dominating tendency in economic life too. Men may differ about the extent to which the socializing process ought to go, and about the chemical formula according to which the two ingredients of individualism and socialism are to be mixed, but the new ingredient will have to go in. It takes no prophet to foretell that.

What then shall the attitude of Christian disciples be to this great ideal of social reformers? I feel that it will have to be friendly. The law of laissez faire, if untempered by any force of loyalty and association, would have found little grace in the sight of Old Testament lawgivers and prophets, and still less in the sight of Jesus. One of the deepest principles of the New Testament is the principle of κοινωνία, of fellowship, of association. One of the two ordinances of the church is a meal of fellowship. The early church made a bold attempt to realize this principle of fellowship in regard to property also, and the attempt has been repeated again and again in the face of overwhelming obstacles, wherever a serious effort has been made to live according to Christ's law of life. The power of association and cohesion was implanted by the Spirit of God; its theory was formulated by Paul in his illustration of the body and its members, an illustration so true, that men like Schäffle and Dr. G. D. Boardman, in developing a theory of a true social life, could do no better than to unfold that illustration in detail.[8] True Christianity emphasizes to the utmost the value of the individual, and has been the real motive power back of the efforts to secure personal liberty. But it contains more than individualism; it also contains the principle of association, and implants the trustworthiness, love, and unselfishness which cement men together and make association a workable idea. In so far, therefore, as socialism is the effort to translate into facts of political economy the Christian tendency to association, in so far it has a right to claim our approval.

It will be my task now to criticize the ideals of social reformers by mentioning the dangers to which they seem to me liable. Of course not all are liable to the same mistakes. Considering the space at my disposal, I can only sketch in a broad way the dangers to which large sections of men devoted to social progress seem to tend.

First, there is a real menace to individual liberty in the schemes of socialism. For working purposes I am myself a socialist. We want more socialism than we have at present, anyway. Our present individualism is no real individualism. It is a race between men on horseback and men on foot. As long as public functions are in the hands of private corporations and they can tax the public, individualism means tyranny. So I am in favor of at least enough socialism to take natural monopolies out of private management.[9] But when we consider the socialistic program that lies beyond that practical necessity, we cannot escape the impression that it is full of danger to personal liberty. When the entire nation is organized as a colossal machine, and every cog is dependent on its connection with the machine for its chance to work, will there be freedom enough to make life tolerable? If a man is harried by a tyrannous foreman or a spiteful fellow workman now, he can quit his job and try elsewhere. He may be out of a job for a while, but there are at least other employers to try. In the socialistic state there is to be only one employer, the state. If a man there quits his job, he cannot even employ himself. All the instruments of production are to be owned by the state. He cannot escape the bullying foreman or spiteful mate, except by setting the official machine in motion and securing a transfer.

8. Albert E. F. Schäffle (1831–1903) was the author of *The Quintessence of Socialism*, which went through many editions in the original German. George Dana Boardman (1828–1903), pastor of the First Baptist Church of Philadelphia, wrote on many themes, including international peace, the doctrine of the church, and the kingdom of God.

9. [ED.] For a fuller discussion of Rauschenbusch's attitude toward socialism, see below, 291–92, 308–22.

Only those who have lived where liberty is scarce know its sweetness. As a young man I spent four years in Germany. On my return to my native country I was conscious not only of the thrill of a young patriot, but also of an invigorating ease and freedom in dealing with men. I studied the cause of the sensation and concluded that it was due to the larger freedom accorded here by everybody to everybody. Later I crossed the sea again with a number of Germans of the middle classes, and heard with astonishment how little love they had for their fatherland and how ready they were to transfer their allegiance to their new home. Outwardly New York cannot compare with Berlin. Our streets are dirty and ill-paved, our tenements squalid, and the opportunities for easy and pleasant recreation and for the enjoyment of music and art are much fewer. Yet it seems that there is something in New York life that makes it more attractive than Berlin. I know no other cause than the greater freedom.

Freedom gives the real zest to life. Freedom is also necessary to develop a nation of vigorous characters. A high level of culture and ability can be produced without freedom, as we can see from the educational work of the Jesuits. But it will be the commonplace usefulness of barnyard fowl, assiduously laying eggs, but without wing enough to fly over the fence. The Jesuits have developed no new thoughts; no Jesuit has ever led humanity onward into the unexplored country of the future. If socialism takes away our freedom, it stifles the future leaders of humanity before their birth.

On the other hand, it is well for the advocates of personal liberty who urge this objection against socialism to remember that liberty is today the possession of a favored few. Few boys in New York really choose their profession. A job is the great arbiter of their destinies. Would a boy like to become an engineer? But his father gets a job for him in a butchershop, and a butcher he becomes. Can the tyranny of socialism be much worse than that which locks the door on factory operatives now at the stroke of a bell, as if they were convicts, and docks them an hour's wages if a passing train makes them five minutes late in the morning?

A second danger in social reform tendencies threatens the stability and importance of family life. This danger is often exaggerated by conservatives who are in need of a bugaboo. An aged brother once assured me that the application of the single tax would inevitably lead to a communism of wives. Communism of nonsense! Yet I think there is a considerable inclination among social reformers to loosen the rigor of the family bond. The wrongs of women are preached to us by determined voices, voices that are often painfully vibrant with the memory of personal wrongs. And because to such the walls of the house were a fiery square of torture, they ask to see the walls torn down, forgetting that these same walls to innumerable others are the breakwaters of God's most blessed haven.

Socialists also frequently aim at an easing of the marriage bond, because they recognize in the family the great bulwark of individualism. They see men absorbed in securing a competence for their families, and in pushing their children one degree higher up in the social scale, and there is no interest left for the elevation of their city. Most men would sell out their interest in social questions to secure $5000 a year for their families. But how is the interest in the general welfare, which the socialist state will demand, ever to be secured if it has to work against this family selfishness? So it is that in the socialist pictures of the future, the state is more and the family less; the public buildings are opulent, but the family lives in narrow quarters; the children are less the property of the parents and more the property of the state. I recently read a book by Solomon Schindler giving the autobiography of Young West, the son of Mr. Julian West and Edith Leete, of *Looking Backward* fame.[10] Young West's earliest recollections are of the public kindergarten in which he, like all other children, was brought up. He was very fond of one of his teachers. A lady came to see him once a week, and he was told that this was his mother, but he didn't know what that might mean. As he grows older he occasionally goes to see Dr. Leete, and his mother and her second or third husband, but these visits are about as warm as if a boy of our times paid a visit of respect to his second cousin's uncle. Generally the boy and his companions act like young prigs and Philistines, which is no wonder, seeing they were brought up in a succession of model orphan asylums. Later, when Young West marries, he has a child and is very fond of it, but he and his wife love it too well to keep it long under their own ignorant care, so they pass it on to a public institution where trained professionals are sure to do much better by it.

Is it not a curious and solemn Nemesis that has come upon us? We have

---

10. [ED.] Solomon Schindler (1842–1915), *Young West: A Sequel to Edward Bellamy's Celebrated Novel, Looking Backward* (Boston, 1894). There was much discussion of the utopian and "nationalist" thought of Bellamy (1850–98) in social-Christian circles during the 1890's, stimulated especially by his widely read *Looking Backward, 2000–1887* (Boston, 1888). Schindler's novel is a rather gentle criticism of the commonwealth so glowingly described by Bellamy. Life in such an "ideal" state, Schindler suggests, would be flat and passionless for those reared in the more exciting atmosphere of the nineteenth century.

housed the working people in tenements, worked them in factories, raised their children in institutions, and sent them to homes and almshouses to die. And of these ingredients glorified the working classes have built their ideal of the New Jerusalem: a vast industrial army in ideal factories with plenty of wages promptly paid; great asylums as educational institutions, splendid public pleasure resorts, and little dwarfed homes.

It is true that marriage is often an instrument of torture today. But the remedy does not lie in making marriage a pleasurable friendship to be dissolved at will, or a pedotrophic partnership; that would twist the sexual relation into a scourge to lash us all. It lies rather in securing such a diffusion of fair prosperity and such a stability of economic conditions that the money motive will be practically eliminated from marriage, and that the worry and stress will be eased which now create nervous exhaustion, irritability, and discord. It is true, also, that the exclusive love of family is a real hindrance to social progress. But here too the remedy does not lie in paring down the family, but in preaching the civic as well as the domestic virtues, the kingdom of God as well as individual religion, and in getting women interested in something outside their own families and churches.

Let us ward off any social ideals that impair the stability and scope of the family and home. There is no need of impairing them. Even with a socialist system of industry there is ample room for a private home. If it were not so, if there were no place there whither a man could withdraw from the press of the world to the restful society of a beloved woman and his own children, it is a question if any gain in external comforts purchased by the change would be worth so great a price.

In the third place, certain tendencies of social reformers contain a danger to national life. We have spoken of the inclination to international union among workingmen. This inclination has been planted and watered by the jingoism and commercialism of bourgeois politics. The national flags have so often had to serve as a cover for lust of conquest, in which the people furnished food for the cannon, that a hatred has grown up against nationality and its symbol, and the red flag of socialism has been substituted — not to denote bloodshed, as some think, but the common blood of humanity. In Germany national history and pride have been so much used to prop the monarchy and existing institutions that socialists are now creating a new historical literature which reverses the old verdicts, calls the national heroes intriguers and butchers, and pours contempt on the great events of the nation's past. This is deplorable. Nationality is a good and holy fact. As the individual has a right to his individuality, so the nation has a right to its nationality. And as human life is infinitely enriched by the differences in individuality, so the life of the race has been enriched by the differences of nationality, and this is destined to be far more the case as increasing intercommunication brings the nations face to face and introduces them.

The internationalism of the working classes is nobly right in protesting against a narrow and warlike patriotism, but we must never lose our loyalty to our own country, nor our reverence for her past, her heroes, and her flag. As the new social enthusiasm must contain in itself the old love of family, so the new love of humanity must contain the old love of the fatherland.

In the fourth place, many social reformers more or less openly look forward to a revolutionary break of development by force. It is not unnatural that they do. Progress is so slow, and resistance so stubborn and subtle; it is so hard to get remedial legislation enacted, and so much harder yet to get it enforced, that men naturally get impatient, especially if they are themselves the grist that is being ground. Especially men whose only strength lies in their brawn are bewildered and enraged to find a just cause bound hand and foot by a smiling lawyer with a bit of red tape, and they feel that if they could only close in a death-grapple for once, there might be some chance for them. The wonder is that force is so seldom used.

Yet those who are dissuading workingmen from efforts for a gradual change, and urging them to try the way of force, are playing fast and loose with the future, and will, in the long run, probably retard social progress. There is a recoil after the use of violence which carries a cause almost back to the line from which it was shot by the explosion. Remember the almost universal jubilation of Europe when the French Revolution began; but remember also how the smoke of blood rose from the guillotine and obscured the judgment of men, so that it took two generations or more for the great ideals of that tremendous uprising to shine out in their first brightness again. If ever there was a grand and holy revolution it was the Puritan revolution under Cromwell. But a certain Charles Stuart, a perfidious traitor, was beheaded; a reaction followed; and today the English Prayer Book still contains prayers for a day of humiliation and fasting for the martyrdom of his blessed majesty, beseeching God not to punish England for his death. Remember the confusion engendered by our Civil War, and the bitter hatred left for these thirty years to poison the springs of our national life.

I do not say that force is never to be used. It is certainly useful as a rod to hang on the wall, and there are bad boys in these United States more alive to the swish of that rod than to all moral suasion. I am only contending that force is not as effective as it looks. The period of agitation and development which has been cut short by it simply comes in afterwards in another form. Not only the violence, but also the suddenness is dangerous. The slow conflict of opposing forces is God's method of educating a nation. He maketh even the stubbornness of conservatives to praise him, though he sometimes does not appear to turn the remainder of it aside. In the peaceful conflict crude schemes are melted down and refined; ideas are elaborated; the public mind is permeated; old fogies die; a young generation grows up with the new ideals bred in their bones; and when the change comes, it has a backing in the people. While if it were forced on an indifferent or hostile majority by a determined minority, there would be a reaction, a repeal, and a great and wise measure would go down to the record of posterity discredited and abolished after trial. Therefore let us counsel patience, not for the sake of the people who might get hurt in a scrimmage, but for the sake of the cause and its ultimate success. Steady progress, measure by measure, is best, feeling our way from step to step with sure-footed Anglo-Saxon caution, keeping our feet on the ground, and not going off in a French balloon of abstract principles and logical schemes.

Right here is a sphere of influence for members of the Brotherhood and others of their kind. We are mostly members of the classes that have money, culture, and power, and have inside influence with those classes. By our influence we can weaken their selfish resistance to the progress of justice, induce them to make piecemeal concessions, and so work off in steady progress the steam which, if accumulated, would burst the boiler.

Fifthly, lastly, and chiefly, many social reformers are practical materialists. In Germany and other continental countries socialists are mostly avowedly materialists. Socialist political economy and materialistic philosophy are there like the two sides of the same cloth. Christian people in Germany seem to regard it as a demonstrated certainty that a Christian workingman will shipwreck his faith if he becomes a socialist. Things are not so bad in this country, but of practical materialism we have enough. We see it in the disproportionate emphasis on the economic side of sociology. Many social reformers do not seem to be aware that there is anything in sociology except taxation, finance, and monopolies. They regard the social body as one of those humble creatures that have no organ except an alimentary canal. How to increase and regulate the production of material goods is the main question with them.

Now it is desirable that men acquire refined tastes and habits, and these presuppose an abundant production of economic goods. It is still more desirable that the goods produced be justly distributed. But the main thing is not more goods, but more justice and equality; not a more luxurious life, but a saner, nobler life. A nation's wealth might grow from three hundred dollars per capita to a thousand dollars, and people might grow unhappier all the time. Scotland and Scandinavia have been poor in goods, but rich in noble hearts and vigorous minds. Greater average luxury may only lead to greater average lasciviousness. "Jerusalem waxed fat and kicked." Jesus parted company with the social reformers of his day on this very point. They wanted material prosperity. He did too, but he wanted first the kingdom of God and God's justice, and prosperity as the natural outcome of that; without that basis prosperity may be a curse. It is true for nations, as well as individuals, that the great thing is not the quantity or quality of meat and drink, but righteousness, peace, and joy in the Holy Ghost; that is, a just, peaceable, and glad life in the Holy Spirit.

This practical materialism is shown not only in picturing the aim of social improvement, but also in planning the means. They put their trust in improved arrangements, voting machines, asphalt pavements, patent streetsweepers, cheaper carfares and telephone rates, etc. Now these things are highly desirable, and I would gladly put in a good shift of work to secure any of them, but any or all of these things will not save a nation. We might have streets as smooth and clean as a Paris boulevard, and the people on it might yet be a libidinous lot, working out their own destruction. If any man says: "Get men converted and never mind how the streets look" I say, "Not a bit of it; as long as children play on them, it matters a lot to me how they look." If another man says: "Let us have ideal streets, and we shall have ideal men," I say, "That is falser yet. You cannot load human cussedness into Colonel Waring's ashcarts and dump it into New York Bay, nor smother the devil under a patent pavement." Material improvements are important, but social reformers must not forget to look deeper than that.

I have tried to sketch the noble desires for personal liberty, equal opportunity, and fraternal association which furnish the material for the ideals of social reformers.

I have also tried to point out the dangers to the liberty of the individual, the integrity of the home, and the just pride of nationality to which some of them are prone; also how they may frustrate the realization of their own hopes by revolutionary methods and the fostering of a materialistic covetousness and trust in material improvements.

I have made similar criticisms before to audiences of socialists, but never to a religious audience, because religious people are inclined to accept such criticisms as ground to excuse themselves from participation in the movement. I hope that will not be the effect of this paper upon Christian readers. We ought to join in it exactly to avert these dangers. For my part, at least, I am a social reformer, though with feeble strength and sad cowardice. I am also a Christian disciple, and in this double quality I have tried to hold the balance even.

❖ ❖ ❖ ❖ ❖ ❖ ❖ ❖

STATE-HELP VERSUS SELF-HELP,
OR PATERNALISM IN GOVERNMENT[1]

Editor's introduction. The Baptist Congress for the Discussion of Current Questions was founded in 1882, and for over thirty years it provided a forum for debate on theological and social issues by both Northern and Southern Baptists. Rauschenbusch addressed the Congress in 1888 — the first of many such occasions.[2] He was elected promptly to the executive committee, and later served a term (1892–95) as corresponding secretary of the Congress.

In 1898 Rauschenbusch gave one of three papers on the subject of paternalism in government. His associates on the platform were Shailer Mathews of the University of Chicago and a Brooklyn writer, George William Douglas. Charles Evans Hughes was also to have addressed the assembly on the same topic, but his law practice interfered. In emphasizing the role of the state in industrial society, Rauschenbusch was no doubt attempting to overcome the individualistic views that were strong among many Baptists, especially those of rural background. Some of the points he made call to mind the work of Gladden and Ely — for example, his stress on equal rights for labor, and his interest in state ownership of natural monopolies.

❖ ❖ ❖ ❖

1. *We define our terms.*

"Paternalism" is a mildly contumelious term used by orthodox political economists to designate something kind but foolish. More picturesquely yet, it is called "grandmotherly legislation." It designates legislative inter-

1. *Sixteenth Annual Session of the Baptist Congress for the Discussion of Current Questions, held in the Delaware Avenue Baptist Church, Buffalo, N.Y., November 15th, 16th and 17th, 1898* (N.Y., 1898), 107–16.
2. In *A Rauschenbusch Reader,* Benson Y. Landis gives half a dozen samples from Rauschenbusch's addresses to the Congress, including about a third of the one reprinted here.

ference by the state on behalf of single classes, proceeding from benevolent motives, but running counter to so-called natural economic laws.

Its alternative is "self-help," which leaves every man to do the best he can for himself in the industrial struggle for existence. On this latter theory the state is to confine itself to the maintenance of order. The Germans wickedly call this "die Nachtwaechtertheorie vom Staat," [3] because it conceives of the state as a magnified policeman, patrolling the streets for thieves, but without further obligations.

The topic fails to state a third alternative: socialism. Socialism is not paternalism. Common ownership is not state interference. There is nothing grandmotherly in it, if the citizens of a town come to the conclusion that they can furnish their own water, make their own gas, or run their own streetcars more cheaply and profitably than by allowing a stock company to do it for them. On the contrary, when New York City, unable to provide rapid transit for itself, has to look with meek and imploring eyes to the Manhattan Elevated and Russell Sage [4] to come to its rescue, then we have that helpless dependence on a beneficent and omnipotent power above us which constitutes the essence of paternalism. A national postal service and municipal waterworks are not measures of state interference, but measures of cooperative self-help on a large scale.

It is true, there are isolated cases of public ownership which are paternal in their nature, the South Carolina liquor monopoly, for instance. But in the same way abstinence from public ownership may be paternal in its nature, too. When our postal department limits the weight of packages to four pounds in order not to compete with the express companies, or discourages the sending of large amounts by money order lest it draw business away from the banks, that refusal to extend state functions is a paternal guarding of certain classes at the expense of the rest, and it is in defiance of natural economic laws. No private business would abstain from extending itself in these directions, if it had such a chance.

I place so much emphasis on this distinction between paternalism and socialism, between state interference and state ownership, because in a loose fashion all extensions of state functions are frequently lumped and stigmatized as paternalism.

There are, then, three possible lines of action: on the one extreme, self-help or economic individualism; on the other extreme, state ownership or

---

3. [ED.] "The nightwatchman theory of the state."

4. [ED.] Russell Sage (1816–1906) amassed a huge fortune from his speculations in railway securities.

socialism; and between the two, state interference or paternalism, which seeks to stand on the basis of individualism, but to mitigate the evils thereof by measures largely borrowed from socialism. But these measures are often applied sporadically and without the saving spirit of democracy. The very name "state-help" is a relic of an undemocratic theory of government; it indicates that the state is still regarded as an entity apart from the people, which can stoop down to them and do things for them.

II. *We are now living under a régime of state-help.*

The era of laisser faire has passed. Its advocates are still puissant voices in economic literature, but in practical politics all civilized nations are committed to a policy of benevolent interference. I shall give a few instances of paternal legislation. They are merely samples, just enough to bring the situation before us. It must be remembered, too, that there is no uniformity of legislation in our various States.

The United States counteract the law of supply and demand, and interfere with the free flow of labor in favor of the laboring classes at home, by forbidding the importation of labor under contract. They exercise paternal care over the immigrants immediately on their arrival, by giving only a few licensed hotelkeepers access to them and by maintaining a free labor bureau for them.

Most States, I believe, have "Truck Acts," forbidding the payment of laborers in anything but money in order to guard them against the "company stores." The state, even in America, has begun to interfere with the conditions of labor; to fix a maximum working day or week and a minimum wage; to secure a Saturday half-holiday; to prescribe how often and when workingmen shall be paid; and to insist on proper space and ventilation in factories. It excludes children below a certain age entirely, and regulates the employment of older children. It is beginning at last to compel retail stores to furnish seats for their saleswomen and to provide places where they can eat their lunches without being nauseated. It compels factories to fence their dangerous machinery and in unhealthful employments enforces other sanitary safeguards. The state interferes to secure one rest day in seven; a measure borrowed from the paternalism of Moses, in the maintenance of which religious custom fortunately gives its powerful backing to economic interests.

All this is evidently state-help. Self-help would leave it to the self-interest or humanity of employers to provide for the health and efficiency of their hands, or to the individual or combined initiative of the employees to insist on proper conditions of labor under penalty of refusing to work for the undesirable employer.

The state further interferes by the inspection of articles used by its citizens. It inspects and marks herrings in Scotland, gun-barrels in Birmingham, silver plate in London, slaughtered hogs in Germany, and ships, boilers, elevators, building plans, sewerage, banks, bakeshops and insurance companies in America.

The state in paternal helpfulness furnishes free information to citizens in need thereof; consular reports on foreign countries to its merchants seeking an outlet for trade; free seeds and information about bugs and beets to its farmers; and weather reports to sailors and picnic parties. It establishes libraries for our instruction and parks for our recreation; provides brass bands for our edification, and stocks rivers with trout and bass for the betterment of our morals. It tries to save us from temptation by restricting or forbidding the liquor traffic and the sale of indecent books and pictures. It keeps us clean in New York by forbidding the use of soft coal, and (alas!) dirty in Chicago by permitting it. It insists on fire escapes for hotels and tenements down which we can climb, and provides firemen to carry us down if we haven't enough self-help in us to be able to climb. It stands ready to teach us if we are blind; to feed us if we are poor; to care for us if we are sick or old; to rescue us if we are shipwrecked, and to bury us if we are dead. In most countries it even provides for our safety after death by supporting a state church.

It may be objected that some of the functions named are not paternal, but are part of the essential duty of the state in protecting the life and property of its citizens. I have tried to select only fair cases which have been left in the past, and might conceivably now be left, to the self-help of the individual. If there is any question about them, it shows how difficult it is to draw the line between proper and superfluous activity of the state. The state protects the life of a citizen if it arrests a man who tries to shoot him; if it repairs pavements on which he might break his neck; if it inspects and condemns a bicycle or a sausage which might do him to death; and if it tells him when to come in out of the rain to avoid pneumonia. And the last may be more necessary to the saving of his life than the first. Now where does proper state care of life end and fussy paternalism begin?

The most important measures of paternalism are some that are so firmly established in law and custom that they are not usually recognized as such. I shall mention three.

One is the protection of home industries by the tariff. Nursing infant industries is certainly a paternal function — or must we say a maternal function? A tax adjusted so that it will exclude foreign competition, taxes home consumers for the benefit of a limited class of producers, and does not even give government an income for its pains. Let the orthodox American majority voter remember that when next he makes damnatory remarks about paternalism.

A second instance is our public school system. The paternal state provides free schools and free schoolbooks for its children, and may yet provide free lunches. In many states it intervenes even against the parents to compel the education of the child, instead of leaving the desire for education to work out its own fulfillment. I know that this is commonly justified on the ground that the state guards its own welfare in preventing the ignorance of its citizens. But that theory was patched up to hide our blushes when we meet the consistent individualist in the gates. A law prohibiting high-heeled shoes could similarly be justified on the score that healthy mothers are essential to the welfare of the state. No; public education, at least when it is as lavish and loving and constantly expanding as it is with us, cannot be squeezed into the pigeonhole of "the self-protection of the state." When it was first introduced in individualistic England, it was very properly denounced as un-English, fit only for Germans or Americans.

A third important instance of paternalism is the enforcement of private contracts. Suppose A lends money to B, who is untrustworthy. B fails to pay. A can then set in motion the huge machinery of the police and the courts to compel him to pay, and finally use the state as an auctioneer at a sheriff's sale. Now self-help would let the foolish lender suffer for his folly. Henceforth A and all his kin would lend only to good and safe men. Capital would concentrate in the hands of the good, and the bad would go out of business, or reform. That would cut down our state expenses for law courts, reduce the Egyptian plague of lawyers, put a premium on uprightness, and conclusively demonstrate the moral order of the universe. Yet, though there are doubtless many opponents of paternalism here, I doubt if there is a corporal's guard who would favor the abolition of our present system.

I have tried to bring home to us that paternalism is not something new and alien to American life and institutions, which foolish men are now trying to introduce among us; but that we are living under a régime of paternalism, and that it is at most a question whether we are to push out freely in that direction, or to restrict state-help to the absolutely necessary. Our next point addresses itself to the solution of that question.

III. *There are evils on both sides.*

It is justly urged that if the people learn to look to the state instead of their own vigor and initiative for relief from every ill, they will grow less energetic, cautious and self-reliant. Paternalism lessens both the inclination and the opportunity of running risks. It narrows the field of permitted undertakings. It has been wittily said that if the ships of Columbus had been inspected according to modern laws, he would never have been allowed to discover America. State inspection, while it lessens the risk of consumers, frees producers and owners from claims for damages, if damage does happen. And if state inspectors are bribed, the people have neither prevention nor cure.

Again, legislation is sweeping in its nature; it cannot take proper account of local needs. A law that may be useful in one trade or locality may be superfluous in another. And constant legislative interference is irritating and injurious.

These objections are serious. Liberty of action is a precious good in itself, and a mighty educator of men. But it must not be forgotten that there are objections against unrestricted laisser faire too.

Self-help is the remedy of the strong. It may do for the building trades or the locomotive engineers, but it is least effective for those who need help most.

Furthermore, experience has proved that while certain interests can safely be left to private initiative, others simply cannot. For instance, one would suppose that workingmen would look after arrangements guarding them against mutilation and violent death. But actually those who brush the sleeve of Death all day are most callous to his presence. Nor can that matter be left to the humanity or self-interest of the employers. Professor Jevons tells of a manufacturer who was informed by an inspector that he would have to fence certain machinery.[5] He raised no objection; said it was true that a man had been killed there recently; but he had apparently never thought of preventing the danger until he was told he must. It is terrible to read of conditions in England before modern labor legislation began; of young children and half-naked women working in the foul

5. [ED.] W. Stanley Jevons (1835–82) was a productive English statistician and political economist, known for *The Theory of Political Economy* (London, 1871), *Methods of Social Reform* (London, 1883), and many other works. He called attention to individual, subjective factors in economic life, which led to the formulation of a theory of value based on utility as an alternative to the classical theory of value based on labor.

atmosphere of coal mines; of infants under ten years old working at the loom in the heated air of cotton mills for fifteen hours a day and kept awake by the overlooker's lash. That was *not* paternalism. Every step in the Factory Laws was met by indifference or opposition, sometimes from both sides. The Mercantile Inspection Bill in this State was defeated repeatedly by a lobby representing the department stores of New York, who, in their capacity as heavy advertisers, muzzled even the news departments of the daily papers. This is not suspicion, but a fact.

The remedies of paternal legislation are often irritating and burdensome. But how about the remedies of self-help? The strike and boycott are the militant measures of self-help — the only ones it offers after moral suasion has failed. But think of the expense of a strike to both sides; of its indirect injury to trade; of the class hatred it breeds; of the damage it often inflicts on an innocent public. Its results, when there are any, are less permanent than the enactment of a law. It may lead to riot and open battles. Homestead, Brooklyn, Hazleton, and Virden[6] have cost our country dear, by decreasing patriotism, weakening the respect for law and its interpreters, and demoralizing us all by shame and the sense of our impotence. Yet that was the struggle of self-help. Would compulsory arbitration be much worse?

The alternative of state inspection to prevent accidents is the granting of damages after the accidents have happened, in order thus to prevent future accidents. But do not forget how difficult it is for the poor to collect damages at law. I once served as intermediary between a family that had lost its head and provider by an accident, and the corporation concerned. The officers stated their case with entire frankness. It was worth two hundred dollars to them to compound the claim; if the family sued and won, they would appeal; in any case they could make the case run several years; the corporation lawyer was engaged by the year and the case would not cost them much, so they had a longer wind that the plaintiffs. The family was convinced, and two hundred dollars was paid for the man's life. I am not judging that corporation. Its business involves an almost daily succession of accidents, and they are not a benevolent society. I am only pointing out the drawbacks of the remedies offered by self-help.

If, then, there are evils on both sides, it becomes largely a question of

6. [ED.] These sites of acute labor conflicts would have been instantly recognizable to an audience in the 1890's.

wisdom to find the lesser evil in any given case, and in such matters a cubic inch of experience is worth a cubic mile of theory.

IV. *We seek to draw the lessons of economic history.*

I shall try to summarize the experience of the past and the probable trend of the future in a few statements.

1. We shall never go back to unrestricted laisser faire. Evolutionary philosophy might permit it. But we also have a heart educated by Christianity, and a lively, though spasmodic, sense of human solidarity. It is not a question today whether we are to return to self-help, but whether we are to stop at state help or pass on to state ownership. The Duke of Argyll [7] wisely says: "The two great discoveries of the present age in economic practice have been the desirability of removing restrictions on the free exchange of goods, and the absolute necessity of imposing conditions on the free disposal of labor."

2. It is no longer open to question that the state must interfere against the industrial exploitation of children, to safeguard their right to unstunted physical growth and a fair measure of education.

3. Likewise the state must interfere on behalf of women. Experience has shown that women rarely organize in trade, and singly they are helpless. Moreover, their case differs from that of men in that they do not merely represent working capacity, but are the mothers of the race. When England declared it unfit that women work in mines, the usual objections were made both by mine owners and by the women; now everybody has acquiesced. But neither is it fit that young girls be kept standing all day in retail stores and enter marriage physically broken. Nor is it fit that nursing mothers work in factories while their babies are fed on artificial food at home, to die early or grow up puny.

4. The state must look after the sanitary condition of all places where larger numbers of people work together. It must regulate the air space, ventilation, heating, length of working time, meal hours, etc., in factories and stores. In our present huge organization of labor, in the shifting character of our working population, and in the absence of social bonds between employers and employees, these matters cannot be left to private

---

7. [ED.] George Douglas Campbell, Eighth Duke of Argyll (1823–1900), wrote extensively in the fields of religion and science, evolution, and economics. The "radical duke" was prominent in politics, serving liberal British administrations in a number of cabinet posts.

contract. There must be laws to regulate, and especially there must be an adequate force of inspectors to enforce the laws.

5. There must be state inspection of important articles, on the safety or genuineness of which the public is not competent to pass, e.g. the safety of boilers or steamboats, the quality of milk, water, or lighting gas, etc. On the other hand, all questions of mere taste or convenience should be left to individuals.

6. Self-help is ineffective against corporations holding natural monopolies. The individual cannot cheapen carfares by refusing to ride, nor compel purer or cheaper gas by burning kerosene. The state by its franchise creates such monopolies; it is a partner in them; and it is responsible for their behavior.

7. But experience has shown that constant state interference is irksome to the corporations, corrupting to the state, and not always satisfactory to the public. Where state interference yields no remedy, state ownership should be fearlessly tried. The success of modern experiments in it amply justifies the trial. It is true that there are great potential dangers in it; but it is also true that there are great actual dangers and evils in our present system of farming out franchises. Public ownership may build up a great bureaucracy; but our present system has actually built up in the great corporations a huge administrative organization, which is less amenable to public interest and public opinion than state officials. A great body of officeholders may indeed become a menace to free institutions; but our great corporations, dependent on legislatures and officials for privileges, are actually now the chief source of corruption in our public life. It is true that state ownership would do away with competition, check private initiative, and eliminate the element of personal ownership and management. But all that is being done now. Competiton between railroads or gas companies is difficult to begin and more difficult to maintain. The minor stockholders of a railway have next to no voice in the management. If it is our industrial destiny to submit to industrial centralization and its evils anyway, let us at least have the profits of centralization too, and the sense of ownership which public proprietorship would awaken in the people. If the state has often done its work badly, perhaps the remedy is not to withhold further work from it, but to make its work so large and so important to public comfort that its performance will be jealously watched, and a higher standard of efficiency and fidelity will be set for our public servants. I believe it is fair to say that the experience of the past points

away from state interference with natural monopolies and toward state ownership of them.

In conclusion, I would offer three suggestions to those who are afraid of socialism, dissatisfied with paternalism, and desirous to retain the largest possible measure of industrial individualism:

1. See that any lingering inequalities in our laws are purged out, so that if the workingman is to fight for himself, he will, at least, not have to fight with one hand strapped to his back. Brentano says: All statutes of laborers in the Middle Ages were framed with regard to the powers and wants of the landed proprietors.[8] Our legislation has come to us in unbroken continuity from a past when the lower classes did not help to make the laws. It is on the face of it unlikely that the short span of time during which the common people have had a voice in legislation, has sufficed to secure real equality in principle and practice. But until there is equality of law, self-help is unfair.

2. Help self-help. Help cooperative stores and profit-sharing along. Offer your services for the peaceful settlement of labor disputes. Extend the organization of labor. Back up just strikes. These are the means offered by self-help. If you trust in this Caesar, strengthen Caesar's hands.

3. Strengthen public opinion in its demands for justice and humanity. That is the silent arbiter in all our struggles for the right, the compulsory power in all progress. As long as the walking delegate is sneered at and labor leaders vilified by the religious and secular press; as long as good men concede it as self-evident that employers can do as they will with their own, and that "there is nothing to arbitrate," unless they please, so long self-help is helplessness. Remember that every great strike that fails, strengthens the impression that self-help is futile, and that salvation comes only by state help or socialism. If you wish to stave off socialism, stiffen the public opinion which backs up the labor movement. And that, gentlemen, is not done by silence.

8. [ED.] Lujo Brentano (1844–1931), a German political economist, wrote standard works on the Christian socialist movement of Britain and on the history of the English trade union movement, and aroused wide interest in the study of medieval guilds.

ENGLAND AND GERMANY [1]

Editor's introduction. Because of their emphasis on awakening the churches of America to the domestic social crisis, it can easily be overlooked that the social gospel leaders were men of wide interests. Gladden, Ely, and Rauschenbusch, with many other social Christians, had a deep interest in international affairs, and were themselves widely traveled. A knowledge of other nations and their problems is more or less evident in the major social-Christian writings of all three men. Occasionally they dealt with these matters directly, revealing a concern for international justice and peace.

In the article reprinted here, Rauschenbusch discussed the international situation at the outbreak of the Boer War (1899–1902) in which England fought for control of the Orange Free State and the Transvaal. Rauschenbusch had spent time in both England and Germany, and had a premonition of their eventual conflict. The international superiority of European and North American powers is taken for granted.

What will happen if England proves unable to conquer the two South African republics? If the giant slips and goes to his knees a moment, will the powers take the opportunity? What will happen if England conquers and annexes the two republics? Will the other powers demand compensation elsewhere, and will England have to yield it? Back of the local struggle in Africa looms the sinister possibility of a concerted movement of the great powers against England.

Public attention has been fixed for several years on the conflicting interests of Russia and England. The relations of France and England were also discussed in connection with the recent Fashoda incident.[2] On the

1. "England and Germany," *The Watchman*, VIII (November 16, 1899), 9–11.
2. [ED.] In 1896, the movements of English and French troops toward Fashoda on the Nile brought the two nations to the brink of war. The French, harassed by the Dreyfus affair, decided to back down, but anti-English feeling in France became intense.

other hand, the relation of Germany and England has not received, in this century, the consideration which it deserves.

I was surprised, during a recent visit in Germany, to find how unfriendly the feeling of Germans toward England has become. It is not France that is distrusted and denounced; it is England. The Dreyfus affair gave opportunity enough for harsh judgments and for malicious pleasure in the weakness of France, but the tone of the German newspapers seemed to me far more courteous and forbearing than that which prevailed in America.[3] But England! Selfish, greedy, lying, perfidious Albion! The free civil institutions of England are still admired as models by the radical political parties. But for England in its international relations I found only angry distrust. This is a serious fact. National likes and dislikes are powerful factors in modern politics. How has this feeling arisen?

One cause is the commercial rivalry between the two countries. Germany's progress in manufacturing and commerce during the last twenty years has been astonishing. Her foreign carrying trade is immense. She is treading on England's heels all over the East, in Australia, South America, Africa, and in the home country. The English law requiring imported goods to be marked with their origin was an act of self-defense against Germany, but the prevalence of the sign, "Made in Germany," only demonstrated the headway which German trade has gained. This progress is due largely to the admirable technical education furnished in Germany. The German schoolmaster is again winning her wars. It is also due to the fostering care of a paternal government. The German steamer lines to East and West Africa, to Australia and the East Indies, have been built up by government subsidies, and the policy pays. German young men have long been the trusted clerks and managers of business houses all over the world. But formerly they were absorbed by the English population. Individually they grew rich, but they furnished no increment to German power. Germany made no attempt to hold her children on foreign shores; they were regarded as lost. That is different now. She is carefully strengthening German sentiment abroad, and building the scaffolding of a German world empire by her colonies. England feels the growth

3. [ED.] In 1894 Captain Alfred Dreyfus of the French army was falsely charged with treason. He was convicted; and even when the facts of the affair began to come to light, many of the French, under the influence of anti-Semitic feeling, still regarded him as guilty. The ensuing terrible controversy continued for over a decade before Dreyfus was finally exonerated.

of this rival power, and it is not improving her temper toward Germany. But the other side, too, has its feelings, and they have been rasped. Commercial rivalry would not of itself be so exasperating if it were not roughened by contempt. Your Briton is a capital fellow among equals, but gentleness and courtesy toward those whom he regards as his inferiors is not one of his strong points. And, unfortunately, all who do not speak English as their native tongue are apt to be regarded as his inferiors. The inbred consciousness of being the chosen people is an argument for the descent of the English from the Lost Tribes of Israel which has not, perhaps, received full weight with those who hold that interesting theory.[4] Even we in America have winced when the visiting Englishman has patronizingly criticized our manners. And yet we are fortified in our self-respect by the knowledge of past growth, present greatness, and future destiny. It is almost impossible for an American to realize how it feels to belong to a waning race or a puny nation. Germans ate the bitter herbs of national humiliation with their daily bread for generations. However superior the individual German might be to the individual Englishman or Frenchman, he felt in them that sense of national strength which he lacked, and the foreigner was quite ready to accept the superior position conceded to him. Since the unification of the German empire [1871] that has begun to change. The pride of national greatness is getting into the German blood. He has moved his chair higher up at the council-board of the nations. But the others have not quite realized the change. The old tone lingers, and is resented. The exaggerated determination with which Germans have been bracing their shoulders and setting down their feet in Samoa, in China, and the Philippines, is the natural action of one whose social position is not fully conceded, and who is compelled to shoulder his way to recognition. When English papers advise the German emperor with a "my dear little man" sort of tone to learn sense of his wise English mother, it makes the German hand twitch toward the sword-hilt, for Germans have exceedingly small regard for "Madame Cohn." [5] In short, one element of the ill feeling is the resentment of a strong and growing nation toward another nation, stronger, more self-confident, and always arrogant. And the fact that the two are blood relations does not soothe the quarrel.

4. [ED.] A reference to a movement known variously as Anglo-Israel, British Israel, the Anglo-Saxon Federation, etc., which holds as its principal article of belief that the Anglo-Saxon peoples are the true Israel, and the heirs to the promises of God to Israel as recorded in the Scriptures.

5. [ED.] An uncomplimentary reference to Queen Victoria.

Another cause for the present German aloofness is the posthumous influence of Bismarck. I know of nothing in English or American life that even approximates the reverence paid in Germany to that colossal figure. To the gratitude for the restoration of Germany unity, and the over-mastering influence of the man for so many years, is added the historical bent of the German mind, and the conscious cult of the dead man's memory in the schools. Men look to the political principles of Bismarck as to a sort of authoritative revelation of statesmanship, authenticated by the miracles of its success. Now, one of the fundamental principles of Bismarck's statecraft was that Russia, and not England, is the friend to be sought by Germany. Russia has the stable policy of an autocratic govern-ment, and the traditions of an hereditary house. England is vacillating by the changes of its party government and the succession of its prime minis-ters. Russia's interests rarely conflict with Germany's. England's interests are bound to conflict with Germany's more as Germany becomes a com-mercial power. Russia is the bulwark of monarchical institutions and of the conservative spirit. England's spirit and institutions are democratic, its influence cosmopolitan and unsettling; therefore, tie to Russia, keep clear of England. That was one of Bismarck's leading thoughts, and the con-servative portion of Germany has got the lesson by heart now.

A fourth cause for German dislike of England is religious dissimilarity. It is true, both are in the main Protestant nations, but the type of their Protestantism differs greatly. Religious life, in so far as it affects political life in England, is the humanitarian democracy begotten by Puritanism. German religion has been taught to confine itself to the inner life, the family, and the personal calling. When religion affects political action in Germany, it is by ecclesiastical considerations rather than by an ethical spirit. And so Germany does not understand Exeter Hall.[6] It does not ap-preciate a nation getting angry about the Bulgarian or Armenian atroci-ties, or enthusiastic about universal peace, especially if the same nation somehow uses these popular excitements to slip its foot a little farther forward in Turkey. When Jacob tells his dreams of celestial ladders, and then acquires Laban's herds by devious ways, Germany is disgusted. It has never understood Cromwell; to kill a king and to set up an autocracy, to pray fervently and plot deeply, to seek the glory of the Lord and to make money hand over fist, is a combination baffling to the German mind. It looks too much like hypocrisy. That is an unfair judgment; but

6. [ED.] The London headquarters of the evangelical party of the Church of Eng-land—a reference to the English evangelical spirit in general.

we are trying to see things from the German point of view just now, and we must acknowledge that there are facts enough to support this interpretation, if prejudice first inclines the mind to it.

Sketched with rough and perhaps exaggerating lines, that seems to be the sentiment prevailing in Germany, with a few of the causes that have created it. It is well to keep this sentiment in mind, if we inquire further for the probable policy of Germany in international affairs.

Germany is one of the oldest of the great nations, but the youngest of the great powers. She gained her unity and her European standing by a great feat of arms. She guards both only by perpetual vigilance. Like the builders of Nehemiah, she has to build the walls of her greatness with a trowel in one hand and a sword in the other. She has to reckon always with the wounded pride of France and the demand for revenge. She is superior to France in numbers, but inferior in wealth and more vulnerable in her geographical position. France has only one first-class power touching her borders, namely Germany. Germany has three — France, Austria, and Russia, all of them possible enemies. She has two allies at present, but each of them has its weakness. Italy is akin to France by blood, language, and religion; she is also desperately poor, and getting restive under the military burden imposed on her by the Triple Alliance [7] as her share of the work. Austria is a conglomerate of peoples and languages; like a vessel with a crack across the middle, she has to be handled gingerly. They are not the best possible allies, and Germany knows it well. The three together overmatched either Russia or France; but are they equal to the Dual Alliance? [8] If the old Triple Alliance of the three empires could be restored, or if the anger of France could be allayed, and Germany become the middle member of an alliance reaching from the Pyrenees to the Pacific Ocean, that would indeed be a different matter.

The latter contingency is not as impossible as it looks at first sight. France is not the natural ally of Russia. They are the most heterogeneous states in Europe. It will be remembered how slowly and grudgingly Russia allowed happy France to inform the world of their alliance. France for over a hundred years has stood for the revolutionary movement of the peoples; Russia has for the same length of time almost completely succeeded in barring out that movement. Those who have read Bismarck's Memoirs will remember how the menace of that movement constantly influences the monarchs of the Continent. Think of the incongruity of it, when the "Marseillaise" was played by a Russian band in St. Petersburg,

7. [ED.] Germany, Austria, and Italy.   8. [ED.] France and Russia.

to welcome the president of France. It was only the fear of the Dreibund that drove Russia to this alliance, and even now she carries her obligations rather lightly. France has found no countenance with Russia for her war of retaliation. On the contrary, she has been held down to peace by being yoked to Russia. Would she make further concessions for fear of losing her only ally? The Kaiser has lost no opportunity of showing the polite attentions which the feminine pride of France values. His messages of condolence, his recent visit to a French schoolship, his generous reference to her brave dead at the dedication of a battlefield monument, perhaps, too, his reticence in the Dreyfus matter, all show that he is carefully employing a monarch's power of gratifying and honoring, in order to assuage the bitter memories of France. His efforts and the good offices of the passing years have not been quite in vain. There is a stir of hopefulness in Germany, that a war of revenge may yet be averted; but the strongest force to draw the two together would be a common foe. A new hatred would obliterate the old. Suppose Germany were needed in a combination against England? The world has already been astonished by seeing France and Germany appear side by side to back Russia against England and Japan in China. Under Russia's leadership that might happen again.

Germany has everything to gain by peace on the Continent. Every year adds to her commerce and wealth and navy. Every year she outstrips France farther in the number of fighting men. She has unassimilated elements along her borders: the French in Alsace and Lorraine; the Danes in Schleswig; the Poles in the eastern provinces; she needs only time for them. She has nothing to gain from a new war with France. She desires peace between Russia and Austria; for if Austria breaks up, the German portion, it is true, would almost certainly fall to the share of Germany, but the Slavonic portions and the Balkan states would gravitate to Russia. By that composite character of hers Austria is the great dike protecting the Teutonic portion of Central Europe against the flood of Pan-Slavism. This is one of the reasons why Germany is propping the Turk. She cannot afford to have the Eastern question opened, and Russia and Austria in collision about it; at least not yet, for as yet Russia and England would be the only gainers. But give Germany time and she, too, may get her share. The influence of Germany is very strong at the Sublime Porte.[9] German capital is coming to take that leading position in the Levant which long belonged to France. There are prosperous colonies of Ger-

9. [ED.] The Ottoman Turkish court and government.

man settlers in Syria who are doing more than any outsiders to revive agriculture. The pilgrimage of the Kaiser was not all piety, nor all love of display. England has Egypt; Russia will have Constantinople. It may be Germany's part some day to reconstruct Syria; but her interests in the Mediterranean are not yet sufficient for that, therefore she needs time.

Germany is not yet a really first-class power. There are only three powers in the world that have both intelligence and energy enough and a sufficient territorial base for world empires of the largest kind; they are England, Russia, and the United States. But Germany comes first in the powers of the next rank. Surrounded by enemies, not greatly favored by nature, weakened by generations of disunion, she has by intelligence, thrift, and foresight nursed her commercial and military forces till they occupy a truly commanding position. Her women furnish the first requisite of national greatness, the living force of men. Her schools train them. But who will create additional territory on which they may live and work? Germany wants foreign possessions. She needs them as points of support for her foreign commerce and naval power. She needs them if the overflow of her population is not to be lost to her. Her sons and daughters have gone for a hundred years to enrich the blood and brains of other nations, especially of the English-speaking nations. These German emigrants have kept their colonies almost intact against Russian influence; they have been absorbed slowly by France; but they melt into English and American life. The more possessions Germany has abroad, the more permanent nuclei of German life will be formed and serve as points of support to buttress the lengthening span of German foreign power.

But wherever Germany goes, she finds England there before her. England has three centuries the start of her, and there is little left to take. Jacob has the blessing; let Esau go and mourn. The one great branch of the Teutonic family has vastly outstripped the other. But "we be of one blood, you and I." Is it strange or ridiculous that the Continental Teutons, now that they have at last found their organic unity, should seek to do what the insular Teutons have been doing for ages?

This, then, is the situation. England has pre-empted the world. The significance of her foreign possessions has not been fully realized, except perhaps by the most prescient minds, until now that modern means of communication have widened out the arena of international action. In the future, their home territory will be only the standing point from which the European nations will play their world-wide game. The Eastern question no longer centers in Turkey, but in China; so large has the world become. Will the other nations consent to remain cramped in their expansion by the sprawling limbs of the British empire, if they can help it? If ever the giant is wounded in one place, and for a moment relaxes his hold on the outlying possessions — that will be the historic moment for the others. The very vastness of England's power will drive her opponents into coalition, if it has not already done so. As for Germany, if a common war with England would draw Russia to her side, cause France to forget her older feud, and hold out promise of the world empire which can be gained in no other way, would it not be worth while for Germany? And, on the other hand, if the English government knows the state of public sentiment in Germany, and realizes what is at stake in keeping the Continental powers disunited at this juncture, would it not be worth while for England to secure the full neutrality of Germany even at the price of a large concession? Why is the German government so entirely unresponsive to the public indignation against England's Transvaal war? Why has the attitude of protecting friendship and kinship toward the Dutch republic been abandoned?

So we repeat the questions with which we set out: What will happen if England proves unable to conquer the Boer republics? And again, what will happen if she does conquer and annex them?

DOGMATIC AND PRACTICAL SOCIALISM [1]

Editor's introduction. Rauschenbusch was interested in the socialist movement because of its concern for social justice. In 1912 he could call it "far and away the most powerful force for justice, democracy, and organized fraternity in the modern world." Yet, he added, Christian people found that "these moral elements were fused with an alloy that is repellent to their Christian instincts." [2] Rauschenbusch himself was generally known as a Christian socialist, but his socialism was mild, revisionist, evolutionary, and non-doctrinaire. For him, Christian socialism was a "peculiar genus" of the movement, consciously antagonistic to its prevailing tendencies at a number of points, and especially to its materialistic philosophy, while insisting on the role of religion in the betterment of society, and asserting the moral responsibility of the individual. [3] Basically a reformer himself, he called for immediate practical steps toward alleviating social injustice and promoting improved living and working conditions. He opposed scientific and doctrinaire socialism. His views were carefully set forth in an address given at Rochester in 1901, which attracted wide attention. For example, Joseph O'Connor declared in an editorial, "The address of Walter Rauschenbusch at the Labor Lyceum yesterday was clear, candid, scholarly — a masterly discussion of the great theme of the day." He thought Rauschenbusch had hit "the socialist element in the Labor Lyceum very hard." [4] Many newspapers printed the address in full.

This paper is not a random shot. For more than a year I have wished to address this Labor Lyceum on this topic, because I felt that the questions I am going to discuss are of very great practical importance; and further, that their discussion is especially needed right here. I take it that the

1. *Rochester Democrat and Chronicle*, February 25, 1901.
2. *Christianizing the Social Order*, 397.
3. See his posthumously published article, "Christian Socialism," *A Dictionary of Religion and Ethics*, Shailer Mathews and Gerald B. Smith, eds. (N.Y., 1921), 90–91.
4. *Rochester Post-Express*, February 25, 1901.

great majority of us would be classed as socialists. There may be a few old-school individualists here, a sprinkling of new-school individualists in the shape of single-taxers or philosophical anarchists; but in the main this audience, like similar audiences in the cities everywhere, is composed of socialists.

As such, we would probably agree in the following fundamental positions: That the instruments of production are today in the hands of a limited number, that this limited number of persons absorbs the chief advantages arising from machinery and the social organization of labor; that labor does not receive its fair share of what it produces; that the wages of labor are determined not so much by its productiveness as by its needs; that the small producer is more and more eliminated, and production concentrated under the direction of a few men; that these men thereby wield a power which is dangerous to the people; that while production becomes more social, the appropriation of its benefits is by individuals, and that the issuing of the products is anarchic and haphazard, resulting in industrial and commercial crises and spasms, with enormous waste of wealth and labor.

In view of these facts, we believe in replacing the competitive system of production and distribution by a system in which not only the production of wealth, but its distribution shall be social. I have purposely stated these points in general terms to give as many as possible standing ground in this platform and make us realize our essential unity.

The clear recognition of these evils, and the outlook toward this escape from the troubles of our present social order, have been of immense value to us all. They have saved us from the frantic ignorance in which we might otherwise seek an escape by aimless violence, and have turned political economy from a dismal into a hopeful science. I had occasion recently to read a primer on political economy by Jevons. It represents the old-school liberalism with all its cocksure and smiling demonstration that two times two is five, and that the working classes are getting all they ought to get, and that this is the best of possible worlds, if only people would stop interfering with natural laws. It made me laugh, and I realized how far we have really advanced beyond that.

EVOLUTION OF SOCIALISM

But while the chief ideas of the new political economy are now clearly wrought out on a solid historical basis of facts, there are minor questions still at issue. Socialism does not pretend to be a cast-iron system of economic doctrine, once for all revealed to Karl Marx. In Germany, where the scientific thinking of socialism has chiefly been done, there has been a steady evolution of the party program; some ideas have been dropped; others have been inserted. As one of the German leaders has expressed it, the party is always molting its feathers. In our country we have had the school of socialism represented by Edward Bellamy, who held that all men, women, and children should share alike in the results of social production, not on the basis of work done, but on the basis of their humanity; while most of us, I suppose, hold that men should be paid on the basis of the quantity and quality of their work. So, because there are such minor questions still unsettled, and because there are different tendencies of socialist thought, we find different schools or even separate socialist parties working side by side, and at times butting against each other.

I want to raise one of these family quarrels this afternoon, not about some question of detail, but about a deep-seated difference in tactics. To formulate this difference I divide socialists into dogmatic socialists and practical socialists. By dogmatic socialists I mean those who do not believe in any immediate partial realization of the socialist aims, but expect to see them all realized at once in a coming social catastrophe, and meanwhile confine themselves to the discussion of socialist doctrine and theory. By practical socialists I mean those who believe in immediate social reforms, which would approximate to the socialist commonwealth, and at the same time prepare for its complete realization. This difference is so deep and far-reaching that all other differences are slight compared to it.

It was natural that in its infancy socialism confined itself to working out its ideas. It began by criticizing the present social order; it investigated its historical origin, showed its effects on the people and its necessary outcome. It also developed a theory of the true economic system of production. It elaborated these ideas, gathered a mass of historical material to buttress the theory, and popularized the whole for the people. That was all that could be done at first.

After Two Generations

Meanwhile two generations have passed. In Germany the social-democratic party is the largest in point of votes among the group of parties. In England and America the socialist parties as such are insignificant in numbers, but socialist ideas and sentiments have spread on the wings of free thought and a free press, and have become very influential in public life. In a number of the civilized nations there is at least a possibility of immediately realizing the social program by installments. But there are many socialists who refuse to make any effort in that direction. They are holding off until the present economic order shall have decayed so far, and socialist convictions have spread so thoroughly, that socialists can seize political power and at once put an end to the whole system and inaugurate the new order. They criticize every practical measure proposed. Talk to them about the reform of the land system, and they tell you that the working class owns no land and has no interest in it, and that such reform would still leave the wages system intact. Advocate public ownership of natural monopolies, and they tell you that you will only put more power into hands of the capitalistic state. Talk of finance and bimetallism, and they tell you that that is a quarrel between two classes of capitalists and of no concern to the proletariat. Say a good word for trades unionism and the organization of labor, and they assure you that the unions are impotent, and useful only as platforms for the preaching of socialism and as object lessons to workingmen, that nothing but socialism will do.

The only thing that will do is the complete expropriation of the capitalist class by the working class and the ownership of all the means of production by the people. The attitude of the dogmatic socialists constantly reminds me of certain Christians whom we call millenarians. They believe that this is a bad world and getting worse all the time; that it is folly to try to improve it by social reforms; that any apparent improvements are promptly captured by the devil, and only make things worse. They stake all their hope on the return of Christ, who will come when things have got to the worst, and make all things new. Meanwhile there is nothing to do but gather some who will watch and wait for it, and share in the glory when it comes. In the same way the revolutionary socialists regard the present order as hopelessly bad; they are pleased to see it getting worse; they expect their new Jerusalem to come suddenly, and they stake all on that hope; meanwhile they sit and wait for the decay of the old order, gathering a party of socialist believers who will be ready for it when it comes. Of course the dogmatic socialists will repudiate with scorn any relationship to these Christians, just as these Christians reject with horror the insinuation that they are like these socialists; but they are first cousins all the same.

Causes of Dogmatic Socialism

How have dogmatic socialists come to take this position? I think there are four main causes for it: (1) They trace all economic evils to a single cause, the appropriation of surplus value by capital; hence they also concentrate their hope on a single measure of cure. (2) They concentrate their interest on the industrial proletariat and are indifferent to reforms that touch others. (3) They believe that the present economic system is hastening to its end with ever-increasing speed and it is a waste of time to attempt minor reforms. (4) They believe that reforms would only make the present system more tolerable and would prolong its life; they prefer to see it become intolerable and break into pieces as soon as possible. For these four reasons they belittle reforms and stake their hope entirely on the social revolution. I shall now take up these four reasons one by one, and see whether they are good reasons for abstaining from action and confining themselves to theory.

(1) I said that socialists trace all economic and social evils back to a single cause, the ability of capital to appropriate the surplus value of social production. It was the great service rendered to economic thought by Marx that he worked out the theory of surplus value and pushed it to the front. But most men who discover a great new fact or idea are so much in love with the child of their brain that they exaggerate its importance and expect from it the solution of everything. Every new science has started out with an excess of confidence in itself, and has had to learn modesty by experience. Marx was especially exposed to the temptation of reducing everything to a single cause, because, like most German philosophic thinkers of the first half of the nineteenth century, he had been trained in the philosophy and dialectics of Hegel. Now it is almost impossible to convey to those who have not had the misfortune to do a good deal of philosophic reading, a conception of the fatal fascination of Hegelianism to reduce everything to a single proposition. It is magnificent exercise in thinking, and often sheds a brilliant light on questions; but it is apt to force things out of their true proportion for the sake of getting a clean-cut system. Posterity will, I think, ascribe a very high position to Marx and accept on the whole his fundamental doctrines, but I do not believe that it will ascribe to his doctrine of industrial exploitation so exclusive an importance as he did. Anyone who has been trained by history and knows the immense complexity of forces in human society will

be suspicious of a scheme which reduces everything to a single cause and a single remedy. It looks too much like a patent medicine that undertakes to regulate your liver and also promote the growth of your whiskers, strengthen your heart action, and cause all warts to disappear. There is a story of an old German soldier who knew only a single tune, and no matter what hymn was given out, he would bawl it to that old tune. Is there not something of the same one-sidedness in dogmatic socialists who meet every complaint, whether of city or country, of manufacturing or commerce, with the same single tune? For my own part I hold that there are two primary factors of production, land and labor; and that there are two great methods of exploitation, the one by appropriating the land and charging rent, the other by organizing labor and absorbing profits. Therefore I regard the two questions, the question of the land and the question of capital, as coordinate and equal. I wish that socialists and land reformers would understand each other instead of belittling each other. Let each school emphasize the reform which seems to it the most important or the easiest to attain, but let us recognize that either would mean an immense gain for the cause of justice and the cause of the people. When sectarianism is rapidly dying out in the churches, must we have it all over again in the cause of social reform?

The Industrial Proletariat

The second reason why dogmatic socialists take no interest in gradual reforms is that they concentrate their attention on the "industrial proletariat." The idea is that all land and all capital will soon be united in a few hands; the middle class will be eliminated; there will be only two classes left, the small capitalist class owning everything, and the huge proletarian class having nothing but its labor to sell. When society has been simplified in these two classes, the industrial revolution is inevitable; the proletariat will seize the power, expropriate the capitalists, and socialism will have arrived. Meanwhile socialists may be sorry for the small tradesman or farmer who is ground up in the industrial mill, but they see no use in helping him prolong the agony by any legislation that would relieve him for a while. Hence socialists in Europe often refuse to help land reform, peasant proprietorship, or similar measures of reform. The sooner the middle classes join the class-conscious proletariat the better.

But in this argument of theirs, it is taken for granted that the middle class is actually disappearing and that the working class is homogeneous, the same all the way through, with identical interests. That is the course of development foretold by Marx, and dogmatic socialists have regarded that as self-evident. But actual development since Marx has not substantiated that. There has been a concentration of industrial enterprises; they have grown relatively fewer and fewer. But there has not been in the same measure a concentration of wealth. The two things are quite distinct. Through the device of the stock companies, a great many individuals seem to share in the proceeds of our modern concentrated industries. At any rate, the middle class is not disappearing, though the small business is. In England there were estimated to be in 1851, 300,000 families with an income of $750–$5000, that is, belonging to the upper working class and lower middle class. In 1881 there were 990,000 of that range of income. The population in thirty years had increased about 30 per cent; this middle class had increased 233⅓ per cent (*British Review*, May 22, 1897). Giffen estimates the same class now at a million and a half. According to Lassalle, Prussia in 1854 had 16,300,000 inhabitants and only 44,407 persons with an income of over 1000 thaler (about $750).[5] In 1894–95 the population had increased to 33,000,000, and 321,296 persons paid taxes on more than 1000 thaler income. Population had only doubled in forty years, but this middle class of persons with good income had increased sevenfold. I could give figures for other countries, but do not want to weary you.

I have no figures for this country, and I am not sure that anybody else has. I am, of course, familiar with the frequently published tables showing what percentage of the total wealth of the country is held by the plutocrats, how much by the middle class and how much by the working class, but I do not know where they get their figures. In Europe the income tax furnishes a fairly trustworthy basis of calculation. In this country neither the census nor any other system furnishes trustworthy figures. In statistics of commerce and industry we must remember that the big figures of large production for the market are pretty sure to be counted in, while the small amounts of the common people are easily neglected. Yet in their aggregate they rise to immense amounts, and for this comparison they are absolutely necessary, if it is to have any sense at all. There is a lot of loose reasoning going on with insecure figures. Thus

5. [ED.] Robert Giffen, *The Progress of the Working Classes in the Last Half Century* (N.Y., 1885). Ferdinand Lassalle (1825–64) was a brilliant, controversial socialist labor leader, who in 1863 founded the first real political party of German workers. Though he was acquainted with Marxist thought, he remained a Hegelian, and was a vigorous proponent of state socialism.

Reverend Charles H. Vail in his *Principles of Scientific Socialism* (p. 29), after showing how many small farms failed in one year, concludes: "But as the supply of these aspirants to bankruptcy is not unlimited, they will soon terminate, and the middle class will be known only by tradition." [6] But things do not move quite as fast in practice as they do in theory. The fact is that social reform in Europe has begun to cut across the scheme of developments foretold by Marx. Factory legislation has cut into profits; the shifting of taxation has cut into rent and interests. And today we do not yet see any such simple division into a small class of capitalists and a large class of proletarians as is required by the dogmatic socialists. There is no great gulf fixed between the two, but there is still a strong middle class, ranging in many gradations of wealth from the working class up to the very rich. I am not defending this or commending it; I am simply trying to guard us against being blinded by a theory and fooling ourselves as to the facts. We are so fond of thinking that because a thing must be so according to our theory, therefore it is so.

No Uniform Poverty

Furthermore, even among the working class there is no such uniform poverty as the conception of a class-conscious proletariat demands. Even among the population of a factory town there is a considerable scale of differences in wages and position and no great solidarity of interest, and I am not sure that they will present a united front in a great army of class-conscious proletarians. The Knights of Labor made a brave attempt to unite workers, skilled and unskilled, without regard to their special trade interests, on the basis of the solidarity of all labor. But their attempt on the whole failed. The labor unions are organized according to special interests, and you all know how hard it is to bring them together for a great common fight.

The third reason why dogmatic socialists withhold their support from immediate reforms is because they believe the present economic order to be very near its collapse, and therefore it is a waste of time to tinker it. Their tactics are based on that belief. If the belief is correct, their tactics are sensible; if the belief is incorrect, their tactics are bad.

It is very natural for men who are intensely convinced of a truth to think that all men must soon see it too. It is natural for men who suffer by

6. Vail was a radically inclined minister who openly espoused political socialism; his book was published in New York in 1899.

the present order, and desire its end, to persuade themselves that they already hear it straining and cracking to its downfall. The wish is often the father of the thought. In 1847, when the political revolution of 1848 was brewing in Europe, Marx in the Communistic [*sic*] Manifesto declared that the political revolution would be merely the prelude to the social revolution which would immediately follow. That is more than fifty years ago. In his last work (*Vorwort zu den Klassenkampfen in Frankreich*, 1895), Engels frankly confessed that he and Marx had been mistaken in forecasting the time required for the industrial revolution to do its work. Do we have to make their mistake over again? Can we not begin where they left off? Three years ago, if I remember correctly, the gentleman who was then candidate for governor of the Socialist Labor party predicted that socialism would be established in seven years. Half of that time is gone. Does any sober man care to back that prediction now? There are several factors necessary for a collapse of our present social order.

FACTORS OF A COLLAPSE

The materialistic view of history ranks as first factor the material conditions. An industrial order must outlive itself, and become insufficient and impossible, before a new order can be born out of the old. The mere desire to have a new order cannot produce it. The material basis in cold facts must be present. Now, I think candid students of socialist literature will have to concede that the progress of industry toward its own dissolution has not been as rapid as the great theorists of socialism once expected. While capital has concentrated, it has not concentrated as fast as was expected. The middle class, as I have shown, has not disappeared. In agriculture it is questionable if there has been any general progress toward farming on a large scale. In some countries, where it has been tried, the movement is rather away from it. Marx expected that the industrial and commercial crises would become more and more violent and destructive, and cover larger and more world-wide areas in their earthquake shocks, and thus make the present order impossible. Certainly we have had serious crises, but they do not seem to follow each other in more rapid spasms, leaving society constantly more exhausted. The interval has lengthened rather than shortened. I think it not impossible that by the extension of the world market, by our rapid means of communication and transportation, and by the general extension of the credit system, the local shocks can be distributed as if through an elastic medium, so that the crises will be less serious in the future.

Materialistic socialism lays the chief stress on the material factors of change, but it recognizes that there must be a preparation in the minds of men by the spread of socialist ideas before the revolution can be accomplished. How far have we got along in that direction? Socialism has made the most compact and enduring progress in Germany. The party polled about 2,100,000 votes last time, I believe. But the non-socialist votes still numbered about 5,500,000 votes. Moreover, socialists readily concede that many men vote with them who are not really dyed-in-the-wool socialists. A prominent socialist author estimated the socialists of real conviction at about 900,000. But if only one-third of the non-socialist parties are class-conscious anti-socialists, that would give twice the other figure. Perhaps it may be hoped that socialist votes will increase immensely at the next elections in Germany. That may be; passing events have a good deal to do with that. But during recent years the number has not grown as fast as formerly. From 1870 to 1890 they increased eighty-seven per cent; 1890 to 1893, twenty-five per cent; 1893 to 1898, eighteen per cent. At that rate they will not get a working majority of the people for a long time.

In this country, after a good many years of agitation, and in spite of a widespread sentiment in favor of radical reform, the two socialist parties polled only 135,670 votes out of a total of 13,969,770, or not quite one per cent. Of course that is not a full indication of the spread of general socialist ideas. The socialists of the larger cities, chiefly belonging to foreign nationalities by birth and associating with their comrades in the faith, must not fool themselves about the state of public sentiment. The number of people in the United States who could give any account of socialism which would not be ridiculous is still very, very small, and a good share of that number belongs to the professional classes and not to the proletariat. Nor is there any hope of an immediate change. The people of the United States are notoriously conservative in politics, not in spite of our democratic institutions, but in consequence of our long training in democracy and our trust in those institutions.

RISING OF THE PEOPLE

Perhaps there are some who think that matters can be hastened by an armed rising of the people. According to materialistic socialism, force cannot create a new order; it can at most break down obstacles to a new order which is practically already in existence. Force can act as midwife; it can not be the mother of the new era. But it could not do even that unless the majority of the people were in sympathy. The time when a determined minority in a center like Paris can begin a revolution and control the rest of the country is gone by. With modern arms and transportation the chances of a force revolution are greatly diminished. Engels recognized this in 1895. He said a conflict with the military power would throw back socialism, and that social-democracy would thrive better by legal means that by attempting a forcible overthrow.

It is not my wish to discourage anyone by this discussion. I want us all to recognize the actual state of things, and then fix on the right course of action accordingly. If only a short time intervenes before the collapse of the present order, then social reform is a useless patching of a rotten hulk. If, on the other hand, we have to take a long outlook yet under the present system, reformatory measures will be useful, both to make the intervening time more tolerable, and also to lead up to the final change by organic evolution.

The fourth reason why dogmatic socialists refuse to help in immediate reforms is that they do not care to make the present system more tolerable and give it a longer lease of life. The more rapidly it goes to pieces the better. The more intolerable the condition of the people becomes, the sooner will they make an end of things. So they take a certain savage delight in cases of acute distress, in the breaking down of the small business man and farmer, in the concentration of population in the cities, etc.

All this is permissible tactics if the suffering is short anyway. If, however, the development before us is still a long one, it is both cruel and unwise. The starved and helpless poor, flabby of flesh, thin of blood, weak in energy and will, alternating between fits of rage and long despair, are not good material even for a force revolution, and they will not do at all for a peaceful revolution, in which patience, staying power, intelligence, and practical sagacity count. What sort of revolution could you work with an army of hobos? And the more the people approximate that condition, the less hope is there. The bone and sinew of the social movement here and everywhere are the men who earn good wages, or small storekeepers and professional men, not the unskilled and unintelligent workingmen. The idea of profiting by the misery of the people is suicidal. The true way is to secure every advantage that can be gained for the physical welfare of the people and their education, and meanwhile to spread ideas. That has been done and can be done by reforms in the interest of the working class, looking toward shorter hours, better pay, better conditions of labor, housing, recreation, education, etc. And at the same time, by weakening the opposing forces through appropriating rent by taxation, making natural monopolies contribute to the public rather than the private wealth, and shutting as many as possible of the sluices by which the river of public wealth has been drained into the races that have turned private millwheels. The men who are holding off in hopes of a speedy catastrophe are gambling for sudden success, but if they do not realize on their venture they will have gambled away their stakes, the life-blood of the people.

THE NECESSARY PREPARATION

Furthermore, these men forget that the time which is left us before the collapse of capitalistic society is of inestimable value in getting ready. They seem to think that the main work will have been done when the crash comes. I tell you the real work will then only begin. Socialism will not then have succeeded; it will then be on trial; and if it does not succeed inside of four weeks, the clock of time will be turned back, nobody knows how far. The difficulty of the transition seems to me to be vastly underestimated by socialists. They skate over it very lightly, perhaps because they feel that they are on thin ice with deep water below them. Mr. Vail in the *Principles of Scientific Socialism* (p. 34) ends his account of the industrial evolution by this forecast of the final victory: "When the socialists have wrested the power of government from the capitalist class, they will at once proceed to transform private business into socially managed concerns. Just as rapidly as practicable, trust after trust, and industry after industry, would pass under public administration — the officials in charge being made responsible to the whole people — until all production and exchange are socialized and the consummation of the industrial revolution completed."

Hurrah! Isn't it easy? And I suppose each industry will patiently wait till its turn comes to be socialized, and private owners will go on running their factories, paying their men and turning out the necessaries of life until they too are expropriated. In the French Revolution, production and exchange were almost entirely local; individuals were ruined, but there was no general stoppage of production. It was like the time when every house had its own pump and burned candles. Breaking six pumps left all the others still in shape. In 1848 things were different. The mere talking of the clubs produced a feeling of insecurity which paralyzed industry. Work stopped. Every day increased the ruin. Expropriation was impossible; there were no social organs to assume control of industry. Individuals might have been replaced by individuals, experienced men by men who had enthusiasm but no experience. Today it would be still worse. The age of pumps and candles has nearly gone; our water and light is centralized. Blast a water conduit and explode a gas-house, and the whole city will be waterless and in darkness.

We need some sort of rudimentary organization of the people on whom the management of industry and commerce can devolve when the present despotic managers step out. Marx said that during the transition the proletariat would have to exercise dictatorial power. What does that mean? Unless there is a real social organization of the people already in existence, it would mean that the club orators, the men who spout in places like this, would be entrusted with power, and the Lord have mercy upon us! Workingmen are still fascinated by the man who can do what they can't do — talk fluently. I am a talker myself, and consequently I prefer the silent man who does things to the man who is like a roof gutter in a rainstorm. It is no easy thing to run a satisfactory democracy. We have been testing methods in this country for a century and a quarter, and we haven't learned yet. Running an industrial democracy is harder than a political democracy. The history of trade unionism by Sidney Webb shows how long it took the unions in England to evolve an organization that would really work.[7] The great cooperative societies in England have more money than they can profitably invest, because they haven't got the men who can manage things successfully.

What I am trying to show is this: that the plan of just holding off from reforms and letting the present order go to pieces by its own weight and rottenness, means that the people in the course of the years will be weakened in body and mind and will, and be less fit for the task they will have to face; and they will be without social organization and experience when the time comes. On the other hand, steady improvement by reforms will better the health and intelligence of the people, will train them in social organization, and will weaken the opposing forces.

7. [ED.] Sidney (1859–1947) and Beatrice (1858–1943) Webb, British investigators of social and economic problems, were the authors of *The History of Trades Unionism* (rev. ed., N.Y., 1920). They were central figures in the Fabian socialist movement, and exerted great influence on the rise of the Labour Party in Britain.

Practical Socialism

Doubtless I may be mistaken in the details of my argument, but as a whole I think it can hold water. And if so, it all goes to show that we should not abstain from practical reform work in the expectation of a speedy collapse of the present economic order, meanwhile only dogmatizing and theorizing; but that we should get to work to keep the people in good condition during the inevitable years of evolution, to create the social organization that will make socialism practicable when it does come, and to win for the people by peaceful and gradual means at least a part of the social wealth now taken by individuals.

It had been my intention to submit a practical program of certain reform measures, all of which are now being discussed and agitated and none of which is outside of the possibility of speedy realization if all reform forces would unite on them. But my paper is already longer than it ought to be, and I shall have to omit that part. I will only enumerate the measures without entering any defense of my faith in them: (1) appropriation of economic rent by the taxation of ground values apart from improvements; (2) appropriation of some of the chief sources of profit by municipal ownership of natural monopolies, e.g. water, gas, electric light and power, and surface roads; (3) extension of the industrial machinery and capacity of the organized people by control of the express and telegraph business through the machinery of the post office; (4) by the income derived from these sources, extension of education, libraries, museums, parks, playgrounds, baths, etc., to promote the welfare of the people; (5) breaking up the accumulations of great capital by a steeply graduated inheritance tax; (6) organization of trades, partly to maintain wages and improve the condition of labor, and partly to create a social organization of the people, on which the social management of industry can devolve when it becomes necessary; (7) labor legislation to shorten the working time, improve the sanitary conditions of labor, prevent child labor, restrict female labor, etc.

In all this the ultimate aim of socialism need not be lost sight of. On the contrary, these reform measures would gain intelligent direction and the swing of hope, if they were all regarded as steps in the great process of regaining the rights of the people and of evolving a social organization in which liberty, equality, and fraternity would be possible.

Such an attitude I call practical socialism. I am not alone in being tired with everlasting dogmatizing and theorizing which when the people ask for bread, offers them, not a stone, but a theory. In Germany it has become clear for several years that the theory of collectivism is not the all-absorbing topic in socialist literature that it used to be. Practical measures are no longer inserted in the party program merely as a tail to the all-important kite of theory. Practical reforms are coming to the front, and the most experienced and most intelligent members of the party are the ones who are moving farthest away from the old-fashioned revolutionary socialism. In England, so far as I can see, revolutionary socialism is weak and confined to foreigners mostly, and Fabian socialism is pervading England. They expect no immediate catastrophe and wouldn't have it if they could, but go in for municipal reform, labor unions, and cooperation, and they have prodded the old parties into socialism knee-deep already.

In America the current of socialist thought and sentiment does not run in the channel of the socialist parties, but is leavening the ideas of the people and will transform our social organization in the direction of socialism quietly and gradually. If dogmatic socialists choose to sit on the fence and criticize the men who do this work, that is their look out. The work will be done almost as fast anyway. In the countries having the largest measure of political liberty, socialism is today least revolutionary. I predict that within ten years the drift in the Teutonic nations will be altogether away from the idea of catastrophe, and toward socialist reform work.

❖ ❖ ❖ ❖ ❖ ❖ ❖ ❖

THE NEW EVANGELISM [1]

Editor's introduction. "This article is timely and of great power," William R. Richards, pastor of the Brick Presbyterian Church of New York City, commented in *The Independent* concerning Rauschenbush's "The New Evangelism." Aware that the older evangelism associated with such figures as the late Dwight L. Moody was losing its power, church leaders were scanning the religious horizons for fresh signs of awakening. Spokesmen for the social gospel, in an attempt to explain the failure of the churches to reach and to hold the working classes, often criticized the churches for their bondage to commercial and professional interests. Russell Conwell, pastor of Grace Baptist Church in Philadelphia, then the largest Protestant church in America, concurred with what he saw as the negative conclusions of Rauschenbusch's article. "It looks to the writer," he said, "as if the confusion is to be greater, the darkness deeper and the fermentation more violent, before the 'future' church will begin to crystallize into definite form." But William S. Rainsford, rector of New York's great "institutional" church, St. George's Episcopal, thought Rauschenbusch had been unduly pessimistic:

> The paper seems to me to be altogether admirable. It is, however, a practical denial of its opening statement — namely, that there is no new evangelism before us which we might adopt. There is a new evangel. It is here today. It is leavening the Church, it is salting the world, and it cannot be trodden under the foot of men.[2]

Three years later Rauschenbusch was to find himself in the vanguard of this new evangelism, when *Christianity and the Social Crisis* became a religious best-seller. With it, the social gospel came of age.

❖ ❖ ❖ ❖

The present interest in the "new evangelism" is almost wholly an expression of dissatisfaction with the old evangelism, the waning power of

1. "The New Evangelism," *The Independent*, LVI (January–June 1904), 1054–59.
2. The comments directly followed the article, *ibid.*, 1059–61.

which is generally conceded. There is as yet no new evangelism before us which we might adopt; we are only wishing that there might be. Our conceptions of what it ought to be are vague, as all ideas about the future necessarily are, but that is no cause for belittling the current inquiry. It is one of the most important topics that could be discussed. I shall attempt in the following discussion to apply the same method of historical investigation to this great and threatening fact of contemporary religious history which would be applied to a fact of equal importance in a past era.

The gospel of Christ is one and immutable; the comprehension and expression of it in history has been of infinite variety. No individual, no church, no age of history has ever comprehended the full scope of God's saving purposes in Jesus Christ. Neither has any proclaimed it without foreign admixtures that clogged and thwarted it. A fuller and purer expression of the evangel has therefore always been possible and desirable. It is on the face of it unlikely that the gospel as commonly understood by us is the whole gospel or a completely pure gospel. It is a lack of Christian humility to assume that our gospel and *the gospel* are identical.

Every individual reconstructs his comprehension of life and duty, of the world and God, as he passes from one period of development to the next. If he fails to do so, his religion will lose its grasp and control. In the same way, humanity must reconstruct its moral and religious synthesis whenever it passes from one era to another. When all other departments of life and thought are silently changing, it is impossible for religion to remain unaffected. The gospel, to have power over an age, must be the highest expression of the moral and religious truths held by that age. If it lags behind and presents outgrown conceptions of life and duty, it is no longer in the full sense the gospel. Christianity itself lifts the minds of men to demand a better expression of Christianity. If the official wardens of the gospel, from selfish motives or from conservative veneration for old statements, refuse to let the spirit of Christ flow into the larger vessels of thought and feeling which God himself has prepared for it, they are warned by finding men turn from their message as sapless and powerless. The most familiar instance is that of the revival of learning, and the repudiation of medieval religion and theology, in the fifteen and sixteenth centuries.

We are today passing through an historical transition as thorough and important as any in history. The last one hundred twenty-five years have swept us through profound changes in every direction. World-wide commerce and the imperialistic policy of the Christian nations have made the problems of international and interracial relations urgent. The church responded by a new movement of world-wide missions, but it has failed hitherto to Christianize international politics. The monarchical system, so intimately connected with ancient religion, has crumbled, and democracy has taken its place; but the church has not broadened its ethical teaching to any great extent to meet the new duties of the citizen-kings. It still confines its ethics to the *personal* and *family* life. In industry and commerce there has been a vast increase in the production of wealth and a shifting in its distribution, but the church has furnished no adequate principles either for the distribution or the consumption of wealth. We are emerging from the era of individualism. The principle of coordination, cooperation, and solidarity is being applied in ever widening areas and is gaining remarkable hold on the spirits of men. The church is applying that principle in its organization, but its message is still chiefly on the basis of individualism.

It is not strange if the message of the church has failed to keep pace with a movement so rapid. But neither is it strange if humanity, amid the pressure of such new problems, fails to be stirred and guided by statements of truth that were adequate to obsolete conditions. The church is in the position of a mother talking to her son of seventeen as if he were still twelve. What she says is good and loving, but it is not what the boy with his new passions and problems needs.

The present paralysis of the churches affects all Western Christendom and only a cause coterminous with modern civilization will explain it. Communities are affected in just the degree in which they are affected by the progress of civilization — the backward countries and rural communities least, the industrial cities most. State churches and free churches alike feel the drag. It is not because the religious spirit has failed. It runs surprisingly strong, but it runs largely outside of the churches. Neither is the trouble due to lack of piety in the ministry, for, on the whole, we are as good as our fathers. We are told that the gospel has always met with indifference and hostility. But is this today a persecution for righteousness's sake, so that Jesus would call us blessed for enduring it, or is it a case where the salt is trodden under foot of men, because it has lost its saltness? The worst explanation is that which shrugs its shoulders and regards the present alienation of the people from the church as a mysterious dispensation of Providence against which we are helpless. Effects do not happen without causes, and God's reign is a reign of law. In short, no small or local or passing cause will explain so large a fact as the present condition of the church.

Now, apply this to evangelism. Evangelism is only the cutting edge of the church, and it is driven by the weight back of it. The evangelizing power of the church depends on its moral prestige and spiritual authority. Every evangelist banks on the accumulated moral capital of the church universal.

There are two kinds of evangelization. The one proclaims new truth, as Jesus did to his nation, or Paul to the Gentiles, or as a missionary does to the heathen. The other summons men to live and act according to the truth which the church has previously instilled into their minds and which they have long accepted as true. The latter is, on the whole, the kind which we have to do. To be effective, evangelism must appeal to motives which powerfully seize men, and it must hold up a moral standard so high above their actual lives that it will smite them with conviction of sin. If the motives urged seem untrue or remote, or if the standard of life to which they are summoned is practically that on which they are living, the evangelistic call will have little power. The two questions which every Christian worker should investigate for himself are these: Are the traditional motives still effective? And is the moral standard held up by the church such as to induce repentance?

The motives urged at any time will vary with the preacher and the audience, and there will always be a large measure of truth and power even in the most defective preaching that touches human nature at all. Yet there is a change in emphasis from age to age. Within our own memory the fear of hell and the desire for bliss in heaven have strangely weakened, even with men who have no doubt of the reality of hell and heaven. On the other hand, the insistence on present holiness and Christian living has strengthened. Good men give less thought to their personal salvation than our fathers, but their sympathy for the sorrows of others is more poignant. Past Christianity has developed in us a love for our fellows and a sense of solidarity so strong that they demand to be considered in every religious appeal. On the other hand, we cannot conceal from ourselves that the old "scheme of salvation" seems mechanical and remote, and its effectiveness as a motive depends largely on the past teaching of it, which is stored in our minds. The sense of great coming changes, begotten by a better knowledge of the plastic possibilities of mankind, is strong upon us. We have a new hope for humanity such as has long existed only where the millennial hope was a vital thing.

Even so brief an enumeration must make us feel that some motives are dropping away, because they were narrow and incompletely Christian, and larger and more truly Christlike motives are offering themselves. It should be the scientific effort of every Christian worker to observe what motives are today really effective with the young and thoughtful minds who represent the present and future. The fact that some evangelists who are determined in repudiating anything that savors of "modern thought" are so effective in urging the old motives does not invalidate what we have said. In every large city there are many men who belong to the old time and are untouched as yet by the new. They respond joyfully to the ideas in which their Christian life was nurtured, and in which their holiest memories are enshrined. But there are other men who come once and then stay away, because they hear nothing to which they can respond. And these men are not counted. Moreover, the strong personality of the evangelist may count for more than anything he says.

What about the moral standard held by the church in its teaching and in its collective life? Can she summon men to repentance by it?

The moral teaching of the church in the past has dealt with private and family life. It has boldly condemned drunkenness, sexual impurity, profanity; it has fostered gentleness and pity, and it has been largely successful in this teaching. It has also drawn the line against Sabbath-breaking, dancing, card-playing and theater-going, but it has not been successful in maintaining that line. In general, the community has risen toward the level of the church in private and domestic virtue, and the church has drifted toward the level of the respectable community in regard to amusements. As a result of both movements the gap has lessened. The morality of the church is not much more than what prudence, respectability, and good breeding also demand. Nor is the morality of church members generally distinguished by the glow of spiritual fervor. There is less family worship and prayerful life than with our fathers. But with this moral outfit can the church authoritatively say to the world, "Repent and become like me?"

When we pass from private and domestic life to political and business life, the matter is worse. About the most pressing questions arising there the church as a body is dumb. It has nothing to say about the justice of holding land idle in crowded cities, of appropriating the unearned increment in land values, of paying wages fixed by the hunger of the laborers and taking the surplus of their output as "profits," or of cornering the market in the necessaries of life. It feels restless about some glaring evils like child labor, but only moderately so. Individuals in the church are intelligent and active, but the church, both as an organized body and as a corporate spiritual force, is inert. The moral guide of humanity is silent where authoritative speech is today most needed. Where it does speak, it is often on the wrong side. When we consider the ideas prevalent in the churches, their personnel, and their sources of income, has the church a message of repentance and an evangel for this modern world?

One important and growing class in our population is largely alienated from the church — namely, the industrial wage-workers. The alienation is most complete where the industrial development under the capitalistic system has most completely run its course. In our country that alienation has begun within the last generation, during which this class has become a class, and the process is not yet complete. This constitutes the spiritual barrier to evangelistic efforts as soon as they go beyond the young people of the families already in the churches. Our evangelistic call strikes an invisible wall and comes back in hollow echoes. It is an untrue and cruel charge to say that the church workers have not done their best to reach the people. The efforts of the churches in the great cities for the last generation have perhaps never been paralleled. And yet they are futile. This is one of the most stunning and heart-rending facts in all our life.

The church has passed under the spiritual domination of the commercial and professional classes. I do not mean that they alone compose its membership; but they furnish its chief support, do its work, and their ethics and views of life determine the thought of the church more than we realize. This is not due to any wrongful attempt to make the church subservient, but rather to the fact that they are the dominant classes in all industrial nations, in literature and politics as well as in the church. Now the stratification of society is becoming more definite in our country, and the people are growing more conscious of it. The industrial conflicts make them realize how their interests diverge from those of the commercial class. As that consciousness increases, it becomes harder for the two classes to meet in the expression of Christian faith and love — in prayer meetings, for instance. When the Christian business man is presented as a model Christian, working people are coming to look with suspicion on these samples of our Christianity. I am not justifying that, but simply stating the fact. They disapprove of the Christianity of the churches, not because it is too good, but because it is not good enough. The working people are now developing the principle and practice of solidarity, which promises to be one of the most potent ethical forces of the future, and which is essentially more Christian than the covetousness and selfishness which we regard as the indispensable basis of commerce. If this is a correct diagnosis of our condition, is it strange that the church is unable to evangelize a class alienated from it by divergent class interest and class morality?

Let us sum up. The powerlessness of the old evangelism is only the most striking and painful demonstration of the general state of the churches. Its cause is not local nor temporary. It does not lie in lack of hard work or of prayer or of keen anxiety. It lies in the fact that modern life has gone through immense changes, and the church has not kept pace with it in developing the latent moral and spiritual resources of the gospel which are needed by the new life. It has most slighted that part of the gospel which our times most need. It lacks an ethical imperative which can induce repentance. In private life its standard differs little from respectability. In commerce and industry, where the unsolved and painful problems lie, it has no clear message, and often claims to be under no obligation to have one. In the state churches the state has dominated; in the free churches the capitalist class dominates. Both influences are wordly — in favor of things as they are and against the ideals which animate the common people. The people are becoming daily more sensitive to the class cleavage of society. The church suffers under the general resentment against the class with which it is largely identified. To this must be added the fact that the spirit of free inquiry engendered by modern science neutralizes the dogmatic authority with which the church has been accustomed to speak.

The new evangelism which shall overcome these barriers and again exert the full power of the gospel cannot be made to order nor devised by a single man. It will be the slow product of the fearless thought of many honest men. It will have to retain all that was true and good in the old synthesis, but advance the human conception of salvation one stage closer to the divine conception. It will have to present a conception of God, of life, of duty, of destiny, to which the best religious life of our age will bow. It will have to give an adequate definition of how a Christian man should live under modern conditions, and then summon men to live so.

A compelling evangel for the working class will be wrought out only by men who love that class, share its life, understand the ideals for which it is groping, penetrate those ideals with the religious spirit of Christian-

ity, and then proclaim a message in which the working people will find
their highest self. They will never be reached by a middle-class gospel
preached down at them with the consciousness of superiority.

If we personally are to have a share in working out the new evangel,
we shall have to be open to two influences and allow them to form a vital
union in our personalities. We must open our minds to the spirit of Jesus
in its primitive, uncorrupted, and still unexhausted power. That spirit is
the fountain of youth for the church. As a human organization it grows
old and decrepit like every other human organism. But again and again it
has been rejuvenated by a new baptism in that spirit. We must also keep
our vision clear to the life of our own time. Our age is as sublime as any
in the past. It has a right to its own appropriation and understanding of
the gospel. By the decay of the old, God himself is forcing us on to seek
the new and higher.

This attempt at a diagnosis of our ills is not offered in a spirit of condemnation, but of personal repentance and heart-searching. We all bear
our share of guilt. I have full faith in the future of the Christian church.
A new season of power will come when we have put our sin from us. Our
bitter need will drive us to repentance. The prophetic spirit will awaken
among us. The tongue of fire will descend on twentieth century men and
give them great faith, joy and boldness, and then we shall hear the new
evangel, and it will be the old gospel.

❖ ❖ ❖ ❖ ❖ ❖ ❖ ❖

THE NEW APOSTOLATE [1]

Editor's introduction. Christianity and the Social Crisis catapulted its author into the national spotlight; the book eventually sold over 50,000
copies and was widely discussed. "The popularity which came overnight
to Walter Rauschenbusch was evidence that Americans from all walks of
life — not just the clergy — recognized that he was responding to a central dilemma that had developed in American cultural and religious life,"
writes Robert D. Cross of the most famous social gospel book of them all.
"Certainly, *Christianity and the Social Crisis* is a persuasive book," he
continues. "Though the larger argument is complex and at points even
disingenuous, each chapter is a model of clarity, put together with the
skills of a platform orator." [2] Indeed, many parts of the book had been
pretested on the platform or in the pages of journals. The climactic
passage reprinted here had been given as an address before a session of the
Amity Missionary Conference in 1896. It marks the high point of a work
that was itself the climax of two decades of thought and work in social
Christianity.

❖ ❖ ❖ ❖

The first apostolate of Christianity was born from a deep fellow-feeling
for social misery and from the consciousness of a great historical opportunity. Jesus saw the peasantry of Galilee following him about with their
poverty and their diseases, like shepherdless sheep that have been scattered and harried by beasts of prey, and his heart had compassion on
them. He felt that the harvest was ripe, but there were few to reap it.
Past history had come to its culmination, but there were few who understood the situation and were prepared to cope with it. He bade his
disciples to pray for laborers for the harvest, and then made them answer
their own prayers by sending them out two by two to proclaim the king-

---

1. *Christianity and the Social Crisis* (N.Y., 1907), 414–22.
2. Introduction to the Torchbook edition (N.Y., 1964), viii, xvii.

dom of God. That was the beginning of the world-wide mission of Christianity.[3]

The situation is repeated on a vaster scale today. If Jesus stood today amid our modern life, with that outlook on the condition of all humanity which observation and travel and the press would spread before him, and with the same heart of divine humanity beating in him, he would create a new apostolate to meet the new needs in a new harvest time of history.

To any one who knows the sluggishness of humanity to good, the impregnable intrenchments of vested wrongs and the long reaches of time needed from one milestone of progress to the next, the task of setting up a Christian social order in this modern world of ours seems like a fair and futile dream. Yet in fact it is not one tithe as hopeless as when Jesus set out to do it. When he told his disciples, "Ye are the salt of the earth; ye are the light of the world," he expressed the consciousness of a great historic mission to the whole of humanity. Yet it was a Nazarene carpenter speaking to a group of Galilean peasants and fishermen. Under the circumstances at that time it was an utterance of the most daring faith — faith in himself, faith in them, faith in what he was putting into them, faith in faith. Jesus failed and was crucified, first his body by his enemies, and then his spirit by his friends; but that failure was so amazing a success that today it takes an effort on our part to realize that it required any faith on his part to inaugurate the kingdom of God and to send out his apostolate.

Today, as Jesus looks out upon humanity, his spirit must leap to see the souls responsive to his call. They are sown broadcast through humanity, legions of them. The harvest field is no longer deserted. All about us we hear the clang of the whetstone, and the rush of the blades through the grain, and the shout of the reapers. With all our faults and our slothfulness, we modern men in many ways are more on a level with the real mind of Jesus than any generation that has gone before. If that first apostolate was able to remove mountains by the power of faith, such an apostolate as Christ could now summon might change the face of the earth.

The apostolate of a new age must do the work of the sower. When the sower goes forth to sow his seed, he goes with the certainty of partial failure and the knowledge that a long time of patience and of hazard will intervene before he can hope to see the result of his work and his venture. In sowing the truth a man may never see or trace the results. The more

3. See Matthew IX, 32–X, 42.

ideal his conceptions are, and the farther they move ahead of his time, the larger will be the percentage of apparent failure. But he can afford to wait. The powers of life are on his side. He is like a man who has scattered his seed and then goes off to sleep by night and work by day, and all the while the seed, by the inscrutable chemistry of life, lays hold of the ingredients of its environment and builds them up to its own growth. The mustardseed becomes a tree. The leaven assimilates the meal by biological processes. The new life penetrates the old humanity and transforms it. Robert Owen was a sower.[4] His cooperative communities failed. He was able to help only a small fraction of the workingmen of his day. But his moral enthusiasm and his ideas fertilized the finest and most self-sacrificing minds among the working classes. They cherished his ultimate hopes in private and worked for realizable ends in public. The Chartist movement was filled with his spirit. The most influential leaders of English unionism in its great period after the middle of the nineteenth century were Owenites. The Rochdale Pioneers were under his influence, and the great cooperative movement in England, an economic force of the first importance, grew in some measure out of the seed which Owen had scattered. Other men may own the present. The future belongs to the sower — provided he scatters seed and does not mistake the chaff for it which once was so essential to the seed and now is dead and useless.

It is inevitable that those who stand against conditions in which most men believe and by which the strongest profit, shall suffer for their stand. The little group of early Christian socialists in England, led by Maurice, Kingsley, and Hughes, now stand by common consent in the history of that generation as one of its finest products, but at that time they were bitterly assailed and misunderstood. Pastor Rudolf Todt, the first man in Germany who undertook to prove that the New Testament and the ethics of socialism have a close affinity, was almost unanimously attacked by the church of Germany.[5] But Jesus told his apostles at the outset that opposition would be part of their day's work. Christ equipped his church with no legal rights to protect her; the only political right he gave his disciples was the right of being persecuted.[6] It is part of the doctrine of

4. [ED.] Robert Owen (1771–1858), a British manufacturer, philanthropist, and social reformer, was the founder of the New Harmony, Indiana, communitarian society, and the inspiration for a number of like experiments.

5. [ED.] Todt invoked state intervention on behalf of the exploited in *Der radikale deutsche Sozialismus und die christliche Gesellschaft* ("Radical German Socialism and the Christian Society"; Wittenberg, 1877).

6. Nathusius, *Mitarbeit der Kirche*, 476. [ED.] Martin von Nathusius (1843–1906), professor of practical theology at the University of Greifswald, wrote *Die Mitarbeit*

vicarious atonement, which is fundamental in Christianity, that the
prophetic souls must vindicate by their sufferings the truth of the truth
they preach.

> Disappointment's dry and bitter root,
> Envy's harsh berries, and the choking pool
> Of the world's scorn, are the right mother-milk
> To the tough hearts that pioneer their kind
> And break a pathway to those unknown realms
> That in the earth's broad shadow lie enthralled;
> Endurance is the crowning quality,
> And patience all the passion of great hearts;
> These are their stay, and when the leaden world
> Sets its hard face against their fateful thought,
> And brute strength, like a scornful conqueror,
> Clangs his huge mace down in the other scale,
> The inspired soul but flings his patience in,
> And slowly that outweighs the ponderous globe —
> One faith against a whole earth's unbelief,
> One soul against the flesh of all mankind.[7]

The championship of social justice is almost the only way left open to a
Christian nowadays to gain the crown of martyrdom. Theological heretics are rarely persecuted now. The only rival of God is mammon, and it
is only when his sacred name is blasphemed that men throw the Christians
to the lions.

Even for the social heretics there is a generous readiness to listen which
was unknown in the past. In our country that openness of mind is a
product of our free intellectual life, our ingrained democracy, the denominational manifoldness of our religious life, and the spread of the Christian
spirit. It has become an accepted doctrine among us that all great movements have obscure beginnings, and that belief tends to make men respectful toward anything that comes from some despised Nazareth.
Unless a man forfeits respect by bitterness or lack of tact, he is accorded
a large degree of tolerance, though he will always be made to feel the
difference between himself and those who say the things that please the
great.

The certainty of opposition constitutes a special call to the strong. The
ministry seems to have little attraction for the sons of rich men. It is not

---

der Kirche an der Lösung der sozialen Frage ("The Cooperation of the Church in
the Solution of the Social Question"; 2 vols., Leipzig, 1893–94).
  7. James Russell Lowell, "Columbus."

strange when one considers the enervating trials that beset a rich man in a pastorate. But here is a mission that ought to appeal to the rich young man if he has heroic stuff in him. His assured social standing would give him an influence with rich and poor alike which others attain but slowly if at all. The fear of being blacklisted for championing justice and mercy need have no terrors for him. To use his property as a coat of mail in fighting the battles of the weak would be the best way of obeying Christ's command to the rich young ruler to sell all and give it to the poor. When Mr. Roosevelt was still police commissioner in New York, he said to the young men of New York: "I would teach the young men that he who has not wealth owes his first duty to his family, but he who has means owes his to the state. It is ignoble to go on heaping up money. I would preach the doctrine of work to all, and to the men of wealth the doctrine of unremunerative work." [8] The most "unremunerative work" is the work that draws opposition and animosity.

Mr. Roosevelt implies here that a man's duty to his family is the first and dominant duty, and that this exempts him in some measure from service to the larger public. It follows that the childless have a call to the dangerous work of the kingdom of God. A man and woman who are feeding and training young citizens are performing so immense and absorbing a service to the future that they might well be exempt from taxes to the state and from sacrificial service to the kingdom of God. If nevertheless so many of them assume these duties in addition, the childless man and woman will have to do heroic work in the trenches before they can rank on the same level. It is not fair to ask a man with children to give his time and strength as freely to public causes as if he had none. It is still more unfair to expect him to risk the bread and the prospects of his family in championing dangerous causes as freely as if he risked only himself. The childless people should adopt the whole coming generation of children and fight to make the world more habitable for them as for their own brood. The unmarried and the childless should enlist in the new apostolate and march on the forlorn hopes with Jesus Christ.

In asking for faith in the possibility of a new social order, we ask for no utopian delusion. We know well that there is no perfection for man in this life: there is only growth toward perfection. In personal religion we look with seasoned suspicion at any one who claims to be holy and perfect, yet we always tell men to become holy and to seek perfection. We make it a duty to seek what is unattainable. We have the same paradox in

8. Jacob A. Riis, *Theodore Roosevelt, the Citizen* [ED.] (N.Y., 1904), 14.

the perfectibility of society. We shall never have a perfect social life, yet we must seek it with faith. We shall never abolish suffering. There will always be death, and the empty chair and heart. There will always be the agony of love unreturned. Women will long for children and never press baby lips to their breast. Men will long for fame and miss it. Imperfect moral insight will work hurt in the best conceivable social order. The strong will always have the impulse to exert their strength, and no system can be devised which can keep them from crowding and jostling the weaker. Increased social refinement will bring increased sensitiveness to pain. An American may suffer as much distress through a social slight as a Russian peasant under the knout. At best there is always but an approximation to a perfect social order. The kingdom of God is always but coming.

But every approximation to it is worth while. Every step toward personal purity and peace, though it only makes the consciousness of imperfection more poignant, carries its own exceeding great reward, and everlasting pilgrimage toward the kingdom of God is better than contented stability in the tents of wickedness.

And sometimes the hot hope surges up that perhaps the long and slow climb may be ending. In the past the steps of our race toward progress have been short and feeble, and succeeded by long intervals of sloth and apathy. But is that necessarily to remain the rate of advance? In the intellectual life there has been an unprecedented leap forward during the last hundred years. Individually we are not more gifted than our grandfathers, but collectively we have wrought out more epoch-making discoveries and inventions in one century than the whole race in the untold centuries that have gone before. If the twentieth century could do for us in the control of social forces what the nineteenth did for us in the control of natural forces, our grandchildren would live in a society that would be justified in regarding our present social life as semi-barbarous. Since the Reformation began to free the mind and to direct the force of religion toward morality, there has been a perceptible increase of speed. Humanity is gaining in elasticity and capacity for change, and every gain in general intelligence, in organizing capacity, in physical and moral soundness, and especially in responsiveness to ideal motives, again increases the ability to advance without disastrous reactions. The swiftness of evolution in our own country proves the immense latent perfectibility in human nature. Last May a miracle happened. At the beginning of the week the fruit trees bore brown and greenish buds. At the end of the week they were robed in bridal garments of blossom. But for weeks and months the sap had been rising and distending the cells and maturing the tissues which were half ready in the fall before. The swift unfolding was the culmination of a long process. Perhaps these nineteen centuries of Christian influence have been a long preliminary stage of growth, and now the flower and fruit are almost here. If at this juncture we can rally sufficient religious faith and moral strength to snap the bonds of evil and turn the present unparalleled economic and intellectual resources of humanity to the harmonious development of a true social life, the generations yet unborn will mark this as that great day of the Lord for which the ages waited, and count us blessed for sharing in the apostolate that proclaimed it.

❧ ❧ ❧ ❧ ❧ ❧ ❧ ❧

OUR SEMI-CHRISTIAN SOCIAL ORDER [1]

Editor's introduction. Rauschenbusch's most "secular" book was *Christianizing the Social Order,* in which he drew on the large volume of progressivist, reformist, and socialist thought of his time. At its conclusion, evidently sensing that the analysis he had undertaken might be misunderstood, he declared:

> In looking back over the field traversed in this book, it may seem to some as if our argument had fallen away from the high religious ground taken at the outset and had sagged down to the level of mere economic discussion. That impression would be superficial. This is a religious book from beginning to end. Its sole concern is for the kingdom of God and the salvation of men. But the kingdom of God includes the economic life; for it means the progressive transformation of all human affairs by the thought and spirit of Christ.[2]

Reprinted here are the first three chapters of Part II entitled "Our Semi-Christian Social Order." It was here that Rauschenbusch made the oft-quoted and oft-criticized statement that while four great sections of the social order had been largely christianized, one major area — businesss — remained unredeemed.

❧ ❧ ❧ ❧

CHAPTER I: WHAT DO WE MEAN BY "CHRISTIANIZING"
THE SOCIAL ORDER?

We often hear the assertion that no one can tell whether Christianity would work, because Christianity has never been tried.

I deny it. Christianity has been tried, both in private and in social life, and the question is in order whether anything in the history of humanity has succeeded except Christianity.

It is true enough that there has never been a social order which was Christian from top to bottom. But large domains of our social life have come under the sway of Christ's law in their spirit and in their fundamen-

1. *Christianizing the Social Order* (N.Y., 1912), 123-68. Used by permission of The Macmillan Company.
2. *Ibid.,* 458.

tal structure, and these are by common consent the source of our happiness and the objects of our pride, while those portions of the social order which are still unchristianized are the source of our misery and the cause of our shame.

It is unjust to Christianity to call our civilization Christian; it is unjust to our civilization to call it un-Christian. It is semi-Christian. Its regeneration is in process, but it has run in streaks and strata, with baffling inconsistencies and hypocrisies, even as with you and me. But so far as the process has gone, it will warrant us in taking the completion of the job in hand with serene confidence that it will work. Christian history is not a dismal failure to date. The largest and hardest part of the work of christianizing the social order has been done.

In the next chapter I shall try to show how the Christian portions of our social order were christianized. This will furnish us a working conception of the means by which the unregenerate parts can be put through the same saving process. In several subsequent chapters I shall then analyze the unchristianized portions of the social order in order to make clear why and in what respects they are still un-Christian.

But first we shall have to define what we mean by "christianizing" the social order or any part of it.

I do not mean putting the name of Christ into the Constitution of the United States. Some descendants of the Scotch Covenanters still refuse to vote or hold office under our government because Jesus Christ is not formally acknowledged as the head of our nation. But in the present stage of our life that would only be one more act of national hypocrisy. Moreover, Jesus himself does not seem to have cared much about being called "Lord, Lord," unless there was substance to the word. To put a stop to child labor in our country would be a more effective way of doing homage to his sovereignty than any business of words and names.

Neither do we want to renew the attempts made in the past by both Catholicism and Protestantism to set up a theocracy ruled by the church, and making Christian belief and worship a compulsory duty of citizenship. All the experience of history protests against coercion in religion. The small amount of compulsion still surviving in the established churches of Europe and South America is felt by outsiders to be a relic of past evil and a present-day scandal.

Christianizing the social order means bringing it into harmony with the ethical convictions which we identify with Christ. A fairly definite body of moral convictions has taken shape in modern humanity. They express our collective conscience, our working religion. The present social order denies and flouts many of these principles of our ethical life and compels us in practice to outrage our better self. We demand therefore that the moral sense of humanity shall be put in control and shall be allowed to reshape the institutions of social life.

We call this "christianizing" the social order because these moral principles find their highest expression in the teachings, the life, and the spirit of Jesus Christ. Their present power in Western civilization is in large part directly traceable to his influence over its history. To the great majority of our nation, both inside and outside of the churches, he has become the incarnate moral law and his name is synonymous with the ideal of human goodness. To us who regard him as the unique revelation of God, the unfolding of the divine life under human forms, he is the ultimate standard of moral and spiritual life, the perfect expression of the will of God for humanity, the categorical imperative with a human heart. But very many who do not hold this belief in a formulated way or who feel compelled to deny it, including an increasing portion of our Jewish fellow citizens, will still consent that in Jesus our race has reached one of its highest points, if not its crowning summit thus far, so that Jesus Christ is a prophecy of the future glory of humanity, the type of Man as he is to be. Christianizing means humanizing in the highest sense. I ask the consent of both classes to use his name for the undertaking which he initiated for us. To say that we want to moralize the social order would be both vague and powerless to most men. To say that we want to christianize it is both concrete and compelling. Christ's spirit is the force that drives us. His mind is the square and plumb line that must guide us in our building.

The danger in using so high a word is that we shall be led to expect too much. Even a Christian social order cannot mean perfection. As long as men are flesh and blood the world can be neither sinless nor painless. For instance, how can any form of social organization keep the tremendous electric current of sex desire from going astray and dealing misery and shame? The law of growth, which is essential to human life, itself makes any static perfection impossible. Every child is born a kicking little egotist, and has to learn by its own mistakes and sins to coordinate itself with the social life of every successive group which it enters. If perfection were reached today, new adjustments would be demanded tomorrow by the growth of new powers. The justest and most sympathetic human society conceivable would unknowingly inflict injury and wrong, and only slowly realize it when it heard the insistent cry of pain. The structure of society can never be up to date. It is necessarily a slow historical growth, and men will always have to labor hard to rid it of antiquated and harmful customs and institutions brought down from a worse past.

I must ask my readers to keep these limitations of human life in mind as axioms in all the discussion that follows, even when they are not stated, and to assume that we are keeping within hailing distance of common sense. We shall demand perfection and never expect to get it. But by demanding it we shall get more than we now have. Straight-cut insistence on moral duty is quite compatible with the largest patience, as human frailty limps up to God's judgment seat and pleads guilty for a thousand sins. Jesus is the classical example of the combination between high-voltage moral demand and the tenderest understanding.

But within the limitations of human nature I believe that the constitutional structure of the social order can be squared with the demands of Christian morality. At every new step of moral progress the clamor has gone up that fairness and decency were utopian fanaticism and would ruin society, but instead of making the social machinery unworkable, every step toward collective Christian ethics proved an immense relief to society.

An un-Christian social order can be known by the fact that it makes good men do bad things. It tempts, defeats, drains, and degrades, and leaves men stunted, cowed, and shamed in their manhood. A Christian social order makes bad men do good things. It sets high aims, steadies the vagrant impulses of the weak, trains the powers of the young, and is felt by all as an uplifting force which leaves them with the consciousness of a broader and nobler humanity as their years go on.

Having now explained what we mean by christianizing the social order, we might draw from the gospels a list of the Christian principles of social life and test the existing social order by them. But we shall find it more fruitful to trace the moral evolution of those social institutions which have to some degree been christianized and in this way amplify our conceptions of the christianizing process. History will give us a better comprehension of the problem than the closest definition of terms. If we know how a thing has been done, we see how it can and ought to be done.

CHAPTER II: THE CHRISTIANIZED SECTIONS OF OUR SOCIAL ORDER

The simplest and most familiar social organization is the family. It is also the most Christian. It is so Christian that the word "Father" has become the most satisfactory symbol of a loving God, and the word "child" the most trustful expression of our relation to him. When Jesus substituted these family terms for the old royal conceptions with their connotations of despotism, the change meant a redemption of religion.[3] Wherever the members of a social organization have taken to calling one another "brother," it has stood for higher social ideals. "The fatherhood of God and the brotherhood of man" is one of the cherished phrases of our time; it expresses the faith that the same solidarity and tenderness which we know in family life will yet become common in our wider social relations. As for the word "mother" — that carries a mystic breath of religious sweetness to which we all do homage. Thus the social institution of the family is so Christian that we can use all its terms freely as symbols and vehicles of spiritual thought and feeling. Could we do the same with the terms of business life, "boss," "hands," "foreman," "clerk"?

The cheering fact about this is that the family did not set out with so much love and beauty, but had to go through a long sanctifying process. In its early stages the patriarchal family from which our own family organization is derived was held together by stern force and selfishness, quite as much as by love and kinship. The slaves and servants were worked and ruled for the good of the owner and master, and however kind a man he might be, the whip was a matter of course and the infliction of death was his right. Wives were dragged off as the booty of war, or purchased. They represented sex desire and love, but also labor force and the breeding of children. A patriarch with a lot of wives was a capitalist and became rich on the "surplus value" they created for him. His sons were his fighting outfit with which he gained and protected his wealth and power. Around the hall of Priam were fifty apartments for his sons and their wives, and the prowess of the young men was the constitutional basis of his kingship. Daughters too were capital, and beauty might prove a bonanza. When Jacob fled from Esau and fell in love with Rachel at the well, he had no cattle or jewelry to buy her, so he bound himself to work for Laban seven years. Since his children were born in Laban's family, that excellent business man claimed them as his unearned increment, and felt as sore as an outraged landlord when Jacob finally made off with them all. The old gentleman felt a conscious glow of virtue when he let them go unscathed.[4]

3. Note Paul's sense of relief when he contrasted the spirit of the old religions with the spirit prevailing in Christianity. When you became Christians, "you did not receive a slavish spirit so that you had to be afraid again, but you received a filial spirit which impels us to cry out, Abba, Father!" Romans viii, 15.

4. Genesis xxxi. The whole story is very interesting material for the early history of the family.

The life and welfare of every member of the patriarchal family were controlled by its head. He was their economic manager, directing their work, allotting their goods, and selling the common product to his own advantage. They took their religion from him as the household priest. He was ruler and judge over his own, and law and custom upheld his despotic power, for the law was made and the precedents were set by him and his peers. He could divorce his wife or bring in other women to share her most precious rights. If she was unfaithful, he could kill her. She had no corresponding claim on his fidelity, for it was his right to do as he liked. Over his children too he held the power of life and death. The practice of exposing crippled or female children, which still exists in some non-Christian nations, is merely a remnant of larger powers in the past. The Romans were proud that the *patria potestas* was nowhere more absolute than with them.

This despotic family organization contained very large ingredients of good. It furnished the weak protection against enslavement and death. It coerced the savage to work, sweated the idleness out of him, and made his labor more productive by forcing him into cooperation with others. It placed the capable in the position of leadership, and killed them off when they failed. To expand a family of two into a patriarchal tribe of fifty or five hundred, to keep sons and slaves together, to beat off hostile competition and attack, and beat down domestic intrigues and conspiracies, was quite as great a feat of leadership then as to organize a department store or a trust nowadays. The patriarchal family in its tyrannous beginnings can claim the gratitude of posterity with the same right as our present industrial organization. For thousands of years it was the social system within which the larger part of the race found food and protection, education and religion.

Nevertheless the fact remains that the family as an institution was based on despotism and exploitation. The relation of husband and wives, of father and children, of master and slaves, could be made fine and noble by personal goodness, but the personal virtue was constantly vitiated by the wrong inhering in the social order in which they lived. The Old Testament gives us an intimate insight into a number of families, either as they actually lived, or as the admiring and idealizing tradition of later times imagined them, and not one of them shows us a good home from a modern point of view. Abraham was a true gentleman, whose acquaintance would be a benediction in any civilization; Jacob would surely be a millionaire and church elder if he lived today; David is one of the most brilliant and spiritual figures in history. Yet the family relations of these men were such that no self-respecting church could retain them as members if they did the same today. An unregenerate social institution put these good men into positions where they did wrong. We see them now as posterity will see our Christian business men.

The history of the family tells of a slow decrease of despotism and exploitation. Gradually wives were no longer bought outright. The right of divorce was hedged about. The wife gained an assured legal status and some property rights. When polygamy ceased, and adultery was considered a crime in man as well as in woman, the basis was laid for equality between man and wife. But only within the last hundred years has woman risen toward acknowledged equality with swift and decisive steps. Most other countries are still far from conceding what our American women have now learned to take as a matter of course. The present agitation for woman's suffrage is one of the final steps of this ascent. The suffrage will abolish one of the last remnants of patriarchal autocracy by giving woman a direct relation to the political organism of society, instead of allowing man to exercise her political rights for her.

In the same way the relation of the father to the children became less autocratic and more loving. The killing of a child by the father became rare, then illegal, and finally a crime. Marrying off his daughters has ceased to be a lucrative business and has become an expensive joy. Instead of exploiting the children for his own enrichment the father has learned to sacrifice himself for their education and advancement. Changes in the legal status of children have followed the change in family feeling. Here again the course of evolution has come to a swift culmination. Our own generation has witnessed a remarkable advance toward democracy in the relation between parents and children.

Imagine that a Syrian village had fallen asleep in the year 4000 B.C., like the palace of the Sleeping Beauty in the old fairy tale, and were waked to life today. The elders in the village gate resume their discussion of current affairs — of the slave who has run away to escape a beating; of the ten sons of a neighboring sheik who conspired to kill their father and take his slaves and harem to set up for themselves; and of the sad poisoning of a favorite wife's son by some other wife "to this jury unknown." The elders agree that a pernicious social unrest is abroad which makes their life a burden and threatens the foundations of civilization. To them enters a modern tourist, pastor in a staid Pennsylvania town, a man who prides himself on being untainted by radical social notions. As he listens to their woes, he promptly sees the cause and expounds the orthodox American conception of the family, advising them to treat their wives as their equals, to live for their children, and to give their servants one night off per week. They listen to the stranger with patient courtesy at first, explaining that his views are utopian; that all authority would be undermined if a man could not beat his wife; that the women like being beaten, and would take it as a sign of diminishing affection if they were no longer chastised; that polygamy is an index of high morality, since the best citizens have most wives, and you would have to change human nature to make monogamy compulsory; that slaves would have nothing to eat if they had no masters to feed and employ them; that theology rightly teaches that a father, being the author of a child's life, has a right to take its life if he considers it superfluous. The American, aglow with Christian indignation, describes how wisely his wife manages the common finances and selects his neckties; how he sends his girls to Vassar, though it ruins his bank account; how fond the girls are of their dad, and how he would hate himself if he thought that his family regarded him as a tyrant. But he sees dark frowns gathering on their faces and ominous whispers running about. He pales as he hears the ancient Hittite equivalent for "socialist and anarchist" applied to himself. The scene is full of tragic possibilities, and we abandon the unhappy extremist to the imagination of the reader.

Doubtless the head of a patriarchal family, if he could have foreseen the later democratizing of the institution, would have felt that while wife and child might gain, the father would certainly lose by the change. Yet in fact the father too has gained. He has lost in power, but gained in love. In the beginning children seem to have formed a permanent attachment only for the mother. When the father ceased to be a tyrant, he won his share of love.

Thus the constitutional structure of the family has passed through an ethical transformation by slow historical processes. The despotism of the man, fortified by law, custom, and economic possession, has passed into approximate equality between husband and wife. The children have become the free companions of their parents, and selfish parental authority has come under the law of unselfish service. Economic exploitation by the head of the family has been superseded by economic cooperation and a satisfactory communism of the family equipment. Based on equal rights, bound together by love and respect for individuality, governed under the law of mutual helpfulness, the family today furnishes the natural habitation for a Christian life and fellowship. There is no conflict of the Christian spirit with the accepted laws of family life; only with the transgressions of those laws. We can therefore say that the family has been assimilated to Christianity. As an institution it has been christianized.

That does not, however, mean that Christian living has become automatic in the family and requires no religious effort. To make the family a place of permanent love, peace, and spiritual beauty is now, and always will be, a great moral achievement and one of the highest triumphs of personality. The number of really beautiful families is still small. Yet the traditions of the institution, as religion, custom, public opinion, law, and neighborhood examples have shaped it, make it an ennobling and restraining force in the life of all. The despotic and polygamous family life of the past caused saints to do shameful things. The christianized family holds even selfish and wayward individuals to some measure of decency, serviceableness, and love. The fact that the institution as such has been christianized predisposes the individuals living in it to be Christians. If they are personally temperate, reasonable, loving, and swayed by religious convictions and duties, they will find the family responsive to their highest desires; if they are not, they will at least find it a restraining, educational, and disciplinary influence.

The process through which the family has been transformed can justly be called a christianizing process, not only in view of the results achieved, but of the forces that accomplished the results. So far as the Greco-Roman world is concerned, Christianity saved and regenerated the institution of the family just as much as it ever saved any sinner. Among the wealthy classes of the ancient world, marriage had reached a stage of decomposition compared with which the divorce scandals of some of our millionaires seem decorous, and, as usual, the upper classes infected the lower with their bacteria. The young Christian church attacked the sexual evils of heathen society, its prostitution, concubinage, ease of divorce, and unnatural vices, with the same convinced ardor with which socialists smite our industrial vices; and in the degree in which the church gained spiritual control, it cemented the family with new religious sanctions, made it once more permanent, and filled it with higher meanings and values. However derelict the church has been about other social relations, it has always been deeply concerned in the family. It has often taken reactionary positions, for instance, about the public activities and the emancipation of women, but it has always stood for fidelity, cleanness, and tenderness.

Moreover, the influence of the Christian spirit on the home life has been more searching and intimate than mere church influence. It did its work within the four walls of innumerable homes, unrecorded by public observation, and the actors in the readjustments were not aware that they were sharing in a great social transformation. If any one will pass in review the families he has known intimately, he will realize that religion is often the decisive factor in the character of a home. If we go through a tenement house full of slovenly, quarrelsome, and discouraged families, and find one home which seems an oasis of cleanliness, order, and peace, we shall be safe in assuming that we have struck a religious family. But every christianized family leaves traditions in the hearts of its children which they will seek to realize in their own homes, and it sets the standard a little higher for all who come in contact with it. By such precedents public opinion and custom are formed, and ultimately law follows custom. So the ethical transformation of the family becomes comprehensible only through the persistent atmospheric pressure of Christianity exerted on countless families through many generations. We can watch its swift decay today wherever the influence of Christianity has lapsed.

On the other hand, religion did not do the work singlehanded. Social and economic changes did their part. For instance, the suppression of polygamy was helped by the cessation of slavery. The home became a place of rest and love when household production changed to joint labor in the shop and factory, relieving the family of the coercion of productive toil. Religion always does its most powerful and permanent social work when it supports and invigorates the wholesome tendencies in the common life of men.

Today this christianized family is being attacked by new disintegrating forces, against which it is all the more defenseless because it now rests so exclusively on the finer and more fragile moral instincts. High rents in the cities narrow the home and crush its charms. High prices and high standards of living combine to make family life expensive and to suppress child life. Industrialism is emptying the home of its womenfolk. A theory of education which imposes no law except the law of pleasurableness on the young is sapping the virtues of self-restraint and patience. The materialistic spirit developed by modern commercialism is weakening the organization of the spiritual life, the church, and therewith the power of organized religion over the home is failing. Unless these destructive forces are checked in this generation, the institution of the family will have been christianized only to perish like a flower in full bloom bitten by frost. Unless the rest of society is christianized, the christianized family cannot survive in it.[5]

5. Some of these causes of decadence have been discussed more fully in *Christianity and the Social Crisis*, 271–79.

A similar christianizing process has taken place in the church, which is the social organization of the religious life of humanity.

At the beginning of the modern era the church was a despotic and exploiting organization. Instead of being the great exemplar of fraternity, it was ruled by a monarchical and aristocratic hierarchy, which used its immense powers to lord it over the people and to enrich itself. Though founded on the principle of love and freedom, it coerced belief and terrorized men into uniformity by physical constraint. But coercion is in religion what rape is in love. The church owned nearly a third of the landed wealth of Europe, and in addition to its rents extorted tithes and fees by civil process. It had commercialized heaven, hell, and purgatory, and did a thriving business in assorted religious commodities. Because many of its positions were rich sinecures, they were bestowed on favorites, granted for a rake-off, and often held by absentees, while hungry vicars did the actual work. Every effort to reform the church before the Reformation turned, not, as we would suppose, on the restoration of evangelical doctrine, but on the abatement of simony, which was the ecclesiastical term for what we call "graft." A hundred years before Luther all the best minds of Europe were exerting themselves to reform the church "in head and members," an equivalent of our efforts to get at "those higher up" in political corruption. Three international councils were convened in rapid succession and sat for years, but the net outcome for decency was slight. The ecclesiastical Tammany Hall was able to counter every move. The forces of corruption were so solidly entrenched, and the forces of moral indignation were so carefully gagged, that even the almost universal condemnation of all honorable men was unable to work a permanent change. Instead of being a great, free, mobile force available to work righteousness, the church was itself the chief object of contempt and reform. Scientific Catholic historians today agree in confessing the practical abuses prevailing, and they would be less guarded in their condemnation of them if Protestants did not point to this degradation of the church to justify the terrible split of the Reformation.

If any one in the year 1500 had prophesied that the time would come when the type of the lazy and fat-bellied priest would disappear from literature and the stage, and when the ministry of the church would be wholly free from any charge of general sexual impurity; when the church itself would be without governmental powers, without legal privileges, without power to collect its tithes and execute its verdicts by the aid of the state, without endowed wealth, and depending entirely for support on the free gifts of those who loved her; when corruption and graft would be unknown and impossible in church life, and ministers, with few exceptions, would be sincere and hard-working men; when any attempt to repress or force religious belief would arouse general condemnation, and every man would be free to follow the inner light — if any one had prophesied all this, it would have been read as a delightful utopian dream, and very likely the church would have suppressed the book.

Yet that is the condition actually attained in our country. Our ministers as a class are a clean, laborious, and honorable profession. They are anxious to serve the community, and do so according to their best light, even when they derive no tangible benefit whatever. If there is any graft in the ministry, it is the graft practiced by the churches in underpaying their pastors, using their wives as unpaid workers, and turning them off on a pittance or on nothing when the magnetism of youth has been worked out of them. That is graft, but the old graft reversed. The church itself is almost without special privilege except the tax exemption which it shares with other benevolent organizations. Very few churches have any endowment; they all live from hand to mouth, and rejoice when they end a year without debt. In all the criticism of the church today, is there any charge that the church is doing conscious and positive wrong? The substance of all charges is that it fails to rise to its highest opportunities. May none of us have a blacker mark than that when we stand at the judgment bar!

All this means that the church has become a Christian. It was christianized when it got rid of its elaborate and profitable superstitions, and made salvation both simple and free. It was christianized when it lost its power and its will to tyrannize. Some Protestant churches have entirely democratized their organization; others, which have retained a monarchical or aristocratic form of organization in our country, have at least been steeped in the democratic spirit. The clergy was christianized when it lost the opportunity to live on easy money and learned to do hard work for plain pay. The church is hated today only in countries where it suppresses religious and intellectual freedom and resists the moral aspirations of the people. It is loved where it is a cooperative organization, resting on a basis of liberty and equality, held together by good will, and serving the highest ends known to the people. Let no one say that the churches of our country are not loved. What other nationwide organization is there which is supported freely by the people with such an output of money and of voluntary service, and which can offer them so little in return in the way of financial help or of pleasurable excitement? Why do the people do it if they do not love their churches?

For centuries before the Reformation, the instinct of Christian men had located the fundamental cause for the corruption of the church. It was a common conviction that the debasement of the church had set in with the "Donation of Constantine," by which the Emperor Constantine was supposed to have conferred large territories and sovereign rights on Pope Sylvester in the fourth century. That had been "the poisoned bone which the devil had thrown and which the church had swallowed." Since then the church has become an antichristian power. Constantly the bolder reformatory spirits taught that the church could be saved only by surrendering its wealth and political power and returning to apostolic poverty, supported only by the free gifts of those who loved her. And that has, in fact, been the way by which the salvation of the church has come. Church historians have overestimated the purifying influence of Luther's and Calvin's doctrine, and underestimated the tremendous fact that in consequence of the terrible punishment of the social and political changes accompanying the Reformation, the power of the church to tyrannize and exploit was stopped, and rent and profit began to disappear from church life. That took the church out of the captivity of mammon, and brought her back to God and the people.

The church did not welcome its salvation. When the princes of the church lost their temporal sovereignty; when the property of the church was "secularized"; when the constitutionalized "pull" and graft of the clerical aristocracy was canceled; the classes affected always felt that the cause of religion had received its death blow. Even today the papacy is not reconciled to the loss of the little state which had given the Pope the status of a sovereign prince, and even American Catholics feel compelled to demand the restoration of the papal sovereignty in order to enable the papacy to get back into the game of international politics which has always been so ruinous to the spiritual power of the papal institution. The process by which the church was stripped of power and wealth was no beautiful act of self-renunciation, but a shameless holdup by the powers that be. The ruling classes, the princes and aristocracy, found the church ditched with punctured tires on the road from Jerusalem to Jericho and proceeded to help themselves to what Providence had provided, being careful to show their governmental badge of authority to prove that it was all done legally. Some fractional part was usually devoted to endow education and charity, but the bulk of the landed wealth of the church made the everlasting fortune of those who were "on the inside" at the time. The despotic power of the Protestant princes was also greatly augmented by seizing the ecclesiastical powers hitherto exercised by the bishops and the Pope, so that the Reformation helped to create the era of absolutism to which the French Revolution began to make an end. Yet, in spite of its evil side effects, the revolution by which the political power and the unearned wealth of the church were fatally broken and started on the way toward extinction proved to be the moral salvation of the church. Wherever remnants of the old conditions survive, the church is under the challenge of the modern spirit, and wherever that spirit becomes conscious and militant, the church is distrusted and hated as a constitutional foe of truth and liberty. On the other hand, wherever the church has been set free from even the chance to tyrannize, it has become a powerful member in the alliance of forces that are redeeming the social order.

Here, then, we have another great section of the social order which has passed through a moral transformation and redemption, still incomplete, but far-reaching and tremendous. Like the family, the church was christianized by unlearning despotism and exploitation, and coming under the law of love and service. Its salvation came, not merely by multiplying the number of good men in it, while leaving the social invitations to tyranny intact; not merely by purifying the gospel preached, while the clergy continued to live abnormal and parasitic lives; but by stripping the church of its unearned wealth, depriving its leaders of special privilege and the food of arrogance, wresting from their hands the means of coercion, and making them answerable to those whom they served and from whom they got their living. When coercion ceased, a purer gospel followed. When the ministry was democratized, Christian ethics had a chance. When the official servants of the church stepped out of the classes that fatten on rent and profit, and entered the honorable poverty of the wage-earners, the lust of rule passed into the will to serve. Because evil had entrenched itself in the church and fought against betterment, salvation had to come by a disastrous revolution which created new evils in place of those which it abolished. It took several centuries of organic development to complete the process, and even now it is not completed. But a constitutional change has been wrought which amounts to a christianizing of the church.

This christianized church is now, like the christianized family, in danger for its very existence. Its financial needs, the supply and hopefulness of its ministry, its hold on the mass of the working people, its stability in the rural districts, are all threatened by modern conditions.[6] Its very value is called in question by the materialistic spirit created by our commercialism. The poor who are reduced to barbarism by poverty, and the rich whose higher life is drowned out by excess, alike stare at the church with dull and apathetic eyes. If the income of the church were big enough for graft, there would be solid "interests" to fight for it. If it could still terrorize the people, it could coerce them into attendance, support, and obedience. Because it appeals only to the free impulses of a mature spiritual life, it languishes where the spiritual life of the nation is atrophied. Unless it helps to save and christianize the national life, large sections of the church will wither away, and it will survive only in those lower forms which still appeal to superstition, dogmatism, and emotionalism.

A third section of the social order which has gone through a christianizing process is the organization which serves the purposes of education.

In its unregenerate days, education was a perquisite of the secular and religious aristocracy. Those families and classes which had gained leisure and taste for the intellectual life cultivated and refined it further. But instead of being a missionary force which impelled the cultured minds to put themselves at the service of the ignorant, it was an added influence to put the upper classes out of sympathetic contact with the lower. In every aristocratic society the possessing class has watched the spread of education downward with jealousy and has yielded the means for it grudgingly, realizing that education breeds unrest and discontent and makes the servile and laboring class less respectful and dependent. Governor Berkeley voiced the attitude of the Cavaliers in England and Virginia in his famous report of 1670: "I thank God there are no free schools, nor printing, and I hope we shall not have them these hundred years; for learning has brought disobedience and heresy and sects into the world, and printing has divulged them, and libels against the best government. God keep us from both!" The prohibition of Negro education in some of our slave States before the war was simply an extreme expression of the unregenerate spirit in education. Even when popular education becomes common, the upper classes maintain special educational privileges for their children. In Germany, for instance, there are two sets of government schools, even

6. These points are fully discussed in Chapter vi of *Christianity and the Social Crisis.*

for the very young: one for the children of the common people, who expect to go to work as soon as they have reached adolescence; the other for the children of parents who can afford to give them a higher and longer education. As long as the social order is divided into these classes, this is a very practical system, but it neither expresses nor creates democracy.

The spirit in which education was imparted was also autocratic and even tyrannous. The novels and biographies of the early Victorian era are full of the flogging of schoolboys. Corporal punishment was so constant that children were under a reign of fear, witness Shakespeare's "whining schoolboy, with his satchel and shining morning face, creeping like snail unwillingly to school." The final escape from school life was often marked by a wild bound for liberty. Maturer students too were mentally coerced by the authority of the teacher and the great names of learning. Freedom and originality in the student were regarded with suspicion, and a purely receptive attitude was encouraged. In the higher walks of intellectual life freedom of investigation and teaching was always an individual conquest, and the yoke of orthodoxy, religious, political, and social, lay heavily on the neck of teachers.

It would be idle to claim that even a single one of these evils has been fully outgrown by education. But there has been a revolutionary change. Corporal punishment has fallen into disuse, and within one generation the reign of fear has so far ceased that the majority of children now seem to love school. In the higher schools habits of intellectual freedom are encouraged. Scientific investigation in the universities has become almost autonomous.

Except in private schools patronized by the wealthy, manifestations of social exclusiveness call for apology, and every advance in democracy is proclaimed with pride. The Christian missionary impulse has taken possession of the teaching profession and the great organization of education. Institutions eagerly create extension courses and implore the intellectually lost to come in and be saved. The presence of even a fraction of one per cent of persons who cannot read and write is felt as a reproach by civilized nations. Individual teachers may be lazy and stale, but the teaching profession as a whole is under the law of Christ. It seeks to serve, and the road to greatness in it is by pre-eminent service.

Profit-making is not unknown in educational life, but it is limited in scope and always felt to be a degradation. Medical schools run for profit, for instance, are inferior institutions and often a disgrace to the profession. Compared with the prizes of business life, even the highest incomes of teachers are modest. Yet for plain pay, men and women give faithful and efficient work and take satisfaction in doing it.

The financial support of the public school system is always niggardly compared with the real needs, and it has often been the nesting place of graft. Nevertheless it is on an essentially Christian basis. Louis Blanc's maxim, "from every one according to his ability, and to every one according to his need," [7] is so lofty and unselfish that even socialists think it would not work in a society just emerging from capitalism. Yet that is the principle on which our schools are maintained. Every family is taxed for their support according to its financial ability, and it gets the benefits of the schools according to its needs. A rich man contributes heavily to the school tax though he may have neither child nor grandchild to profit by them. A man with ten children gets ten times as much good from the schools as the man with one child, and — other things being equal — pays no more for their maintenance. Every enlargement of the functions of the schools makes this Christian principle more striking.

Thus our educational system has passed through a regenerating process. As with the family and the church, the line of progress ran from tyranny to freedom, from aristocratic privilege to democracy of opportunity, from self-seeking to the enthusiasm of service. In detail the bigger part of the change is still before us, but here too a constitutional change has taken place which may justly be called a christianizing of the educational organization. The love of the people has put its approval on the result. It works. The support of the common schools is the largest item in the tax bills of our communities. We have learned to be ashamed of some powerful elements of our national life, but we are proud of our schools. When we annexed the Philippines, and our astonished American conscience inquired how we could create foreign dependencies and subject peoples by conquest and purchase like any other bloody tyrant, we hugged the consolation that at any rate the school would follow the flag. In sizing up the future for our Filipino brothers, the commercial corporation was our biggest anxiety, the public school our best justification. The school is Christian; the corporation — not yet.

In the case of the school, as in the case of the family, organized Christianity contributed a large part of the forces which worked the change. Before the educational appetite had pervaded the people sufficiently to

7. [ED.] Jean Joseph Charles Louis Blanc (1811–82) was a French journalist and politician, theorist of utopian socialism, and historian of the French Revolution.

run on its own strength, and before the democratized state had bent its larger resources to the task of popular education, the church was the chief agency that fostered it. Wherever in its earlier stages the school sought out the poor and neglected classes, the missionary impulse was furnished by religion. That pioneering service of the church is in danger of being obscured today in some countries because the church is so reluctant to be superseded by the state, and because it has often blocked the emancipation of the intellect. But taking the whole history of education in the Christian nations, a fair judgment will allow the church a large balance to its credit.

In our own country, education certainly owes an immense debt to Christianity. Most of our American colonies were organized and developed by financial corporations that were in the colonizing business for the profits they hoped to make out of the colonists. I fail to remember any noteworthy efforts by these dividend-makers to put education on its feet in the new country. The high standards set by the New England colonies were set by religious men and under religious motives. In the westward march of our population, when the life of the frontier absorbed the energies of the settlers in a hard struggle to get a footing, and reduced even the educated individuals to the monotony and the fierce passions of primitive civilization, the churches stood almost singlehanded for the higher interests of mankind. They were always hard pushed to build their simple edifices and support their ministers, yet they founded academies and colleges and encouraged their young people to deny themselves for years and "get an education." The educators who molded the earlier generations of American manhood by their earnestness and heroic devotion, and to whom we look back now wistfully as an almost extinct race of life-givers, simply embodied the spirit of Christianity applied to the intellectual life. That enthusiasm for education, which is one of the finest characteristics of our country and has gone far to redeem us from the charge of gross mammonism, was kindled and fed by the churches and ministers, by the denominational academies and colleges, and by the men and women who were bred in both. These forces have infused that missionary spirit into our educational system which reaches out a summoning hand to the needy and aspiring. Our country has been distinguished for the immense gifts to the cause of education. How many were directly prompted by religion? How many at least indirectly by the moral impulses surviving in the children of religious families? The friendly helpfulness of churches and ministers toward the public schools and high schools has been all the more creditable because there has been no organic connection to call out the sense of responsibility.

A fourth great section of our social order which has been christianized is the political life. To Americans this may seem a staggering assertion, for of all corrupt things surely our politics is the corruptest. I confess to some misgivings in moving that this brother be received among the regenerate, but I plead on his behalf that he is a newly saved sinner. Politics has been on the thorny path of sanctification only about a century and a half, and the tattered clothes and questionable smells of the far country still cling to the prodigal.

The fundamental redemption of the state took place when special privilege was thrust out of the constitution and theory of our government and it was based on the principle of personal liberty and equal rights.

When the rich and the poor have justice meted to them in our courts with an uneven hand, and the fact is made plain and comprehensible, it is felt to be an outrage and a betrayal of the spirit of our institutions. When powerful interests receive special consideration and benefits from Congress or the State legislatures, all concerned are careful to mask the fact and disguise the action as if it were done for the public interest. When the property of the rich is partly exempted from taxation by unequal methods of assessment, and the burden of public expenditure is thrown on the poorer classes, we feel free to protest against it as a departure from the clear intent of our fundamental laws. In short, inequality and oppression, the denial of equal rights and of the equal humanity of all, is felt to be a backsliding and disgrace.

But the time was when these things were sanctioned as just and honorable by law and public opinion. Inequality and privilege were part of the constitution of states. Feudalism shaped the social order of the Middle Ages, just as democracy and capitalism make up the social order of our own age. But in feudalism class differences and class privileges were essential to the very theory of government. The nobleman was on a wholly different footing before the law from the common man. He had to be tried by men of his own class, who were disposed by class feeling to side with him, and the baser forms of punishment did not exist for him. Some remnants of this inequality still linger wherever feudal rank survives. A Russian noble and a moujik who commit the same offense do not receive the same punishment. In Germany two workmen who cut each other up with knives, and two army officers who cut each other up with swords in a duel, are treated in a very different manner by the law. In Italy two cardinals recently claimed their right as Italian princes to have their deposition as witnesses taken in their own houses, instead of coming into a public court like common people. Within certain limits the feudal nobles usually had the right of judicature in their territories; when a peasant was oppressed by the servants of the baron and claimed justice in the court, he found the baron or his appointee sitting in the court to decide the case. Imagine that the constitution of Illinois provided that a director of a corporation could be tried only by a jury of corporation officers, and that every public service corporation had the right to operate its own court of justice to settle all difficulties with its employees and the ordinary public, and could put the offensive citizen who protested against the size of his gas bill into the corporation jail! In the feudal age, landed property was almost the only form of property, and the landed nobility corresponded very fully to what we call "the Interests," so that the illustration is not at all fanciful.

A hundred other special privileges were claimed and exercised by the nobility, not "on the side," but frankly as their natural right. Even a petty noble could declare and wage war, a right of such momentous importance for the people that in our vast nation only a single public body is vested with that power. At one time about a hundred and fifty peers and barons of France could coin and circulate money, another right of profound importance to public welfare. The higher civil and military careers were open only to nobles and churchmen. Political rights were restricted to landowners; consequently it was made hard for the baseborn to acquire land at all. The system of restricting the suffrage on property lines is a remnant of the feudal system of granting political power to those who already had economic power, and of depriving the economically helpless of the political means of asserting their rights. Even in so enlightened a country as Prussia, a three-class system of suffrage prevails, by which one heavy taxpayer in the first class may count for as much as a hundred workingmen in the third class.

Only by comparison with the past do we realize that our political system has really entered on a decisive moral change. The foundations of our commonwealth were fortunately laid when the democratic idealism of the eighteenth century was gathering strength. Soon afterward it got its tremendous utterance in the French Revolution. In every revolutionary movement the highest political and social conceptions of that age are seized by the revolutionary party, and put forward in order to enlist moral support and enthusiasm. When the plowshare tears open the soil, new seeds can gain lodgment. The American Revolution, like the French, was essentially a movement of the capitalist class and was impelled by their economic interests, but as long as the struggle lasted the leaders were inspired by higher enthusiasms, and the necessity of rallying all available spiritual forces gave the convinced radicals and idealists a comparatively free hand for the moment. Between 1776 and 1786 the ardent sentiments of the Declaration of Independence had cooled down into very calculating class interest, and the fundamental law of our country was by no means framed to promote and extend democracy in coming days. But at least we had no king, and no landed and hereditary nobility. The young capitalist class still had its milk teeth. So by the favor of Providence and by our political and economic babyhood the principles of liberty and equality got a solid footing in our traditions. Some of the inherited immoralities, such as the restrictions of the suffrage under which the Constitution was adopted,[8] were overcome, and even when immense inequalities of possession grew up, appeal still lay to the primitive decalogue of our liberties.

In practice we are a nation of backsliders. The whisper of awe and surprise that runs through the country when a powerful malefactor is actually brought to justice is proof that the rich and the poor are not equal before our courts. The real decisions in politics are made by small cliques, and except in seasons of popular revolt the votes of great numbers of citizens count for almost nothing. In actual practice the administration of public affairs is full of favoritism to the powerful, and even more full of damnable neglect for those things which are really vital to the common people.

Yet all these things are in the nature of a derailment of justice; the roadbed and the trackage are still there, even when the train is ditched. These apostasies from the American standards of right have to cloak their real nature in order to exist at all. The means of dethroning the usurpers of public power are always within reach. Graft is at least not embodied in the Constitution, nor declared to be the hallowed foundation of the commonwealth. When some of our States concluded to curb the extralegal power of the bosses by direct primaries, uniform accounting, direct legislation, and the recall, these enormous changes were secured by only a few years of moderately vigorous agitation. On the other hand, when great bodies of voters in Berlin in 1908 tried to make a peaceful protest against the iniquitous Prussian three-class system of suffrage by parading in the

8. Of 3,000,000 inhabitants about 120,000 had the suffrage.

streets, they were dispersed and cut down with sabers. Slavery was the one great social institution contradicting the democratic principle which was able to secure recognition and protection in the federal Constitution. It long jutted into our American life as a disturbing remnant from an earlier and evil age. From the terrible sacrifice which it cost our nation to get rid of it we can learn the difference between a suppression of human rights that is supported by the fundamental law, and a frustration of human rights that circumvents the law.

The backslidings of our politics are partly due to the youth of democracy. It is still in its adolescence. For ages government was managed for the people by a select group, and all the expedients and theories of government were evolved to suit that condition. The people have to learn how to do it. The running of cooperative stores and factories is a new art which has to be learned with losses and suffering, whereas management by corporations is well understood and effective. Democracy stands for the cooperative idea applied to politics; monarchy and aristocracy represent in statecraft the same ideals and methods which corporations represent in business.

Another cause for the frequent breakdown of popular government is the fact that the state very directly affects the property interests of the country. But these interests do not in the least acknowledge the principle of equal human rights, and balk at every attempt to conform them to that doctrine. Consequently politics is the battleground of two opposing forces, of the Christian principle of liberty and equality lodged in our democracy, and of the mammonistic principle lodged in our business life. The family, the church, and the school are only indirectly affected by this struggle; politics is involved directly. The state is like a breakwater, pounded by hungry seas. As long as it holds, let us thank God and not wonder if it is wet and slippery with ooze. When our business life is christianized, the fundamental Christianity of our political structure will become clearer and more effective.

In spite of all failures we can assert that our political communities are constitutionally on a Christian footing. Instead of legalizing class inequality, they at least try to be an organized expression of the equal rights of all. Instead of being a firmly wrought system for holding down the weak and depriving them of the natural means of self-help and even of a voice to utter their wrongs, our government tries to be a guarantee of freedom and a protection to the helpless. Instead of being constitutionally an organization of a clique for their private advantage, it is planned as an organization of all for the common good, and only falls into the hands of marauding interests through the ignorance and laziness of the citizens. Democracy is not equivalent to Christianity, but in politics democracy is the expression and method of the Christian spirit. It has made the most permanent achievements in the younger communities of the Anglo-Saxon group, but it is making headway throughout the world, and is the conquering tendency in modern political life.

If politics has been christianized, how much did Christianity help in converting it? It is possible to make out a strong case for the proposition that democracy has come in spite of the church and that its best champions were avowed infidels. But Christianity is more than the church. The reactionary doings of ecclesiastical machines can be put down in black and white and quoted by scoffers to the end of time. But the decisive movements of the Christian spirit are subtle and hard to record; like the wind it bloweth where it listeth, and few listen to it even while it is blowing; fewer still can trace its effect after the wind has hushed. The struggle for political democracy in its infancy was so closely connected with the struggle for religious toleration and freedom that it is impossible to disentangle the two and decide how much strength each factor would have had by itself. Certainly the success of political democracy was most early and durable where radical and pure types of Christianity had gained a footing and influence. The sense of human worth, the sensitive response to the rights of the poor and helpless, the fighting courage bred by bold religion, are pervasive ingredients in the national life which silently cooperate with all efforts to christianize public life. Democracy has been best led in Protestant countries where a free type of religion ranged men of distinctively Christian character on the side of popular liberty. On the other hand, where free Christianity was suppressed by church and state, the lovers of liberty were ranged against both church and state, and the hatred of tyranny took on the colors of irreligion. In that case the infidels really voiced the spirit of Christianity better than the church: Christ once more found better friends among the publicans than among the Pharisees. Voltaire, for instance, was a destroying angel who mocked and lashed an apostate and unbelieving church with the Christian weapons of humanity, charity, and fraternity. But the fact that such cases are abnormal impresses them on the public notice and memory. The more broadly and justly we view the history of the last eight centuries, the more influence will we attribute to Christianity in the rise of modern democracy. In the Anglo-Saxon communities especially, the spirit of religion has blended with the spirit of freedom; or rather, here the spirit of Christianity has been set free sufficiently to do its work in the field of political life, and has found one great outlet for its power in creating a passionate love for freedom and equality.

Four great sections of our social order — the family, the organized religious life, the institutions of education, and the political organization of our nation — have passed through constitutional changes which have made them to some degree part of the organism through which the spirit of Christ can do its work in humanity. The analysis of these redeemed parts of our social order has explained by historical object lessons in what sense we can speak of christianizing the social order, and has also brought home to us with what gradualness and through what complex forces such a process has to work its way. The presumption is that other portions of the social order will have to submit to similar changes if they are to be christianized.

If this analysis is even approximately correct, it ought to create an immense hopefulness in all Christian minds. Social Christianity is not, then, an untried venture. The larger part of the work of christianizing our social order is already accomplished, and the success which has attended it ought to create a victorious self-assertion in all who stake their faith on its effectiveness. These redeemed portions of our social life are the portions to which our hearts go out in loving pride and loyalty. Christianity works. Moreover, every part of the social order which has come even a little under the law of Christ has immediately served as a vantage ground for further progress. There has been a speeding up of redemption. When a man is gagged, bound, and tied to a stake, the hardest part is to get one hand free: every further gain is easier and makes ultimate freedom surer.

What is next?

Chapter III: Our Present Economic Order

The next thing is business.

Our business life is the seat and source of our present troubles. So much ought to be plain to all who care to see. It is in commerce and industry that we encounter the great collective inhumanities that shame our Christian feeling, such as child labor and the bloody total of industrial accidents. Here we find the friction between great classes of men which makes whole communities hot with smoldering hate, or sets them ablaze with lawlessness. To commerce and industry we are learning to trace the foul stream of sex prostitution, poverty, and political corruption. Just as an epidemic of typhoid fever would call for an analysis of the water supply, so these chronic conditions call for a moral analysis of the economic order and justify the presumption that it is fundamentally un-Christian. Business men themselves concede that it is; some by calmly denying that Christian principles have anything to do with business; others by sadly confessing that Christianity ought to govern business, but that it would mean loss or ruin to put Christian ethics in practice.

Business life is the unregenerate section of our social order. If by some magic it could be plucked out of our total social life in all its raw selfishness, and isolated on an island, unmitigated by any other factors of our life, that island would immediately become the object of a great foreign mission crusade for all Christendom. Our argument, therefore, will now concentrate on this unredeemed portion of the social order.

Our first need is to analyze our economic system so that we may understand wherein and why it is fundamentally un-Christian. Most of us have accepted our economic system as we accept our stomach, without understanding its workings. Nor it it easy to understand the moral essentials of this huge and complicated social machinery. We have no such historical perspective of it as our great grandchildren will have when they study the Great Industrial Transition of the Twentieth Century in college. We are like a swimmer in a stormy sea. To negotiate the next wave is the great object of his concern, but whether that wave is part of a tidal current sweeping him toward shore or out to sea, his narrow horizon does not tell him. So amid the swift changes of our age we find it hard to distinguish between incidental troubles and the essential drifts of our economic system.

We stumble along untraveled trails when we attempt an analysis of our economic system from a Christian point of view. The collective intelligence of the Christian church has not really come to any clearness about the fundamental moral relations involved in modern economic life. It instinctively condemns some of its worst excrescences, but even among its leaders many have no clear grasp of the moral nature and genius of our industrial and commercial world. We have been neglecting the doctrine of sin in our theology. We might look to Christian business men for an incisive comprehension of the moral conditions amid which they work, but most of them are so driven by business that they have no time to consider their situation broadly and with historical insight. They see keenly what is immediately necessary, but in the broader tendencies of their life a vast collective will bids them go, and they go. They are slaves of the lamp. Business imposes its point of view on them, just as the Catholic Church molds the ideas of the priests who labor in it. When "practical men" do theorize, they are often the dizziest theorizers of all.

Nevertheless, a moral analysis of our economic life is now in the process of making. Our whole nation has of late constituted itself a commission of investigation, and is engaged in a profoundly earnest attempt to understand the morals of business. Nothing calls out such serious thought and discussion at present as the unsatisfactory relation of the economic life to the higher laws and values of humanity. This book is part of this collective effort to understand. I propose throughout to think from the point of view of a Christian man. The tests that I shall apply are not technical but moral. Does our business system create sound and noble manhood? Does it make it fairly easy to do right and hard to do wrong? Does it call men upward or tempt them downward? Does it reward or penalize fraternal action? Does it furnish the material basis for the reign of God on earth? As a Christian man I shall have to judge more patiently and forbearingly than if I were inquiring why high prices are making it hard for me to feed my family and rear my children. I shall also have to probe more incisively and condemn more sweepingly than if I were arguing as a lawyer or an economist. Christ would pardon many of those whom we send to cruel years in prison, and would consign to the Gehenna of wrath some of those who sit in our seats of judgment and respectability.

We should get the most enlightening comments on our economic life if we could bring to life some able mind that went to sleep in A.D. 1700, or if some one could live in the year 2000 like the hero of *Looking Backward* and come back to us. By comparing our present system backward with the order out of which it has developed, or forward with the order into which it is silently passing, we should get a realization of the distinctive qualities of the life in the midst of which we are moving. But even if the range of our experience is short, yet the movement of society has been so rapid that even twenty or thirty years of observation allow us to measure the curve of the road along which we are all swinging.

When I was a boy in the 1870's, I spent several happy summers working on the farm in a German community in Lycoming County, Pennsylvania. The tools of our work were very simple. There was a horserake and a mowing machine, but the sheaves of grain were raked and bound by hand, and the hoe was the pillar of agriculture. Except for the buzz saw in the old sawmill by the creek, there was no power machine in sight. Most of the products of the farm were consumed by those who raised them. We took the grain to the mill and waited till it was ground. The miller took his pay in grain. Occasionally we butchered a sheep and had fresh meat to eat. The spinning wheel still buzzed in the kitchen, and a hand loom pounded in the "shop." On market days we took butter, eggs, and berries to Williamsport and sold them to the housewives on the street curb, or we went from house to house offering what we had. The old farmer liked to have me along because multiplying pounds by cents was a confusing operation for which a city boy came in handy. The calculating age had not yet struck him. There was little money to handle.

On that farm we lived the economic life of the pre-capitalistic era. All who have ever worked on an old-fashioned farm can have a living comprehension of the industrial era that is slowly sinking out of sight.

Since that time modern methods have invaded and revolutionized farming at some points. Think of the great wheat farms where gasoline engines and power machines have become the farmer's pets; or the truck farms where they raise asparagus, cranberries, or peaches in quantities that make the digestive apparatus of the onlooker seem puny and behind the times. In the busy season these farmers become employers of gang labor. They have learned to figure and to calculate their expenses and profits in fractional percentage. Their produce is raised "for the market" and not for their home. The farmer's family eats flour milled in Minneapolis and canned stuff that he buys in town. He ships his produce to commission merchants in a distant city, who sell it to dealers, who sell it to hotel men and housekeepers whom the farmer never sees. He has become a cog in the vast machinery of modern production. He feeds the world, and the world feeds him. On these modernized farms we can watch the industrial revolution invading the backward domain of agriculture. Farming has begun to travel the same road which industry began to travel a century earlier.

My own boyhood has also supplied me with a lively impression of the patriarchal régime of the old handicraft system. On a visit to Germany I spent some days in the home of a master tailor in the ancient town of Altena in Westphalia, where my father and grandfather had been Lutheran pastors. His shop was upstairs in his home. Half a dozen journeymen and a couple of apprentices squatted cross-legged on tables, plying the needle. The master worked with them and shared their talk. At noon all ate at his table, and he cut the bread and served the soup to them with due respect to seniority. When he said grace before and after meat, all bowed their heads with him. Downstairs in a tiny store, like a hall bedroom, he kept a few bolts of stuff. From these his customers selected their cloth, or they brought him their own goods to make up. A stock of readymade clothing, made for potential and invisible buyers, probably never entered his mind.

This is a miniature picture of industry in the pre-capitalistic era, of its narrow market, its simple methods, and its direct relations between men. Such little shops continue to supply the bulk of economic products throughout the Orient and to a large extent in continental Europe. Very recently I found only one small shoe store selling factory-made shoes in a German city of twenty thousand inhabitants, but more than a hundred small shops ready and able to take any order that dealt with leather and feet.

Contrast with this simple form of industry the great centers of the shoe or clothing trade in America. Huge factories whirr with specialized machinery. Every turn of the process has its machine; every man has his trick. Thousands of men cooperate under centralized direction. The old patriarchal relations between master and men are gone; they no longer work together, nor talk together, nor eat together, nor pray together. The most competent manager of a shoe factory may not be able to make a shoe to save his life. But he is an expert in organization. The men who own the factory may be still farther remote from its actual work. Some of them may never have seen the place; they have bought stock because it is earning eight per cent and has a good rating. While the goods are being made, no one knows who will wear this coat or those shoes. They are made for the market, seized by the roaring wheels of commerce, and carried to the ends of the earth.

In the old order the aim was to make a living, to give the children an education and a start in life, to lay something by for a rainy day, and to rise a step in life if possible. The range of possibilities and the range of ambition were both narrow. There was always a big difference between the thrifty man and the shiftless man; between the mechanic who sent his boy to college, and his cousin who went fishing and let his job wait for him. But the richest and the poorest in our old-time village communities were only a few thousand dollars apart. In the cities, men of business sagacity equal to any that we now have were content if a lifetime of success won them a few hundred thousand dollars.

Today the range of possibilities is enormous, and the unsatisfied thirst for wealth has grown correspondingly. The poorest and the richest are as far apart as the molehill and the peaks of the Sierras. In the higher reaches of business getting a living drops out of sight. The dominant concern is to get profit, and to invest it to get more profit. In its main river bed the current of business has become a torrent.

Thus the modern economic order is developing right before our eyes. We younger men and women have seen the revolution proceed in American industry and commerce. We have seen the great department stores, the manufacturing centers, and the trusts sprout and shoot up like magic. Our children will see similar transitions in farming. Within one generation our country has become the classical demonstration of capitalistic industry. A similar transition took place a century earlier in England, and more slowly on the continent of Europe.

This modernizing of industry has largely been a simple expansion in size, a sort of adolescence of the industry previously existing. The essential thing in it was not the application of steam power, but the utilizing of human association on a large scale. More men were coordinated under one management, more wealth combined in joint-stock enterprises. A vaster market was opened up. Organization became a science, and the chief of all crafts. The tendency to combine and mass human labor was in full swing before the invention of the steam engine, and would have gone on without it, but the power machine immeasurably intensified it and furnished the technical basis for the combination and division of labor. Gradually the machine has become a sort of new partner in production. The old hand tools merely aided the hand that plied them, and never made that hand unnecessary. The new machine tools tend to become the real workers. They supplant some men entirely, and reduce others to the position of feeding and tending the machine.

Now, in so far as our present economic order is simply the perfecting of human association, Christianity can have no quarrel with it. The massing of industrial units, the specializing of functions, the mastery of natural forces by science and technical skill, are henceforth part and parcel of every social order that will develop on this planet, unless the race reverts to barbarism. The attempts to check this process by prohibiting department stores or enforcing the Sherman antitrust law have bucked against manifest destiny and the law of evolution. An ideal social order would have the serious problem of counteracting the monotony and one-sidedness which are inseparable from machine work, and of protecting the freedom and individuality of the single worker in the centralized pressure of industrial organization, but it could not turn its face back to patriarchal simplicity. An enlarged and diversified industrial organization is not an evil but a good.

The moral objection lies, not against the size and complexity of the modern system, but against the fact that this wonderful product of human ability and toil with its immense powers of production has gravitated into the ownership and control of a relatively small class of men. This group is always changing; some drop out, others enter. But these personal changes are of little importance for the makeup of society. The group is permanent, and the men in it have acquired a proportion of power over their fellows which — human nature being what it is — must lead to injustice, to inequality, and to the frustration of the Christian conception of human fellowship.

In the old handicraft system ownership and power were widely distributed. Every little shop was an industrial unit, and every master mechanic was an independent power. Every apprentice could hope in time to become the owner of so simple a plant. This is the condition still prevailing generally in our farm life in America. Our farmers are workmen who own their instruments of production. They are workmen and capitalists combined in one. That makes them strong, and it is no wonder that they work like grim death before they will let a mortgage force them from the hold which their farm gives them on God's universe. On the other hand, our factory operatives have no right nor claim in the place, the tools, or the output of their work. They are propertyless men who own only their body and its working force. Even if they own a home and have a savings-bank account, that property does not aid them in their work and gives them no share in the control of their shop. In such cases they have property, but no capital.

In the modern industrial order ownership and control are not vested in the workers, but in an entirely different social group which stands apart from them by its interests, social status, habits of life, and modes of thought — the group of investors or capitalists. A man may work twenty years for a corporation, and contribute the most valuable service in building it up, yet have no part nor lot in it at the end, and be liable to dismissal at any time. Another man who has never contributed a hard day's work to it, either of body or mind, is a part owner of it and shares in its control because he has invested money in it. It is true that in most cases the two groups overlap. A number of individuals are usually both owners and active intellectual workers in the concern, and this is the redeeming

feature in the situation. But even that is not essential. The managing officers of a corporation may all be salaried men. And in any case the power
which the managers wield comes to them from the owners and not from
the workers. The capitalist group is in control.

It is the extent and thoroughness of this two-class adjustment which
differentiates the modern industrial order from the old. It is this also
which creates its chief moral dangers. No one will understand the moral
side of our economic relations unless he comprehends this two-group system. Wherever any industrial undertaking is really modernized, the separation of these two groups becomes clearly marked. On the one side, we
have a growing body of workers to whom possession of the plant in
which they work becomes a more and more remote possibility; on the
other side, a scattered group of owners, of whom only a few share in the
productive labor of the concern. But the former group is under the control of the latter. For this reason our modern system is called the capitalistic system.

Divergent points of view and a conflict of interests follow with absolute necessity from this two-class system. The interests of the worker revolve around his job, for a job is his only chance to apply his working
force, and his working force is all he has. So the job is his sole hold on
life. His entire system of ethics becomes job-centric. To get a job, to hold
it against those who might take it from him, and to make it yield him as
much as possible of pay, leisure, and comfort, is the absorbing concern of
his soul. As the sun is the source of warmth and life to the earth, so is the
job to the worker.

On the other hand, the economic interests of the capitalist revolve
around his profits, and since the capitalist class is the controlling and
dominant class, the desire for profit dominates our whole industrial organization. All its efforts converge on one end, to make dividends. All the
parts of the great organism of production move toward profit with an
overwhelming singleness of purpose. Whenever profit has collided with
the higher interests of humanity, the latter have hitherto gone down with
sickening regularity. This triumphant sway of profit as the end of work
and existence puts the stamp of mammonism on our modern life.

Another essential feature of our modern business life is its speculative
method. In large sections of industry, production is not in response to an
actual demand but in anticipation of a possible demand. Business has to
forecast the future, not only in the size and quality of a season's output,
but in the erection of great plants. This means risk and venture. Now

there is an element of risk in any productive labor, even in baiting your hook for a fish or planting cabbages in your back yard. But when production is on so vast a scale as today, when competition is so keen, and when the lure of possible profit is so dazzling, the wholesome natural tingle of daring becomes a consuming fever. The speculative character of business causes enormous waste, and to that extent stamps business as technically inefficient. But what concerns us here is that it creates a feverish heat of desire in which the higher qualities of life are melted and burned. If covetousness is a valuable quality in human nature, business is a superb institution to stimulate and educate it. But if "the love of money is the root of evil," what is business?

When we try to judge our economic system from the point of view of Christian morals, we must not forget that it has biased the moral judgment by which it is to be measured. Recent as the capitalistic system is in human history, it has been in operation long enough to mold the laws and policies of all industrial nations, and to put a deep impress on the ethical and religious ideas of the modern world. On the cut-stone front of a skyscraper are mighty caryatids that seem to hold up its vast weight on their bent shoulders. But we know that it is really supported by the steel girders and trusses of the framework, and all other features of the building must adjust themselves to the mechanical necessities of this essential structure. So in every social order that has ever existed, the economic system then in force was one of the determining influences. Dogmatic socialists often run the theory of "economic determinism" into the ground, but no student of history can question the tremendous importance of the economic factor. In the old handicraft order, generations of small producers had built up a system of municipal laws and guild regulations which sheltered them and their interests against powerful and greedy competitors. The aim of Christian legislation at that time was to secure to every business man a moderate circle of customers and a decent living, and to shackle those who would try to secure inordinate wealth by snatching the bread of their fellows. When the capitalistic method gathered force and headway, it swept away these protective laws which hampered free competition and the massing of capital and labor. It created a new philosophy of economics. It secured control of political power, and enacted laws that threw the field open to those who were strong enough to seize the vantage points. If anything, it favored the strong against the weak, and gave to him that hath. The fierce struggle which followed speeded up the machinery of production, increased the material wealth of the industrial nations boundlessly, and put a generation of strong executive intellects in the saddle. But it trampled down the humane considerations of mercy and fraternity which had to some extent prevailed, and created a general temper of lawlessness and ruthlessness which has now become second nature of us all, so that we hardly realize how hard and inhuman it all is. To limit female labor to ten hours a day in the interest of humanity is today a great moral achievement, and the idea of a legal living wage is a startling innovation to a generation that has inherited the moral point of view of the competitive era.

In a rough and preliminary way we have now sketched the chief moral features of our economic system. We have found the business man in the seat of power. He and his class own and control the immense enginery of modern production. All moral relations run back to him. In the chapters that now follow, we shall take up the various relations which he sustains to his fellows in the organism of business life: first, his relation to other men of his own class with whom he competes or associates; second, his relation to the workers whom he employs; third, his relation to the consumers whom he supplies.

THE SOCIAL PRINCIPLES OF JESUS [1]

Editor's introduction. The most widely circulated of Rauschenbusch's works was a handbook for college and voluntary study groups, written under the direction of a committee on college courses of the Sunday School Council of Evangelical Denominations and the committee on voluntary study of the Council of North American Student Movements, for use as part of a four-year curriculum cycle. Although convinced of an increasing realization "that the salvation of society lies in the direction toward which Jesus led," Rauschenbusch also found that "there is no clear understanding of what he stood for." [2] In an attempt to remedy this lack, he drew upon the evangelical liberal biblical scholarship typified by Ritschl and Harnack, for whom it seemed possible to know the mind of the historical Jesus. Rauschenbusch divided the book into twelve chapters consisting of selected biblical passages, plus commentaries, for each day of the week, followed by a major discussion headed "Study for the Week." The discussion for Chapter XII, entitled "The Social Test of Religion," is given here. The tendency of the social gospel to hold an instrumentalist view of the church is evident, along with an intense concern for Christian unity.

❖ ❖ ❖ ❖

Jesus Christ was the founder of the highest religion; he was himself the purest religious spirit known to us. Why, then, was he in opposition to religion? The clash between him and the representatives of organized religion was not occasional or superficial. It ran through his whole activity, was one of the dominant notes in his teaching, culminated in the great spiritual duel between him and the Jewish hierarchy in the last days at Jerusalem, and led directly to his crucifixion.

---

1. *The Social Principles of Jesus* (N.Y., 1916), 139–46. Used by permission of The Association Press.
2. *Ibid.,* introduction.

I

The opposition of Jesus was not, of course, against religion itself, but against religion as he found it. It was not directed against any departure from the legitimate order of the priesthood; nor against an improper ritual or wrong doctrine of sacrifices. In fact, it did not turn on any of the issues which were of such importance to the church in later times. He criticized the most earnest religious men of his day because their religion harmed men instead of helping them. It was unsocial, or anti-social.

The Old Testament prophets also were in opposition to the priestly system of their time because it used up the religious interest of the people in ceremonial performances without ethical outcome. It diverted spiritual energy, by substituting lower religious requirements for the one fundamental thing which God required — righteousness in social and political life. They insisted over and over that Jehovah wants righteousness and wants nothing else. Their aim was to make religion and ethics one and inseparable. They struck for the social efficiency of religion.

At the time of Jesus the Jewish sacrifices had lost much of their religious importance. During the Exile they had lapsed. They were professional performances of one class. The numerous Jews scattered in other countries perhaps saw the Temple once in a lifetime. Modern feeling in the first century was against bloody sacrifices. The recorded sayings of Jesus hardly mention them. On the other hand, the daily life of the people was pervaded by little prescribed religious actions. The Sabbath with its ritual was punctiliously observed.[3] There were frequent days of fasting, religious ablutions and baths, long prayers to be recited several times daily, with prayer straps around the arm and forehead, and a tasseled cloth over the head. The exact performance of these things seemed an essential part of religion to the most earnest men.

We have seen how Jesus collided with these religious requirements, and

---

3. Edersheim, *Life and Times of Jesus the Messiah*, Appendix XVII, gives a detailed account of Sabbath regulations. [ED.] Alfred Edersheim (1825–89) was born in Vienna of Jewish parents. He was converted to Christianity, studied at the universities of Edinburgh and Berlin, and was ordained first into the Presbyterian ministry, later into that of the Church of England. He was a productive biblical scholar who wrote many books. His *opus magnum*, the two-volume *Life and Times of Jesus the Messiah*, first published in 1883, was an omnibus study of great richness, if somewhat uncritical in its details.

on what grounds. If men were deeply concerned about the taboo food that went into their bodies, they would not be concerned about the evil thoughts that arose in their souls. If they were taught to focus on petty duties, such as tithing, the great ethical principles and obligations moved to the outer field of vision and became blurred. The Sabbath, which had originated in merciful purpose toward the poor, had been turned into another burden. Religion, which ought to bring good men into saving contact with the wayward by love, actually resulted in separating the two by a chasm of religious pride and censoriousness. A man-made and artificial religious performance, such as giving toward the support of the Temple, crowded aside fundamental obligations written deep in the constitution of human society, such as filial reverence and family solidarity.

Other reformers have condemned religious practices because they were departures from the holy Book or from primitive custom. Jesus, too, pointed out that some of these regulations were recent innovations. But the real standard by which he judged current religious questions was not ancient authority but the present good of men. The spiritual center on which he took his stand and from which he judged all things, was the kingdom of God, the perfect social order. Even the ordinances of religion must justify themselves by making an effective contribution to the kingdom of God. The Sabbath was made for man, and its observance must meet the test of service to man's welfare. It must function wholesomely. The candle must give light, or what is the use of it? The salt must be salty and preserve from decay, or it will be thrown out and trodden under foot. If the fig tree bears no fruit, why is it allowed to use up space and crowd better plants off the soil? This, then, is Christ's test in matters of institutional religion. The church and all its doings must serve the kingdom of God.

II

The social efficiency of religion is a permanent social problem. What is the annual expense of maintaining the churches in the United States? How much capital is invested in the church buildings? (See U.S. Census Bulletin No. 103, of 1906.) How much care and interest and loving freewill labor does an average village community bestow on religion as compared with other objects? All men feel instinctively that religion exerts a profound and subtle influence on the springs of conduct. Even those who

denounce it, acknowledge at least its power for harm. Most of us know it
as a power for good. But all history shows that this great spiritual force
easily deteriorates. *Corruptio optimi pessima.*[4]

Religion may develop an elaborate social apparatus of its own, wheels
within wheels, and instead of being a dynamic of righteousness in the
natural social relations of men, its energies may be consumed in driving
its own machinery. Instead of being the powerhouse supplying the kingdom of God among men with power and light, the church may exist for
its own sake. It then may become an expensive consumer of social wealth,
a conservative clog, and a real hindrance of social progress.

Live religion gives proof of its value by the sense of freedom, peace,
and elation which it creates. We feel we are right with the holy Power
which is behind, and beneath, and above all things. It gives a satisfying
interpretation of life and of our own place in it. It moves our aims higher
up, draws our fellow men closer, and invigorates our will.

But our growth sets a problem for our religion. The religion of childhood will not satisfy adolescent youth, and the religion of youth ought
not to satisfy a mature man or woman. Our soul must build statelier
mansions for itself. Religion must continue to answer all our present
needs and inspire all our present functions. A person who has failed
to adjust his religion to his growing powers and his intellectual horizon,
has failed in one of the most important functions of growth, just as
if his cranium failed to expand and to give room to his brain. Being
microcephalous is a misfortune, and nothing to boast of.

Precisely the same problem arises when society passes through eras of
growth. Religion must keep pace. The church must pass the burning
torch of religious experience from age to age, transmitting the faith of the
fathers to the children, and not allowing any spiritual values to perish.
But it must allow and aid religion to adjust itself. Its inspiring teaching
must meet the new social problems so effectively that no evil can last long
or grow beyond remedy. In every new age religion must stand the test of
social efficiency. Is it passing that test in Western civilization?

Religion is a bond of social coherence. It creates loyalty. But it may
teach loyalty to antiquated observances or a dwarfed system of truth.
Have you ever seen believers rallying around a lost cause in religion? Yet
these relics were once a live issue, and full of thrilling religious vitality.

Society changes. Will religion change with it? If society passes from
agriculture and rural settlements to industry and urban conditions, can

4. [ED.] "The corruption of the best is the worst."

the customary practices of religion remain unchanged? Give some instances where pre-scientific conceptions of the universe, embodied in religion, have blocked the spread of scientific knowledge among the people. The caste distinctions of Hinduism were the product of a combination between religion and the social organization of the people; can they last when industrialism and democracy are pervading India? The clerical attitude of authority was natural when the Catholic clergy were the only educated class in the community; is it justified today? Protestantism won the allegiance of industrial communities when the young business class was struggling to emancipate itself from the feudal system. It developed an individualistic philosophy of ethics. Today society tends toward solidaristic organization. How will that affect religion and its scheme of duty? Thus religion, by its very virtues of loyalty and reverence, may fall behind and lose its full social efficiency. It must be geared to the big live issues of today if it is to manifest its full saving energies.

How does this problem of the efficiency of religion bear on the foreign missionary movement? How will backward or stationary civilizations be affected by the introduction of a modern and enthusiastic religion?

We may feel the defects of our church life at home, but there is no doubt that the young men and women who go out from our colleges under religious impulses, are felt as a virile and modernizing force when they settle to their work in Turkey or Persia. Christian educational institutions and medical missions have raised the intellectual and humane standards of young China. Buddhism in Japan has felt the challenge of competition and is readjusting its ethics and philosophy to connect with modern social ideals. The historical effects of our religious colonization will not mature for several generations, but they are bound to be very great. The nations and races are drawing together. They need a monotheistic religion as a spiritual basis for their sense of human unity. This is a big modern social task. It makes its claim on men and women who have youth, education, and spiritual power. Is the religious life of our colleges and universities efficient enough to meet the need?

Here are the enormous tasks of international relations, which the Great War has forced us to realize — the prevention of armed conflicts, the elimination of the irritant causes of war, the protection of the small nations which possess what the big nations covet, the freedom of the seas as the common highway of God, fair and free interchange in commerce without any effort to set up monopoly rights and the privilege of extortionate gain, the creation of an institutional basis for a great family of nations in days to come. These are some of the tasks which the men and women who are now young must take on their mind and conscience for life, and leave to their children to finish. What contributions, in your opinion, could the spirit of the Christian religion make to such a program, if it were realized intelligently and pressed home through the agencies of the Christian church? In what ways has American religion shown its efficiency since the war broke out?

Christianity has been a great power in our country to cleanse and fraternalize the social life of simple communities. Can it meet the complex needs of modern industrialism in the same way? It cannot truthfully be claimed that it has done so in any industrial country. Its immense spiritual forces might be the decisive element, but they have been effectively organized against a few only of the great modern evils. On the fundamental ethical questions of capitalism the church has not yet made up its own mind — not to speak of enforcing the mind of Christ. Nor have the specialists in the universities and colleges supplied the leaders of the church with clear information and guidance on these questions. We cannot make much permanent progress toward a just social order as long as the masses of the working people in the industrial nations continue in economic poverty and political helplessness, and as long as a minority controls the land, the tools, and the political power. We shall linger on the borders of the Inferno until a new accession of moral insight and spiritual power comes to the nations. How will it come?

III

What could the churches in an average village community accomplish if they intelligently directed the power of religion to foster the sense of fraternal unity and to promote the institutions which make for unity? How could they draw the new, the strange, and the irregular families into the circle of neighborly feeling? In what way could they help to assimilate immigrants and to prevent the formation of several communities in the same section, overlapping, alien, and perhaps hostile? How would it affect the recreational situation if the churches took a constructive rather than a prohibitive attitude toward amusements, and if they promoted the sociability of the community rather than that of church groups?

With the rise of land prices and the control of transportation and markets, the rural population is moving toward a social crisis like that which transformed the urban population in the industrial revolution.

Agriculture will become capitalistic, and the weaker families will drop to the position of tenants and agricultural laborers. Cooperation is their way of salvation. Its effectiveness has been amply demonstrated in older countries. It requires a strong sense of solidarity, loyalty, and good faith to succeed. It has made so little headway in America because our national character has not been developed in these directions. What could the churches do to save the weaker families from social submergence by backing cooperation and developing the moral qualities needed for it?

The strong religious life of our people might be more effective if the churches were less divided. Their economic and human resources are partly wasted by useless competition. Our denominational divisions are nearly all an historical heritage, imported from Europe, and coming down from a controversial age. Their issues all meant something vital and socially important in the midst of the social order of that day; but in many cases the real significance has quietly crumbled away, and they are not really the same issues that deeply engaged our forefathers. We are all "tithing mint, anise, and cummin," and forgetting the weighty matters, such as social justice and Christian fraternity. Everybody is ready to acknowledge this about every denomination except his own. We need a revaluation of our religious issues from the point of view of the kingdom of God. That would bring us into harmony with the judgment of Jesus. Nothing else will.

IV

The social efficiency of religion — what call is there in that to the college men and women of this generation? Shall they cease to worship and pray, seek the salvation of society in ethics and sociology, and abandon religion to stagnation? Or shall they seek a new experience of religion in full sight of the modern world, and work by faith toward that reign of God in which his will shall be done?

❖ ❖ ❖ ❖ ❖ ❖ ❖ ❖

THE KINGDOM OF EVIL [1]

Editor's introduction. The most important theological statement for the social gospel movement as a whole was Rauschenbusch's last book, *A Theology for the Social Gospel.* In substance, it was given as the Taylor lectures at Yale in April 1917 — the month the United States entered World War I. In view of later criticism of the social gospel as having been much too optimistic in its estimate of man, it is noteworthy that many chapters of this book concerned the doctrine of sin. Indeed, it suggests many themes which Reinhold Niebuhr was to restate in his own emphatic repudiation of the liberal theology of which Rauschenbusch was an exponent.[2]

The chapter reprinted here is preceded by half a dozen chapters on the doctrine of sin, and on how sin is transmitted and perpetuated. Rauschenbusch made his most distinctive contribution to theology in these chapters, and the latter part of the book contains his most mature explication of the hopeful doctrine of the coming kingdom of God on earth. By that time, of course, such biblical scholars as Wilhelm Wrede (1859–1907), Johannes Weiss (1863–1914), and especially Albert Schweitzer (1875–1965) had sharply challenged the liberal view of Jesus, calling attention to the eschatological elements in his teaching on the kingdom of God. Rauschenbusch somewhat peevishly dismissed their work with these words:

My own conviction is that the professional theologians of Europe, who all belong by kinship and sympathy to the bourgeois classes and are constitutionally incapacitated for understanding any revolutionary ideas, past or present, have overemphasized the ascetic and eschatological elements in the teachings of Jesus. They have classed as ascetic or apocalyptic the radical sayings about property and non-resistance which seem to them impractical or visionary. If the

1. *A Theology for the Social Gospel* (N.Y., 1917), chap. IX, 77–94. Used by permission of The Macmillan Company.
2. Cf. Richard Dickinson, "Rauschenbusch and Niebuhr: Brothers Under the Skin?" *Religion in Life,* XXVII (1957–58), 163–71; Reinhold Niebuhr, "Walter Rauschenbusch in Historical Perspective," *loc cit.,* 527–38.

present chastisement of God purges our intellects of capitalistic and upper-class iniquities, we shall no longer damn these sayings by calling them eschatological, but shall exhibit them as anticipations of the fraternal ethics of democracy and prophecies of social common sense.[3]

So he remained in the main stream of liberal thought, as his references to Schleiermacher and Ritschl in the selection suggest. The social gospel in America after World War I tended, however, to move in the other direction, toward a humanistic interpretation of Jesus, which in its turn was sharply attacked by the neo-orthodox theology which in the 1930's and 1940's came to dominate the theological scene.

This chapter will be the last step in our discussion of the doctrine of sin. We have sought to show that in the following points a modification or expansion is needed in order to give the social gospel an intellectual basis and a full medium of expression in theology.

1. Theological teaching on the first origin of sin ought not to obscure the active sources of sin in later generations and in present-day life, by which sin is quickened and increased. An approximation to the reticence of Jesus and the prophets about the fall of man, and to their strong emphasis on the realistic facts of contemporary sin, would increase the practical efficiency of theology.

2. Since an active sense of failure and sin is produced by contrast with the corresponding ideal of righteousness, theology, by obscuring and forgetting the kingdom of God, has kept the Christian world out of a full realization of the social sins which frustrate the kingdom. The social gospel needs above all a restoration of religious faith in the reign of God in order to create an adequate sense of guilt for public sins, and it must look to theology to furnish the doctrinal basis of it.

3. The doctrine of original sin has directed attention to the biological channels for the transmission of general sinfulness from generation to generation, but has neglected and diverted attention from the transmission and perpetuation of specific evils through the channels of social tradition.

4. Theology has not given adequate attention to the social idealizations of evil, which falsify the ethical standards for the individual by the authority of his group or community, deaden the voice of the Holy Spirit

3. *A Theology for the Social Gospel,* 158.

to the conscience of individuals and communities, and perpetuate antiquated wrongs in society. These social idealizations are the real heretical
doctrines from the point of view of the kingdom of God.

5. New spiritual factors of the highest significance are disclosed by the
realization of the super-personal forces, or composite personalities, in society. When these backslide and become combinations for evil, they add
enormously to the power of sin. Theology has utilized the terminology
and results of psychology to interpret the sin and regeneration of individuals. Would it stray from its field if it utilized sociological terms and results in order to interpret the sin and redemption of these super-personal
entities in human life?

The solidaristic spiritual conceptions which have been discussed must
all be kept in mind and seen together, in order to realize the power and
scope of the doctrine to which they converge: the kingdom of evil.

In some of our swampy forests the growth of ages has produced im-
penetrable thickets of trees and undergrowth, woven together by creep-
ers, and inhabited by things that creep or fly. Every season sends forth
new growth under the urge of life, but always developing from the old
growth and its seeds, and still perpetuating the same rank mass of life.

The life of humanity is infinitely interwoven, always renewing itself,
yet always perpetuating what has been. The evils of one generation are
caused by the wrongs of the generations that preceded, and will in turn
condition the sufferings and temptations of those who come after. Our
Italian immigrants are what they are because the church and the land system of Italy have made them so. The Mexican peon is ridden by the
Spanish past. Capitalistic Europe has fastened its yoke on the neck of
Africa. When Negroes are hunted from a Northern city like beasts, or
when a Southern city degrades the whole nation by turning the savage
inhumanity of a mob into a public festivity, we are continuing to sin because our fathers created the conditions of sin by the African slave trade,
and by the unearned wealth they gathered from slave labor for generations.

Stupid dynasties go on reigning by right of the long time they have
reigned. The laws of the ancient Roman despotism were foisted by ambitious lawyers on medieval communities to which they were in no wise
fitted, and once more strangled liberty, and dragged free farmers into
serfdom. When once the common land of a nation, and its mines and
waters, have become the private property of a privileged band, nothing
short of a social earthquake can pry them from their right of collecting

private taxes. Superstitions which originated in the third century are still faithfully cultivated by great churches, compressing the minds of the young with fear and cherished by the old as their most precious faith. Ideas struck out by a wrestling mind in the heat of an argument are erected by later times into proof texts more decisive than masses of living facts. One nation arms because it fears another; the other arms more because this armament alarms it; each subsidizes a third and a fourth to aid it. Two fight; all fight; none knows how to stop; a planet is stained red in a solidarity of hate and horror.

The entomologist Fabre [4] investigated the army caterpillar, which marches in dense thousands, apparently under some leadership which all obey. But Fabre found there is no leadership. Each simply keeps in touch with the caterpillar just ahead of it and follows, follows on. The one article of faith is to follow the leaders, though none of the leaders knows whither they are going. The experimenter led the column to march in a circle by getting the front rank in touch with the rear, and now they milled around helplessly like lost souls in Dante's hell.

If this were the condition of humanity, we should be in a state of relative innocency and bliss. The front-rank caterpillars are at least not trying to make something out of the rest, and are not leading them to their destruction by assuring them that they are doing it for their good and for the highest spiritual possessions of the caterpillar race. Human society has leaders who know what they want, but many of them have manipulated the fate of thousands for their selfish ends. The sheep-tick hides in the wool of the sheep and taps the blood where it flows warm and rich. But the tick has no power to alter the arterial system of the sheep and to bring the aorta close to the skin where it can get at it. Human ticks have been able to do this. They have gained control of legislation, courts, police, military, royalty, church, property, religion, and have altered the constitution of nations in order to make things easy for the tick class. The laws, institutions, doctrines, literature, art, and manners which these ruling classes have secreted have been social means of infection which have bred new evils for generations.

Any reader who doubts these sad statements can find the facts in the books, though mostly in footnotes in fine print. It is also going on in real life. We can watch it if we look at any nation except our own.

This is what the modern social gospel would call the kingdom of evil.

4. [ED.] Jean Henri Fabre (1823-1915) was a French entomologist and popular writer on insect life.

Our theological conception of sin is but fragmentary unless we see all men in their natural groups bound together in a solidarity of all times and all places, bearing the yoke of evil and suffering. This is the explanation of the amazing regularity of social statistics. A nation registers so and so many suicides, criminal assaults, bankruptcies, and divorces per hundred thousand of the population. If the proportion changes seriously, we search for the disturbing social causes, just as we search for the physical causes if the rhythm of our pulse-beat runs away from the normal. The statistics of social morality are the pulse-beat of the social organism. The apparently free and unrelated acts of individuals are also the acts of the social group. When the social group is evil, evil is over all.

The conception of a kingdom of evil is not a new idea. It is as old as the Christian church, and older. But while our modern conception is naturally historical and social, the ancient and medieval church believed in a kingdom of evil spirits, with Satan at their head, which is the governing power in the present world and the source of all temptation.

The belief in evil spirits is so common in ethnic religions that the relative absence of that belief in the Old Testament is proper cause for wonder. There are only a few passages referring to evil spirits, and a few referring to a spiritual being called Satan. It is altogether likely that the belief in dangerous and malicious spirits held a much larger place in the popular religious life of the Jewish people than we would gather from their literature. If the higher religious minds, who wrote the biblical books, purposely kept the popular beliefs down and out of sight, that gives remarkable support to those who regard the belief in personal evil spirits as a seamy and dangerous element of religion.

After the Exile the religion of the Jews was filled with angels and devils, each side built up in a great hierarchy, rank above rank. Evidently this systematized and theological belief in a satanic kingdom was absorbed from the Eastern religions with which the Jews came into close contact during the Exile. The monotheism of the Hebrew faith held its own against the dualism of the East, but the belief in Satan is a modified dualism compatible with the reign of Jehovah. The apocalyptic system is a theology built up on this semi-dualistic conception, describing the conflict of the kingdom of Satan against God and his angels and his holy nation, and the final triumph of God.

The belief in the satanic kingdom and the apocalyptic theology were transferred from Judaism to Christianity as part of the initial inheritance of the new religion from the old, and any one familiar with patristic literature and with popular medieval religion needs no reminder that this was one of the most active and effective parts of the religious consciousness. The original belief was reinforced by the fact that all the gods and the daimonia of the Greco-Roman world were dyed black and classified as devils and evil spirits by the aggressive hostility of the church. This process was repeated when the medieval church was exorcising the pagan gods from the minds and customs of the Teutonic nations. All these gods remained realities, but black realities.

Popular superstition, systematized and reinforced by theology, and inculcated by all the teaching authority of the medieval church, built up an overwhelming impression of the power of evil. The Christian spirit was thrown into an attitude of defense only. The best that could be done was to hold the powers of darkness at bay by the sign of the cross, by holy water, by sacred amulets, by prayer, by naming holy names. The church buildings and church yards were places of refuge from which the evil spirits were banned. The gargoyles of Gothic architecture are the evil spirits escaping from the church buildings because the spiritual power within is unbearable to them. I recently witnessed a cornerstone-laying at a new Catholic church. The bishop and the clergy thrice moved in procession around the foundation walls, chanting; an acolyte carried a pailful of holy water, and the bishop liberally applied it to the walls. So the rectangle of masonry became an exempt and disinfected area of safety. Under the sunshine of an American afternoon, and with a crowd of modern folks around, it was an interesting survival.

The belief in a demonic kingdom was in no wise attacked in the Reformation. Luther's sturdy belief in devils is well known. Indeed, the belief which had been built up for centuries by the church came to its terrible climax during the age of the Reformation, in the witch trials. From A.D. 1400 to 1700, hundreds of thousands of women and girls were imprisoned, tortured, and burned. These witch trials were grounded on the belief in the satanic kingdom. Thomas Aquinas furnished the theological basis; the Inquisition reduced it to practice; Innocent VIII in 1484, in the bull *Summis desiderantes*, lent it the highest authority of the church; the *Malleus Maleficarum* (1487 or 1488) codified it; lawyers, judges, informers, and executioners exploited it for gain; information given by malice, fear, or the shrieks of the tortured made the contagion self-perpetuating and ever spreading. It prevailed in Protestant countries equally with Catholic. To believe in the machinations of evil spirits and their compact with witches was part of orthodoxy, part of profounder piety. If the devil and his spirits are not real but a figment of social imagination, yet at that time the devil was real, just as real as any flesh-and-blood being, and far more efficient. Theology had made him real. The Reformation theology did not end this craze of horror. Aside from the humane religious spirit of a few who wrote against it, it was the blessed skepticism of the Age of Enlightenment and the dawn of modern science which saved humanity from the furies of a theology which had gone wrong.

The passive and defensive attitude toward the satanic kingdom of evil still continues wherever the belief in evil spirits and in the apocalyptic theology is active. Bunyan's *Pilgrim's Progress* presents a dramatic record of the Calvinistic religious consciousness in its prime. In all the wonderful adventures and redoubtable combats of Christian and his companions and heavenly aids, they are on the defensive. The only exception that I can remember occurs in the second part, when Christian's wife and children, personally conducted by Great-Heart, pass by Doubting Castle where Christian and Hopeful were imprisoned by Giant Despair.

> So they sat down and consulted what was best to be done: to wit, now they were so strong, and had got such a man as Mr. Great-Heart for their conductor, whether they had not best to make an attempt upon the giant, demolish his castle, and if there were any pilgrims in it, to set them at liberty, before they went any further. So one said one thing, and another said the contrary. One questioned if it was lawful to go upon unconsecrated ground; another said they might, provided their end was good; but Mr. Great-Heart said, "Though that assertion offered last cannot be universally true, yet I have a commandment to resist sin, to overcome evil, to fight the good fight of faith; and pray, with whom should I fight this good fight, if not with Giant Despair? I will therefore attempt the taking away of his life and the demolishing of Doubting Castle.

So they passed from the defensive to the offensive attitude, and demolished the castle. The serious deliberations of the party show that Bunyan realized that this was a new departure. He was, in fact, at that moment parting company with the traditional attitude of theology and religion, and putting one foot hesitatingly into the social gospel and the preventive methods of modern science. Note that it was Mr. Great-Heart who made the move.

Today the belief in a satanic kingdom exists only where religious and theological tradition keeps it alive. It is not spontaneous, and it would not originate anew. Its lack of vitality is proved by the fact that even those who accept the existence of a personal Satan without question, are not influenced in their daily life by the practical belief in evil spirits. The demons have faded away into poetical unreality. Satan alone remains, but he has become a literary and theological devil, and most often a figure of speech. He is a theological necessity rather than a religious reality. He is needed to explain the fall and the temptation, and he reappears in eschatology. But our most orthodox theology on this point would have seemed cold and skeptical to any of the great theologians of the past.

No positive proof can be furnished that our universe contains no such spiritual beings as Satan and his angels. Impressive arguments have been made for their existence. The problem of evil is simplified if all is reduced to this source. But the fact confronts us — and I think it can not be denied — that Satan and his angels are a fading religious entity, and that a vital belief in demon powers is not forthcoming in modern life.

In that case we can no longer realize the kingdom of evil as a demonic kingdom. The live realization of this belief will be confined to narrow circles, mostly of premillennialists; the church would have to use up its precious moral authority in persuading its members to hold fast a belief which all modern life bids them drop. Yet we ought to get a solidaristic and organic conception of the power and reality of evil in the world. If we miss that, we shall see only disjointed facts. The social gospel is the only influence which can renew the idea of the kingdom of evil in modern minds, because it alone has an adequate sense of solidarity and a sufficient grasp of the historical and social realities of sin. In this modern form the conception would offer religious values similar to those of the old idea, but would not make such drafts on our credulity, and would not invite such un-Christian superstitions and phantasms of fear.

The ancient demonic conception and the modern social conviction may seem at first sight to be quite alien to each other. In fact, however, they are blood-kin.

The belief in a satanic kingdom, in so far as it was not merely theology but vital religious faith, has always drawn its vitality from political and social realities. The conception of an empire of evil fastened on Jewish thought after the Jews had an opportunity during the Exile to observe imperialism at close range, and to be helpless under its power. The splendor of an Oriental court and its court language deeply influenced the Jewish conception of God. He was surrounded with a heavenly retinue, and despotic ideas and phraseology were applied. The same social experiences also enlarged the conception of the reign of evil. The little evil spirits had been enough to explain the evil of local Jewish communities. But a great malign power was needed as the religious backing of the oppressive international forces in whose talons the Jewish race was writhing. Satan first got his vitality as an international political concept.

The political significance of the belief in the satanic kingdom becomes quite clear in the relation of the early church to the Roman empire. The Apocalypse of John is most enlightening on this fact. The empire is plainly described as the creature and agent of the satanic powers. The Beast with the seven heads had received its dominion from the great Dragon. The great city, which is described as the commercial and financial center of the world, falls with a crash when Satan and his host are overthrown by the Messiah. Evidently the political system of Rome and the demonic powers are seen as the physical and spiritual side of the same evil power.

Early Christianity is usually described as opposed to paganism, and we think of the pagan religion as a rival religious system. But it was also a great social force penetrating all community life, the symbol of social coherence and loyalty. Its social usages let no one alone. It became coercive and threatening where religious actions had political significance, especially in the worship of the emperor. Christians believed the pagan gods to be in reality demon powers, who had blinded and enticed men to worship them. Whoever did worship them came under their defiling power. Idolatry was an unforgivable sin. All the life of the church aimed to nerve Christians to suffer anything rather than come under the control of the dark powers again from which baptism had saved them. When the choice confronted them and they were pinned to the wall, the hand that gripped them was the hand of the Roman empire, but the face that leered at them was the face of the adversary of God. So the belief in a satanic kingdom of evil drew its concrete meaning and vitality from social and political realities. It was their religious interpretation.

In the Middle Ages, when the Roman empire had become a great memory, the papacy was the great international power, rich, haughty, luxurious, domineering, commanding the police powers of states for its coercive purposes, and claiming the heritage of the emperors. The democratic movements which sprang up during the eleventh and twelfth centuries, and headed toward a freer religion and a more fraternal social life, found the papacy against them. Then the Apocalypse took on new life. The city on the seven hills, drunk with the blood of the saints and clad in scarlet, was still there. The followers of Jesus who suffered in the grip of the international hierarchy did not see this power as a Christian church using oppressive measures, but as an antichristian power, the tool of Satan and the adversary of God. This belief was inherited by Protestantism and was one of its fighting weapons. Once more it was a political and social reality which put heat and vitality into the belief in the reign of Satan.

Today there is no such world-wide power of oppression as the Roman empire or the medieval papacy. The popular superstitious beliefs in demonic agencies have largely been drained off by education. The conception of Satan has paled. He has become a theological devil, and that is an attenuated and precarious mode of existence. At the same time belief in original sin is also waning. These two doctrines combined — the hereditary racial unity of sin, and the supernatural power of evil behind all sinful human action — created a solidaristic consciousness of sin and evil, which I think is necessary for the religious mind. Take away these two doctrines, and both our sense of sin and our sense of the need of redemption will become much more superficial and will be mainly concerned with the transient acts and vices of individuals.

A social conception of the kingdom of evil, such as I have tried to sketch, makes a powerful appeal to our growing sense of racial unity. It is modern, and grows spontaneously out of our livest interests and ideas. Instead of appealing to conservatives, who are fond of sitting on antique furniture, it would appeal to the radicals. It would contain the political and social protest against oppression and illusion for which the belief in a satanic kingdom stood in the times of its greatest vitality. The practical insight into the solidarity of all nations in their sin would emphasize the obligation to share with them all every element of salvation we possess, and thus strengthen the appeal for missionary and educational efforts.

The doctrine of original sin was meant to bring us all under the sense of guilt. Theology in the past has labored to show that we are in some sense partakers of Adam's guilt. But the conscience of mankind has never been convinced. Partakers in his wretchedness we might well be by our family coherence, but guilt belongs only to personality, and requires will and freedom. On the other hand, an enlightened conscience cannot help feeling a growing sense of responsibility and guilt for the common sins under which humanity is bound and to which we all contribute. Who of us can say that he has never by word or look contributed to the atmospheric pressure of lubricious sex stimulation which bears down on young and old, and the effect of which after the war no man can predict without sickening? Whose hand has never been stained with income for which no equivalent had been given in service? How many business men have promoted the advance of democracy in their own industrial kingdom when autocracy seemed safer and more efficient? What nation has never been drunk with a sense of its glory and importance, and which has never seized colonial possessions or developed its little imperialism when the temptation came its way? The sin of all is in each of us, and every one of us has scattered seeds of evil, the final multiplied harvest of which no man knows.

At the close of his great invective against the religious leaders of his nation (Mt. xxiii), Jesus has a solidaristic vision of the spiritual unity of the generations. He warns his contemporaries that by doing over again the acts of their forefathers, they will bring upon them not only the blood they shed themselves, but the righteous blood shed long before. By solidarity of action and spirit we enter into solidarity of guilt. This applies to our spiritual unity with our contemporaries. If in the most restricted sphere of life we act on the same sinful principles of greed and tyranny on which the great exploiters and despots act, we share their guilt. If we consent to the working principles of the kingdom of evil, and do not counteract it with all our strength, but perhaps even fail to see its ruinous evil, then we are part of it and the salvation of Christ has not yet set us free.

I should like to quote, in closing this discussion, a remarkable passage from Schleiermacher's systematic theology, which describes the kingdom of evil without calling it by that name. I need not say that Schleiermacher was one of the really creative minds in the history of Protestant theology, a man who set new problems and made old problems profounder, thus fertilizing the thoughts even of those who know nothing of him. Speaking of the universal racial sin of humanity, he said:

> If, now, this sinfulness which precedes all acts of sin, is produced in every individual through the sinful acts and condition of others; and if on the other hand every man by his own free actions propagates and strengthens it in others; then it is something wholly common to us (*gemeinschaftlich*). Whether we view this sinfulness as guilt or as conscious action, or as a principle and condition of life, in either aspect it is something wholly common, not pertaining to every individual separately or referring to him alone, but *in each the work of all, and in all the work of each*. In fact we can understand it justly and completely only in this solidarity. For that reason the doctrines dealing with it are never to be taken as expressions of individual self-consciousness, but they are expressions of the common conscious-

ness. This solidarity is a unity of all places and all times. The peculiar form which this racial sinfulness takes in any individual, is simply an integral part of the form it takes in the social group to which he belongs, so that his sin is incomprehensible if taken alone and must always be taken in connection with the rest. This principle runs through all the concentric circles of solidaristic consciousness, through families, clans, tribes, nations, and races; the form which sinfulness takes in any of these can be understood only in connection with the rest. Therefore the total force exerted by the flesh against the spirit in all human actions incompatible with the consciousness of God, can be truly realized only when we see the totality of all contemporary life, never in any part alone. The same holds true of the succession of generations. The congenital sinfulness of one generation is conditioned by the sinfulness of those who preceded, and in turn conditions the sin of those who follow." [5]

Ritschl, another incisive and original theological thinker, adopted this solidaristic conception of sin, and its correlated ideas in the doctrine of salvation, as the basis of his theological system. He thinks that this, and not the theory of subjective religion which is commonly quoted in connection with his name, is Schleiermacher's epoch-making contribution to theology.[6] Certainly the passage I have quoted shows what a capacity of religious vision is evoked by a religious comprehension of the solidarity of human life. "The consciousness of solidarity is one of the fundamental conditions of religion, without which it can neither be rightly understood nor rightly lived." [7]

---

5. Schleiermacher, *Der Christliche Glaube*, 71, 72. 3rd edition. The translation and italics are mine. A few unessential phrases are omitted to shorten the quotation. [ED.] The third German edition of *The Christian Faith* by F. D. E. Schleiermacher (1768– 1834) (2 vols., Berlin, 1835–36).

6. Ritschl, *Rechtfertigung und Versöhnung*, I, 555. [ED.] *The Christian Doctrine of Justification and Reconciliation*, Ritschl's chief theological work (Bonn, 1870–74).

7. Ritschl, I, p. 496.

Selected Bibliography

ABELL, AARON IGNATIUS. *The Urban Impact on American Protestantism, 1865–1900* (Cambridge, Mass., 1943).

BODEIN, VERNON PARKER. *The Social Gospel of Walter Rauschenbusch and Its Relation to Religious Education* (New Haven, 1944). Vol. XVI, Yale Studies in Religious Education.

BURR, NELSON R. *A Critical Bibliography of Religion in America* (Princeton, 1961). Vol. IV, Religion in American Life. See especially Part III, "Religion and Society."

CARTER, PAUL A. *The Decline and Revival of the Social Gospel: Social and Political Liberalism in American Protestant Churches, 1920–1940* (Ithaca, N.Y., 1954).

CAUTHEN, KENNETH. *The Impact of American Religious Liberalism* (N.Y., 1962). See especially Chapter 5, "The Social Gospel: Walter Rauschenbusch."

DOMBROWSKI, JAMES. *The Early Days of Christian Socialism in America* (N.Y., 1936).

DORN, JACOB H., III. "Washington Gladden, Prophet of the Social Gospel, 1836–1918" (typed Ph.D. dissertation, University of Oregon, 1965).

ELY, RICHARD T. *French and German Socialism in Modern Times* (N.Y., 1883).
———. *The Labor Movement in America* (N.Y., 1886).
———. *Social Aspects of Christianity, and Other Essays* (N.Y., 1889).
———. *Outlines of Economics* (1st ed., N.Y., 1893).
———. *Socialism: An Examination of its Nature, its Strength and its Weakness, with Suggestions for Social Reform* (N.Y., 1894).
———. "Fundamental Beliefs in My Social Philosophy," *The Forum*, XVIII (September 1894–February 1895), 173–83.
———. *The Social Law of Service* (N.Y., 1896).
———. *Ground Under Our Feet: An Autobiography* (N.Y., 1938).

EVERETT, JOHN RUTHERFORD. *Religion in Economics: A Study of John Bates Clark, Richard T. Ely, Simon N. Patten* (N.Y., 1946).

GLADDEN, WASHINGTON. *Working People and Their Employers* (Boston, 1876).
———. *The Christian League of Connecticut* (N.Y., 1883).
———. *Applied Christianity: Moral Aspects of Social Questions* (Boston, 1886).
———. *Burning Questions of the Life that Now Is, and of that Which Is to Come* (N.Y. [1889]).
———. *Who Wrote the Bible? A Book for the People* (Boston, 1891).
———. *The Cosmopolis City Club* (N.Y., 1893).
———. *Tools and the Man: Property and Industry Under the Christian Law* (Boston, 1893).
———. *The Church and the Kingdom* (N.Y., 1894).

391

————. *Ruling Ideas of the Present Age* (Boston, 1895).

————. *Seven Puzzling Bible Books. A Supplement to "Who Wrote the Bible?"* (Boston, 1897).

————. *Social Facts and Forces: The Factory, the Labor Union, the Corporation, the Railway, the City, the Church* (N.Y., 1897).

————. *How Much Is Left of the Old Doctrines? A Book for the People* (Boston, 1899).

————. *Social Salvation* (Boston, 1902).

————. *Where Does the Sky Begin* (Boston, 1904).

————. *Christianity and Socialism* (N.Y., 1905).

————. *The Church and Modern Life* (N.Y., 1908).

————. *Recollections* (Boston, 1909).

————. *The Labor Question* (Boston, 1911).

————. *Ultima Veritas and Other Verses* (Boston, 1912).

————. *Present Day Theology* (Columbus, 1913).

————. *The Forks of the Road* (N.Y., 1916).

————. *The Interpreter* (Boston, 1918).

HOPKINS, CHARLES HOWARD. *The Rise of the Social Gospel in American Protestantism* (New Haven, 1940). Vol. XIV, Yale Studies in Religious Education.

HUDSON, WINTHROP S. *The Great Tradition of the American Churches* (N.Y., 1953). Chapter x, "A Lonely Prophet: The Continuity of the Great Tradition," is on Rauschenbusch.

HUGHLEY, J. NEAL. *Trends in Protestant Social Idealism* (N.Y., 1948).

LANDIS, BENSON Y. ed. *A Rauschenbusch Reader: The Kingdom of God and the Social Gospel.* With an Interpretation of the Life and Work of Walter Rauschenbusch by Harry Emerson Fosdick (N.Y., 1957).

MAY, HENRY F. *Protestant Churches and Industrial America* (N.Y., 1949).

MAYS, BENJAMIN E., ed. *A Gospel for the Social Awakening: Selections from the Writings of Walter Rauschenbusch* (N.Y., 1950).

MEYER, DONALD B. *The Protestant Search for Political Realism, 1919–1941* (Berkeley, 1960).

MILLER, ROBERT M. *American Protestantism and Social Issues, 1919–1939* (Chapel Hill, N.C., 1959).

MOEHLMAN, CONRAD H. "Life and Writings of Walter Rauschenbusch," *Colgate-Rochester Divinity School Bulletin*, I (1928–29), 32–37. In "The Rauschenbusch Memorial Number," with other articles on Rauschenbusch by Justin Wroe Nixon and Henry B. Robins.

MÜLLER, REINHART. *Walter Rauschenbusch: ein Beitrag zur Begegnung des deutschen und des amerikanischen Protestantismus* (Leiden, 1957).

NOBLE, DAVID W. *The Paradox of Progressive Thought* (Minneapolis, 1958). Chapter VII deals with Ely, and Chapter x with Rauschenbusch.

RAUSCHENBUSCH, WALTER. *Christianity and the Social Crisis* (N.Y., 1907).

————. *For God and the People: Prayers of the Social Awakening* (Boston, 1910).

———. *Christianizing the Social Order* (N.Y., 1912).

———. *"Unto Me"* (Boston, 1912).

———. *Dare We Be Christians?* (Boston, 1914).

———. *The Social Principles of Jesus* (N.Y., 1916).

———. *A Theology for the Social Gospel* (N.Y., 1917).

———. *The Rochester Theological Seminary Bulletin* (Sixty-Ninth Year: November 1918). A "Rauschenbusch Number," containing reports of the funeral and memorial services, various tributes, and some items by Rauschenbusch himself.

SHARPE, DORES R. *Walter Rauschenbusch* (N.Y., 1942).

SINGER, ANNA M. *Walter Rauschenbusch and His Contribution to Social Christianity* (Boston, 1926).

SMUCKER, DONOVAN E. "The Origins of Walter Rauschenbusch's Social Ethics" (typed Ph.D. thesis, University of Chicago, 1957).

———. "Multiple Motifs in the Thought of Rauschenbusch: A Study in the Origins of the Social Gospel," *Encounter*, XIX (1958), 14–20.

STACKHOUSE, MAX L. "Eschatology and Ethical Method: A Structural Analysis of Contemporary Christian Social Ethics in America with primary reference to Walter Rauschenbusch and Reinhold Niebuhr" (typed Ph.D. thesis, Harvard University, 1964).

THOMPSON, ERNEST TRICE. *Changing Emphases in American Preaching. The Stone Lectures for 1943* (Philadelphia, 1943). Chapters IV and V deal with Gladden and Rauschenbusch respectively.

VISSER 'T HOOFT, W. A. *The Background of the Social Gospel in America* (Haarlem, 1928).

Index